SPORT MATTERS

Sport Matters offers a comprehensive introduction to the study of modern sport. It covers a wide range of issues including why modern sport developed first in England, the role of sport in European civilizing processes, the development of soccer as a world game, spectator violence in the UK, North America and the rest of the world, and the increasing commercialization and professionalization of sport. It also addresses issues surrounding gender and sport, and sport and racial stratification.

By building upon a number of theoretical perspectives, particularly the writing of Norbert Elias, as well as systematically analysing further approaches, including Marxism and Foucauldian post-structuralism, *Sport Matters* provides an engaging and informative introduction to sport from a sociological perspective and will be essential reading for all students in this area.

Eric Dunning is Emeritus Professor of Sociology at the University of Leicester and Visiting Professor of Sociology at University College Dublin. He is author of a number of works, including *Quest for Excitement* (1989) and *Sport and Leisure in the Civilizing Process* (1992).

SPORT MATTERS

Sociological studies of sport, violence and
civilization

Eric Dunning

London and New York

First published 1999
by Routledge
11 New Fetter Lane, London EC4P 4EE

Simultaneously published in the USA and Canada
by Routledge
29 West 35th Street, New York, NY 10001

Routledge is an imprint of the Taylor & Francis Group

© 1999 Eric Dunning

Typeset in Bembo by Routledge
Printed and bound in Great Britain by TJ International Ltd,
Padstow, Cornwall

British Library Cataloguing in Publication Data
A catalogue record for this book is available from the British Library

Library of Congress Cataloging in Publication Data
Dunning, Eric.
Sport Matters: sociological studies of sport, violence and civilization /
Eric Dunning.
Includes bibliographical references and index.
1. Sports – Sociological aspects. 2. Sports – Cross-cultural
studies. 3. Violence in sports. I. Title.
GV706.5.D85 1999 98-47958
306.4'83–dc21 CIP

ISBN 0–415–06413–9 (hbk)
ISBN 0–415–09378–3 (pbk)

FOR MICHAEL AND RACHEL AND
IN MEMORY OF NORBERT ELIAS

CONTENTS

ILLUSTRATIONS

Figures

Tables

PREFACE

Sport Matters is the third book in a series. It should be seen as a sequel to *Quest for Excitement* (1986) and *Sport and Leisure in the Civilizing Process* (1992). My aims in writing it have been primarily threefold: (1) to illustrate the fruitfulness of, to clarify and test in relation to a body of sports-related issues the figurational/process-sociological paradigm developed by Norbert Elias, especially the theory of 'civilizing processes'; (2) to produce a book which will hopefully make a contribution towards persuading more 'mainstream' sociologists of the importance of sport as a field of sociological enquiry; and (3) by writing, not only about sport in Britain but about sport in other countries as well, including aspects of the globalization of sport forms, to contribute towards making the sociology of sport more cross-cultural and less 'natiocentric' than it has been up to now.

If I have met with success in achieving any of these aims, it will reflect the help I have received from a number of friends and colleagues, central among them: Pat Murphy, Ken Sheard, Ivan Waddington, Joe Maguire, Joop Goudsblom, Stephen Mennell, Richard Kilminster, Cas Wouters, Chris Rojek, Chris Shilling, Mike Attalides, Melba Sweets, Syd Jeffers, Bero Rigauer, Hubert Dwertmann, Günther Lüschen, Helmut Kuzmics, Michael Krüger, Nuria Puig, Klaus Heinemann, Paco Lagardera, Francisco Sobral, Beatriz Ferreira, Ademir Gebara, Raschid Siddiqui, Allen Guttmann, Koichi Kiku, Richard H. Robbins, Roger Rees, Jay Coakley, David Miller, Liam Ryan, Peter Donnelly, Kevin Young, Earl Smith, Nancy Bouchier, Frank Kew, Martin Roderick, Dominic Malcolm, Jason Hughes, Graham Curry and Ian Stanier. My thanks to all of them. Last, but by no means least, my thanks go to Sue Smith for undertaking with unflagging cheerfulness and great efficiency the laborious task of typing the manuscript. Anne Smith and Lisa Heggs also made heroic contributions in the final stages.

INTRODUCTION

Sport as a field of sociological enquiry

The social significance of sport

The idea of calling this book *Sport Matters* came from Chris Rojek. I was thinking of the more conventionally academic *Sport, Society and Civilization* but when Chris suggested *Sport Matters* as a title, I jumped at it on account of its signifying ambiguity. It appeals to me because it implies something about the book's subject matter whilst simultaneously conveying the idea that this subject matter is important.

There is no need to support the contention that sport is important by reference to facts and figures. It is enough to suggest a few measures which even people who are indifferent to sport or actively dislike it would find it difficult to deny. Think, for example, of the following: the attention regularly devoted to sport in the mass media; the amounts of money, public and private, spent on sport; the dependency of business on sport for advertising; the growth of state involvement in sport for reasons as diverse as a desire to combat spectator violence and contribute to health or national prestige; the numbers of people who regularly take part in sport as performers or spectators, to say nothing of those who are directly or indirectly dependent on it for their livelihoods; the fact that sport functions as something akin to a lingua franca which permits not only the consolidation of bonds among friends but also the breaking of ice between strangers (this, of course, is primarily a male phenomenon, although that may be slowly changing); the abundant use of sporting metaphors in such apparently diverse life-spheres as politics, industry and the military, a fact which is indicative of the emotional and symbolic resonance of sport; and finally the ramifications, national as well as international, 'social' as well as 'economic',[1] negative as well as positive, of international tournaments such as the Olympics and soccer's World Cup. No activities have ever served so regularly as foci of simultaneous common interest and concern to so many people all over the world.

Clues regarding why sport has come to be significant are offered by the psychology of sports participation and spectatorship. Writing from a 'post-structuralist' or 'Foucauldian' standpoint, John Fiske recently suggested that

1

'one reason for the popularity of sport as a spectator activity is its ability to slip the disciplinary mechanism of the workaday world into reverse gear'. Sport, he argued, is an 'inverted panopticon' where fans whose behaviour is 'monitored and totally known' at work become monitors of the players who, through their 'total visibility', become 'epistemological bobo doll(s) upon which the fans can punch away their frustration'. Along with popular culture more generally, sport provides according to Fiske:

> peaks of intense experience when the body identifies with its external conditions, and thus shakes itself free from the repressive difference between *their* control and *our* sense of identity. This intensity is often experienced by fans as a sense of release, of loss of control. Fans often use metaphors of madness to describe it, and madness, as Foucault has shown us, is what lies just outside the boundary of civilization and control.
>
> (Fiske, 1991a: 11–20)

This argument is perceptive but limited. It is not only 'popular culture' but 'high culture' which provides opportunities for 'peaks of intense experience'. Moreover, 'the controllers' and not only those who are 'controlled' are often 'mad' on sports, a fact which suggests that modern sport is not class specific in quite the way that Fiske implies. Nor are modern societies structurally divided simply between 'the controllers' and the 'controlled'. People who are controlled in one context are often controllers in another. Thus, factory workers may be controlled by managers but they are (or try to be!) controllers in relation to their children. Similarly, although schoolteachers are subordinate to heads (principals) and the local and national educational authorities, they are – officially at least – controllers in relation to their pupils. And, to take an example from British professional sport, soccer managers may be formally subordinate to boards of directors but they are controllers in relation to the players. Moreover, as concern over crowd disorderliness has grown around the world in recent years, mainly but by no means solely in soccer, sports stadia have grown to be increasingly panopticon-like in the sense of involving the close monitoring by police and stewards – often using closed-circuit TV – of the spectators whom Fiske describes as monitors. Finally, formal structures of control in all spheres of life are not infrequently subverted. Nevertheless, despite his apparent failure to appreciate complexities such as these, Fiske has made a valuable contribution in drawing attention to the need to consider sport in relation to social control.

As early as the 1960s, Norbert Elias and I undertook a preliminary examination of sport from a perspective which is in some ways similar to that of Fiske (Elias and Dunning, 1986).[2] It, too, was primarily concerned with issues of sport and social control. More particularly we suggested that one of the main functions performed by playing and watching sport consists in the fact that it enables people generally – 'controllers' as well as 'controlled', those from the higher as well as the lower classes – to engage in a 'quest for excitement'. It appears to serve as a counter to the routines and controls which, generally speaking and not just in the world of work, have become ubiquitous in the everyday life of the relatively 'civilized' advanced industrial societies of today, routines and controls which tend to be conducive to the regular generation, not only of simple boredom but, perhaps more importantly, of feelings of emotional 'staleness' as well. More specifically – and we were writing primarily with sport as, on balance, a voluntary rather than compulsory activity in mind because that is its dominant present-day form – we hypothesized that sport involves a search for pleasurable and de-routinizing emotional arousal via what we called 'motility', 'sociability', 'mimesis' or some combination of all three.[3] That is, voluntary sport appears to be largely about obtaining satisfaction from engaging in physical movements, from the social contacts that are made in sports, and from the arousal of affects which bear a playful and pleasurable resemblance to the emotions which are generated in seriously critical situations. Of course, blended with such affects are cognitive satisfactions such as the intellectual pleasures which can be obtained from devising sports strategies and memorizing sports statistics, and aesthetic pleasures such as those which can be derived from accomplishing or witnessing the skilful and/or graceful execution of a sports manoeuvre. As Maguire (1992) has expressed it, sport fundamentally involves 'a quest for exciting significance'.

Sports can also be said to be a form of non-scripted, largely non-verbal theatre, and emotional arousal can be enhanced by spectacular presentation, the emotional 'contagion' which derives from being part of a large, expectant crowd, and from the 'performances' which spectators and not just athletes put on. But to experience excitement at a sports event, one has to *care* in one or more of three senses. One has to care about the sport *per se*. If one is a direct participant, one has to care about one's own performance. And if one is a spectator, one has to care about the performance of one or another of the contenders or contending sides. In order, as it were, for the 'gears' of one's passions fully to engage, one has to be *committed*, to want to *win*, either as a direct participant for one's own sake because one's *identity* is at stake, or as a spectator, because one *identifies* with one of the individual performers or competing teams. Questions of identity and identification are of critical importance both for the routine functioning of sports and for some of the problems recurrently generated in connection with them.

Fiske again captures this aspect of the problem when he writes: 'Release is not just pleasurable in itself, it also produces spaces in which fans can construct identities and relationships which enable them to know themselves differently from the way they are known by the monitoring order' (Fiske, 1991a: 15, 16). Arguably, a more satisfactory way of putting this would be to say that an important aspect of sports in modern societies consists in their development as an enclave where people are permitted to experience a relatively high – but crucially variable – degree of autonomy as far as their behaviour, identities, identifications and relationships are concerned. The variations, of course, depend fundamentally on the degree to which behaviour in or at a particular sport is perceived by powerful groups as problematic. Let me probe the questions of identity and identification more deeply.

It is sometimes overlooked in philosophically influenced sociological theories[4] that one of the few universal features of human societies consists of the fact that, from the start to the finish of their lives, humans are orientated towards and dependent on fellow humans[5] (Elias, 1978). It is also universally the case that, in the context of the interdependencies which form the basic stuff of human life, people's autonomy tends to increase and their dependency to decrease as they mature. Then, as they enter old age, their autonomy tends to decrease and their dependency to increase once again. In other words, and ignoring for the moment, for example, the class contouring which takes place in societies such as Britain or the veneration heaped on the aged in countries such as China, degrees of human dependency vary partly as a function of biological age. However, the increasing dependency which tends to accompany entry to old age is an aspect of interdependence which is less relevant for present purposes than the growing autonomy which tends to accompany the physical and social maturation of the young.

Centrally involved in the maturation and growing autonomy of a person is a process of individualization during the course of which he/she gradually learns to think of himself/herself as an 'I', to acquire an identity and sense of self. Such individualization and identity formation occur through processes of interaction between the developing self and others, and degrees of socially produced individualization vary, *inter alia*, with the structural differentiation of societies.[6] However, more to the point for present purposes is the fact that one of the preconditions for the occurrence of individualization in what is considered in modern societies to be a 'healthy' way is the formation of bonds with others that are neither too distant nor too close and in which a balance is struck between autonomy and dependence. It is a question of forming a socially appropriate 'we–I balance' (Elias, 1991a) in which a person comes to be considered by others as neither too self-absorbed nor too dependent on the groups to which he/she belongs.

The bonds which humans form involve both direct interdependence with concrete persons such as parents, children and friends, and indirect interdependence within collectivities such as cities, classes, markets, ethnic groups and nations. Whether direct or indirect, such bonds tend to be simultaneously inclusive and exclusive. That is, the membership of any 'we-group' (Elias, 1978) tends to imply generally positive feelings towards other members of the group and pre-fixed attitudes of hostility and competitiveness towards the members of one or more 'they-groups'. Although such a pattern can be modified – for example, through education – it is easy to observe how frequently the very constitution of 'we-groups' and their continuation over time seem to depend on the regular expression of hostility towards and even actual combat with the members of 'they-groups'. That is, specific patterns of conflict appear to arise regularly in conjunction with this basic form of human bonding and simultaneously to form a focus for the reinforcement of 'we-group' bonds. Conflict patterns of this type are readily apparent in the sphere of sport, for example in soccer hooliganism where, in Britain and a number of other countries, social controls have recently been augmented to a level where the relative autonomy of soccer as an enclave for the regular enjoyment of a sports experience has been jeopardized.

In modern industrial societies, sport has come to be important at the individual, local, national and international levels. Depending on how highly sport in general and particular forms of it are valued in a given society or group, it plays an important part in the identity formation of individuals, for example in the ranking and hence self-conceptions of males – and increasingly of females, too – as 'good' or 'bad' footballers, baseball players, cricketers or whatever. In other words, modern sports are more than just contests to see who can run fastest, jump highest or score the highest number of runs, points or goals; they also involve forms of identity testing which, because the people involved have learned of the social value attached to sport, are crucial for the self-concepts of these individuals and their rank ordering as members of a group. In fact, there is reason to believe that, in industrial societies over the past 200 years, sport has come to be increasingly important in the identity formation of males and that in recent years, with the increasing entry of females into this formerly exclusive male preserve, sport has come to be a site where significant battles over gender identities and gender roles are being fought.

Of course, sport is not only important with regard to the testing of individual identities but in the related processes of intergroup testing within countries and in the rank ordering of countries as well. In order to see how, it is only necessary to think of the sports competitions that take place between, for example, schools in particular towns or cities, teams or clubs that represent the towns and cities in question, and nations in such world events as the Olympics or the soccer, cricket and rugby World Cups. Not everybody feels this way. Some people hate sport, others are indifferent to it, and there are sports lovers who are 'turned on' by some sports and not by others. Nevertheless, it remains the case that feelings of elation and pride are generated in many people when their or their children's school wins, for example, a high-school football tournament, a team or club representing their city wins the Superbowl or FA Cup, one of their national sides wins an international tournament or a member of their nation or ethnic group is victorious in an Olympic or other world event. Feelings of dejection and inferiority follow when a team or individual with whom they identify at any of these levels loses.

In short, in modern societies, sport has come to be important in the identification of individuals with the collectivities to which they belong; that is, in the formation and expression of their 'we-feelings' and 'we–I' balances. Through their identification with a sports team, people can express their identification with the city that it represents or perhaps with a particular subgroup within it such as a class or ethnic group. There is even reason to believe that, in the context of a complex, fluid and relatively impersonal modern industrial society, membership of or identification with a sports team can provide people with an important identity-prop, a source of 'we-feelings' and a sense of belonging in what would otherwise be an isolated existence within what Riesman (1953) called the 'lonely crowd'. It has been suggested that sport can perform such functions in the urbanizing areas of 'Third World' countries, too (Heinemann, 1993). In other words, sport today provides a context in countries all over the world where people can meet and bond, if sometimes only fleetingly, and – although this will obviously depend *inter alia* on the degree of organizational stability of the sports in question – it can help to give people a sense of continuity and purpose in contexts which are highly impersonal and beset by what many experience as a bewildering pace of change.

Especially since the end of the 'Cold War' and with the deployment of the so-called 'new technology', rapid social change has increasingly become a global and not just a national phenomenon. An important part of this process involves the disappearance across the globe of many older patterns of work and social integration and the emergence of newer ones. In that context – although, again, one is not dealing with continuities which are absolute – allegiances with sports teams can provide a useful anchor in an increasingly uncertain world. To concretize this with just a few examples: the former Soviet Union may have collapsed; Yugoslavia may have been embroiled in civil war; many French Canadians may wish to secede from their 'anglophone' fellows, and Scots from the rest of the UK; the nations of Western Europe may or may not be about to form a federal state but, in the midst of all these anxiety-provoking imponderables, Moscow Dynamo, Rangers, Celtic, the Minnesota Twins, the Toronto Blue Jays, the Montreal Canadiens, the Arsenal, Schalke 04, Marseilles, Juventus, FC Barcelona and Red Star Belgrade, live on!

The people most committed to sport are commonly called 'fans', an abbreviation of the term 'fanatic'. For the most committed fans, and perhaps for others besides, sport can be said to function as a 'surrogate religion' (Coles, 1975). Indications of this are provided by the reverential attitudes of many committed fans towards the teams they support and their idolization of particular players. Indeed, it is not uncommon for such fans to turn their bedrooms into shrines. Of course, unlike the major world religions, sport does not have an elaborate theology. Nevertheless, to the extent that sports fans can be said, through their involvement in and identification with a particular club, to 'celebrate' or 'worship' one or more of the collectivities to which they belong, sport can be said to possess some of the characteristics of a religion in Durkheim's (1976) sense. In fact, according to Diem (1971), all sports were originally cultic. More to the point, Durkheim's analysis of the 'collective effervescence' generated in the religious rituals of the Australian aborigines which he saw as the root of the experience and concept of 'the sacred' can be transferred, *mutatis mutandis*, to the feelings of excitement and communal celebration that constitute a peak experience in the context of a modern sport. It may even be the case that part of the explanation for the growing significance of sport in modern societies lies in the fact that it has come to perform some of the functions performed earlier by religion. That is, it may in part be catering for a type of need which, for increasing numbers of people, is not met elsewhere in the increasingly secular and scientific societies of our age.

The sociological neglect of sport

From the arguments I have adduced so far, one might have supposed that the study of sport would occupy a place of some importance in the social sciences. In sociology, for example, one might have expected it to feature as a research subject in at least three ways: as a subject covered in its own right; as a topic taught under the broad heading of 'the sociology of leisure'; and as a subject covered within the framework of one or more of the subject's traditional subdivisions, for example education, deviance or gender. Instead, what one encounters is a situation in which sport is virtually ignored. Possible reasons are not difficult to find. The neglect appears to stem largely from the fact that a principal impetus behind the development of sociology has been more ideological than scientific in character in at least two senses.

The first sense consists in the fact that many of the people who have so far contributed to the subject appear to have been motivated more by a short-term desire to 'do something' about the world here and now than by a desire to contribute to knowledge. Many Marxists, for example, appear to have taken Marx's eleventh thesis on Feuerbach literally. That is, their view of sociology has been influenced by Marx's contention that 'philosophers have *interpreted* the world...the point, however, is to *change* it' (Marx and Engels, 1942) as if 'interpretation' and 'change' were somehow antithetical. As a result, moral and political considerations rather than scientific concerns have tended to be to the forefront in their occupational motivations. They do not seem to have appreciated that the fact that Marx sought to develop the basis for a 'scientific socialism' in which political action could be based on an empirically substantiated theory of social change contradicted his 'eleventh thesis'. In fact, although the theses on Feuerbach are best construed as an attack on the mechanistic materialism of Feuerbach and the idealist philosophy of Hegel, one could argue that Marx's work implied the direct opposite of the eleventh thesis, namely something to the effect that: 'political actors have tried to *change* the world in various ways; the point, however, is to *understand* it'.

For sociologists, theory and understanding – and they can only be fundamentally developed through continuous interplay with empirical enquiry – ought to take precedence over action intended to change the world. This is an argument in favour of theory, of deepening our fundamental understanding of the complex world in which we live. It is *not* an argument against political action or research intended to make a here-and-now intervention. In fact, I was engaged in attempting to make just such a practical intervention in England in the 1980s as far as football hooliganism is concerned. But this intervention was based on *theory-guided research* and *that* is the point (Williams *et al.*, 1989).

In the 1960s, a common Marxist argument was that sociology is a 'bourgeois' subject which originated through 'a debate with the ghost of Marx' and hence as a defence of capitalism. Such an argument was not without merit, perhaps especially in relation to the dominance at that time of Parsonian functionalism and empiricism. However, in Britain in the 1980s – and perhaps elsewhere – the opposite idea gained ground, namely that sociology is a 'subversive' subject, concerned with promoting revolutionary change. Again, such an idea had some substance, for example to the extent that some sociologists who had been involved in the student movement of the 1960s were, by then, being promoted to senior positions and gaining power in the framing of teaching and research agendas. However, if one looks at the development of the subject in the longer term, it is clear that, *pace* the claims of the ideologists of left and right, sociology originated from more than one point on the political spectrum. In the USA, for example, the term 'sociology' was first used before the Civil War by so-called 'Southern Comteans' such as Hughes and Fitzhugh as part of a defence of slavery (Lyman, 1990; see also Chapter 8)! In some periods and countries, the subject may have been more dominated by the supporters of one political position than by others but its origins cannot legitimately be described as deriving solely from a right-wing, left-wing or, for that matter, 'middle-of-the-road' position. Its core is concerned with the development of knowledge, and people of most political persuasions have made contributions in that connection.

The widespread commitment of sociologists to a view of the subject which sees it as concerned mainly with contributing to the solution of problems here and now arguably leads to a downgrading of the concern with sociology as being about contributing to the development of a reliable fund of basic knowledge about humans and their societies in all their aspects. As Elias (1987) showed, the development of the natural sciences indicates that striving for freedom from 'heteronomous evaluations' – from allowing non-scientists to dictate the research agenda and non-scientific concerns to occupy pride of place – and taking the 'detour via detachment' – striving to hold one's emotions and value-commitments momentarily in check in order to focus on the research object *per se* – increases the chances that one will be able to come up with adequate diagnoses and find workable solutions. More to the point for present purposes, however, a dominant orientation towards the immediate solution of 'problems' was almost bound to have as a consequence a neglect of areas of social life such as sport. That is because, in large part precisely on account of such an orientation, the study of sport has tended to be seen as 'trivial' compared with the 'really important' issues with which 'mainstream' sociologists are concerned. If this 'Eliasian' line of reasoning has any substance, however, a focus mainly on the solution of 'here-and-now' problems is liable to be self-defeating and to contribute to the production of undesirable unintended consequences to the extent that it leads the concern with understanding *per se* to be sidelined. Vice versa, an orientation principally towards understanding *per se* is likely to be conducive, not only to an avoidance of the arbitrary neglect of important areas of social life such as sport, but also to the realistic solution of problems in sport and elsewhere. It is also likely to be suggestive of policies and forms of action through which the production of undesirable unintended consequences can be minimized. But, of course, such a concern with relatively detached understanding has to be tempered by a motivating and familiarity-conferring *involvement*. In other words, it is a question of striving, not for total 'value-freedom', whatever that may mean, but for a judicious balance between detachment and involvement.

The entrapment of sociology in political struggles has probably been unavoidable. This is not to deny that, to the extent that they have been directed into scientific channels, political motivations have played a positive part in the growth of sociological knowledge. However, the ideological cast of sociology's dominant paradigms and the consequent downgrading of sport as a subject for theorization and research cannot be traced simply to political sources. Two patterns of taken-for-granted thinking which appear to be deeply rooted in the modern West have arguably played a part as well. The first is a tendency towards 'economism', that is a predisposition to take it for granted that 'the economy' constitutes the 'social realm' of the greatest value and 'causal' significance, coupled with a tendency to explain even non-economic phenomena reductively in economic terms. This pattern is not only found in Marxism but in work influenced by the ideologies of the centre and right as well. The second taken-for-granted thinking pattern is a tendency to think dualistically: that is, conceptually to split interdependent phenomena such as individuals and societies, action and structure, body and mind, rationality and emotion, involvement and detachment into absolute dichotomies in which the polarized opposites are conceived as having a separate existence. Again, this tendency is shared by left, right and centre, and also by many 'positivistically' inclined sociologists who share the figurational view of the subject as concerned with knowledge.

It is reasonable to suppose that the roots of this taken-for-granted tendency towards economistic thinking lie in part in the Protestant ethic to which Weber (1930) drew attention. However, just as Weber was crystal clear in arguing that this ethic was just as much a product of capitalism as vice versa,

so it seems plausible to suggest that the taken-for-granted character of economism is associated consequentially and not just causally with the dominance in
the modern world of capitalist modes of production. It is correspondingly
reasonable to suppose that economism is both a product and a buttress of the
power in capitalist societies of bourgeois groups and the values they espouse.
Among the casualties of the taken-for-granted character of these values are the
difficulties faced in persuading people of the significance of ecological issues,
including the ecological effects of sport.

This already complex argument can be taken further. The tendency towards
economistic thinking may also be connected with the ways in which Western
civilizing processes have involved a tendency for military values to be relegated
to a subordinate position relative to values connected with non-violent production. This is not meant to imply that military values have disappeared in the
West but rather that, within Western societies – compared, say, with the societies of their feudal past – military and political roles have tended to become
differentiated and that, correlatively, military personnel have tended to be
subordinated to politicians. One of the consequences of this is that, when military actions are engaged in by Western countries, they tend to be justified in
terms of a rhetoric of 'defence' and to be described as matters of 'regrettable
necessity' rather than 'glory' and 'national honour'. Similarly, in these societies,
especially in their more recent 'neo-' or 'post-colonial' stages, the maximization
of economic prosperity by peaceful means rather than conquest and the violent
exploitation of human labour tends to be an unquestioned goal of domestic
political life. This is not to deny the continued involvement of specific groups
in these societies, including governmental groups, in the international arms
trade and violent exploitation. It is to stress that there is a tendency for such
activities to be conducted in a clandestine way and for it to be a cause of political embarrassment when they are brought to light. But, independently of the
degree of substance behind this line of reasoning, it is indisputable that a
tendency towards economistic thinking is deeply rooted in the modern West
and that it has as one of its undesirable consequences the downgrading by sociologists of the study of sport because many of them judge sport as being 'trivial'
and 'unproductive', a 'waste of time'.

Civilizing processes also contribute to the prevalence in Western societies
and Western sociology of dualistic thinking. They do so by constraining many
people to have an experience of self as what Elias called a socially detached
Homo clausus rather than as one of a number of *Homines aperti*, open people
who live in a context of pluralities and interdependencies from the start to the
finish of their lives (Elias, 1978: 119ff.). According to Elias, the social controls
which are internalized as self-controls in the course of a civilizing process
tend to be experienced as a barrier, on the one hand, within the self between
one's 'rationality' and 'feelings', and on the other, between the self and others.
That is, a *Homo clausus* has an experience of self as a detached and isolated ego
who possesses a 'mind' which is experienced as somehow separate both from

his/her 'body' and the other humans with whom he/she is inextricably inter-dependent. Together with the tendency towards economistic thinking, the *Homo clausus* experience of self arguably contributes to the downgrading of the study of sport in mainstream sociology because, between them, these tendencies lead sport to be seen as falling on the negatively valued side of a complex of overlapping dichotomies such as those between work and leisure, 'mind' and 'body', seriousness and pleasure. As a result, despite its manifest importance as indicated by the various 'measures' which I discussed earlier, sport is not seen as posing sociological problems of comparable significance to those associated with the 'serious' business of economic, political and domestic life or even with such aspects of leisure as 'the arts'. That is, the value of sport even tends to be downgraded as a leisure activity because it is perceived as being 'phys-ical' in character and not engaging with the supposedly higher 'mental' and 'aesthetic' functions.

The emergence of the sociology of sport as a contested field

Some headway has been made in mainstream sociology in Britain in recent years with regard to the teaching of and research into one sports-related topic: soccer hooliganism. This has clearly been connected with the rise of soccer hooliganism in Britain to 'social problem' status. The fact that no other sports-related problem conceived as having comparable socio-political significance has arisen thus far helps to explain the unique, if still marginal, status of soccer hooliganism as a subject within the mainstream sociology curriculum. Nevertheless, there are one or two other areas where some kind of breakthrough might have been expected, particularly the sociologies of religion and education. I alluded earlier to some reasons why one might have expected studies of sport to have been undertaken under the rubric of the sociology of religion. That one might also have expected them in the soci-ology of education is suggested by the fact that physical education is a school subject of some significance and because sports have traditionally constituted one of the main vehicles by means of which schools have interacted. Notwithstanding the pioneering researches into physical education which have been conducted by scholars such as John Evans (1993), the fact that studies of sport feature at best marginally in *mainstream* books and courses on the sociology of education provides further testimony to the extent to which the sociology curriculum has been driven by ideological rather than scientific concerns. However, the major field in which this arguably holds good is the sociology of gender. That is because, as I hinted earlier, sport has arguably become one of the main sites in modern societies for the inculcation and expression of traditional masculine identities and, with the increasing involve-ment of women in the field, one of the key sites of struggle over gender issues. It follows that sport ought to feature alongside work, politics, education and the family in texts and courses on the sociology of gender. In this case, the ideological bias against sport appears to have contributed to the neglect of an area of social life which is arguably one of the most crucial as far as gender issues are concerned.

It is important to stress that this discussion relates to the status of the sociology of sport within the *parent subject* and not to the sociology of sport *per se*. This subdiscipline has experienced a growth over the past thirty years which is nothing short of remarkable. In an attempt to explain why, Rojek (1992: 2) refers to what he calls 'the economic growth of the sport and leisure sector'. The expansion of 'the pleasure industry', he suggests, has multiplied employment opportunities and elevated sport and leisure in social life. This has been bound up with such wider changes as the decline in the centrality of work as a source of 'self-realization' and the growth of the view that it is a means of financing 'free-time'. This argument is convincing except that it neglects that one of the consequences of feminism has been to increase the centrality of occupational careers for females just at the time when some sociologists (such as Gorz) were arguing that work is declining as a 'central life interest'. In other words, there are 'malestream' elements in this argument. Moreover, it seems to me that Rojek misses something of importance, namely the degree to which the sociology of sport, if not perhaps the sociology of leisure, is a specialism which has developed mainly within physical education rather than the parent subject. I do not mean this in an entirely negative sense. It is, however, worth questioning what the sociology of medicine would have looked like had it been developed primarily by doctors or the sociology of law primarily by lawyers. In the preface to an earlier book, I wrote:

> [The sociology of sport] is largely the creation of physical education-alists, a group of specialists whose work, because of their practical involvement in the area, sometimes lacks, firstly, the degree of detachment that is necessary for fruitful sociological analysis, and secondly, what one might call an 'organic embeddedness' in central sociological concerns. That is, much of what they have written focuses mainly on problems specific to physical education, physical culture and sport, and fails to bring out wider social connections. Moreover, it tends to be empiricist in character.
>
> (Dunning, in Elias and Dunning, 1986: 2)

This was interpreted by Jenny Hargreaves (1992: 162) as a condemnation of work in the sociology of sport by physical educationalists as 'inferior'. However, that was not my meaning. Empiricist work can be of value, though this only becomes fully apparent when it is interpreted in theoretical terms. By the same token, theoretical work, even if it is 'embedded in central sociological concerns', can be valueless, particularly to the extent that it is either orientated more towards ideological issues than towards adding to knowledge, or abstract and orientated around the sorts of metaphysical issues that are the life-blood of many philosophers. More to the point for present purposes, however, it remains in my opinion true that much work in the sociology of sport continues to be empiricist. Nevertheless, although the charge of empiricism retains a degree of validity, it is less apposite for the 1990s than it was in the 1960s and 1970s. In Britain, just to take a couple of examples, this is shown very clearly in the work of John Evans (1993) and Jenny Hargreaves (1994).

In my judgement the sociology of sport has recently emerged as one of the liveliest areas in the subject. A central part of its liveliness consists in the fact that the subdiscipline has become a terrain contested by protagonists of all the main sociological paradigms. There are now on offer in the sociology of sport functionalist, symbolic interactionist, Weberian, figurational and varieties of feminist and Marxist approaches. Latterly, post-structuralism and post-modernism have been added to what, paraphrasing William James, one might call the 'blooming, buzzing confusion'. It is a situation full of potential for further development but also fraught with danger, particularly the danger that representatives of the different paradigms will misconstrue the positions of their rivals, in that way contributing less to fruitful debate than to sterility and perhaps destructive conflict. It is certainly the case that the figurational sociology of sport – to which *Sport Matters* is intended as a contribution – has been frequently misconstrued.[7] And figurational sociologists in their turn have undoubtedly misconstrued the work of others. So, in the hope of contributing to research based on a properly informed debate and helping to avoid a situation of destructive interparadigm rivalry, let me bring this introduction to a close by setting forth what the central tenets of figurational sociology are and how the present book is an exemplification of such an approach.

Figurational sociology and the sociology of sport

The 'figurational' approach to sociology was initiated by Norbert Elias. It is an approach which focuses, above all, on social processes and interdependencies or 'figurations'. I shall explain the meaning of these terms later and illustrate what I take their sociological usefulness to be throughout the book. For the moment, let me stick to some of the more general characteristics of the figurational approach, particularly the fact that it aims to contribute to a synthesis in at least two senses.

The first sense consists in the fact that figurational sociology is concerned with exploring the links between the biology, psychology, sociology and history of human beings. It is fundamentally based in this respect on the recognition that evolution has equipped humans biologically as social beings, above all as a symbol-creating, symbol-learning and symbol-using species, a fact which makes it possible for their knowledge to grow and for the societies and cultures they form to develop and change. Of course, knowledge can be forgotten, and societies can 'regress', but that is less important for present purposes than the fact that figurational sociology recognizes that what we call 'history', whether it involves 'progress' or 'regression' or some combination of both simultaneously, depends, at bottom, on the fact that the blind or unplanned process of evolution has equipped humans biologically with a capacity for learning. A central point made by Elias in this connection is that the term 'evolution' should be restricted to the biological level and that 'development' is preferable as a means of bringing out the distinctive character of learned, socio-cultural changes. In Elias's words: 'A possible way to make the distinction quite clear is the limitation of the term "evolution" as symbol of the biological process achieved through gene-transmission and to confine the term "development" to intergenerational symbol-transmission in all its various forms' (Elias, 1991b: 23).

The sociological relevance of this synthesizing perspective is considerable. One of its advantages consists in the fact that it offers a mode of conceptualization which points the way towards an equally theoretical and research-based resolution of the sorts of problems – NB: it points the way and does not pretend to have 'solved' such problems – that recurrently arise in the human sciences in conjunction with the deep-rooted tendency to dichotomize 'nature' and 'nurture', to see them as totally separate and even opposed in the development of humans. For example, the figurational synthesis offers a way out of the sort of sterile, fundamentally ideological conflict between, on the one hand, schools such as ethology and sociobiology which stress the animal nature of humankind at the expense of those human properties which are unique, and, on the other hand, sociological schools which stress the unique characteristics of humans at the expense of those they share with other animals. Kilminster expressed this well and identified the ideological dimension clearly when he wrote:

> on Elias's agenda [was] the intention to steer between the two extreme ideological positions which commonly permeate research on the animalic dimension of human beings. On the one hand lies the reductionist view of the ethologists and sociobiologists...which effectively says that we are basically apes. On the other hand is the philosophical-religious view that human beings constitute a complete break with the animal world, forming a level of soul or spirit.
>
> (Kilminster, 1991: xiv)

Problems in the sphere of sport which could be illuminated by this synthesizing perspective include that of the relationship between genetic inheritance, social learning and social structure in the determination of sporting talent. Another is that of the relationship between genetic inheritance, social experience and sports practice in the determination of injuries of various kinds. Yet another is that of the part played by unlearned relative to learned forms of body language in sporting encounters. Perhaps more importantly, however, the figurational synthesis points squarely at the heart of the problem of how and why it has come to be that humans have a need for activities such as sports, namely the fact that the unplanned process of biological evolution has led *Homo sapiens* to be, not just a symbol-using species who depend largely on socio-cultural learning for their survival, but also creatures whose 'organism requires stimulation in order to function satisfactorily, particularly stimulation through the company of other human beings' (Elias, 1986b: 114). If we are right, sport has arisen as one of the means of providing such stimulation. Indeed, as Elias and I pointed out as long ago as 1969, sport appears to be a leisure activity of decisive significance in the context of the highly controlled and routinized urban–industrial societies of today where work increasingly has a sedentary character and people are increasingly reliant on mechanized transport of various kinds (Elias and Dunning, 1969: 50ff.).

The second sense in which figurational sociology constitutes a synthesizing endeavour consists in the fact that it involves an attempt to meld the best features of classical and modern sociology. It differs from other attempts to construct a synthesis, however – for example, the 'structuration theory' of Giddens (1984) – because, while it is currently fashionable to restrict the classical sociologists whose contributions are held to constitute a *sine qua non* for constructing such a model to the 'holy trinity' of Marx, Weber and Durkheim, Elias (1978) added the currently unfashionable Comte. He did so because a theory of knowledge – the 'law' of the three stages of intellectual growth – was central to Comte's contribution; and because, for Comte, problems of social development or, as he called them, 'social dynamics', stand at the heart of the sociological enterprise. A concern with social development and, as part of it, the development of knowledge and the development of sport stands at the core of figurational sociology, too.

In a modified form, elements of the theories of Marx, Weber and Durkheim also figure centrally in Elias's synthesis. The concept of class, for example, occupies an important place in figurational sociology, together with the idea of the part played by conflict in social dynamics. However, Elias departed from Marx in arguing that ownership and control of the means of production are not universally the dominant source of social power – which does not mean, of course, that they are *never* the dominant source. He also developed the theory of what he called 'established-outsider figurations' (Elias and Scotson, 1994) in an attempt to lay the foundations for a more general theory of power capable of shedding light on the common features of class, racial–ethnic and gender inequalities as well as those experienced by people who are discriminated against on account of their sexual orientations (Van Stolk and Wouters, 1987).

From Weber, Elias took the concept of the state as an organization which has a monopoly over violence in a given territory. However, unlike interpreters of Weber such as Dahrendorf (1959), Elias did not stress the legitimate character of this monopoly but recognized that states and their agents often use their power illegitimately and for their own rather than societal ends. Elias also went beyond Weber in establishing the linkage between the violence monopoly of states and their monopoly over taxation. Finally, he went beyond Weber by adapting Marx's theory of economic monopolization to political conflicts, showing, for example, how processes of state formation occur through hegemonial struggles and how, in their 'civilizing processes', the societies of Western Europe have moved from private ownership of the means of ruling to more public forms (Elias, 1994: 345ff.).

The main Durkheimian concept integrated into the figurational synthesis is that of 'interdependence' and, yet again, in Elias's hands it was radically transformed. Thus, while for Durkheim (1964), bonds of interdependence do not figure in simpler societies where 'mechanical solidarity' constitutes the dominant form of social cohesion but are produced only by a complex division of labour which gives rise to 'organic solidarity', for Elias (1978), although interdependency chains vary in their density, visibility and length, interdependence *per se* is a social universal, one of the principal building blocks of social life.[8] Nor did Elias use the concept of interdependence in a harmonistic sense. On the contrary, it was central to his concept of power[9] and he also wrote of the interdependence of enemies, even of 'survival units' such as tribes and states that are at war with each other (Elias, 1978: 74ff.).

A further way in which the figurational synthesis is rooted in the classical legacy consists in the concern of its practitioners with historical or long-term processes and their opposition to what Elias (1983) called 'the retreat of sociologists into the present'. What he arguably achieved in this connection were the foundations for a synthesis which, while maintaining the emphasis on social dynamics of theories such as those of Comte and Marx, was shorn of their evaluative concepts of inevitable 'progress' and their teleology, that is their ideas of social development as moving inexorably towards a specific goal – the scientific–industrial society in the case of Comte; the classless 'communist' society in the case of Marx. According to Elias (1978: 158ff.), the direction of social development is discernible but, at the present level of knowledge, only retrospectively.[10] Critics (Giddens, 1984; Horne and Jary, 1987) have often called this theory 'evolutionary', but, if it is, it is only 'evolutionary' in a weak sense. Elias wrote in this connection of 'blind' or 'unplanned' long-term processes and, without pretending to have done much more than point in the direction in which a better understanding must be sought, he replaced abstract teleological concepts such as Hegel's 'cunning of reason' and Marx's 'logic of capital' with the suggestion that the dynamics of long-term social processes derive from the interweaving of aggregates of individual acts. Each of these acts involves a measure of intentionality but the collective outcome, the direction of the long-term social process, is not planned. Engels anticipated aspects of such an idea when he wrote in 1890 that history makes itself in such a way that the final result always arises from conflicts between many individual wills....There are innumerable intersecting forces, an infinite series of parallelograms of forces which give rise to one resultant – the historical event. This...may...be viewed as the product of a power which, when taken as a whole, works unconsciously and without volition. For what each individual wills is obstructed by everyone else, and what emerges is something that no one willed. Thus past history proceeds in the manner of a natural process and is also essentially subject to the same laws of movement.

(Engels, 1942: 382)

History, of course, does not 'make itself' or 'act', only interdependent human individuals do. Nor is it a question of 'a power' 'working unconsciously' and 'without volition'. What is involved is a social process pure and simple. However, in Engel's case, this insight was lost because it became submerged within a reductionist, economistic theory and because Marx's collaborator did not see with sufficient clarity that the balance of similarities and differences between 'natural' and social processes is a subject which requires investigation. By contrast, although little more than a first approximation, Elias's concept has the merit of pointing us in a direction in which more 'reality-congruent' and testable (i.e. research-orientated) models can be sought.

What of the specifically twentieth-century elements in the 'Eliasian' synthesis? In the present context, it must be enough to mention two: Elias's modification of the sociology of knowledge from Mannheim (1953) and his adaptation of the concept of function. Since the charge of 'functionalism' is one of the criticisms most frequently laid at Elias's door (Horne and Jary, 1987; Critcher, 1988), it is on this latter aspect of his synthesis that I shall dwell.

For Elias, 'function' is an inherently relational concept and essential for any subject concerned with relationships. Perhaps the best way of clarifying Elias's distinctive adaptation of this concept is by means of a quotation. According to Elias:

[L]ike the concept of power, the concept of function must be understood as a concept of *relationship*. We can only speak of social functions when referring to interdependencies which constrain people to a greater or lesser extent....It is impossible to understand the function A performs for B without taking into account the function B performs for A. That is what is meant when it is said that the concept of function is a concept of relationship.

To put it at its simplest, one could say when one person (or a group...) lacks something which another person or group has the power to withhold, the latter has a function for the former. Thus men have a function for women and women for men, parents for children and children for parents. Enemies have a function for each other, because once they have become interdependent they have the power to with-hold from each other such elementary requirements as that of preserving their physical and social integrity, and ultimately of survival....

To understand the concept of 'function' in this way demonstrates its connection with power....People or groups which have functions for each other exercise constraint over each other. Their potential for withholding what they require is usually uneven, which means that the constraining power of one side is greater than that of the other.

(Elias, 1978: 77–8)

In Elias's hands the concept of function thus became inherently relational and geared towards power, constraint, conflict, struggle and exploitation. At its heart lies a radical and multi-levelled concept of interdependence. That is, according to Elias interdependence is not simply involved in the exchange of goods and services but is a more deeply rooted feature of human life. Goudsblom expressed this clearly when he wrote:

Living together in mutual dependencies is a basic condition for all human beings. From the moment it is born a child is dependent upon others who will feed, protect, fondle, and instruct it. The child may not always like the constraints exerted by its strong social depen-dencies, but it has no choice. By its own wants it is tied to other human beings – to its parents in the first place, and through its parents to many others, most of whom may remain unknown to the child for a long time, and perhaps for ever. All of the child's learning, its learning to speak, to think, to feel, to act, takes place in a setting of social dependencies. As a result to the very core of their personalities [people] are bonded to each other. They can be understood only in terms of the various figurations to which they have belonged in the past and which they continue to form in the present.

(Goudsblom, 1977: 7)

In fact, interdependence precedes birth and, as Goudsblom shows, is constitu-tive in the construction of the personality and individual habitus or 'self'. Each of us is born through the sexual interdependence of our parents into the interdependency ties of some form of family. Our family is locked into the chains of interdependence of a 'survival unit' such as a nation-state and, in the modern world, into interdependency chains that are increasingly global in scope. A crucial part of the socialization of individuals, furthermore, involves the learning of a language and, since languages are produced collectively over time, in this way people's interdependence with earlier generations is expressed. In the words of Elias, 'there is no one who is not and has never been interwoven into a network of people' (1978: 131) and it was in order to capture the idea of such networks that he coined the concept of 'figurations'. It is a term which, as Elias put it, 'can be applied to relatively small groups just as well as to societies made up of thousands or millions' (1978: 131). Put like that, it sounds deceptively simple. Arguably, however, it provides a means for avoiding a major problem that has plagued sociology and philosophy for years, what is called in philosophical terms the 'agency–structure dilemma', the problem of finding a way of conceptualizing the relations between individuals and societies in a way that is neither reifying nor reductionist; that is, which neither metaphysically postulates the existence in societies of supra-individual structures that are 'real', nor sees societies simply as aggregates of detached and independent individuals.

In a critique of the figurational sociology of sport, Horne and Jary (1987) quoted with approval an argument by Bauman that there is a clear affinity between 'the idea of figuration and such other household notions as "pattern" or "situation"' (Bauman, 1977: 117). This is in part a truism and in part a misconception. One can talk of a 'figuration of humans' but one cannot use the terms 'pattern' and 'situation' in this way. One has to refer to a pattern 'formed by' humans or to a situation 'in which they find themselves'. In other words, these more standard sociological terms separate the structures formed by humans from the humans themselves. In using the term 'pattern', for example, it is comparatively easy to reify, to convey the idea that one is talking of some 'thing' which exists in its own right, independently of the constituting human beings. In its turn, the term 'situation' is as vague and abstract as the terms 'background' and 'environment'. Like the latter, it conveys no connotation of structure. It can hardly have been accidental that one of the contexts where it was recommended was by Popper (1957) in his anti-structural advocacy of a sociology based on 'methodological individualism' and concerned with studying what he called the 'logic of situations'. That it is an issue of political and not simply academic relevance is suggested by the fact that former British Prime Minister Margaret Thatcher once said there is no such thing as society, only individuals and families. In so far as she was attacking the reifying usage of 'society', she was right. However, she was only half-right since an obvious counter to her assertion is that there are no 'individuals' in her sense, that is individuals who are completely detached and isolated except in the sense of belonging to families. On the contrary, humans are ineradicably interdependent as a species. Without interdependency ties they could neither be born nor survive. Individuals and figurations complement each other. They are part and parcel of the same phenomenon, what Elias (1991a) referred to as 'the society of individuals'.

Of course, the concept of figurations could be used in a reifying or reductionist manner but, in Elias's usage, it refers simultaneously to living individuals and their bonds of interdependence. It implies a reference both to 'action' and 'structure'. It was chosen on account of its linguistic properties compared with such less apposite terms as 'pattern', 'situation', 'system' and 'structure'. It was also forged in the context of a programme of research concerned with shedding light onto how 'agents' and 'structures' are *mutually* produced and *mutually* transformed. Abrams grasped Elias's contribution in this regard when he wrote:

> The most remarkable recent attempt to contain the social and the individual within a unified scheme of sociological analysis is probably that made by Norbert Elias. In *The Civilizing Process* Elias gives us both a principled critique of the dualism of conventional social analysis and, by way of a minutely documented case study of the 'history of manners', a thoroughly substantiated presentation of an alternative theoretical position.
>
> (Abrams, 1982: 230–1)

The theory of 'civilizing processes' to which Abrams was referring was described by Elias as a 'central theory'. He (Elias) regarded it as a testable theory towards which sociological research more generally could be orientated, in that way hopefully endowing the research process with a degree of continuity of a kind that has so far been rare and which will allow the fund of reliable knowledge to grow. The present book is orientated towards the theory of civilizing processes in this spirit. Although neither Elias nor any other figurational sociologist would want to suggest that anything any of us has so far done comes anywhere near matching the reliability of the knowledge claims made in the natural sciences – Elias was always at pains to stress how comparatively primitive knowledge in the social sciences remains – it is, I think, not too far fetched to express the hope that the various chapters in *Sport Matters* may be seen as adding at least some weight to Elias's claim. That is, the reader ought to judge what follows in terms of whether or not the arguments and evidence put forward in particular chapters provide confirmation of the basic tenets of the theory of civilizing processes, while at the same time illustrating the fruitfulness of this theory as a focus for and facilitator of a wide range of sociological research. In Chapter 1, I shall attempt to substantiate this claim by means of an exploration of some of the problems of the emotions in sport and leisure.

1

ON PROBLEMS OF THE EMOTIONS IN SPORT AND LEISURE

The subject of this chapter is the emotions aroused in sport and leisure.[1] The chapter is primarily conceptual and theoretical and advances the claim that a figurational approach, above all Elias's theory of civilizing processes (Elias, 1994), whilst not by any stretch of the imagination representing a panacea for all of sociology's current difficulties, is a means of avoiding some of the traps, for example that of thinking in terms of a crude 'work–leisure' dichotomy, into which practitioners of our specialism recurrently fall. In effect, what I shall do is revisit some of the tenets of the figurational perspective regarding sport and leisure as we set them forth in the 1960s, and assess how they have withstood the test of time. I shall start with an example which relates to football.

Describing the match between Portugal and North Korea in the World Cup Finals of 1966, sports journalist Brian Glanville wrote:

> the beginning of Portugal v. North Korea was sensational; a goal in a minute, followed by a second and a third; and all for North Korea. Their opening was extraordinary, a thunderclap of dazzling, attacking football, Pak Seung Jin driving home after a cutting right–wing move.
>
> Portugal had some twenty minutes to ride the punch, but could not do so, Li Dong–Woon scoring a second, Yang Sung Kook, the outside-left, a third. The Portuguese team, conquerors of Brazil, seemed now quite *bouleversés*. It would take genius to revive them; and Eusebio provided it, running, shooting and fighting with indomitable flair, long legs threshing past the little Korean defenders.
>
> After twenty-eight minutes Simoes put him through for his first goal. Three minutes from half-time a Korean brought Torres tumbling like a forest giant. Eusebio belted in the penalty, then urgently picked up the ball and galloped back to the centre-spot, to be intercepted and upbraided by an obscurely outraged Korean.
>
> Eusebio would, in the event, have the best of the argument. Fifteen minutes from half-time, he sprinted through again to equalize,

then, after another of his exhilarating left-wing runs, in which he negotiated tackles with electric ease, he was hacked down – and scored another penalty. At a corner kick Augusto got the fifth, and the Koreans, too generous and ingenuous to sit on their lead, were out.

(Glanville, 1980: 150)

Glanville captures here some of the excitement generated by this match. Elias and I watched it together on TV, as we did most of the 1966 World Cup matches which were screened. We had already been studying football for some seven years but it was our experience of the 1966 World Cup which helped to crystallize our focus on the significance of emotions in leisure. Elias, in fact, became so agitated when West Germany defeated Russia 2–1 in the semi-finals that he was led to expostulate: 'The Germans will claim this as revenge for their defeat at Stalingrad!' At that time, he was still only in the early stages of the partial reconciliation which he underwent with the country of his birth from which he had been forced to flee in 1933. Elias became even more agitated during the England–Germany Final when, towards the end of normal time, West Germany equalized – so agitated, indeed, that he was unable to watch the extra time. He had wanted first Russia and then England to win or, perhaps more accurately, he had wanted Germany to lose. More importantly for present purposes, however, our mutual reflection afterwards on Elias's agitation and my jubilation at England's one and only World Cup triumph, and the fact that, despite neither of us being particularly identified with either side, both of us found the Portugal v. North Korea match highly exciting, provided one of the early stimuli for our work on the social and psychological importance of emotions in sport and leisure. As I shall suggest later, in our joint work Elias and I tended, not to ignore, but to underplay the importance of identifications as far as emotional arousal in sport is concerned. There are, I think, three possible reasons why. The first was connected to our lack of identification with either side referred to above. The second was connected with Elias's painful experiences of nationalism and his ambivalence in that regard, especially towards Germany. The third is the fact that personal and collective identities are more important in sport than in many other leisure forms and we were trying to lay the foundations for a more general theory.

Let me move closer to my central theme. In his important, but in my view marginally flawed, *The Tourist Gaze* (1990), Urry defines tourism as follows:

Tourism is a leisure activity which presupposes its opposite, namely regulated and organized work. It is one manifestation of how work and leisure are organized as separate and regulated spheres of social practice in 'modern' societies. Indeed acting as a tourist is one of the defining characteristics of being 'modern' and is bound up with major transformations in paid work. This has come to be organized within particular places and to occur for regularized periods of time.

(Urry, 1990: 2–3)

Simply to have recognized that tourism is important and has been neglected by 'mainstream' sociologists represents an achievement. So does Urry's stress on the relationship between tourism and status. Nevertheless, his dichotomizing distinction between tourism and leisure and organized work is problematic. As Moorhouse (1989) pointed out, replication of the taken-for-granted dichotomy between work and leisure has for some time been *a*, if not *the*, major shortcoming of British empiricist–functionalist, Marxist and some feminist work in the sociology of leisure.[2] There are strong elements of this in Urry's analysis. Suggesting that 'the real orthodoxy of leisure studies is a conceptual and theoretical confusion coupled with an unwillingness to break out of its own isolation', Moorhouse argues that the subdiscipline ought, first, 'to abandon the commonsense categories of "work" and "leisure"' and, second, 'that social analysis must start taking a serious interest in fun and pleasure' (Moorhouse, 1989: 27–31). This is similar to what Elias and I argued in the 1960s. In fact, whilst Moorhouse's critique of the conventional sociology of leisure can be said to rest on a nuanced understanding of the differentiated character of work in 'advanced industrial' societies, Elias's and my critique involves an attempt to pinpoint the equally nuanced and differentiated character of their leisure. Thus, whilst Moorhouse argues that the sociology of leisure needs to pay greater attention to 'the real rhythms and experiences of life on the shop or office floor' (Moorhouse, 1989: 24), it was our contention that it ought to pay greater attention to the complexity of the experienced and otherwise empirically observable rhythms of life in various leisure contexts. It was also our contention that greater attention ought to be paid to pleasure and fun since they are crucial aspects of human life, even though, particularly in societies with a puritanical inheritance, they are not seen according to dominant conceptions as posing important problems for the social sciences.

Despite the manifest ways in which state, class, gender, 'racial'/ethnic and other forms of oppression are operative in the leisure field, it is also arguably the case that a primary requirement for advancing knowledge of their operation is a basic understanding of the ways in which various leisure institutions are structured *vis-à-vis* performing the function of providing satisfactions of various kinds. That is, for a full understanding of their use as vehicles of exploitation, one has to know what it is that makes them enjoyable. This was the principal issue which Elias and I addressed in our essays 'The Quest for Excitement in Leisure' and 'Leisure in the Sparetime Spectrum'. In summarizing what we argued I shall offer my own gloss on what we wrote and, later, propose some criticisms.

Our starting point was the suggestion that mainstream sociologists have for the most part sidelined leisure and sport because few of them have yet detached themselves sufficiently from the dominant thinking patterns, categories and values of Western societies to be able to grasp the social significance of leisure and sport and hence the sociological problems which they pose. More particularly, leisure and sport appear to have been neglected as objects of sociological reflection and research – I am thinking here of their absence or low status as topics covered in mainstream textbooks and theories – because they are seen as falling on the negatively valued side of a set of conventionally perceived and overlapping dichotomies such as those between work and leisure, mind and body, seriousness and pleasure, economic and non-economic phenomena, the 'rational' and the 'irrational', 'real life' and 'fantasy', and 'the useful' and 'the useless'. That is, in terms of the pervasive Western tendency towards reductionist and dualistic *Homo clausus* thinking, sport tends to be perceived as a trivial, irrational, pleasure-orientated sphere of life which engages 'the body' rather than 'the mind' and is of little or no 'practical' economic utility and value, whilst leisure activities such as visiting museums, art galleries and attending 'classical' concerts tend to be seen as engaging the other half of the dualism, that is 'the mind'. Alternatively, sport and leisure are reduced to economic terms and hence devalued as activities with their own significance and meaning. As a result, they are not seen as posing sociological problems of comparable significance to those associated with the 'necessary' and 'serious' business of economic and political life. So pervasive, indeed, are these *Homo clausus* tendencies that, even when sociologists such as Urry and those mentioned by Moorhouse grasp the growing significance of leisure and sport in the modern world, they tend to vitiate their analyses by reproducing the conventional dualisms, hence devaluing the leisure side of the equation and producing explanations which are mechanistic and overly simple.

What would a non-dualistic, *Homines aperti*-orientated sociological theory of sport and leisure look like? It would focus in the first instance on sport and leisure activities *per se* and it would be a theory in which an attempt is made to synthesize elements of biology, psychology, sociology and history. And it would have to be a theory which focuses equally on people's emotional and cognitive processes, seeking to understand their sport and leisure activities in the context of the fluid and diachronically changing 'figurations', that is spatio-temporal interdependency chains and networks, which they form and in which a labile balance of power and a corresponding lattice-work of tensions always form a crucial part (Elias, 1978: 128).

Although such terms tend to be used interchangeably both in popular usage and the sociology of sport and leisure, Elias and I suggested, first, that it is critical to draw a distinction between 'sparetime', the general, all-inclusive category – we rejected 'free time' in this connection on account of its ideological overtones – and 'leisure' which, we argued, ought to be treated as more specific. In other words, we proposed that, with the obvious exception of people employed occupationally in the sport and leisure industries, whilst all leisure activities are sparetime activities, not all sparetime is leisure. Non-leisure sparetime and leisure tend to differ in terms of the interplay between two dimensions both of which are continua rather than dichotomies: the continuum of choice and the continuum of routinization. Thus some non-occupational and in that sense 'sparetime' activities such as performing the duties involved in voluntarily running an amateur sports club, carrying out housework and catering for one's own and others' bodily needs – in patriarchal societies up to now the latter has primarily been a sphere to which females are confined and this includes the provision of refreshments in male amateur sports clubs – tend to involve a high degree of compulsion, to be highly routinized and to be performed with a high degree of emotional restraint. Leisure activities, by contrast, tend to involve a stronger element of choice, together with an element of what we called, at least as far as relatively 'civilized' societies are concerned, 'the controlled de-controlling of emotional controls'. We also suggested that occupational work can involve leisure-like elements, that it would be possible to construct a 'work spectrum' which overlaps and dovetails with the 'sparetime spectrum' (Elias and Dunning, 1986: 292–3) and that there appear to be three basic elements of leisure: sociability, motility and imagination/emotional arousal. Of course, in particular leisure activities, two and sometimes all three of these elements are fused. To these elements, there appear to correspond two main classes of leisure events: sociable activities and 'mimetic' or 'play' activities. Again, in particular activities these categories can be fused and there is also a miscellaneous category.

It is not a profound discovery to suggest that, although some are highly individualized and privatized, sociability is a basic element in most leisure activities. That is, a key element in the enjoyment is pleasurable emotional arousal through being in the company of others without any obligations apart from those which are taken on largely voluntarily. However, in some leisure activities such as parties, pub-going and visits to friends, sociability is the primary element. We referred to sociable gatherings of this type as 'leisure-gemeinschaften' because they provide opportunities for closer integration between people on a level of overt and, in intent, friendly emotionality which differs markedly from the forms of integration which are regarded as normal in the occupational and other non-leisure parts of life in contemporary industrial societies. It goes without saying that we were not using the concept of Gemeinschaft in the traditional sense where it involves a romantic yearning for a mythical lost past in which communities were supposedly conflict-free. And we suggested that taking risks with social norms – 'playing with norms' as one 'plays with fire' – tends to be a central characteristic of 'leisure-gemeinschaften'. As we expressed it: 'approaching the border of what is socially permissible and sometimes transgressing it, in short a limited breaking of social taboos in the company of others, probably adds spice to these gatherings' (Elias and Dunning, 1986: 121ff.). The sorts of things we had in mind were flirting at parties and such primarily male activities as telling risqué jokes, singing 'dirty' songs and playing at drinking games of the type which, in Britain, became traditionally associated with rugby clubs. Of course, as with every kind of risk taking, we recognized that in this sort of context people sometimes go too far and do serious social, psychological and even physical damage to themselves, to others and to their relationships.

By 'motility', we meant movement and were referring to such leisure activities as dance and a crucial dimension of sports. What we had in mind was similar in some ways to Csikzentmihalyi's (1975) concept of 'flow activities', that is activities in which one of the principal immediate sources of satisfaction is the pleasure taken through absorption in movement *per se*. Aerobics provides an example. We used the term 'mimetic' in order to underscore the idea that a number of leisure activities which otherwise appear to have little in common seem to share specific characteristics. We were thinking of activities which it is usual to classify under such different headings as 'sports', 'entertainment', 'culture' and the 'arts', and where the evaluation by 'intellectuals' of some as 'highbrow', some as 'middlebrow' and others as 'lowbrow', tends to express an unwillingness to perceive their common characteristics. More particularly, we suggested, activities in all these spheres arouse emotions of a specific type which are physiologically related to but experientially different from the emotions people experience in the ordinary course of their non-leisure lives and in seriously critical situations. In the context of mimetic activities and events – at the theatre or the cinema, at a concert or playing and watching a sport or game – people can experience and, for example in amateur dramatics, act out fear and laughter, anxiety and elation, sympathy and antipathy, and many other emotions which they experience in their non-leisure lives. Such activities are about emotional arousal but, in these mimetic contexts, all the sentiments and emotionally charged acts are transposed. Especially in comparison with the emotions generated in critical situations, they lose their 'sting'. To paraphrase Milton's commentary on Aristotle, they are blended 'with a kind of delight' (Elias and Dunning, 1986: 80). Even fear, horror, hatred and other ordinarily far from pleasant feelings can be associated in mimetic settings with enjoyment. Think of horror and murder films. Not everybody likes them and they can be a source of nightmares, perhaps particularly in children. Nevertheless, for many people watching 'spinechillers' is an enjoyable experience which they actively seek out. The experiences and behaviour of people in mimetic contexts such as these appear to involve a specific transposition of experiences and behaviour which are characteristic of the so-called 'serious' business of life, whether this term is used in relation to warfare, politics, occupational work or sparetime routines. Of course, 'serious' and 'mimetic' functions can be blended, as in the case of 'Live Aid' concerts, but let me stick to the task of clarification. Elias and I used the term 'mimetic' to express this special relationship between the non-mimetic business of life and this specific class of leisure activities. We did not mean by it 'imitative' in a literal sense. Sports such as rugby, football and cricket, for example, although they may be kinds of war-games, are not literally forms of military combat. Similarly, plays and films are often concerned with imaginary settings or they may deal with settings which no longer exist.

It was in order to capture complexities such as these that we used the concept of mimesis in a figurative sense akin to the usages of Aristotle and Milton (Elias and Dunning, 1986: 77). We did not mean by it that mimetic events are imitations of or that they 'mirror' 'real' life. As we used it, the term refers to the fact that, in mimetic contexts, emotions take on a different 'colour'. In these contexts people can experience and in some cases act out strong feelings without running the risks usually connected in the societies of the 'developed' world with emotional arousal. In fact the arousal of a specific type of excitement appears to stand at the core of all mimetic leisure. Outside mimetic contexts, the *public* arousal of strong excitement – and 'public' is a key term in this context – is, in the relatively civilized industrial societies of today, usually hedged in by social controls as well as by controls internalized at the level of individual conscience. In mimetic contexts by contrast, pleasurable excitement can be shown with social approval and without offence to individual conscience as long as it does not overstep specific limits. One can vicariously experience hatred and the desire to kill, defeating opponents and humiliating enemies. One can share making love to desirable men and women, experience the anxieties of threatened defeat and the open triumph of victory. In other words, one can – up to a point – tolerate the arousal of strong feelings of a great variety of types in societies which otherwise impose on people a life of relatively even and unemotional routines, and which require a high degree and great constancy of emotional control in all spheres of life.

It was our further contention that the feelings aroused by sociable and mimetic activities, particularly the latter, are tensed between opposites such as fear and elation and that they move, as it were, back and forth from one to another. Traditional concepts make it difficult to understand that, in leisure activities, seemingly antagonistic feelings such as fear and pleasure are not simply opposed to one another as they seem logically from a *Homo clausus* standpoint to be, but are inseparable parts of processes of leisure enjoyment. In that sense, we suggested, only limited satisfaction can be had from leisure occupations without short wisps of fear alternating with pleasurable hopes, brief flutters of anxiety alternating with anticipatory flutters of delight, and in 'ideal' cases, for example in a sports context when the side one is identified with wins, working up through waves of this kind to a cathartic climax in which all fears and anxieties are temporarily resolved, leaving people for a short while with an aftertaste of pleasurable satisfaction.

We further suggested that emotional arousal plays a central part in sport and leisure because it performs a de-routinizing function. Routines embody a high degree of security and we hypothesized that, without people exposing themselves to a degree of insecurity, to some more or less playful risk, the encrustation of routines could not be lessened. However, leisure activities can lose their de-routinizing function. They can become routinized through repetition or through too strict a measure of control and hence lose the capacity for generating excitement. That is, they can lose the function of providing a degree of insecurity, of satisfying people's expectation of something unexpected, and the risk, the tension, the flutter of anxiety which accompany it. These up and down, shorter and longer waves of playfully antagonistic feelings appear to be the mainspring of the emotional refreshment which can be provided by sport and leisure.

The preliminary theory of sport and leisure which Elias and I developed is related to the theory of civilizing processes (Elias, 1994). In a generally constructive discussion of our work, Chris Rojek suggests that we failed to take sufficiently into account Freud's arguments in *Civilization and its Discontents*. There is, writes Rojek, 'a danger of being overcomplacent'. Freud established that civilization is 'founded upon the repression of instinctual gratification' and contended that psychoanalysis shows that 'what we call our civilization is largely responsible for our misery' (Freud, 1939: 23). The possibility, continues Rojek, that civilizing processes may increase 'the sum of human unhappiness by generating mental discontent and illness…is not a proposition which Elias's work necessarily discounts, but at least one can say that it is hugely underdeveloped' (Rojek, 1995: 54). This misses two crucial points. First, that, in the course of the unplanned European civilizing processes which have been under way since the eleventh century, people have been constrained more and more to abandon the pleasures of unbridled emotional expression and increasingly to seek satisfactions of a longer-term, often more sublimatory, kind. In other words, this process has been a question of a balance between losses and gains. The second point is that the European civilizing processes have been inherently democratizing in the sense of involving – though not in any simple, unilinear way – an accretion of controls on those – rulers in relation to ruled, employers in relation to employees, males in relation to females, adults in relation to children – with the greatest power. The whole point about studying civilizing processes sociologically is to increase our understanding of them so that we shall hopefully be able in the future to bring them under greater conscious control, thereby reducing their 'blind' character and increasing the 'sum of human happiness'.

Nor would any figurational sociologist seek to deny that our work is 'hugely underdeveloped'. Just as Elias once described the work of Marx as 'one manifestation of a beginning' (Elias, 1994: xxxii), so he would have accepted that as describing his own work, too, with the possible proviso that the latter is perhaps in some ways more advanced because, coming later, he was able to integrate into his synthesis insights, not only from the work of Marx but also from authors such as Weber, Simmel, Mannheim and Freud. Above all, Rojek confuses the highly involved popular concept of 'civilization' with the more detached technical concept of a 'civilizing process' when he seems to accuse 'Eliasians' of 'over-complacency'. The theory of civilizing processes should be judged in terms of such testable criteria as whether civilizing processes are related to processes like state formation and the lengthening of interdependency chains and the balance between civilizing and de-civilizing tendencies in the development of sports. Alternatively, it should be judged over whether Elias's diagnosis of the relatively continuous civilizing and state-formation processes of Britain and France until recent times, compared with the relatively discontinuous and therefore, on balance, more 'de-civilizing' and 'barbarizing' development of Germany (Elias, 1996), can be supported by evidence and reasoning. Moral criteria such as the alleged 'over-complacency' of Elias and those striving to build on his work should not come into it.

Elias was far from 'complacent' about modern 'civilization'. He took seriously threats such as nuclear annihilation and ecological disaster, suggesting that people in the future may well come to see our times as part of an extended Middle Ages (Elias, 1994: 307–8) and people such as ourselves as 'late barbarians' (Elias, 1991b: 146–7). More to the point, Rojek apparently fails to realize that, whilst we would not seek to deny the ways in which 'civilizing processes' have so far increased in specific ways 'the sum of human unhappiness by generating mental discontent and illness',[3] Elias's and my work on sport and leisure was intended as an empirically supportable counter to the gross pessimism of Freud. What we tried to show is that, although unintended long-term processes were central to their development, it is possible for humans to create institutions which are genuine providers of recurrent short-term pleasure for people in large numbers and which, although they appear wasteful in terms of one of today's hegemonic values – the value-preference for work over leisure – are, in fact, less wasteful of human lives and resources than, for example, the high rates of unemployment, alienation and anomie which tend to result from the unbending prosecution of such values.

Our work on sport and leisure was not offered as some kind of 'fixed and final' theory but rather as a contribution which we believe(d) suggests ways in which recurrent difficulties in the field might possibly be circumvented. More particularly, it was our hypothesis that, in the most 'civilized' societies of the contemporary world, the routinization of social life has proceeded to such a degree that life for many people has become emotionally stale, and that some, for example working single mothers and many in the older age groups where retirement leads to degrees of social detachment, suffer from 'leisure starvation'. We also hypothesized that, as part of the same overall and, on balance, civilizing development, a complementary development has occurred in the sport and leisure field: the development of emotionally stimulating and arousing activities and institutions. It is important, though, to grasp that these have been subjected to the same sorts of civilizing constraints as the other spheres of modern life. That is why we spoke of the *controlled* de-controlling of emotional controls' (Elias, 1986b: 44 and 49). In other words, in the 'normal' course of events in the more 'civilized' societies of today, mimetic activities can act, for people fortunate enough to be able to avail themselves of the available opportunities, as counters to the routinization and emotional staleness of non-leisure life by providing a limited and controlled emotional arousal. Think of the standards by which the behaviour of modern theatre and concert audiences is controlled compared with the standards in operation in the eighteenth century. Or think of how violent and rough the antecedents of modern soccer and rugby were compared with contemporary forms. One indication of this is provided by a newspaper report from 1898 which Patrick Murphy came across in the early stages of our research into football hooliganism. The report in question reads:

> Herbert Carter has died at Carlisle from injuries received while playing football last week, when he was accidentally kicked in the abdomen. Two other football players also died on Saturday from injuries received in the course of play, vis Ellam of Sheffield, and Parks of Woodsley. These, together with the case of Partington, who died on Wednesday last, make a total of four deaths during the past week.
>
> (*Leicester Daily Mercury*, 15 November 1898)

It could have been a chance set of circumstances which led to the deaths of four soccer players being reported in a single week in 1898. However, it is our contention that the degree of civilization of sport and leisure varies with the levels of civilization of societies. That is, sport and leisure pursuits perform a de-routinizing function in *all* societies *via* the de-controlling of emotional controls but, in societies which grow more civilized and routinized, this de-controlling itself grows more controlled.[4] In fact, a balance has to be struck between the rules and norms which lead to de-controlling behaviour and those which are concerned with emotional controls. If the controls become too rigid, sport and leisure events can grow too routinized and boring. If they become too lax, this can lead to behaviour which transcends the bounds of what is regarded as civilized. As Elias expressed it with primary reference to soccer: 'Like other varieties of leisure-sport...soccer is precariously poised between two fatal dangers, boredom and violence' (Elias, 1986b: 51). When a sport or other leisure activity grows too violent or is perceived as doing so, the state and other powerful groups are liable to intervene. When it is perceived as recurrently producing boredom, intervention is undertaken by the authorities responsible for the activity in question, and/or, in sports and leisure activities which are commercialized/professionalized, by those who claim ownership rights.

It is not our contention that every leisure event in more civilized societies succeeds all the time in securing de-routinization. On the contrary, some are flops, whilst in other cases people's excitement rises to levels which lead them to contravene the accepted canons of civilized behaviour. As we expressed it, again using the example of football:

> a game of football constitutes a form of group dynamics with a built-in tension. If this tension, if the 'tonus' of the game becomes too low, its value as a leisure event declines. The game will be dull and boring. If the tension becomes too great, it can provide a lot of excitement for the spectators but it will also entail grave dangers for players and spectators alike. It passes from the mimetic to the non-mimetic sphere of serious crisis....[I]n this context one has to discard the negative undertones of the conventional concept of tension and... replace it by another which allows for a normal optimum tension which can, in the course of the figurational dynamics, become too high or too low.
>
> (Elias and Dunning, 1986: 89)

A degree of uncertainty thus has to be built into the structure of a leisure event by means of written rules and informal conventions to enable it to perform its de-routinizing function; that is, to enable it recurrently to generate a level of tension and hence emotional arousal which is neither too high nor too low. But, perhaps especially in the highly individualized and competitive societies of the industrialized world today, people constantly take risks with these rules and conventions, trying to stretch them in order to gain some sort of competitive advantage, in the world of sport to win a championship or match, in the arts by establishing a new 'school'. The dynamics of leisure events thus involve perpetual risk taking and the struggle to control it, as well as a tendency for such events to vacillate between levels of tension–excitement which are either too high or too low and the consequent efforts to restore their 'tonus' to an optimum level.

It was also our contention that

> [t]his more dynamic concept of tension applies not only to [leisure events] as such but also to the participants. Individual people, too, can live with a built-in tension which is higher...or lower than normal, but they are only without tension when they die. In societies such as ours which require an all-round emotional discipline and circumspection, the scope for strong pleasurable feelings openly expressed is severely hedged in. For many people it is not only in their occupational but also in their private lives that one day is the same as another. For many...nothing new, nothing stirring ever happens. Their tension, their tonus, their vitality...is thus lowered. In a simple or complex form, on a low or a high level, leisure activities provide, for a short while, the upsurge of strong pleasurable feelings which is often lacking in the ordinary routines of life. Their function is not, as

31

is often believed, a liberation from tensions but the restoration of that measure of tension which is an essential ingredient of mental health. The essential character of their cathartic effect is the restoration of normal mental 'tonus' through a temporary and transient upsurge of pleasurable excitement.

(Elias and Dunning, 1986: 89)

Thus *pace* Rojek and *pace* Freud, specific 'contents' and not only 'discontents' appear to have developed in the civilizing processes of the West. However, we have been criticized in this connection for relying on Aristotle's concept of catharsis. Allen Guttmann, for example, has written that he has doubts about our

> use of the concept of catharsis as it relates to sports. After all, the most 'dramatic' ball game is very different from the experience that Aristotle analyses in the *Poetics*. Social psychologists have done an enormous amount of work devoted to testing the catharsis theory…[and it all] seems to indicate that sports spectacles increase rather than decrease propensities to commit acts of violence.…
>
> There are also empirical data which raise questions about the theory that the quest for excitement in sports is an escape from the routinization of modern life. If this is the case…then how can we explain…that the advantaged rather than the disadvantaged members of society are likely to do and to watch sports? In other words, those whose lives are least routinized – that is, professionals – are more likely to seek excitement in sports than those whose lives are most routinized: factory workers and clerical personnel. Perhaps the answer lies in the *kinds* of sports that are popular with different groups.
>
> (Guttmann, 1992: 157)

These criticisms deserve an answer. The first thing worthy of note is that Guttmann fails to appreciate that our hypothesis that sport and 'the arts' have common properties as leisure forms does not entail a claim that they are identical. Indeed, different sports, arts and leisure forms generate different levels of tension and they generate them differently. But despite their differences they share structures geared to performing the mimetic function of emotional arousal. The point is that this balance of similarities and differences needs to be investigated empirically. However, research in the sociology of sport and leisure to date has tended to take the structural properties of sports and leisure forms for granted, failing to examine the minutiae of how they are structured and how they work.

Pace Guttmann, Elias and I were also well aware of the research on catharsis in sport and the fact that it indicates that sports tend to increase rather than reduce propensities to aggression. However, such research is based on a concept of catharsis which is different from Aristotle's and our own. More particularly, it is based on an overly simple frustration–aggression hypothesis and seeks to test – often under artificial laboratory conditions – the idea that sports, especially contact and combat sports, represent a context where people can vicariously discharge the frustration-engendered aggressiveness generated in their everyday lives. By contrast, our hypothesis holds that sports are concerned with the *creation* rather than in any simple sense the relief or discharge of tensions. Furthermore, as figurational sociologists we focus on sports as events which can only be understood in relation to their *total* context, the often different meanings attached to them by different groups and individuals, and the different structurally generated interests, values and power resources of such personnel. We also stress such facts as that modern societies remain predominantly patriarchal, that modern sport started out as a male preserve and that many sports continue to act as vehicles for the expression and reproduction of male aggressiveness (Dunning and Sheard, 1973; Dunning, 1986; Dunning and Maguire, 1996). We have also sought to show how, in contexts such as soccer hooliganism, aggression and violence can be experienced as pleasurable and exciting (Dunning *et al.*, 1988), and how modern sports are embedded in a complex set of political and economic nexuses which are increasingly becoming global in scope (Dunning and Sheard, 1979; Maguire, 1990, 1991, 1993a, 1993c, 1994a, 1994b, 1996).

Guttmann also seems to have understood our concept of routinization in a popular sense where it equates to the performance of simple and repetitive tasks which tend to be experienced as boring. However, while that is part of it, our definition is more sociological. We defined 'routines' as

> recurrent channels of action enforced by interdependence with others, and which impose upon the individual a fairly high degree of regularity, steadiness and emotional control in conduct and which block other channels of action even if they correspond better to the mood, the feelings, the emotional needs of the moment.
>
> (Elias and Dunning, 1986: 98)

In other words, our definition stresses the compelling character of routines, the fact that they are, on balance, directed towards and controlled by others rather than oneself and that they involve not only regularity but social pressure towards emotional control. Such a definition seems fully compatible with Guttmann's observation – which, I think, holds good more for North America than Britain and perhaps the other societies of Western Europe and probably fails to take spectatorship and TV viewing sufficiently into account – that sport tends to be engaged in more by middle- than working-class groups. That is, whilst manual and routine non-manual workers may have occupations which are highly routinized in the sense of involving simple and repetitive tasks, people who work in professional and managerial occupations tend to experience greater psychological and social pressure to exercise nuanced and differentiated self-control in the public phases of their work.

Guttmann is on safer ground in criticizing us for neglecting 'the enormously important role played by the psychological process of identification, which turns athletes into symbolic representations of social groups' (Guttmann, 1992: 158) That is true of our joint work but less true of the work I carried out with my Leicester colleagues where we suggested that, in sports spectatorship, identification with a team or individual sportsperson is a precondition for fully 'engaging the gears' of one's passions (Murphy *et al.*, 1990: 3ff.; see also the introduction to the present volume). As I have noted, Maguire (1992) refers cogently to a 'quest for exciting significance' in this regard. What he means is that, in sport, quests for identity, identification, meaning and prestige are interwoven in complex ways with the quest for emotional arousal. In an early essay, I used the fact of team identifications to cast doubts on the conventional concept of catharsis, pointing out that passionately committed sports fans are liable to be deeply frustrated if the team they support loses and may well aggressively 'take it out' on others through verbal and/or physical violence (Dunning, 1972).

A further criticism can be levelled at one aspect of what Elias wrote independently on leisure. In his introduction to *Quest for Excitement*, he made a number of references to 'stress tensions'. What he meant are the tensions people are liable to experience as a result of being socially constrained to strive to maintain an even control over their drives and affects. According to Elias, such tensions tend to be widespread in societies 'where fairly high civilizing standards all round are safeguarded and maintained by a highly effective state-internal control of physical violence' and he continued:

> Most human societies...develop...counter-measures against the stress-tensions they themselves generate. In the case of societies at a relatively late level of civilization, that is with relatively stable, even and temperate restraints all round and with strong sublimatory demands, one can usually observe a considerable variety of leisure activities with that function, of which sport is one. But in order to fulfil the function of providing release of stress tensions, these activities must conform to the comparative sensitivity to physical violence which is characteristic of people's social habitus at the later stages of a civilizing process.
>
> (Elias, 1986b: 41–2)

Elias was discussing here some of the unsolved 'problems of civilization' which he raised towards the end of *The Civilizing Process*. They were the sorts of issues raised by Freud in *Civilization and its Discontents* (1939) and which Marcuse discussed from a Marxist standpoint in *Eros and Civilization* (1955) through such concepts as 'surplus repression'. Elias was more open-ended in his approach than these scholars, never pretending that we have sufficient knowledge at present to solve such problems. They are serious problems for which practical solutions are urgently required and will only be resolvable with the help of theory-guided research. For present purposes, however, it seems more pertinent to note that, by introducing the serious issue of 'stress tensions' into our theory of leisure, Elias was departing from the theory as originally constructed. That was concerned, not with the relationship between leisure and stress tensions, but with the need for the arousal of controlled tensions which are experienced as pleasurable in societies which are highly routinized and in that sense 'unexciting'. 'Stress tensions' are a different matter and, at least in their more serious forms – one is not dealing here with a simple dichotomy but with a complex continuum – are perhaps better addressed by means of calming activities such as basket weaving, gardening and listening to soothing music, and not by highly competitive, intensely arousing, physically combative activities such as sports.

In what is in many ways a balanced discussion of the figurational contributions to the study of sport and leisure, Chris Rojek suggests that

> when pressed, figurational sociologists insist that their work is more 'objectively adequate' than rival theories. By the term 'objectively adequate' is meant that the propositions of figurational sociology correspond more closely to the observable facts of sport and leisure than competing theories in the field. Now few words in the English language carry the same weight as 'objectivity'. By insisting on superior 'object adequacy' figurational sociologists imply that forms of sociology which are concerned with impressions and experience are less valuable....The point to be made here is that in claiming to be objectively adequate figurational sociologists fail to be sufficiently reflexive about their own methods.
>
> (Rojek, 1995: 54–5)

Figurational sociologists make no such claims. Nor do terms such as 'objectivity' and 'objectively adequate' appear in our vocabulary. We see the gaining of knowledge as a conflictful process and eschew what one might call the political/ideological or philosophical 'quick fix'. We stress the need to carry out theory-guided research and to get away from what seems to have become a widespread tendency in sociology in recent years to live parasitically off the work of others, especially that of the latest philosophers who have come to be regarded as 'trendy' whilst eschewing primary research. Our concern is via research to develop more 'object adequate' or 'reality congruent' representations, that is representations which are more 'adequate' regarding their empirically observable 'objects' or more 'congruent' with some aspect or aspects of 'reality' than is the case with existing concepts. We do this by seeking in our research to be as 'detached' as possible. However, while our *aim* in this connection is by means of a 'detour via detachment' (Elias, 1987) in which our feelings are momentarily held in check to add to the sum of 'reality congruent' knowledge, we do not *claim* or *insist* that we have produced such knowledge. Rather, we put our work into the sociological arena in the hope that others will debate, strive to understand and, above all, test it by means of further research.

Conclusion

In this chapter, I have suggested that a figurational/process-sociological approach to the study of sport and leisure has certain advantages relative to more 'conventional' approaches which, whatever contributions they make in other ways, tend to be vitiated by an unreflecting commitment to what Elias (1978) called *Homo clausus* assumptions. Among these advantages are that a figurational/process-sociological approach: (1) pays due attention to the central part played by emotions in leisure; (2) seeks to develop concepts, hypotheses and theories by means of constant cross-fertilization with empirical enquiries – a process in which the empirical and the theoretical are both equally necessary and in which neither should be allowed to gain the upper hand; (3) tries to avoid the oversimplifications and distortions of the diverse and complex sport and leisure world which can result from an unreflecting commitment to conventional dualisms such as those between 'work' and 'leisure', 'body' and 'mind', etc.; and (4) is concerned with an attempt to add to knowledge and seeks to maximize the degree of distanciation in sociological work from short-term pressures, anxieties and concerns. It is probably worth repeating that, whilst this is our aim, we do not claim to have achieved it. That must be an issue on which others judge.

I have also suggested that a basic theory which focuses on sport and leisure behaviour and institutions as social facts in their own right, tracing their connections with but not reducing them to other areas of social life, can help to throw light on the manifold ways in which, for example, agencies of industry and the state, together with class, 'racial'/ethnic, gender and other inequalities, impact on the contouring of leisure. Such a theory might even be a *sine qua non* in this connection, for example by helping to explain how and why people who are far from being 'cultural dopes' play a part in perpetuating institutions (e.g. American football, professional soccer or the popular music industry) through which they are exploited in the sense of allowing others to amass profit or 'surplus value' out of their strong commitments. In other words, the figurational/process-sociological approach is fully attuned to the part played by attempts at exploitation, manipulation and control – which, of course, are sometimes more and sometimes less successful and frequently result in the production of unintended consequences – in sport and leisure as in any other social field. That is, the figurational approach takes it as axiomatic that, as Elias expressed it, power is 'a structural characteristic...of all human relationships' (Elias, 1978: 74). I would only want to add that advances in understanding are less likely to come via a priori theorizing about, for example, the effects of advertising on leisure preferences, than they are from theory-guided research. That is, advance of understanding is less likely to come from mechanically reading and debating conclusions derived from say, Marx, Gramsci, Foucault, Baudrillard, Raymond Williams, Bourdieu and, yes, Elias, than they are from testing hypotheses derived from such authors. Advances will also be more likely if we succeed in shifting the balance in the field in at least two ways: first, between debate and (theory-orientated) research more in favour of the latter; and second, more in favour of debates about sociological research and theories which are systematically focused on the empirically observable social world as opposed to arcane debates about how to interpret the latest musings of non-research-orientated philosophers whose work happens, for the moment, to be fashionable (Mouzelis, 1991). In saying this, I do not wish totally to deny the value of what philosophically influenced sociologists write but rather to suggest that philosophical ideas usually need to be recast and, above all, purged of *Homo clausus* elements before they can become unambiguously useful in a context of theory-guided research and research-orientated theory.

Also central among my arguments has been the contention that Elias's theory of civilizing processes can act as what Elias would have called a 'central theory': that is, be used as a guiding, co-ordinating, synthesizing and hypothesis-forming theory in the sociology of sport and leisure as elsewhere. I realize that, especially in the multi-paradigmatic and conflict-ridden world of present-day sociology, this is liable to give rise to the charge that I am 'privileging' Elias. That is a charge to which I readily accede. I do so because of the slowly growing recognition that Elias was one of the twentieth century's most important sociologists on account of the reality-orientation of his work. I was lucky enough to have worked with him but that is not the point on which I wish to dwell. That concerns the potential fruitfulness of the theory of civilizing processes for the study of sport and leisure. However, a precondition for testing it is that it should not be rejected on 'knee-jerk' grounds on account, for example, of the Holocaust or other examples of twentieth-century barbarism. Elias was born a German Jew, fled from Germany in 1933 and his mother was murdered in Auschwitz. He was thus acquainted with the Holocaust in deeply personal terms and his experiences in that regard influenced him profoundly in developing the theory of civilizing processes in the first place.

In Chapter 2, I shall explore the explanatory value of the theory of civilizing processes as far as the development of modern sport is concerned, focusing in that connection in particular on issues of sport and violence as seen from a long-term perspective.

2

SPORT IN THE WESTERN CIVILIZING PROCESS

It is widely believed that we are living today in one of history's most violent periods. Indeed, it is probably fair to say that, in Western societies, the fear that we are currently undergoing a process of 'de-civilization' is deeply imprinted in the contemporary *Zeitgeist*, one of the dominant beliefs of our times. The psychologists Eysenck and Nias expressed this when they wrote of 'a number of acknowledged facts' which, they claimed, 'have helped to persuade many people that the civilization in which we live may be in danger of being submerged under a deluge of crime and violence' (Eysenck and Nias, 1978: 17). From a figurational standpoint, 'civilization' is *always* potentially faced with such a danger: that is why we lay stress on increasing understanding of the processes involved. It is a moot point, however, whether Eysenck and Nias's contention is based on an analysis which is sufficiently detached.

Arguing from a different psychological perspective, Peter Marsh contended around the same time that recent social developments in Britain have led to a decline in opportunities for 'socially constructive ritual violence' – what he called 'aggro' – with the consequence that uncontrolled and destructive violence has increased. Using a variation of Fromm's distinction between 'benign' and 'malignant' aggression (Fromm, 1977), Marsh argued that there has taken place a 'drift from "good" violence into "bad" violence'. People, he said, are 'about as aggressive as they always were but aggression, as its expression becomes less orderly, has more blood as its consequence' (Marsh, 1978: 142). Marsh even went so far as to claim that, given certain peculiarities of American social development, a tradition of 'aggro' or 'ritualized violence' never emerged in the USA, in a word that violence in the USA has always been 'disorderly' and 'malign' (Marsh, 1978: 80ff.). A possible implication of this argument is that, with the supposed breakdown of 'aggro' in European societies, we are currently witnessing – as part of a more general process of 'Americanization' associated with globalization? – a convergence of the societies of Western Europe towards American forms and levels of violence in sport and elsewhere. Let me turn to more general beliefs about violence in sport.

Writing in 1988, August Kirsch, Director of the Federal Institute of Sports Science in the then Federal Republic of Germany, suggested that: 'spectator riots at big sports events are one of the negative accompaniments of modern sport' (Hahn *et al.*, 1988: 7). Peter S. Greenberg, an American journalist, even went so far as to claim in the 1970s that 'mass recreational violence has never before been so rampant in the sports arenas of America' (in Yiannakis *et al.*, 1979: 217–21). Probably the most extreme statement of this kind was made, also in the 1970s, by Australian journalist Don Atyeo. He detected parallels between modern sports and their counterparts in Ancient Rome, suggesting that a self-destructive trend towards greater violence is occurring world–wide in modern sport, principally as a result of the demands of sensation-seeking spectators. Atyeo expressed his apocalyptic vision thus:

> The future of violent sports seems assured. Games will grow harder and bloodier to feed the rising appetite of an audience which will grow both increasingly more jaded and satiated with violence, and increasingly more violent itself, until, perhaps, something happens to bring it all crashing down. This time around, though, the likelihood is that it won't be the barbarian hordes banging on the gates outside which will destroy the Coliseum. This time the violence will be of sport's own making and will come from within the walls of the Coliseum itself.
>
> (Atyeo, 1979: 377)

This is a rather extreme view. However, more sober and research-based socio-logical diagnoses concur with the view that sports violence is currently increasing. For example, in a comprehensive and insightful literature review Kevin Young recently suggested that

> Sports-related violence is considered to have become a critical social problem in many countries. Fans of European sport, particularly soccer, have gained notoriety for their violence inside and outside stadia. Violent disturbances at sport have occurred with some frequency in Australia, Central and South America, Asia and North America.
>
> (Young, 1991: 539)

What light do figurational theory and research throw onto this complex and contentious field? In order to move towards an answer, I shall provide a thumbnail sketch of the theory of civilizing processes (Elias, 1994) starting with a discussion of two general issues.

The first relates to the fact that there is at least one sense in which the belief that the twentieth century has witnessed a trend towards increasing violence is based on solid foundations. More particularly, as an accompani-ment of the increasing pace and scope of global social change, the twentieth century is the first in which *world* wars have occurred. It has also been a century in which the violence and effectiveness of the technology of mass destruction have increased to hitherto unprecedented levels, a fact evidenced above all in nuclear weapons and the weaponry of chemical and germ warfare. There have also been numerous violent and destructive wars since 1945. However, they have been local in scope, restricted, with the recent exception of the wars associated with the break-up of Yugoslavia and the USSR, mainly to Third World countries, and many areas of the world, particularly in the West, have enjoyed hitherto unprecedented levels of peace and prosperity since the end of the Second World War. A world authority comparable with those of Western nation-states and based, like them, on a monopoly of violence and taxation, has not emerged and perhaps never will. Nevertheless, this process of increasingly localized and destructive wars, coupled with the enjoyment of relative peace elsewhere, has been in some ways reminiscent of the civilizing and state-formation processes of Western Europe since the Middle Ages. More particularly, as Elias showed, whilst changing from feudal through dynastic to nation-state forms, these societies grew increasingly pacified internally whilst engaging in increasingly violent and destructive warfare with each other. What he called the (European) 'civilizing process' took place in that context.

Dutch political scientist Godfried van Benthem van den Bergh uses Elias's theory to hypothesize that the invention and deployment of nuclear weapons have had the unintended consequence of forcing the leaders of the nuclear powers to conduct themselves in more prudent and restrained ways than their predecessors did in pre-nuclear times. In other words, it is van Benthem van den Bergh's contention that, in the absence of world government, nuclear weapons can be considered as an international equivalent of the violence monopolies of nation-states and to have had, on balance, civilizing consequences (van Benthem van den Bergh, 1992; see also Mennell, 1989, 1992). Although Elias disagreed with it, this hypothesis is persuasive. However, it may underestimate the difficulties faced by the initial nuclear oligopolists in retaining their control over nuclear weapons and the degree to which processes of learning in nuclear confrontations which stop short of actual nuclear exchanges and where the outcome is by no means certain are probably a precondition for the emergence of these civilizing restraints in international relations. For present purposes, however, the main point to stress is that figurational sociologists do not engage in 'nuclear' or 'Holocaust denial' but have concerned themselves with such issues at least as much and perhaps even more than the members of other sociological schools. Indeed, facing up to issues of violence constitutes one of their central starting points.

My second point relates to a difference between the theoretical underpinnings of the theory of civilizing processes regarding violence and aggression compared with the work of those who have been influenced by Lorenz (1966) or Freud (1939). The core of the figurational position on the balance between 'nature' and 'nurture' in the production of human violence has been summarized by Elias thus. The idea that humans have an innate aggressive drive which structurally resembles the sex drive, he says, is a false way of posing the problem. What we have is an 'innate potential to shift [our] whole physical apparatus to a different gear if [we] feel endangered'. This is the so-called 'flight–fight mechanism' through which the human body reacts to danger by 'an automatic adjustment which prepares the way for intensive movement of the skeletal muscles, as in combat or flight'. According to Elias, however, human 'drives' such as the hunger or sex drive are released physiologically, 'relatively independently of the actual situation' in which people find themselves. By contrast, the shifting of the body-economy 'to combat-or-flight readiness is conditioned to a far greater extent by a specific situation, whether present or remembered'. Such situations can be 'natural', for example being confronted by a wild animal, or social, especially conflict. However, 'in conscious opposition to Lorenz and others who ascribe an aggression drive to people on the model of the sexual drive, it is not aggressiveness that triggers conflicts but conflicts that trigger aggressiveness'. Of course, there is a degree of rhetorical exaggeration in this. Elias would not have denied that some conflicts are caused by the disruptiveness of aggressive individuals or that, in some cases, the aggressiveness of such individuals has psychological and perhaps even genetic roots. Nor would he have denied the interdependence of different human drives (Elias, 1994: 156). It was simply that he wanted to counter the crude psychological reductionism involved in the notion of an 'aggressive instinct'.[1]

The theory of civilizing processes

An anonymous reviewer of my proposal for *Sport Matters* generally approved of the planned book but expressed reservations regarding a discussion of sport in the Western civilizing process because, he/she said, the topic had 'already been sufficiently debated'. This revealed a view of sociology which seems nowadays to be widespread but which is at variance with that of figurational sociologists. We see the subject as being less about debate – although, of course, public debate is crucial – than building up reliable knowledge through the interplay of theory and research. Seen in this light, it is mistaken to regard a theory as no longer deserving a place on the sociological agenda simply because it has been 'sufficiently debated'. Only if theories have been *refuted* by reasoning and research – a primary requirement of which is that they should be accurately interpreted – should they be consigned to the dustbin and forgotten. It is my contention that, however much it may have been critically *debated*, Elias's theory of civilizing processes has so far stood the test on theoretical and empirical grounds. That is, while neither Elias nor any other figurational sociologist would want to claim that our understanding of civilizing and de-civilizing processes at the moment is anything more than rudimentary, Elias's preliminary theory – and it is to be regarded at present as nothing more than that – has yet to be refuted by observation and reasoning.

English-speaking sociologists, in particular, appear to experience difficulties with Elias's theory. The reasons why may be connected with the translation of his book and, in part, with an emotional reaction to the term 'civilization', which is seen as value laden in a moral sense. Elias's book was first published in 1939 under the title *Über den Prozess der Zivilisation* – 'on' or 'about' the process of civilization. This shows that Elias saw the theory as a *contribution* to the understanding of the development of the West rather than as a fully fledged theory. That is lost in the bald English translation of the title as *The Civilizing Process*.[2] Also lost in the critical reaction is any reference to the context in which the book was originally produced. Writing as he did in exile in Britain after the Nazi rise to power and on the eve of the Second World War, Elias wanted to convey the lost idea of 'civilization' not only as a process rather than, as many people saw it in the West, an already accomplished state, but, particularly at that historical juncture, as a social formation which was massively on trial as well. In short, his work was centrally concerned from the beginning with civilizing (social) controls as a more or less fragile shell and with civilizing processes as developments which are liable, under specific and at present not well-understood conditions, to go into reverse.[3]

In *The Civilizing Process*, Elias started by considering the meaning of the term 'civilization' and reached the conclusion that, since any aspect of human society and behaviour can be judged to be 'civilized' or 'uncivilized', providing such a definition is a difficult if not impossible task. It is easier, said Elias, to specify the function of the term. It has come, he argued, to express the self-image of the most powerful Western nations and acquired in that connection derogatory and racist connotations, not only in relation to what Westerners call the 'primitive' or 'barbaric' non-Western societies they have conquered, colonized or otherwise subjected to domination, but also in relation to 'less advanced', that is less powerful, societies and outsider groups in the West itself. Interestingly, Elias showed how the First World War was fought by Britain and France against Germany in the name of 'civilization', and how, in the eighteenth, nineteenth and early twentieth centuries when the formerly disunited and therefore relatively weak Germans were engaged in a process of catching up with their more united and powerful Western neighbours, many Germans became ambivalent about 'civilization', preferring to express their self-image through the more particularistic concept of *Kultur* ('culture') (Elias 1994: 3 ff.; Williams, 1976).

A further way in which Elias sought to distance his theory from the evaluative connotations of the popular concept was by means of an explicit denial that Western societies have come to represent some kind of 'end-point' or 'pinnacle' (Elias, 1994: 522). People in the present-day West may consider themselves to be 'civilized' and regard Western civilization as 'complete', but, whilst it can be empirically shown that they have grown *more* 'civilized' than their medieval forebears in certain respects (i.e. that, although there is no guarantee that such a process will continue in the future, they can be said to have undergone a 'civilizing process' in a technical sense), Elias was clear that present-day Westerners are far from being civilized in any absolute way and speculated, as I noted in Chapter 1, that future historians may come to judge even the most 'advanced' present-day Western societies as having formed part of an 'extended Middle Ages' (Elias, 1994) and their members as 'late barbarians' (Elias, 1991b).

The reverse side of this coin, according to Elias, is that, with the marginal exception of the unborn and as yet unsocialized child, there is no zero point of civilization, no absolutely uncivilized society or individual. It was also Elias's contention that the level of development of a society can be measured with a relatively high degree of detachment by means of what he called 'the triad of basic controls' (Elias, 1978: 156). These are: (1) the extent of societies' control-chances over natural events; (2) the extent of societies' control-chances over human relationships; and (3) the extent to which societies' individual members have learned to exercise self-control. The theory of civilizing processes is concerned with the second and third of these 'basic controls', and the two volumes of *The Civilizing Process* involve an attempt to trace developments in these regards in the most powerful societies of Western Europe from the Middle Ages to the early twentieth century.[4] In short, far from being some kind of fully fledged and universally applicable construct, the theory of civilizing processes as it stands at present is strictly delimited in terms of time and space. It attempts to account for the different trajectories of development mainly of Britain, France and Germany, and, if one takes Elias's work on the Germans into account, seeks to add to the understanding of how and why German development up to 1945 went, on balance, in a 'barbarizing' direction resulting in Nazism and the Holocaust (Elias, 1996). Whether and how far this theory is applicable in non-Western contexts and, indeed, in societies other than those studied by Elias is a matter for research. Even as far as Britain, France and Germany are concerned, there is a need to test and refine Elias's findings and to probe areas of social life which he did not touch.

It is neither possible nor necessary in this context to specify in detail the entire spectrum of factual developments which Elias saw as constituting the Western civilizing process. It is enough to stress that he was clear about the fact that, as with social developments more generally, it has been based on the intergenerational transmission of learned experiences. Hence it is reversible. In fact, it is useful to think of Elias's theory as operating on two distinct yet interpenetrating levels. On the one hand, it involves an empirical generalization about the overall trajectory of personality structure, habitus formation and social standards in the societies of Western Europe from the Middle Ages until the early twentieth century. On the other, it involves the hypothesizing of an explanatory connection between what Elias sought to establish was an empirically demonstrable civilizing trajectory at the levels of personality, habitus and standards and an equally demonstrable tendency towards more effective forms of state centralization and control. More particularly, Elias's time-series data on what would conventionally be called the 'microsocial' or 'behavioural-normative' level – his principal evidence comes from manners books – consistently reveal a dominant trend which, despite variations in speed and temporary reversals, continued over long periods in the direction of: the elaboration and refinement of manners and socially required standards of behaviour; increasing social pressure on people to exercise an even measure of all-round self-restraint over their feelings and behaviour, that is regarding all aspects of bodily functions and in more and more social situations; a shift in the always socially necessary balance between external constraints and self-constraints in favour of self-constraints; an advancing threshold of repugnance regarding bodily functions such as eating, drinking, defecation, urination, sex and sleeping, a process in terms of which these functions and the connected bodily organs came to be increasingly laden with taboos and surrounded by feelings of anxiety, embarrassment, guilt and shame; an advancing threshold of repugnance regarding engaging in and even witnessing violent acts; and, as a corollary of this generally advancing threshold of repugnance, a tendency to push violence and acts connected with biological functions increasingly 'behind the scenes'. Examples are the abandonment of public executions and the confining of sex and sleeping increasingly to the bedroom. In a word, according to Elias a central tendency of European civilizing processes has involved a trend towards privatization.

Elias sought to explain this empirical generalization principally by reference to empirical data on state formation, that is regarding the unplanned or 'blind' establishment[5] at the 'macro' level of social integration of relatively stable and secure centralized state monopolies on violence and taxation – according to Elias, tax and violence are the major 'means of ruling'[6] – processes in which violent 'hegemonial' or 'elimination' struggles among kings and other feudal lords were decisive. Using more conventional language, what was involved was the gradual transition via competitive struggle from highly decentralized feudal societies to more highly centralized dynastic states and eventually to nation-states.[7]

According to Elias, an important corollary of this unplanned process was the gradual pacification of larger and larger spaces within each developing state. In other words, states which remained externally embattled at each stage – and it is crucial to remember that – became increasingly pacified internally. In turn, internal pacification facilitated material production, the growth of trade, an increase in the amount and circulation of money together with a growing 'monetarization' of social relations, and correlatively with all of this, a lengthening of interdependency chains, that is a shift from bonds of interdependence which were primarily local in scope to bonds which became increasingly national and subsequently international.

According to Elias, the 'macrosocial' consequences of this complex of changes were principally threefold. More particularly, there took place: (1) a further augmentation of state power (in the first instance primarily royal power) because tax revenues and the capacity of governments to equip standing armies increased; (2) a progressive augmentation of the power of middle-class or 'bourgeois' groups, that is initially of town-dwelling groups who lived by trade and whose power and status depended primarily on relatively fluid and expandable monetary resources as opposed to the comparatively fixed resource of land; and (3) a correlative weakening of the 'warrior aristocracy', that is of knights whose power depended fundamentally on land ownership and force of arms. At the point where the power of these rising middle- and falling upper-class groups became approximately equal, kings became able to play off one against the other and uphold a claim to 'absolute rule'.

This development went further in France than elsewhere – Louis XIV in the seventeenth century, for example, is reputed to have said *'l'état ç'est moi'* (the state is me) – and it was at this point, according to Elias, that what he (Elias) called 'the courtization of the warriors' began most significantly to occur; that is, members of this ruling class began to be tamed and transformed from rough-and-ready 'free' or independent 'knights' into urbane and polished 'courtiers' who were dependent on the king. In Britain by contrast, partly because, as an island, it was dependent for military purposes more on a navy than a land army, claims to absolute rule proved impossible to sustain and monarchs were forced to share the business of ruling with parliament. In the British context, the civilizing function of the royal court was shared with parliament and 'Society', the assembly of nobles and untitled 'gentlemen' and 'ladies' whose 'London season' coincided more or less with when parliament met. As I shall show briefly in the present chapter and in greater detail in Chapter 3, there is reason to believe that this overall figuration was crucial to the fact that the initial development of modern sport took place in Britain.

Subsequently, in conjunction with the continuing growth of bourgeois power and, later, of working-class power as well, private ownership of the means of ruling gave way increasingly to more public forms. Another way of putting it would be to say, following Weber, that the patrimonial rule of dynastic and absolute rulers gave way to forms of parliamentary sovereignty and rational–legal rule (Weber, 1946). According to Elias, the fundamental power shifts which produced these changes in forms of ruling were principally a consequence of two things:

1   The disarming of members of the population other than the specialist military and police; that is, depriving them of the right to use the means of violence, which does not mean they were all deprived in fact.[8] This had the effect of diminishing the use of direct force in social relations, hence to a degree equalizing the power chances of those who were physically weaker relative to those who were physically stronger, for example women relative to men, children relative to adults. In this context, a more peaceful habitus began to become increasingly dominant in social relations, especially, but not solely, *within* particular societies.

45

2   The fact that the lengthening of interdependency chains increased the
     dependency of rulers and other powerful groups on those over whom
     they were dominant, hence increasing the power chances of the latter –
     for example, by providing opportunities for the organized withdrawal of
     their labour – and leading, *not* to equality *tout court*, but to a shift towards
     lesser inequality in the relations between them. Elias referred to this as
     'functional democratization' (Elias, 1978: 65ff.).

According to Elias, there were differences between the civilizing and state-
formation processes of Britain and France, though in both cases the processes
were relatively continuous in the longer term. This contrasted markedly with
German developments which were, Elias argued, more discontinuous. In
Germany a number of deep-rooted structural obstacles for a long while
impeded state centralization, the emergence of a powerful and relatively independent middle class and hence the development of more democratic values,
attitudes and institutions. In fact, Germany did not become a relatively unified
nation-state until 1870 and it did so under the hegemony of the militaristic
Prussians. In such a context, the Germans remained subject to forms of absolutist rule until 1918 and this became deeply rooted in the habitus, conscience
and traditions of a majority of Germans. This helps to explain the part played
by Germany in the origins of the First and Second World Wars and the rise of
Nazism and 'the Holocaust'. It also helps to explain why a cult of duelling and
Turnen, a nationalist and militaristically orientated form of gymnastics, originated in Germany rather than modern sport (Elias, 1996).

    Whatever its degree of adequacy, it is difficult to see how such a theory can
be justifiably described as 'evolutionary', even in the relatively weak sense of
displaying 'a tendency towards latent evolutionism' (Horne and Jary, 1987:
100). It is a theory concerned with processes based on the intergenerational
transmission of learned experiences which Elias sought to demonstrate as
having factually occurred. As such, it is testable at both the 'macro' and the
'micro' levels, and regarding the connections which Elias postulated between
them. It is also potentially testable by reference to societies outside a Western
context and in relation to specific spheres of social life such as crime and
punishment (Spierenburg, 1991) and, more germane for present purposes,
sport. In fact, *pace* Horne and Jary and others who have similarly argued that
the theory of civilizing processes is untestable, the body of Leicester work on
sport represents an explicit test and elaboration of the theory. It does so
because, when Elias and I first began our work on the development of sport
in 1959, neither of us knew what the results would be.

    This is an appropriate point at which to begin a discussion of that work.
As I hope to show, the principal strands in the development of modern sport
tend to confirm the theory of civilizing processes as far as both the direction
and the 'causes' or, more properly, the sociogenesis and psychogenesis of this
development are concerned.[9] I shall start by dealing briefly and for compara-

tive purposes with the 'sports' of the ancient world.[10] I shall then discuss the 'sports' of medieval and early modern Europe, and after that, what we have come to define and recognize as 'sports' today.

The sports of the ancient world

There is a tendency in academic discourse and popular mythology to look on the 'sports' of Ancient Greece as representing some kind of pinnacle of civilized sporting achievement (McIntosh, 1993: 27).[11] By contrast, the 'sports' of Ancient Rome are commonly viewed as a regression into barbarism. There is no need to deny what was, from the standpoint of the 'late barbarians' of today who consider themselves to be 'civilized', the high level of cruelty and violence of the 'sports' of Ancient Rome. The brutality of the gladiatorial combats, the mock battles, the massacres and the bloodlust of the crowds are well established. Sociologically, these 'sports' are indicative of an attitude to life, death and the sufferings of others which was very different from that which dominates in the contemporary West (Auguet, 1972). It was probably bound up with the centrality of slavery in the economy and society of Ancient Rome. It is probably not so well known, however, that the violence of the Roman Games was not restricted to events in the arena: crowds throughout the empire often behaved violently as well. Take the circus factions at the chariot races. They were divided principally into 'the Blues' and 'the Greens' after the colours of the charioteers. Gibbon described them thus:

> the blues affected to strike terror by a peculiar and Barbaric dress, the long hair of the Huns, their close sleeves and ample garments, a lofty step and a sonorous voice. In the day they concealed their two-edged poniards (daggers), but in the night they boldly assembled…in numerous bands, prepared for every act of violence and rapine. Their adversaries of the green faction, or even inoffensive citizens, were… often murdered by these nocturnal robbers, and it became dangerous to wear any gold buttons or girdles or to appear at a late hour in the streets….No place was safe…from their depredations; to gratify either avarice or revenge, they profusely spilt the blood of the innocent; churches and altars were polluted by atrocious murders; and it was the boast of the assassins that their dexterity could always inflict a mortal wound with a single stroke of their dagger.
>
> (quoted in McIntosh, 1993: 35)

The Blues and Greens were evidently comparable in some ways with the soccer hooligans of today, though, if Gibbon is to be believed, they were considerably more murderous. That he may have exaggerated the violence of the circus factions to some degree is suggested by the fact that he was trying to establish that Rome's 'decline and fall' occurred largely as a consequence of a rising tide of immorality and vice. In short, whatever degree of conscious deliberation was involved, Gibbon may have exaggerated the violence of the circus factions in order to provide greater support for his thesis. Whatever is the case in this regard, however, more recent research (Cameron, 1976) substantiates the thesis that, judged by present-day standards, their behaviour was often extremely violent. For example, they set the wooden hippodrome in Constantinople on fire in AD 491, 498, 507 and 532, leading the Emperor Justinian to invest in a marble stadium. The evidence suggests that by far the worst of these circus riots was the one in AD 532 when the Blues and Greens joined forces, rescued prisoners who, as was customary, were about to be publicly executed prior to the commencement of the racing, and were eventually put down by troops at an estimated cost of 30,000 lives (Guttmann, 1986: 32). The thirty-nine deaths at the European Cup Final between soccer teams Liverpool and Juventus at the Heysel Stadium, Brussels, in 1985 and even the estimated death toll of between 287 and 328 (Smith, 1983: 181) at the soccer international between Peru and Argentina in Lima in 1964, the worst recorded soccer-related tragedy of modern times, are placed by this comparison with what went on in Constantinople in 432 in a perspective which is rather different from that which would come from looking at them in solely present-centred terms.

What about the 'sports' of Ancient Greece? Were they, as present-day mythology would have it, less violent than the 'sports' of Ancient Rome? Comparative judgements of this kind are difficult to make but the surviving evidence certainly suggests that they were considerably more violent than modern sports. Take the pankration. According to Finley and Pleket (1976: 40), it combined elements of boxing, wrestling and judo, and was one of the most popular events in the Ancient Olympics. In effect, it was equivalent to what has recently come to be called 'ultimate fighting'. In the pankration, we are told:

> the competitors fought with every part of their body....[They] were allowed to gouge one another's eyes out...trip their opponents, lay hold of their feet, noses and ears, dislocate their fingers and arms, and apply strangleholds. If one man succeeded in throwing the other, he was entitled to sit on him and beat him about the head, face and ears; he could also kick him and trample on him. It goes without saying that the contestants in this brutal contest sometimes received the most fearful wounds and that not infrequently men were killed! The pankration of the Spartan epheboi was probably the most brutal of all. Pausanius tells us that the contestants quite literally fought tooth and nail and bit and tore one another's eyes out.
>
> (Elias, 1986b: 136)

Greek boxing was similarly brutal. There were no weight classes and, as in kick-boxing and French *savate*, contestants could use feet as well as hands. Blows could also be delivered with outstretched fingers, and dodging and feinting, especially moving backwards, were regarded as signs of cowardice. Ancient Greek boxers just stood toe to toe and slugged it out (Elias, 1986b: 137–8).

Further testimony to the violence of the Ancient Greek Olympics is provided by the fact that the *hellanodikai*, the managers of the games, employed two classes of assistants: the *mastigophoroi* or whip-bearers, and the *rabdouchoi* or truncheon-bearers, whose task was to keep both competitors and spectators under control (Guttmann, 1986: 17). The need for functionaries of this kind is suggestive of crowds which must frequently have been unruly and which would only respond to a strong measure of externally imposed physical restraint. One measure of how unruly they were is provided by the fact that drunken rowdiness was apparently such a problem at the Pythian Games at Delphi that spectators were forbidden to carry wine into the stadium (Guttmann, 1986: 17). The recent ban on alcohol at soccer matches in Britain and elsewhere is evidently nothing new!

The 'sports' of Ancient Greece were based on the ethos of a warrior nobility. Unlike modern sports, they involved a tradition of 'honour' rather than 'fairness' which helps to explain the high level of violence tolerated within them. This level of violence was consonant with the frequency with which the city-states went to war and the fact that life within them was generally more violent and insecure than that in modern nation-states. In fact, one of the principal justifications given for 'sports' in Ancient Greece was as a training for war. For example, Philostratos wrote that, at one time, people regarded the games as training for war and war as training for the games (Finley and Pleket, 1976: 113), thus indicating a closer connection between war contests and game contests than exists – with marginal exceptions such as Nazi Germany – in present-day nation-states. A similar ideological connection was often made in the European Middle Ages and early modern period.

The sports of medieval and early modern Europe

In the European Middle Ages, there were four principal types of 'sports': tournaments; hunts and other activities involving the brutalization of animals; archery contests; and folk games. There was some imitation across class boundaries and a degree of variation between countries but, in general, such 'sports' tended to be class specific. That is, tournaments and hunts were restricted to knights and squires, archery contests to the middle strata, and folk games, as the name implies, along with such sports as bear-baiting, cock-fighting and dog-fighting, to the 'common people'. I shall confine my discussion to the tournaments and folk games.

The earliest surviving records of the tournaments date from the twelfth century and are indicative of a very violent type of 'sport'. 'The typical tournament', we are told, 'was a mêlée composed of parties of knights fighting simultaneously, capturing each other, seeking not only glory but also ransoms'

(Guttmann, 1986; Barber, 1974). Most significantly for present purposes, between the twelfth and sixteenth centuries the tournaments underwent a civilizing process in the course of which they were transformed increasingly into pageants involving 'mock' rather than 'real' violence; that is, they became centrally concerned with spectacle and display, and as this process unfolded, the role of spectators, especially upper-class females, grew in importance. As Guttmann has expressed it:

> The presence of upper class women at tournaments plainly signals transformation in function. The perfection of military prowess became ancillary and the tournament became a theatrical production in which fitness to rule was associated with fineness of sensibility.
>
> (Guttmann, 1986: 41)

This is consistent with Elias's concept of 'the courtization of the warriors' and with the part he attributed to the growing power of females in that process (Elias, 1994: 326).[12] Despite the taming of the tournaments, however, spectatorship continued to be a hazardous affair and stands are reported to have collapsed in London in 1331 and 1581 resulting in numerous injuries and, on the latter occasion, loss of life (Guttmann, 1986). It is to the folk games that I shall now turn since it is from that source that such more civilized modern sports as soccer and rugby sprang.

Modern soccer and rugby are descended from a type of medieval folk games which, in Britain, went by a variety of names such as 'football', 'camp ball', 'hurling' and 'knappan'. Continental variants included 'la soule' in France, 'sollen' in Belgium and the *gioco del pugno* (game of the fist) in Italy. The ball in such games was carried, thrown and hit with sticks as well as kicked, and matches were played through the streets of towns as well as over open country. They were played by variable, formally unrestricted numbers of people, sometimes in excess of a thousand. There was no equalization of numbers between sides, and the rules were oral and locally specific rather than standardized, written and enforced by a central body. Despite such local variation, the games in this folk tradition shared at least one feature: they were play struggles which involved the customary toleration of forms of physical violence which have now been tabooed and were generally played in ways which involved levels of violence that were considerably higher than would be permitted in soccer, rugby and comparable games today. That this was so will emerge from a few extracts from sixteenth- and seventeenth-century accounts. These two centuries are the richest source of evidence about such games largely as a result of attacks on them by Puritans and counterattacks by the Puritans' opponents. Despite the degree of ideological contamination that was inevitably thus engendered, evidence from earlier and later centuries by and large confirms the sixteenth- and seventeenth-century sources (Dunning and Sheard, 1979: 21–45). As a result, these folk games can be said to have constituted a single tradition, the basic structure of which endured over several centuries in a relatively unchanged form. That is, such changes as occurred did not involve developments of a basic structural kind.

We hear, for example, that, in Chester, a town near Liverpool in England's north-west, a football match between the Shoemakers' and the Drapers' Companies had been played annually on Shrove Tuesday since 'time out of man's remembrance'. By 1533, however, what were described as 'evil disposed persons' – sixteenth-century equivalents of today's soccer hooligans – had apparently come to take part with the result that 'much harm was done, some in the greate thronge falling into a trance, some having their bodies bruised and crushed; some their armes, heades or legges broken, and some otherwise maimed or in peril of their lives' (Dunning and Sheard, 1979: 23). In the description of Cornish 'hurling acrosse countrie' which he published in 1602, Carew hints that this level of violence and physical danger was inherent in the structure of such games and not simply a consequence of the involvement of what we would call 'hooligans' today. Thus he described the game as being 'accompanied by many dangers....For proofe whereof, when the hurling is ended you shall see them retyring home, as from a pitched battaile, with bloody pates [heads], bones broken and out of joynt, and such bruses as serve to shorten their daies' (Dunning and Sheard, 1979: 27). A year later, Owen wrote of Welsh 'knappan' that

> at this playe privatt grudges are revenged, soe that for everye small occasion they fall by the eares, wch beinge but once kindled betweene two, all persons on both sides become parties, soe that some tymes you shall see fyve or vi hundred naked men, beating in a clusture together.
>
> (Dunning and Sheard, 1979: 28)

Just as in Cornish hurling, some of the participants in knappan played on horseback. The horsemen, said Owen, 'have monstrouse cudgells, of iii foote and halfe longe, as bigge as the partie is well able to wild [wield]'. Further testimony to the wildness of such games is provided by Thomas Elyot, the disciple of the humanist Erasmus and friend of Thomas More. Writing in 1531, Elyot condemned 'foot balle' as a game in which there is 'nothynge but beastely furie, and exstreme violence; whereof proceedeth hurte, and consequently rancour and malice do remayne with them that be wounded; wherefore it is to be put in perpetuall sylence' (quoted in Marples, 1954: 66).

Between 1314 and 1667, numerous unsuccessful attempts were made by state and local authorities to ban these wild games (Dunning and Sheard, 1979: 23; see also Chapter 4 of the present volume). In France, too, unsuccessful attempts were made to ban 'la soule' and similar games, at least up until the Revolution in 1797 (Elias, n.d.). That the continental variants were as wild as their counterparts in Britain is suggested by Guttmann's description of

51

the *gioco del pugno*. It was played in Northern Italy and was, according to Guttmann:

> often little better than a pitched battle, a tournament fought with weapons provided by nature. An even rougher version...occurred when the 'players' hurled rocks at each other, a pastime honoured by Savanarola's condemnation. In Perugia, a thousand or more men and women joined in the annual stone fight, which became so violent that the authorities attempted to moderate the bloodshed in 1273 by threatening that those who killed their opponents would henceforth be tried for murder.
>
> (Guttmann, 1986: 52)

How did modern forms of sport develop out of this violent folk tradition? In the next two sections, I shall try to show how this process occurred in conjunction with the 'civilizing spurts' which Britain experienced in the eighteenth and nineteenth centuries.

The initial development of modern sport

In Florence during the Renaissance, a more restrained and regulated game developed, the *gioco del calcio* (game of kicking). It was played by noblemen (Marples, 1954: 67; Young, 1968: 26). It was rough and, as far as one can tell, controlled in the last instance by ranks of pikemen present in case the excitement of the struggle led either the young noble players or members of the crowd to get carried away and lose their self-control (Guttmann, 1986: 51). The *gioco del calcio* is still played in Florence and remains a rough game, perhaps even rougher than rugby.

It has been suggested, for example by Bredekamp (1993: 53, 54), that *calcio* formed the model on which soccer is based, but there is no direct evidence for such a process of diffusion. In support of his claim, Bredekamp cites just one piece of data: the fact that English people associated with the British Consul in Livorno took part in a ceremonial game of *calcio* there in 1776. However, as evidence this is very weak. In Bredekamp's account, the people involved remain nameless; nothing is said about *how* they played *calcio* and how familiar they were with the rules. More importantly, nothing is said about these people trying to introduce the game to friends and acquaintances back in England. In other words, the inferential component in Bredekamp's assertion is so strong that it is better, for the moment, to suppose that the development of soccer – and rugby, too: they were socially co-produced – was a process which occurred autonomously in England. That, at least, is consistent with the judgement of the Dutch historian, Huizinga, who described England 'as the cradle and focus of modern sporting life' (Huizinga, 1971: 13).

Although there are signs of the development of more restrained and regulated sport forms in England as early as the sixteenth century, all the evidence suggests that these did not catch on. The initial development of modern sport was a process which occurred later, principally in two main, overlapping stages: a stage in the eighteenth century when members of the aristocracy and gentry were predominant; and a stage in the nineteenth century when members of ascendant bourgeois groups joined the landed classes in taking the lead. The evidence also suggests that this process was more a function of wider social developments, especially of the peculiarly English variants of the state-formation and civilizing processes, than it was of the properties of these emergent sporting forms. More particularly, the eighteenth century saw the emergence of more civilized forms of boxing, fox-hunting, horse-racing and cricket, while the nineteenth century saw the emergence of more regularized forms of athletic competition, mountain and water sports, but above all, the early development of more civilized ball games such as soccer, rugby, hockey and tennis. The increasing predominance of ball games and non-violent forms of athletic competition over field sports, especially field sports in which the quarry is killed, arguably in itself represented a 'civilizing shift' of some significance. So did the fact that modern sports came over time − at least in non-totalitarian countries − to be justified less as a training for war and more as healthy, enjoyable and socially valuable 'ends in themselves'.

Two other things are worthy of note. The first is that, in the popular consciousness of Western societies in the nineteenth and twentieth centuries, the term 'sport' has increasingly been withdrawn from the hunting and killing types of activities; for example, in Spain bullfighting is not regarded as a sport and, in Britain, increasing doubts have been raised over whether fox-hunting can be regarded as one. Correlatively with this, the term 'sport' has been applied more exclusively to competitive leisure activities involving physical exertion which either do not involve violence as a legitimate component − it can be involved illegitimately, of course, as with bumping, jostling and spiking in running events − or in which violence is centrally involved but subjected more to civilizing controls, for example the no hitting below the belt rule in boxing.

Another aspect of this process has involved the attempt by specific groups to secure the inclusion of more non-violent competitive activities under the rubric 'sport'. An example is provided by activities such as mountaineering and rock-climbing in which the competition is not between humans, or not just between them, but between humans and some physical obstacle, usually involving an element of physical risk. Such activities are consistent with the theory of civilizing processes because they presuppose the bringing of what was hitherto wilderness under greater human control. Moreover, the dangers in such cases are almost always controlled by means of special techniques and equipment. Engaging in risky activities which are then controlled, followed once again by the 'shift to risk', has been a central characteristic of the development of sport and leisure forms in the relatively civilized societies of Western Europe in the nineteenth and twentieth centuries. Let me examine the two initial phases in the development of modern sport in greater detail. This will necessarily entail a brief consideration of developments in sport and society in the seventeenth and not simply the eighteenth and nineteenth centuries.

An obvious hypothesis by which to explain the initial emergence of modern sport would be to link this process with the fact that Britain in the eighteenth century began to become the world's first industrial nation, in other words to suggest that there was a connection between the 'sporting' and 'industrial revolutions'. That has been proposed by Brailsford (1991), Brohm (1978), Hargreaves (1986) and Rigauer (1969). Such an hypothesis is not wrong but, by placing too much stress on the independent significance of 'economic factors', it is an oversimplification. It is arguably better to trace the 'sporting revolution' to an overall social transformation in which, rather than economic developments, political and normative developments and developments at the level of habitus were predominant. Elias speaks of a number of 'civilizing spurts' in this connection. He writes:

> Just as the pacifying and civilizing spurt of the seventeenth century in France was not the beginning of a process in that direction, so, in England, the comparable spurt of the eighteenth century was only one of several spurts of this kind, though perhaps the most decisive. Henry VIII's successful attempts to tame his barons were a step.... The powerful court life...of Queen Elizabeth I and King James I had a similar function. But in the eighteenth century, the long drawn-out struggle between, on the one hand, monarchs and their representatives, and on the other, the landed upper classes and the urban middle classes, resulted in a condition in which the landed upper classes, nobility and gentry, had gained parity if not supremacy in relation to king and court. Their dominant position in both Houses of Parliament also gave them a superior position in relation to the urban middle classes.
>
> (Elias, 1986b: 36)

The currently available evidence suggests that what one might call a process of 'incipient sportization' can be traced to the 'civilizing spurts' of the sixteenth and seventeenth centuries. For example, Carew wrote in 1602 of a second form of hurling which he called 'hurling to goales' in which teams of equal numbers – fifteen, twenty or thirty a side – competed. He also wrote of the 'lawes' to which the players of this game subjected themselves. According to Carew:

> The Hurlers are bound to the observation of many lawes, as that they must hurle man to man, and not two set upon one man at once: that the Hurler against the ball, must not *but* nor hand-fast under the

girdle: that hee who hath the ball must *but* onely in the others brest:...
The least breach of these lawes, the Hurlers take for a just cause of
going together by the eares, but with their fists onely; neither doth
any among them seek revenge for such wrongs or hurts but at the
like play againe.

(Carew, 1602: 73–5)

Carew defined 'butting' as 'thrusting an opponent in the brest' with one's
'closed fist'. Thus, hurling to goales was a rough game, played according to
agreed-on customary rules rather than written ones, and these rules included
a prohibition against hitting or grasping an opponent 'below the belt'. There
were, however, no external officials. Breaches of the rules were simply decided
by fist-fights among the participants.

Other evidence also points to the emergence in England as early as the
seventeenth century of a traditional form of fighting with the fists alone. It
seems to have been shared by men of all classes and to have had a degree of
female support. Misson de Valbourg, a Huguenot refugee who came to
England in 1685, offered the following description of the street fights he
observed in London, contrasting them with the equivalent which, he said, was
current in France at that time:

If two little boys quarrel in the street, the passengers stop, make a ring
around them in a moment, and set them against one another, that
they may come to fisticuffs....[D]uring the fight the ring of
bystanders encourages the combatants with great delight of heart,
and never parts them while they fight according to the rules. And
these bystanders are not only other boys, porters and rabble, but all
sorts of men of fashion....The fathers and mothers of the boys let
them fight on as well as the rest, and hearten him that gives the
ground or has the worst. These combats are less frequent among
grown men than children, but they are not rare. If a coachman has a
dispute about his fare with the gentleman that has hired him, and the
gentleman offers to fight him to decide the quarrel, the coachman
consents with all his heart. The gentleman pulls off his sword, lays it
in some shop with his cane, gloves and cravat, and boxes....I once
saw the late Duke of Grafton at fisticuffs in the open street, with such
a fellow, whom he lambed most horribly. In France, we punish such
rascals with our cane, and sometimes with the flat of the sword; but
in England this is never practised. They use neither sword nor stick
against a man that is unarmed, and if an unfortunate stranger...
should draw his sword upon one who had none, he'd have a hundred
people upon him in a moment.

(quoted in Marsh, 1978: 77)

The descriptions by Carew and Valbourg point to an early development in England of notions of 'fair play', one of the basic ingredients of modern sport. However, as Elias suggested, it was in the context of the eighteenth-century 'civilizing spurt' that 'sportization', the 'take-off' into modern sport, began most significantly to occur. During the seventeenth century, Britain became locked into a cycle of violence associated mainly with the Stuart attempt to reimpose Catholicism and to claim 'absolute power' along the lines of Louis XIV in France, for example by raising taxes independently of parliament. This resulted in civil war and the state monopoly of force was severely challenged. By the eighteenth century, however, the effectiveness of the state's violence monopoly had been more or less restored – though under conditions in which aristocratic and gentry groups enjoyed greater autonomy than their counterparts in absolutist France. By that time, too, passions had begun to calm down and parliamentary party forms of conducting political struggles began to emerge. It was in the context of an increasingly pacified society subject to more effective forms of parliamentary rule that recognizably modern forms of sport based upon written rules first began to emerge. That there was a strong connection between these two developments is suggested by the fact that there were close parallels between the emergent party rituals of parliament and the emergent rituals of modern sport. Both, as they came to develop in eighteenth-century England, began to involve less violent ways of conducting struggles than had previously prevailed. In other words, it was not a question of some abstractly conceptualized 'political factor' somehow influencing the development of sport but rather that the habitus of ruling groups in Britain – and to a certain extent of groups lower in the class hierarchy as well – underwent a 'civilizing spurt', leading them simultaneously to transform the political and leisure sides of their lives in a civilizing direction. As Elias expressed it:

> Military skills gave way to the verbal skills of debate…rhetoric and persuasion…which required greater restraint all round and identified this change…clearly as a civilizing spurt. It was this change, the greater sensitivity with regard to the use of violence which, reflected in the social habitus of individuals, also found expression in the development of their pastimes. The 'parliamentarization' of the landed classes of England had its counterpart in the 'sportization' of their pastimes.
>
> (Elias, 1986b: 34)

The fact that the leisure side of this process involved a civilizing spurt emerges clearly from the development of boxing and fox-hunting. Elias comments on the early 'sportization' of boxing thus:

Like many other bodily contests, fighting with bare knuckles assumed the characteristics of a sport in England where it was first subjected to a tighter set of rules....The growth of sensitivity showed itself in the introduction of gloves and, as time went on, in the padding of gloves and the introduction of various classes of boxers which ensured greater equality of chances. In fact, it was only in connection with the development of a more differentiated and...tighter set of rules and the greater protection of the contestants from serious injury which followed...that a popular form of fighting assumed the characteristics of a 'sport'.

(Elias, 1986b: 21)

Elias seems to have got the timing of these innovations slightly wrong. That is, the available evidence suggests that gloves – they were suggestively called 'mufflers' at the time – were introduced after the first written rules. Both were apparently introduced in the 1740s at a London amphitheatre run by a man called Jack Broughton, where he attracted a largely 'gentlemanly' clientele who went there to gamble on prize-fights and/or to be taught to box (Sheard, 1992). What have reductively come to be known as 'Broughton's Rules' were 'agreed by several gentlemen at Broughton's Amphitheatre, Tottenham Court Road, August 16, 1743'. They were as follows:

1. That a square of a yard be chalked in the middle of the stage; and every fresh set-to after a fall, or being parted from the rails, each second is to bring his man to the side of the square, and place him opposite the other; and till they are fairly set-to at the lines, it shall not be lawful for the one to strike the other.
2. That, in order to prevent any disputes as to the time a man lies after a fall, if the second does not bring his man to the side of the square, within the space of half a minute, he shall be deemed a beaten man.
3. That, in every main battle, no person whatever shall be upon the stage, except the principals and their seconds; the same rule to be observed in bye-battles, except that, in the latter, Mr. Broughton is allowed to be upon the stage to keep decorum, and to assist gentlemen in getting to the places; provided also he does not interfere in the battle: and whoever presumes to infringe these rules to be turned immediately out of the house.
4. That no champion be deemed beaten, unless he fails coming up to the line in the limited time: or that his own second declares him beaten. No second is to be allowed to ask his man's adversary any questions or advise him to give out.

5.   That, in bye-battles, the winning man to have two-thirds of the
     money given, which shall be publicly divided upon the stage,
     notwithstanding any private agreement to the contrary.
6.   That to prevent disputes, in every main battle, the principals
     shall, on coming on the stage, choose from among the gentlemen
     present two umpires, who shall absolutely decide all disputes that
     might arouse about the battle; and if the two umpires cannot
     agree, the said umpires to choose a third, who is to determine it.
7.   That no person is to hit his adversary when he is down, or seize
     him by the ham, the breeches, or any part below the waist; a man
     on his knees to be reckoned down.

                                              (Sheard, 1992: 129–30)

Although they were self-evidently aimed at regularizing the gambling
component and with limiting the possibility of wider, gambling-related
disputes, these rules were also formulated with a civilizing intention in a
number of respects. More particularly, they were intended: to regulate the start
of fights in a fair way by decreeing that neither boxer should deliver a punch
until both were properly stationed at the chalked starting square; to prevent
other persons from assisting or otherwise interfering with the direct combatants; to provide fair control by stipulating the necessity for two umpires to
decide on all disputes, with the possibility of them calling on a third should
they fail to agree; and with limiting the target for punches to the upper body
and preventing boxers from striking opponents who were down or on their
knees.

   That what one can retrospectively call a 'civilizing intent' also lay behind
the first introduction of gloves ('mufflers') is shown by an advertisement
placed by Broughton in the *Daily Advertiser* in February 1747 announcing his
intention to open a 'boxing academy'. It reads:

   Mr. Broughton proposes…to open an academy…in the Haymarket,
   for the instruction of those who are willing to be instructed in the
   mystery of boxing, when the whole theory and practice of that truly
   British art, with all the various stops, blows, cross-buttocks etc, incident to combatants, will be fully taught and explained; and that
   persons of quality and distinction may not be debarred from entering
   into a course of these lectures, they will be given with the utmost
   tenderness and regard to the delicacy of the frame and the constitution of the pupil, for which reason mufflers are provided that will
   effectually secure them from the inconveniencing of black eyes,
   broken jaws and bloody noses.

                                                   (Sheard, 1992: 125)

The introduction by Broughton and the 'gentlemen' who supported him of 'mufflers' and rudimentary written rules marked an early stage in a complex, ongoing long-term process which was full of ups and downs. For example, despite Broughton's innovations, bare-knuckle prize-fighting over unlimited rounds until one boxer admitted defeat or was so hurt that he could fight no longer (was unable to 'come up to scratch') continued until the 1880s when, after a long drawn-out struggle in which bare-knuckle fighting was suppressed on several occasions only to resurface, the state authorities finally succeeded in pushing it more or less permanently underground. As part of this overall process, an informal division of boxers into three weight classes – 'heavy-weight', 'middleweight' and 'lightweight' – had emerged by the 1850s and 1860s but it was, again, not until the 1880s that anything approaching the more complex weight gradations of modern boxing was introduced in Britain and the USA (Golesworthy, 1960: 236). A finely nuanced scheme of the modern type, of course, is an essential ingredient in the fairness of boxing as a modern sport and helps to push the balance in contests between skill and strength in favour of the former (Sheard, 1992). Similarly, the more nuanced and finely detailed, so-called 'Queensberry rules' on which modern boxing is based and which, among other things, sought to limit the number and dura-tion of rounds were introduced – originally for amateur rather than professional boxers – in 1865 (Sheard, 1992: 219–21). (I have said 'so-called 'Queensberry rules' because the evidence suggests that their principal drafter was a Cambridge undergraduate, J. G. Chambers, acting under the patronage of the Marquis of Queensberry (Sheard, 1992: 263).)

The Queensberry rules were the first to mention gloves. Although this was not stipulated explicitly in writing, these were to be made of leather and stuffed with not less than four ounces of horsehair (Sheard, 1992: 266). Interestingly, Elias (1986b: 21) described the introduction of boxing gloves as a mark of increasing sensitivity, and Broughton's advertisement of 1747 shows him to have been partly right. However, as Sheard (1992) has convincingly shown, whilst boxing gloves may to some extent protect the skin and facial features of the receiver of a punch, they also protect the hands of the puncher, thus allowing harder blows to be delivered more frequently and often in rapid succession than tended to be possible in bare-knuckle fighting. Hence boxing gloves probably contribute to a greater incidence of brain damage. Thus, while the evidence suggests that modern boxing emerged in England in conjunction with a series of 'civilizing' spurts involving greater sensitivity to injury, pain and the sight of blood, it also suggests that, in one respect at least, the sport has grown more seriously violent and damaging. It is largely on that account that, since the 1940s, there has been a series of medically led campaigns to ban it. It is difficult to avoid the conclusion that if, in the future, there is a substantial increase in the numbers of people who are more civilized than the present-day 'late barbarian' devotees of boxing, the pressure will mount either to disallow the delivery of blows to the head or to ban the 'sport' altogether. If that happens, as has been the case generally in Western civilizing processes so far, boxing would probably not disappear but be driven underground.

Fox-hunting is another sport which is widely considered to be 'uncivilized' today. Like boxing, it, too, has been subject to orchestrated opposition − for example, by 'hunt saboteurs'. Looked at in solely present-centred terms, it seems absurd to suggest that an activity which is judged 'barbaric' by so many people can be said to have undergone a 'civilizing process'. However, that is Elias's contention. It is necessary, he says, to view an activity such as fox-hunting, not from a present-centred perspective but in relation to its antecedents, the forms of hunting of the Middle Ages, especially those engaged in by the upper classes. These, he suggests, were more spontaneous, less elaborate and organized, and more war-like. He continues:

> A glance...at the earlier forms of hunting shows the peculiarities of English foxhunting....It was a form...in which the hunters imposed on themselves and their hounds a number of highly specific restraints. The whole organization...the behaviour of the participants, the training of the hounds, was governed by an extremely elaborate code. But the reasons for this code...were far from obvious. Why were the hounds trained not to follow any scent other than that of the fox and, as far as possible, not of any fox other than the first that they had discovered? The ritual of foxhunting demanded that the hunters should not use any weapons. Why was it regarded as a major social crime to shoot foxes and as improper for gentlemen hunting foxes to use any weapons at all? Fox-hunting gentlemen killed, as it were, by proxy − by delegating the task of killing to their hounds. Why did the foxhunting code prohibit the killing of the hunted animal by the people themselves? In the earlier forms of hunting, when people themselves had played the main role in the hunt, hounds had played a subordinate role. Why was the main role in English foxhunting left to the hounds, while the human beings confined themselves to the secondary role of followers or perhaps of controllers of the hounds?
>
> (Elias, in Elias and Dunning, 1986: 161–2)

It is Elias's contention that these rules and rituals emerged in conjunction with the development of fox-hunting as a modern sport. It was, in fact, one of the earliest activities to which the term 'sport' in its modern sense became attached and the primary function of these rules and rituals was the genera-tion, prolongation and resolution of enjoyable tension–excitement. That a 'civilizing spurt' was involved is suggested above all by the fact that the fox-hunting gentlemen and ladies killed by proxy rather than directly, gaining their pleasure from the excitement of the chase and the resolution of the tension by watching rather than directly performing the kill. Their conscience did not yet involve a generalized revulsion against killing and bloodshed *per se* but only against directly participating in violence.

Early stages in the development of rugby and soccer

By contrast with their folk antecedents and, in most respects, with more advanced but still pre-modern games such as Italian *calcio*, soccer and rugby can be said to exemplify sports which are more civilized in at least six senses. More particularly, they are more civilized in the sense that each involves the following:

1 Strict limitation on the numbers of participants, together with numerical equality between the contending sides. De-limitation of the numbers of participants represents a civilizing development because a game played by unlimited numbers is liable to result in frequent mêlées and brawls. The institutionalization of numerical equality between sides is civilizing, too, because it constitutes a central ingredient of the notion of 'fair play'.
2 Specialization around the practices of kicking, or kicking, handling, carrying and throwing, together with elimination of the use of sticks for purposes of striking either other players or the ball. Similarly, all players play on foot. That is, practices which were often dangerously intermixed in the old folk tradition, such as some players using sticks and some playing on horseback and others on foot, have come to be separately institutionalized in the differentiated games of soccer and rugby, together with related games such as hockey and polo.
3 A centralized rule-making, administrative and rule-enforcing body, the Football Association (FA) in the case of soccer, and the Rugby Football Union (RFU) in the case of rugby.
4 A set of written rules which demand from players the exercise of strict self-control over physical contact and the use of physical force, and which prohibit force in certain forms, for example 'stiff-arm tackling' (striking an opposing player in the throat) and 'hacking' (kicking an opposing player to the ground).
5 Clearly defined 'intra-game' sanctions such as 'free-kicks' and 'penalties' which can be brought to bear on those who break the rules and, as the ultimate sanction for serious and persistent rule violation, the possibility of excluding players from the game.
6 The institutionalization of specific roles with respect to controlling the game, that is the roles of referee and, in soccer, 'linesmen' (recently renamed 'assistant referees' partly in order to accommodate the performance of this role by females) and, in rugby, 'touch judges'. Unlike the 'whip-bearers' and 'truncheon-bearers' of the Ancient Greek Olympics and the pikemen of Florentine *calcio*, these match officials do not rely on

physical force or the threat of it to secure compliance but on non-physical sanctions specific to the game. This suggests that the orderly character of these modern games is fundamentally dependent, not only on non-violent external constraints but also on the exercise of a large measure of self-control by the players. In other words, such sports are indicative of a shift in the balance between external constraints and self-constraints in favour of self-constraints and are thus symptomatic of the sorts of civilizing processes so far undergone in the societies of Western Europe. A corollary of this shift is the fact that arguing with but above all striking a match official is regarded as one of the most reprehensible acts in these as in all other modern sports.

The early development of soccer and rugby occurred as part of a temporally concentrated civilizing spurt. Two significant moments in it were the production in the 1840s of the first written rules, and the formation, in 1863 and 1871, respectively, of the FA and the RFU. Let me elaborate briefly on this civilizing spurt.

The first surviving written rules of football were produced at Rugby, a 'public school' in the English Midlands, in 1845 (Dunning and Sheard, 1979: 91–4). Other public schools committed their football rules to writing shortly afterwards. The developing social context in which such rules were produced was a microcosmic reflection of the state-formation and civilizing processes which were then occurring in British society at large. Most of the leading public schools of Britain can trace their origins to the Middle Ages and early modern periods. They were founded as charitable institutions or local grammar schools but, during the eighteenth century, they were increasingly usurped by members of the aristocracy and gentry. In that context, they came to take on the character which they have today of elite boarding schools catering for the perceived educational requirements of the upper and middle classes.

In conjunction with their usurpation by the aristocracy and gentry, the public schools experienced a cycle of violence which was expressed most strikingly in the frequency with which boys openly rebelled against the school authorities (Dunning and Sheard, 1979: 46–62). Between 1728 and 1832, for example, Eton and Winchester, the two oldest schools, each experienced at least seven rebellions, whilst Rugby, which only became a public school at the end of the eighteenth century, experienced at least four. That it is no misnomer to describe these disturbances as 'rebellions' is shown by the fact that the 1797 revolt at Rugby and the 1818 revolt at Winchester led to the Riot Act being read and could only be quelled by contingents of the army or the militia using drawn swords and bayonets. The first school at which the authorities regained control was Rugby under Thomas Arnold and it is no accident that it was in conjunction with the regularization of authority relations at that school that more regularized and civilized forms of football began to emerge. It was also symptomatic of this development and of British social development more generally that the boys, especially the seniors or 'prefects', were allowed a measure of autonomy in this process (Dunning and Sheard, 1979: 79–99).

Central among the objectives of the senior boys at Rugby who framed the written rules of 1845 – and, perhaps behind them, of the school authorities – was to secure stricter control over the use of physical force in the game. To this end, the rules placed restrictions on the practice of hacking and sought to prohibit altogether the use of what were called 'navvies'. These were iron-tipped boots, sometimes with projecting nails, and had formed a violent part of the game at Rugby and some other public schools. That navvies had also been used in at least some of the folk antecedents of modern football is suggested by an anonymous Old Etonian who wrote contemptuously in 1831 that

> I cannot consider the game of football as being at all gentlemanly. It is a game which the common people of Yorkshire are particularly partial to, the tips of their boots being heavily shod with iron; and frequently death has been known to ensue from the severity of the blows inflicted thereby.
>
> (quoted in Dunning, 1971: 135)

In spite of this dismissive attitude, forms of 'the Wall Game' and 'the Field Game' – early variants of football which continue to be played at Eton today – were well established at the school in the 1830s and 1840s. In fact, the first written rules of Eton football were laid down in 1847,[13] two years after the Rugby rules had been committed to writing. Significantly, they embodied the first known absolute taboo on the use of hands and can thus be considered as having legislated for an embryonic form of soccer. It seems likely that status rivalry between Etonians and Rugbeians lay behind the incipient bifurcation of football into the association and rugby forms. (I shall deal with this process in greater detail in Chapter 4.) The bifurcation only became finally institutionalized, however, when playing football came to be recognized as a legitimate activity for adult 'gentlemen', when members of the upper and middle classes formed clubs specifically or mainly for purposes of playing football, and when associations were formed with a view to framing national rules.

The first of these bodies, the FA, emerged from a series of meetings held in London in 1863 and attended mainly by public school 'old boys' (former pupils) and other 'gentlemen'. At first, those in attendance attempted to form a unified football code. A majority favoured a mainly kicking game from which hacking had been eliminated, but proponents of versions of football modelled on the form played at Rugby preferred a rougher, mainly carrying and throwing game in which the violent practice of hacking retained a central place. Hence they withdrew, themselves banding together in 1871 to form the RFU. The devotees of Rugby took this step partly as a result of a public controversy over what had come to be perceived in some quarters as the excessive violence of their codes, and one of their first acts in framing a unified set of rules was to follow the example of the FA and place an absolute taboo on hacking. I wrote of rugby 'codes' in the plural before the unification of 1871 because, prior to that time, there were considerable variations in the games played by different schools and clubs. There was even one type of rugby in which there was a goalkeeper (Dunning and Sheard, 1979: 113–22).

The available evidence thus suggests that both the first and second main stages in the initial development of modern sport involved a transformation in the direction of greater civilization. That is, as they developed in Britain in the eighteenth and nineteenth centuries, sports such as boxing, fox-hunting, soccer and rugby came to embody the elimination of some forms of physical violence and the general demand that participants should exercise stricter self-control in regard to physical contact and over the socially generated aggressive impulses for which sport can serve as a central avenue of expression, and which, in any case, are liable to be aroused in any competitive activity. As part of this development, too, sports such as boxing, rugby and soccer which involve forms of play-fighting between individuals and groups came, *via* processes of trial-and-error learning, to be subject to forms of control by match officials who use as sanctions, not physical chastisements, but various forms of non-violent, sport-specific penalties which adversely affect the chances in the contest of erring participants and/or their teams. In all these respects, modern sports are different both from their counterparts in Ancient Greece and Rome, and from their antecedents in medieval and early modern Europe. In other words, the development of modern sports can be said to be an exemplification of a civilizing process and to provide support for Elias's theory.

Let me conclude this chapter by making one final point. There is some evidence that in present-day Britain, we may be in the early stages of a civilizing downswing – a de-civilizing process of some as yet indeterminable moment and duration and which is taking place in sport and society at large.[14] In soccer this manifests itself, for example, in the increasing use of elbows and, in rugby, in the increase of practices such as 'raking', that is scraping one's boot-studs across the skin of opponents. In both cases, these de-civilizing developments appear to be largely a consequence of the increasing competitiveness of such games. This, in its turn, appears to be connected with their growing commercialization, professionalization and internationalization, and with the increase in the significance of winning which has been generated in this connection. However, such practices appear to be engaged in mainly for instrumental reasons rather than as pleasurable ends in themselves. They are what one would expect of 'late barbarians' who experience an increase of competitive pressure and do not entail a regression to the forms and levels of mainly expressive violence which were characteristic of the 'sports' of the ancient and medieval worlds.

3

SPORT IN SPACE AND TIME

Trajectories of state formation and the early development of modern sport

Like Chapter 2 with which it overlaps to some extent, this chapter is primarily about sport in the Western 'civilizing process'. It is divided into two broad sections which I have entitled: (1) aspects of time, space and the sociology of sport; and (2) aspects of sport in the state-formation processes of Western Europe. The first section involves a discussion of some complex issues, together with a critique of the ways in which some historians, philosophers and philosophically orientated sociologists have conceptualized 'space' and 'time'. This section starts and finishes with a consideration of sport-related issues. The second section involves an attempt to probe in greater depth why specifically modern sport forms developed in England first. Light will hopefully be shed on this issue by means of a comparative and developmental analysis focused on the different trajectories of state formation of the emergent nation-states of Europe.

Aspects of time, space and the sociology of sport

Dennis Brailsford published a book in 1991 called *Sport, Time and Society: the British at Play*. It is a well-written book, solidly researched, but it is only about 'time' in an unreflexive sense. This means that on the few occasions when Brailsford attempts to be explicitly conceptual, he gets himself into hot water. He does so, not only about time, but about aspects of sport as well. For example, in what I am convinced is a veiled attack on the work of Guttmann (1978), Brailsford writes:

> To see sport as we know it as an entirely modern phenomenon is to take an unduly limited view of its personal and social significance. It is to become over-sophisticated, and to miss sport's simple and eternal essence. Competitive play is scarcely any more 'modern' than, say, hunting, fighting, dancing, singing and sex. In spite of all the change that sport has undergone over the centuries, the same central psycho-social urge has remained at its heart. However larded over the zest

and pleasures of competitive play may have been from time to time by communal, religious, and commercial considerations, this deep chord of personal striving, the pursuit of achievement and satisfaction – even at the expense of pain – has been of its essence. And it can exist vicariously in the spectator as well as in the player.

(Brailsford, 1991: 160)

Brailsford's reference to a 'simple and eternal essence' of sport is *under-sophisticated* and involves a misleading judgement of the balance between continuity and change in the development of modern sport. He is only able to imbue his essentialist contention with meaning as follows: first, by arguing at a high level of generality; second, by asserting the existence of a 'psycho-social urge' which, he contends, has remained unaltered over the centuries; and third, by referring to 'competitive play' and 'the pursuit of achievement and satisfaction' as recurrent elements in the sports of all societies and eras. Such an argument is so highly general that it is almost tautological. In fact it is more useful to see modern sports as involving not only the developmentally specific features pointed out by Guttmann (1978), that is an orientation towards the establishment and breaking of records, plus higher levels of ration-alization, standardization, secularization, specialization and quantification than were characteristic of their antecedents, but also a number of features that are best interpreted as evidence of a 'civilizing process'. Central in this connection are: first, conceptions of 'fair play'; second, violence controls that are poten-tially 'civilizing', though, of course, they can be broken, evaded or fall into abeyance; and third, attitudes towards and uses of space and time that are peculiarly modern and would not have been possible had it not been for developments in knowledge and technology.

Brailsford's formulations are not only questionable regarding his conceptu-alization of the balance between continuity and change in the development of modern sport. His concept of time is debatable as well. 'It is', he says, 'the collapse of the barriers of time that has made the present sporting world a possibility. Sport has conquered the calendar that confined it in the past, and can now invade every hour of every day of the year' (Brailsford, 1991: xi). Brailsford may think he is being metaphorical in this passage but he is closer to being metaphysical. That is, the implication of what he writes is that it is not humans who have made the present sporting world but an impersonal process involving 'the collapse of the barriers of time'. Towards the end of his book, Brailsford suggests in similar vein that

there can be no final reflections on this theme of sport and time. There is no bottom line to be drawn. The pace of the years and the centuries will continue to wreak its changes as long as humans continue to play. The splitting of seconds will become finer and finer.

Time will continue to conquer distance. Sport will more and more create its own environments.

(Brailsford, 1991: 161)

Implicit here is a view of history as inevitable progress which makes Brailsford think he can predict the future. However, that, for present purposes, is less important than the fact that he is using a reified concept of time which serves as a blockage to serious theorization of and research into the processes involved in the development of sport. That is, his mode of conceptualization makes time itself and time concepts such as 'year' and 'century' into 'things' or 'forces' which act. In other words, he is personifying abstractions much as the ancients did when, for example, 'just actions became the goddess Justitia' (Elias, 1992: 42) or as the alchemists did when they said 'nature abhors a vacuum'. Thus Brailsford has time 'conquering distance' and years and centuries 'wreaking change'. However, time and time concepts cannot act, conquer or wreak change, only humans can. 'Time', 'year' and 'century' are human symbols, means of orientation constructed by people to aid their understanding and control their activities in the physical and social worlds. This fact, which is on one level relatively simple, tends not to be seen by scholars such as Brailsford. They are trained in a largely unreflexive, non-theory-orientated historical tradition and hence tend to use popular concepts such as 'time' in a taken-for-granted sense. However, it is not only such atheoretical historians who encounter difficulties on this score. Philosophically orientated sociologists encounter them as well. Consider what Giddens wrote on the subject of time:

> As the finitude of *Dasein* and as 'the infinity of the emergence of being from nothingness', time is perhaps the most enigmatic feature of human experience. Not for nothing [*sic*] was that philosopher who has attempted to grapple in the most fundamental way with the problem, Heidegger, compelled to use terminology of the most daunting obscurity. But time, or the constitution of experience in time-space, is also a banal and evident feature of human day-to-day life. It is in some part the lack of 'fit' between our unproblematic coping with the continuity of conduct across time-space, and its ineffable character when confronted philosophically, that is the very essence of the puzzling nature of time.
>
> (Giddens, 1984: 34–5)

Both sides of this equation are problematic. Time may be a 'banal and evident feature of human day-to-day life' in the modern world where we have inherited a workable calendar and efficient devices for measuring what we call 'time'. However, this has not always been the case as Elias showed when he wrote that:

One forgets that for thousands of years the calendars people used ran into trouble again and again; they had to be reformed and improved repeatedly until one of them reached the near perfection the European calendar has attained since the last calendar reform.

Indeed, so far from being 'banal and evident' is this daily feature of human life that there have been times when people were opposed to calendar reforms because they believed they would shorten their lives!

The other side of what Giddens wrote is problematic because he does not appear to have considered the possibility that the 'daunting obscurity' of Heidegger's terminology may be connected, not with the properties of time *per se*, but with the fact that he (Heidegger) approached the problem philosophically. That seems to be the case because, while the problems associated with 'time' remain *complex* if treated sociologically, they are not 'daunting' and 'obscure'. On the contrary, they are perfectly straightforward. Sociologically, that is, time is a symbolic means of orientation through which humans relate to each other and to events and processes of various kinds. Its only reality is as a social symbol in a universe where only natural – including human–social – processes and events exist, where, if you like, only events and processes of various kinds are 'real'. That, at least, was Elias's view. He expressed it thus:

> Linguistic habits…constantly reinforce the myth of time as something which in some sense exists and as such can be determined or measured even if it cannot be perceived by the senses. On this peculiar mode of existence of time one can philosophize tirelessly, as has indeed been done over the centuries. One can entertain oneself and others with speculation on the secret of time as a master of mystery, although actually there is no mystery.
>
> It was Einstein who finally set the seal on the discovery that time was a form of relationship and not, as Newton believed, an objective flow, a part of creation like rivers and mountains which, although invisible, was like them independent of the people who do the timing. But even Einstein did not probe deeply enough. He too did not entirely escape the pressure of word-fetishism and in his own way gave new sustenance to the myth of reified time, for example by maintaining that under certain circumstances time could contract or expand.
>
> (Elias, 1992: 43–4)

So, processes and events, not symbols, are the only substantives, and 'time' is a symbol, not a process or event. Furthermore, 'every change in "space" is a change in "time"; [and] every change in "time" [is] a change in "space"' (Elias, 1992: 99–100). I shall not elaborate on the concepts of 'space' and 'space–time' here, except to add that, just as people today are the inheritors of more reality-congruent time symbols and time meters than were available to their ancestors, so, too, are they the inheritors of a fund of more reality-congruent knowledge about 'space', especially the 'local space', that is the earth, which they inhabit. That is, they have more reliable maps and devices such as compasses and radar for measuring relative positions in 'space–time', and these are of considerable relevance as facilitators of the development and character of modern sport. Indeed, they actually constitute the very substance of one sport, orienteering.

The principal relevance for the sociology of sport of this argument is that this subdiscipline has to be concerned with the study of events and processes in space and time. This means that the conventional view according to which sociology and history are separate subjects, one concerned with 'the present', the other with 'the past', is arbitrary and wrong. All studies are necessarily studies of the 'past'. A moment's reflection will show that this is so. Human societies exist in space–time, and time, as the old personifying adage has it, 'never stands still'. This means that what we call 'the present' is a constantly shifting reference point in the ceaseless flow of processes and events. What was 'the present' when I started writing this chapter had already become part of 'the past' when I completed it. In a word, 'the present' is an ambiguous concept and it has to be read with an historical connotation. It follows that, if it were to be accepted that sociology is the study of 'the present', some more or less arbitrary judgement about the relatively recent past would have to be made. In other words, one would have to decide whether this term refers, say, to the 1980s and 1990s, the years since the 1960s or the period since the Second World War. However, whatever decision is made, any such study would necessarily involve an attempt to come to grips with aspects of 'the past'. In short, it would inevitably lead one to become involved in a kind of 'historical' study.

It is often argued – for example, by Popper (1957) – that history and historical sociology cannot be 'sciences' because of the uniqueness and unre-peatability of social events. Elias's position was different. He contended that uniqueness and unrepeatability are not inherent in events as 'objects' independently of the values of the people who make such claims (Elias, 1983: 9ff.). On the contrary, Elias suggested, such claims reflect the values of people in highly differentiated industrial societies in which individual uniqueness is highly prized. This raises complex issues. According to Elias, humans have greater scope for individualization in their actions than any other known species. However, each unique human individual is only unique within the recurring, genetically determined pattern of the species. The social relations of ants and bees remain the same for thousands of years because they are dependent on their genetic constitution. As a species, however, *Homo sapiens* is fundamentally different because human patterns of social organization depend on learning. Hence, human social organization changes without biological changes. It is this dependency on learning which enables humans to have a 'history' and which permits their societies and social products such as sports to change and develop. In fact, Elias suggested, the sequences denoted by the terms 'biological evolution', 'social development' and 'history' form three distinguishable but inseparable layers (1983: 13ff.). Rates of change at each of them tend to differ. Thus, social figurations change more rapidly than the genetic structure of biological organisms and individual humans change more rapidly than figurations. For example, the 'knight–page–priest–bondsman' figuration of the European Middle Ages and the 'worker–employer–manager' figuration of more recent times are examples of figurations which have endured for several generations. This is independent of the fact that each and every individual comprising them is, or was, a unique and unrepeatable variation within the common pattern of the species and acted more or less differently, partly in accordance with their species-given capacity for behavioural individualization, and partly in accordance with the level of individualization structurally determined by the stage of development at which their society stood or stands.

Another way of putting this would be to say that figurations have a degree of autonomy relative to the individuals who form them. This is what Durkheim tried to capture when he wrote of the impossibility of modifying social facts by 'a simple effort of the will' (1964: 28). Modern sports appear to have at their core such a character of relative autonomy, a relatively stable structure which makes them comparable with the relatively enduring 'knight–page–priest–bondsman' figuration of the Middle Ages or the equally relatively enduring 'worker–employer–manager' figuration of today. Writing specifically with modern sport in mind, Elias referred provisionally to the 'mature' or, less judiciously, the 'ultimate' form of sports and games, a stage of dynamic equilibrium when changes continue to occur but are liable for a time to be slight and superficial (Elias, 1986b: 156). Such a view is at variance with the beliefs of many writers on such subjects as the commercialization and commodification of sports. They appear voluntaristically to believe that all aspects of the structure of sports are destined to be changed at the whim of entrepreneurs through the entanglement of sports in this process, 'deep-structural' aspects such as constitutive rules as well as 'surface-structural' aspects like matters of scheduling and clothing.

My position on this issue is in some ways closer to that of Hargreaves (1986). He writes of 'the nature of sport as an autonomous means of expression', of the existence of a 'ludic element' which 'is inherently irreducible to programming for profit and control' (1986: 222). However, I only agree with this argument up to a point. As Hargreaves expresses it, it seems to have essentialist undertones, to imply that there is a 'play element' inherent in sport, a kind of 'essence' or 'instinct' which universally imparts to sport a degree of protective autonomy independently of its socio-historical locations, its organization and the socialization, habituses, power ratios, values and interests of the people involved. His position in this regard appears close to Brailsford's.

Figurational sociologists have a concept of the autonomy of sport as well. It is, however, non-essentialist and stresses historically variable relative autonomy, not, as could be taken to be implicit in Hargreaves' formulation, autonomy of a universal and absolute kind. Above all, figurational sociologists do not seek to deny that sports – or for that matter anything else – can be programmed for purposes of profit and control. On the contrary, they seek to explain what happens in such regards by reference to the changing balance of power between the groups involved in sports, the interests and values of these groups, the location and manner of the integration of sports in the wider social framework, and the character and structure, above all the stage of development, of this wider social totality (see Chapter 5).

An important ingredient in the relative autonomy, stability and persistence of sporting forms is the 'deep' or basic structure which is fundamentally produced and reproduced by their written rules and unwritten codes. For example, soccer as it developed in Britain in the nineteenth century came to have a basic structure which enabled it to spread basically unchanged around the world, even into cultural contexts which were vastly different from that where it originated. It is a basic structure, I think, that will survive both the 'Americanization' of the game which was notably exemplified in conjunction with the staging of the 1994 World Cup Finals in the USA and the more general processes of commercialization and commodification associated with the involvement of entrepreneurs. Indeed, it is arguably this basic structure which interests entrepreneurs in soccer and similar sports. It interests them because it explains what engages and excites people in their millions, hence making sport exploitable commercially. Elias arguably began to approach what such a basic structure entails when he wrote:

> In all its varieties, sport is always a controlled battle in an imaginary setting....Take soccer as an example. It is human imagination which makes man-handling a...ball – with the feet only – the object of a heated but controlled struggle between two human groups. The problem to be solved...is how to keep the risk of injuries to the players low, yet keep the enjoyable battle-excitement...high....If the framework of rules and skills...is able, in practice, to maintain this and a number of related balances, the sport can be said to have reached maturity. The varieties of English football reached that condition after a period of growth and functional adjustment, and their design came to give players evenly, again and again, a good chance of a non-violent battle-tension lasting sufficiently long to be enjoyed, as well as a good chance of culmination and release from tension in the form of victory or defeat. If too many games end in a draw, that is, without a tension-resolving victory, the rules of the game require adjustment. In the same way, a sport-game may lose its function if, in too many cases, victory is attained rather too quickly. In that case, the enjoyable

tension-excitement is missing or too short. Like other varieties of leisure-sport…soccer is precariously poised between two fatal dangers, boredom and violence. The drama of a good game of football as it unfolds…has something in common with a good theatrical play. There, too, an enjoyable mimetic tension, perhaps excitement, is built up for some time, then led to a climax and thus to a resolution of the tension.

(Elias, 1986b: 50–1)

In his reference to sports taking place in 'imaginary settings', Elias was lapsing into an idea against which we fought in the 1960s, namely that sports are in some sense 'unreal' or 'hallucinatory' (Dunning, 1972). These settings are 'imagined' rather than 'imaginary'. Apart from that, this passage is insightful regarding the relative autonomy and 'maturation' of sports. Let me use some of Elias's ideas in order to explore further aspects of the unplanned social process in the course of which modern sports in their more 'mature' forms emerged.

Western European state formation and the development of modern sport

Writing in 1976, Ali Mazrui wrote that 'the first laws ever to be voluntarily embraced by men from a wide variety of cultures and backgrounds are the laws of sport' (Mazrui, 1976: 411). He was referring specifically to modern sport and, as Huizinga pointed out, it was England which formed the 'cradle and focus' for the development of this peculiarly modern form of ludic practices (Huizinga, 1971; see also Chapter 2 of the present volume). The broad reasons why are not difficult to discern. They were connected in the first instance with the peculiar dynamism of the West European figuration.

It is sometimes forgotten that the societies of Western Europe were, in a sense, unified at the time of the Roman Empire and continue to bear traces of that experience today. It is usual to talk about 'the Dark Ages' occurring when Roman rule broke down in the West in the fifth century AD and to view this period as one of total anarchy. Viewed from a figurational standpoint, however, it is useful to make a distinction between social unity and social integration, and to see this breakdown of dominion by the Roman state as producing, not disintegration, but the emergence of a new, less unified, more conflict-ridden and violent form of integration between embryonic state-units, together with a shift in the European social order in the balance between centripetal and centrifugal social pressures in favour of the latter (Elias, 1994). That is, according to this conceptualization, the Europe of 'the Dark Ages' was characterized by an unstable, disunited and highly de-centralized form of social integration. This shift towards de-centralized and initially feudal state-units – Elias spoke of 'feudalization' in this connection – was arguably crucial in laying down the structural preconditions for the peculiar dynamism of the West relative to other civilizations, that is for establishing the preconditions for the long-term processes of hegemonial/elimination struggles and monopoly formation which according to Elias were conducive to the eventual rise of nation-states and, correlatively, of science, industrialization and – most significantly of all in the present context – what Elias called 'the sportization of pastimes' (Elias, in Elias and Dunning, 1986). Also involved were wars between nation-states and between the dynastic states and feudal forms of 'survival unit' which preceded them (Elias, 1978). Between them, this complex of interrelated processes contributed to and was reciprocally dependent on the emergent global hegemony of the West, a pattern of global domination which lasted some three to four centuries and which is only now showing signs of coming to a close with the shift of global power – so far, given the retention of military hegemony by the USA, mainly economic power – to the Far East. Western global hegemony, of course, was crucial to the global spread of modern sport. But why, within the overall social field and 'culture complex' of Western Europe, was it in Britain, mainly England, that the 'sportization of pastimes' first occurred?

The broad reasons for this generally accepted fact are easy to discern. They appear to be connected with England's specific trajectory of state formation relative to the state-formation trajectories of the other emergent European nation-states. Germany and Italy, for example, were precluded as sites of 'sportization' by the fact that they remained disunited until well into the nineteenth century. The Italians may have developed *calcio* as early as the sixteenth century, earlier than the English developed soccer and rugby, but, in that relatively disunited country, people valued particularistic local traditions over more universal national ones and *calcio* remained confined by and large to Florence. As far as Germany was concerned, unification was achieved under the aegis of the militaristic Prussians, and a brutalizing duelling culture was centrally involved in the incorporation of the bourgeoisie into the ruling class, a process in the course of which the values of what Elias called *eine satisfaktionsfähige Gesellschaft* – a culture in which the giving and receiving of satisfaction in duels was a key mark of upper- and upper middle-class status – became dominant over their earlier humanistic values (Elias, 1996). Besides this there developed in Germany a highly nationalistic gymnastics movement, *die Turnerbewegung*. In speaking of German resistance to 'English sports', Eisenberg wrote persuasively that:

> The indifference, even occasionally resistance, of the German middle class to modern 'English sports' has been…explained by two arguments. First the *Bürgertum* (the bourgeoisie) had already developed its own form of exercise in the early 19th century. *Turnen* (gymnastics), a form of military drill and not based on the principles of achievement and competition, partly absorbed those resources which in England

and other countries were invested in the development of sports; in addition, it provided an organizational basis for sport's opponents. Second, many intellectuals believed that mind and genius were not compatible with muscular strength. In their view, sports belonged not to German *Kultur* but to western *Zivilisation*, of which they disapproved.

(Eisenberg, 1990: 266)

The fact that, unlike *Turnen*, 'English sport' is based on 'the principles of achievement and competition' – 'fair play' is arguably more important – is of some significance and I shall return to it. First, however, it is necessary to probe further into different trajectories of European state formation and how they are relevant to understanding the development of modern sport.

By contrast with Italy and Germany, France and England were relatively unified nationally as early as the seventeenth and eighteenth centuries and partly – possibly even mainly – on that account they had by that time largely displaced such earlier contenders for the position of European 'superpower' as Spain and Holland. France, however, had become highly centralized and governed by a form of absolute rule in which, in Elias's words, the right of subjects 'to form associations of their own choosing was usually restricted as a matter of course if not abolished' (Elias, 1986b: 38). In England, by contrast, any chances of absolutism and a highly centralized state were smashed in the seventeenth century in the course of the Civil War in which the Commonwealth victory led to severe reductions in monarchical power. This tendency was reinforced by the fact that England was an island/naval power and did not require the sort of large, centralized bureaucracy which tends to grow up in continental states where a substantial land army is needed to defend the frontiers (Elias, 1950). Hence, in England, a variety of socially generated pressures contributed to the fact that the landed upper classes – the aristocracy and gentry – were able to retain a high degree of autonomy and, via parliament, to share the tasks of ruling with the monarch. As I suggested in Chapter 2, in the eighteenth century, as passions generated in conjunction with the Civil War began to cool down, members of these classes gradually developed relatively peaceful 'party political' means of conducting their political struggles. Elias referred in this connection to the 'parliamentarization of political conflict' and went on convincingly to argue, first, that this was central to the English civilizing process, and, second, that there occurred correlatively with this process of parliamentarization what he called the 'sportization' of pastimes, a process in the course of which the more civilized habitus developing among aristocrats and gentlemen as far as the business of ruling was concerned led them to acquire less violent, more 'civilized' ways of enjoying themselves in their leisure. The relationship was correlative not causal. Parliamentarization happened in the political lives of these aristocrats and gentlemen, sportization in their leisure lives.

74

Eisenberg has perceptively observed that the sports which began to be modernized in eighteenth-century England were organized via exclusive 'clubs', those whose modernization began in the nineteenth century in the form of more open and universalistic 'associations' (Eisenberg, 1990, 271–2), a fact which marked a power shift away from landed groups in favour of bourgeois groups. The principal locus of this second wave of sportization was initially provided by the elite 'public schools', a set of schools which, in characteristically English fashion, were allowed to operate with a high degree of independence from the state. Such a high degree of relative autonomy facilitated innovation within the public schools and this, together with the acute status tension and competition between them, was one of the conditions for the sportization of football, the process in the course of which soccer and rugby began to emerge as modern sports (see Chapter 5).

Towards the end of the nineteenth century in conjunction with what Perkin (1989) calls the 'formal' and 'informal' British empires, many of these originally English sport forms began to spread around the world. In fact, just as Italy was the principal home of the musical language employed world-wide today, so England was the principal birthplace of much of the vocabulary and practice of modern sport. As Stiven wrote in 1936:

> England was the cradle and loving mother of sport....It appears that English technical terms referring to this field might become the common possession of all nations in the same way as Italian technical terms in the field of music. It is probably rare that a piece of culture has migrated with so few changes.
>
> (quoted by Elias, 1986b: 126)

A major exception to this pattern of diffusion without the occurrence of significant change is provided by the spread of rugby to the USA where this originally English way of playing football was transformed into the radically different 'gridiron' game, one of the clearest sporting manifestations of American 'exceptionalism'. There was also resistance in Europe to this diffusion of English sports. They were eventually adopted without significant changes of form but Elias refers to a German aristocrat who wrote in 1810 that 'sport is as untranslatable as "gentleman"' (Elias, 1986b: 127) and members of the *Turner* movement sought to halt the spread of soccer in Germany by castigating it as *Fusslümmelei* – 'foot hooliganism' – and *die englische Krankheit* – 'the English disease' (Planck, 1898) – statements of localistic prejudice, not prescience about the soccer hooliganism of the 1970s, 1980s and 1990s! Eisenberg cites a book on sport published in Germany in 1908 which also illustrates this localistic prejudice. In it, sports clubs are compared unfavourably with the student duelling fraternities. 'Contemporaries familiar with both forms of sociability', we learn, 'felt that in sports there was a lot of frictional heat [*Reibung*] but no real warmth [*Wärme*]' (Eisenberg,

75

1990). This was typical of the sort of contrast drawn between *Kultur* and *Zivilisation*.

Such processes of resistance form a so far underresearched area in the sociology of sport. For example, little is known sociologically about the formation of the Gaelic games in Ireland. However, that is less relevant for present purposes than the fact that, by early in the twentieth century, 'sport' had become established, not only as a German word, but – with occasional local modifications such as *deporte* in Spanish and *esport* in Catalan – as part of the lexicon of most European languages. By that time, too, soccer was well on the way towards becoming established as the world's most popular ball game, a process of diffusion which involved the export, not only of the soccer way of playing but also – again with local modifications such as *Fussball* in German, *voetbal* in Dutch and *fútbol* in Spanish – of the name. Only the Italians resisted this linguistic aspect of the diffusion, preferring to keep their own term, *calcio*, presumably on account of their belief that Florence has a claim to having been the birthplace of the modern game. It seems reasonable to suppose that the diffusion of sports such as soccer from England is testimony to the level of maturation they had reached. Let me unpack some aspects of this deceptively simple statement.

I have argued here against a reified concept of time and suggested that recognition of the fact that 'time' is a human symbol and that the only 'reality' consists of processes and events, points towards the idea that sociology ought to be a historical subject. I also contended that Brailsford and Hargreaves are wrong to speak, on the one hand, of sport's 'eternal essence' and, on the other, of a 'ludic element' in sport which is 'inherently irreducible to programming for profit and control'. Such formulations are essentialist. They imply the existence of a 'play instinct' and fail adequately to capture the balance between continuity and change in the development of ludic forms. Arguably more adequate is a figurational concept of modern sport as a developmentally specific and relatively autonomous social phenomenon.

Eisenberg put forward an interesting idea in this connection. After noting that 'one of the most important characteristics of modern sport is its ability to provide and institutionalize a framework of sociability', she applies what she calls Simmel's 'purely theoretical' ideas on competition as a social form in an attempt to explain why competitive sport developed first in England. Crucial in this connection, she says, is Simmel's idea of ' "the pure form of competitive struggle" where…the prize of a contest is not in the hands of either adversary or competitor but of a third party'. Applying this idea to sport, Eisenberg writes:

> In sport, the third party is a governing body presenting a prize, or the coach and a well-informed audience…it is their recognition and applause the sportsmen and -women are striving for. Their fights against each other are merely a means to an end. In order to come as

close to that third party as possible, they have to adjust and establish ties with each other, but not hurt, and in many sports, not even touch each other. In this context, 'the fight of all *against* all' is, according to Simmel, at the same time 'the fight of all *for* all'. Competition in its pure form neutralizes the necessity of assessing victory or defeat in moral terms and helps to establish the assumption that sportsmen and -women are rational, ethical beings who will not cheat.

(Eisenberg, 1990: 269)

The fact that there are sports such as boxing where the explicit aim *is* to hurt one's opponent shows that this fruitful but abstract argument cannot account fully for the development or character of modern sport. Indeed, some of Eisenberg's own data point in this direction. Thus, she tells us how

Even the ideologists of sport in Germany, such as the members of the *Zentralausschuss für Volks- und Jugendspiele* who tried to disseminate football and other games in the 1890s, either did not regard competition as [a] subject at all or expressed negative associations. Many of them feared competition to arouse young persons' passions and to distract them from 'innocuous child[ren]'s games'.

(Eisenberg, 1990: 274)

In other words, such early German proponents of sport did not trust the ability of their protégés to exercise self-control in competitive situations. This suggests that modern sport is not some kind of 'pure form of competitive sociability' in the abstract form envisaged by Simmel but involves human beings who are not simply rational but also emotional and whose personality structures, habituses and internalized social controls reflect a particular stage in a civilizing or de-civilizing process. In the eighteenth and nineteenth centuries, the English generally speaking were evidently more advanced than the Germans in this regard. This is consistent with what Weber (1930) wrote in the *Protestant Ethic*.

As I suggested earlier, modern sport developed first in Britain largely in conjunction with what Elias called 'the parliamentarization of political conflict', a process which marked a crucial stage in the English civilizing and state-formation processes. Moreover, along with parliamentary government, sport in this form came to have many of the characteristics of what Parsons (1964) would have described as an 'evolutionary universal', that is a form which facilitated its spreading to and taking root in all societies at a given level of development. Crucial to this form is the development of constitutive written rules and unwritten conventions which enable a balance to be struck between a number of interdependent polarities such as:

1   the overall polarity between two opposing teams or individuals;
2   the polarity between attack and defence;
3   the polarity between co-operation and tension between the two teams or individuals;
4   the polarity between co-operation and tension within each team;
5   the polarity between the external control of players on a variety of levels (e.g. by managers, coaches, captains, team-mates, referees, linesmen, spectators, etc.) and the flexible controls which individual players exercise on themselves;
6   the polarity between affectionate identification with and hostile rivalry towards opponents;
7   the polarity between the enjoyment of aggression by individual players and the curb imposed upon such enjoyment by the written and unwritten rules;
8   the polarity between elasticity and fixity of rules;
9   the polarity between the interests of players and the interests of spectators;
10   the polarity between the interests of players and spectators and the interests of the authorities and legislators for the sport;[1]
11   the polarity between the interests of players and spectators and the interests of referees, linesmen, touch judges and umpires whose role is concerned with ensuring that the laws or rules of the sport are complied with;
12   the polarity between 'seriousness' and 'play';
13   the polarity between boredom and violence; and
14   the polarity between the interests of those who are involved cognitively and emotionally in the sport and outsiders who are not.

This discussion refers to team sports such as soccer and more individualized sport-games such as tennis. It would have to be modified to take, for example, the various forms of athletic competition into account. It goes without saying that this conceptualization is offered as a guide to further research, not as some kind of fixed and final answer.

The above polarities are interdependent in the sense that changes in any one are liable to have ramifying effects. Take polarities 9 and 12, those between players' and spectators' interests and those between 'seriousness' and 'play'. If the players begin to take part more seriously in a sport, the tension level will be raised and, beyond a certain point, the incidence of hostile rivalry within and between teams is likely to be increased; that is, the game is likely to be transformed from a mock battle in the direction of a 'real' one and players will be liable to transgress the rules and commit acts of 'foul' play. Again, to the degree that spectators become more seriously identified with the teams they support, they will be less liable to contemplate defeat with equanimity and may act in ways intended to affect the outcome of the contest, for example by shouting in favour of their own team and against the opponents. Once a certain point is reached they may directly interfere with play and even invade the playing area in an attempt to secure the contest's suspension. At that point, the authorities of the sport, those with a commercial interest in it and the public authorities are likely to be brought into play.

The sport forms which developed in eighteenth- and nineteenth-century England arguably came to involve a relatively stable balance among polarities such as these. Of course, further research will be necessary to establish how and why. However, for present purposes it is enough to suggest that it is this balance which accounts for their survival for more than a hundred years and their global diffusion in relatively unchanged forms. It is commonly argued that the processes of globalization and commercialization of sports which are currently occurring are a threat to their basic structure but that is doubtful. The basic structure of modern sports appears to give them a high degree of relative autonomy. They are successful 'collective inventions' in the sense that, time and again, they provide people with enjoyable excitement whilst not producing either boredom or degenerating into excessive violence. That is, they fit the temper of the times, of people such as ourselves who, Elias suggested, future historians may well describe as 'late barbarians', that is people who are 'civilized' relative to their ancient and medieval forebears but who are a long way short of reaching any 'pinnacle of civilized self-restraint' (Elias, 1991b).

4

THE DEVELOPMENT OF
SOCCER AS A WORLD GAME

Introduction

The first issue to address in discussing the development of soccer as a world game is the origin and meaning of the terms 'football' and 'soccer'. That is because it is usual in virtually every country to refer to the game as 'football' or by the translation of that English word into the native tongue, for example *Fussball* in German, *voetball* in Dutch, *futebol* in Portuguese, *fútbol* in Spanish, and *fotboll* in Swedish. The only exception in Europe is in Italy where, as I noted in Chapter 3, the term *calcio* is used to reflect the claim of that country to having been the birthplace of the modern game, though this claim is probably false. Although not so widely used as 'football', in England the term 'soccer' is widely understood. It is not so widely understood in continental Europe or Central and South America. In fact, the principal countries where the term 'soccer' is used are those of North America and Australia where its use is made necessary by the fact that Americans, Canadians and Australians use 'football' to refer to the games produced by their citizens of European descent.

This discussion may seem needlessly pedantic. However, it is essential, if only because it is commonly believed outside Australia, Canada and the USA that 'football' implies a solely or mainly kicking game, that is 'soccer'. Such a belief is erroneous. 'Football' is a generic term which refers to a whole class of ball games, central among them Association football (soccer), Rugby football (both Union and League), American football, Canadian football, Australian football, and Gaelic football. 'Soccer' is a corruption of the term 'association' and refers to the highly specific Association way of playing. The term is said to have originated in the late nineteenth century at Oxford University when a student named Charles Wreford-Brown was asked one day by a friend at breakfast: 'I say, Charles, are you playing rugger [Rugby] today?' 'No,' he replied, 'I'm playing soccer' (Glanville, 1969: 29). The practice of adding '-er' to abbreviations was apparently fashionable among the English upper and middle classes at that time. Nevertheless, such a story is probably apocryphal. If not, it represents one of the few instances in the history of sport where the introduction of a specific practice can be authentically traced to a named individual. The key word in the last sentence is 'authentically' for there are numerous mythical accounts which trace the origins of sports to the innovative actions of individuals and do not see the need to locate these individuals socially.

There are two broad kinds of mythical accounts of the origins of sports: those which trace them to the actions of an individual and those which trace them to a collectivity. An example of an individual origin myth is that which traces rugby to the alleged deviant act in 1823 of William Webb Ellis, a Rugby schoolboy. Another traces baseball to an alleged act of General Abner Doubleday in Cooperstown, New York, in 1839 (Gardner, 1974: 60–1; Dunning and Sheard, 1979: 66). Both are implausible.

Most attempts to explain the origins of soccer are myths of the collective rather than the individual kind. Again, they take different forms. For example, it was once believed in Kingston upon Thames, Surrey, that the local game traditionally played there each Shrove Tuesday originated from a Saxon defeat of Danish invaders in the early Middle Ages. The head of the defeated Danish chieftain, it was said, was kicked in celebration around the streets, and the game grew out of that. A similarly implausible belief used to be held in Derby, only this time the game is said to have originated from a defeat of Roman troops by native Britons in the third century AD (Marples, 1954: 6–7). Such beliefs are mythical because there is no evidence to support them from the time when the supposed originating events are said to have taken place. In fact, the reverse of this kind of belief is sociologically more plausible, namely that the Britons and Anglo-Saxons may already have been playing football-like games at the time of their battles against the Romans and the Danes and that, holding football matches as part of their victory celebrations, they may have substituted the defeated leaders' heads for the ball. That they might have done this is consistent with what is known about their levels of civilization in Elias's sense but, again, there is simply no evidence to confirm or refute an hypothesis of this kind.

Origin myths of an anthropologically more plausible kind trace the origins of football to a pagan fertility rite. Writing in 1929, W. B. Johnson noted that it is common in primitive rituals for a globular object to symbolize the sun. In other words, the football is a symbolic representation of the bringer and supporter of life, an hypothesis which receives indirect support from the fact that *la soule*, the French name for a form of football which traditionally flourished in Normandy and Brittany, appears to be cognate with *sol*, the Latin word for 'sun' (Marples, 1954: 12–13). What is not explained in this origin myth is why the symbolic sun should have been kicked and thrown around in what is generally agreed to have been a rough and physically dangerous game.

An earlier variant of this hypothesis was proposed by Chambers who argued that a football symbolically represents, not the sun, but the head of a sacrificial beast (Marples, 1954: 14–15). The object of the game, he conjectured, was for players to get hold of the symbolic head and bury it on their lands in the hope of ensuring abundant crops. Indirect support for such an hypothesis was said to be provided by the fact that the object of some forms of folk football, for example that played at Scone in Scotland, was to place the ball in a hole (Marples, 1954: 12). Further indirect support was said to come from 'the Haxey Hood game', a folk ritual which survives in Haxey, Lincolnshire. The 'hood' in this game is a roll of sacking or leather and the players' aim is to fight for possession of the roll and convey it to their respective village inns. That the roll or 'hood' is the symbolic representation of an animal is said to be indicated by a speech traditionally made by 'the Fool', an official in the ceremony which takes place the day before the game. The relevant part of the Fool's speech goes:

> We've killed two bullocks and a half but the other half we had to leave running field: we can fetch it if it's wanted. Remember it's

> *Hoose agin hoose, toon agin toon,*
> *and if you meet a man, knock him doon.*
> *[House against house, town against town,*
> *And if you meet a man, knock him down.]*
> (Marples, 1954: 14–15)

It is deduced from this that the 'hood' represents half a bullock, that is part of a sacrificial beast. The point about hypotheses of this kind is that it is impossible to support them by direct evidence. They are thus bound to remain more or less plausible speculations and there is no way of determining whether the idea of playing with a football originated from a fertility rite in which the ball symbolically represented the sun, the head of a sacrificial beast, both of these things or, for that matter, neither or anything else. Indeed, there is no way of determining conclusively whether football had a ritual origin or not. However, the traditional speech of the Fool in the Haxey Hood ceremony does point in a sociologically plausible direction. More particularly, while it may not allow one to determine what the origins of football were in any absolute sense, it does permit one to establish its function as a violent and enjoyable means for expressing conflict between rival groups which enabled them to confirm one dimension of their relative superiority/inferiority.

Yet another form of collective origin myth holds that football is a more or less direct derivative of one of the following: the ancient Chinese game of *Tsu chu* (kick ball); Japanese *kemari*; Roman *harpastum*; Greek *episkyros*; or the Italian *gioco del calcio* (game of kicking) (Green, 1953: 5–6; Young 1968: 2). In none of these cases, with the partial exception of *calcio*, is there evidence which allows one to trace a line of descent. A somewhat more plausible explanation was proposed by Jusserand in 1901 and accepted by Magoun in 1938 (Magoun, 1938: 134–7). Noting the existence of parallels between the folk football of England and France, Jusserand suggested they must have had a common origin. And since the records go further back in France than England, he concluded that football must have originated in France and been brought to England in the eleventh century by the Normans. If Jusserand is correct, it is more than a little ironic for he will have proved the French origins of what is widely regarded as having been originally an English sport! My view is that Jusserand's desire to prove the superiority of the French over the English probably helped to tilt him towards this conclusion. This is because – apart from the name which is obviously English – all the evidence suggests that, while football *per se* may not have originated in England, soccer and rugby, the game forms which developed in the nineteenth century, most certainly did. Such a view is not mere speculation but can be supported by reference to data.

Marples accepts the plausibility of the Jusserand thesis but speculates that the existence of football-like games such as 'hurling' and 'knappan' in Cornwall, Ireland and Wales is consistent with what he calls 'the Celtic hypothesis', namely that football-like games underwent an independent but parallel development among the Franks and Anglo-Saxons, and the Celts. Although it is impossible to support it by direct evidence, this line of reasoning is convincing. However, it can be taken further. Since the Chinese, the Japanese, the Greeks, the Romans, the Italians, the English, the French and the Celts all, at some stage in their histories, played forms of game which have been proposed with varying degrees of plausibility as *the* ancestral form of football, it seems reasonable to hypothesize that football-like games most probably had multiple origins, being played in different forms in all or most societies with the technological ability to construct appropriate types of ball and the freedom from material and military necessity to engage in forms of play. It is possible that, the lower the division of labour in such societies, the more closely they approximated structurally to the pattern of social organiza-tion called 'mechanical solidarity' by Durkheim, the more their game forms would have had a ritual and religious character (Durkheim, 1964: 70 ff.). That is because, in societies of that type, the ritual and the sacred are all pervasive.

In short, although it is necessary to maintain a critical distance from the particular anthropological explanations of the origins of football proposed by Johnson and Chambers, there are sociological reasons for believing that hypotheses of this kind may not be totally wide of the mark. However, these reasons remain speculative. They may be more or less plausible but it is impos-sible to support them by reference to data. However, there is evidence about the history and development of football and, if properly interpreted, such evidence begins to allow one to distinguish fact from myth.

Folk football in medieval and early modern Britain

In Britain, reliable evidence for the existence of a game called 'football' does not begin to accumulate until the fourteenth century. However, between 1314 and 1660, orders prohibiting football and other popular games were issued by the central and local authorities on numerous occasions. Table 4.1 gives an idea of the frequency with which it was felt necessary to re-enact such prohibitions, together with an indication of how widely in a geographical sense the folk antecedents of modern football were played.

The 1496 statute of Henry VII was re-enacted several times during the reign of Henry VIII (1509–47), the last English monarch to re-enact such legislation. However, it remained on the statute book until 1845 under the

Table 4.1 Selected list of prohibitions by state and local authorities of the folk antecedents of modern football

Year	Reigning monarch (where applicable)	Place
1314	Edward II	London
1331	Edward III	London
1349	Edward III	London
1365	Edward III	London
1388	Richard II	London
1401	Henry IV	London
1409	Henry IV	London
1410	Henry IV	London
1414	Henry V	London
1424	James I of Scotland	Perth
1450		Halifax
1454		Halifax
1457	James II of Scotland	Perth
1467		Leicester
1471	James III of Scotland	Perth
1474	Edward IV	London
1477	Edward IV	London
1478		London
1488		Leicester
1491	James IV of Scotland	Perth
1496	Henry VII	London
1533		Chester
1570		Peebles
1572		London
1581		London
1594		Shrewsbury
1608		Manchester
1609		Manchester
1615		London
1655		Manchester
1660		Bristol
1666		Manchester
1667		Manchester

Sources: Magoun (1938), Marples (1954), Young (1968)

Note:
Local rather than state authorities were responsible for those prohibitions where the name of the reigning monarch is not included

title 'The bill for maintaining artillery and the debarring of unlawful games' (Marples, 1954: 43).

The prohibition of 1314 and that issued by Edward III in 1365 show the main reasons why the authorities wished to ban football and similar games. The order of 1314 was issued in the name of Edward II by the Lord Mayor of London and referred to 'great uproar in the City, through certain tumult arising from great footballs in the fields of the public, from which many evils perchance may arise'. It aimed 'on the King's behalf' to forbid the game 'upon pain of imprisonment' (Marples, 1954: 439–41). Edward III's prohibition was connected with the belief that playing games like football was having adverse effects on military preparedness. It is significant that this was the time of the Hundred Years War which broke out in 1338 and in which English and French kings were battling over the French possessions of the former. This struggle was decisive in the early stages of the formation of England and France as nation-states. The prohibition of 1365 reads:

> To the Sherriffes of London. Order to cause proclamation to be made that every able bodied man of the said city on feast days when he has leisure shall in his sports use bows and arrows or pellets and bolts...forbidding them under pain of imprisonment to meddle in the hurling of stones, loggats and quoits, handball, football...or other vain games of no value; as the people of the realme...used heretofore to practise the said art in their sports when by God's help came forth honour to the kingdom and advantage to the King in his actions of war; and now the said art is almost wholly disused and the people engage in the games aforesaid and in other dishonest, unthrifty or idle games, whereby the realm is likely to be without archers.
>
> (Marples, 1954: 181, 182)

It is clear, then, that the state authorities in medieval Britain tried to suppress football and other traditional games because they regarded them as a waste of time and a threat to public order. As a result, they tried to direct the energies of the people into what they (the authorities) regarded as more useful channels such as military training.

Official prohibitions may tell us about how the authorities in medieval and early modern Britain viewed folk football but they provide little information about the character of such games. A more detailed discussion of Carew's seventeenth-century account of Cornish 'hurling' than I provided in Chapter 2 will show that these folk antecedents of modern football and related modern sports were forms of intergroup combat-game which were closer to 'real' fighting than is the case with their twentieth-century 'offspring'.

According to Carew, hurling matches were usually organized by 'gentlemen'. The 'goals' were either these gentlemen's houses or two towns or villages some three or four miles apart. There was, he said, 'neither comparing of numbers nor matching of men'. The game was played with a silver ball and the object was to carry it 'by force or sleight' (trickery) to the goal of one's own side. Carew described the game thus:

> Whosoever getteth seizure of this ball, findeth himself generally pursued by the adverse party; neither will they leave, til…he be layd flat on Gods deare earth; which fall once received, disableth him from…detayning the ball: hee therefore, throweth the same…to some one of his fellowes, fardest before him, who maketh away withall in like manner.…
>
> The Hurlers take their next way over hilles, dales, hedges, ditches; yea, and thorow bushes, briers, mires, plashes and rivers whatsoever; so as you shall sometimes see 20 or 30 lie tugging together in the water, scrambling and scratching for the ball. A play (verily) both rude and rough, and yet such as is not destitute of policies, in some sort resembling the feats of warre:…there are horsemen placed…on either party…and ready to ride away with the ball if they can catch it.…But…gallop any one of them never so fast, yet he shall be surely met at some hedge corner, crosse-lane, bridge or deep water, which…they know he must needs touch at: and if his good fortune gard him not…hee is like to pay the price of his theft, with his owne and his horses overthrowe.…
>
> The ball in this play may be compared to an infernall spirit: for whosoever catcheth it, fareth straightwayes like a madde man, strugling and fighting with those that goe about to holde him: and no sooner is the ball gone from him, but hee resigneth this fury to the next receyver and himselfe becommeth peaceable as before. I cannot well resolve, whether I should more commend this game, for the manhood and exercise, or condemne it for the boysterousness and harmes which it begetteth: for as…it makes their bodies strong, hard, and nimble, and puts a courage into their hearts to meete an enemie in the face: so…it is accompanied by many dangers, some of which do ever fall to the players share. For proofe whereof, when the hurling is ended, you shall see them retyring home, as from a pitched battaile, with bloody pates, bones broken and out of joynt, and such bruses as serve to shorten their daies; yet al is good play, and never Attourney nor Crowner troubled for the matter.
>
> (Carew, 1602; quoted in Dunning and Sheard, 1979: 27)

Carew's account gives a good idea of the loose overall structure of this type of game. There was no limitation on numbers of participants, no stipulation of numerical equality between sides and no restriction on the size of the playing area. Hurlers did not play on a demarcated field but on the territory between and surrounding what were agreed on as the goals of the two sides, that is the places to which they had respectively to transport the ball to win. Cornish hurling was a rough but by no means unregulated game. One of the customary rules emerges clearly from Carew's account: when tackled, a player had to pass the ball to a team-mate. There was also a rudimentary division of labour within each team into what Carew, using a then-contemporary military analogy, called a 'fore-ward', a 'rere-ward' and two 'wings'. This shows that use of the terms 'forward' and 'wing' to denote particular playing positions (a practice which survives in present-day soccer and rugby) has a long ancestry and military roots. Carew also mentioned a division between players on horseback and players on foot. This is interesting because it suggests that, in these folk games, elements of what were later to become separate games – in this instance, not only soccer and rugby but also hurling and polo – were rolled together into an undifferentiated whole.

The roughness described by Carew is what one would expect of games played by large numbers of seventeenth-century English people according to loosely defined oral rules. There was no referee to keep control and no outside body to appeal to in cases of dispute. That games of this type continued to be played until the nineteenth century emerges from an account of a kind of football that was played each Christmas Day in the early 1800s in South Cardiganshire, Wales:

> At Llanwennog, an extensive parish below Lampeter, the inhabitants for football purposes were divided into the Bros and Blaenaus....The Bros...occupied the high ground of the parish. They were nick-named 'Paddy Bros' from a tradition that they were descended from Irish people. The Blaenaus occupied the lowlands and, it may be presumed were pure-bred Brythons....[T]he match did not begin until about mid-day....Then the whole of the Bros and Blaenaus, rich and poor, male and female, assembled on the turnpike road which divided the highlands from the lowlands. The ball...was thrown high in the air...and when it fell Bros and Blaenaus scrambled for its possession, and a quarter of an hour frequently elapsed before the ball was got out from the struggling heap....Then if the Bros could succeed in taking the ball up the mountain to Rhyddlan they won the day; while the Blaenaus were successful if they got the ball to their end of the parish....The whole parish was the field of operations, and sometimes it would be dark before either party secured a victory. In the meantime, many kicks would be given and taken, so that on the following day the competitors would be unable to walk, and sometimes a kick on the shins would lead the two men concerned to abandon the game until they had decided who was the better pugilist....The art of football playing in the olden time seems to have been to reach the goal. Once the goal was reached, the

victory was celebrated with loud hurrahs and the firing of guns, and was not disturbed until the following Christmas Day.

(quoted in Dunning and Sheard, 1979: 29–30)

Some authorities have been reluctant to use accounts of 'hurling', 'knappan', 'bottle-kicking' and similar games such as East Anglian 'camp ball' (perhaps 'camp' in this case derives from or is cognate with the German *kämpfen* which means to fight, hence 'fight ball') as evidence regarding the folk antecedents of modern football. That is understandable but arguably based on a failure fully to appreciate the nature of this type of game. They were based on local custom, not national rules; hence the chances of variation in names and playing customs between communities were great because there were neither written rules nor central organizations to unify the name or manner of playing. Given that, references to 'football' in medieval and early modern sources do not imply a game played according to a single set of rules. Identity of names is therefore no guarantee of identity of the games to which these names refer. By the same token, the differences between folk games that were given different names were rarely as great as those between modern sports. That is, as far as one can tell, the differences between hurling, knappan, camp ball, bottle-kicking and, as referred to in the medieval and early modern sources, football, were neither so great nor so clear-cut as those between rugby, soccer, hockey and polo today.

These games may have had different names because they were played with different implements. The 'knappan', for example, was a wooden disc. The 'bottle' in the Hallaton game is a wooden keg. Similarly, references to football in some early accounts seem to refer more to a type of ball than a type of game. Thus, the prohibition of football in Manchester in 1608 referred to playing '*with* the ffotebale' rather than 'playing ffotebale' (Dunning and Sheard, 1979: 22). As far as can be ascertained, the type of ball to which this name was given was an inflated animal bladder, usually, but not always, encased in leather. Balls of this type probably lent themselves better than smaller, solid balls to kicking. This could explain the name 'football'. Alternatively, the term could have signified a game that was played *on* foot as opposed to horseback. Nevertheless, it would still be wrong to assume that, in folk games called 'football', the ball was only propelled by foot, or, conversely, that in games called 'hurling' or 'handball' it was only propelled by hand. That is because prohibitions in these folk games were less clearly defined and less rigidly enforceable than is the case in modern sports.

Such games were traditionally associated with religious festivals such as Shrovetide, Easter and Christmas. However, they could also be played on an *ad hoc* basis at any time in the autumn, winter or spring. They were played across country and through the streets of towns and often by females as well as males. One played as the member of a specific group − for example, for Hallaton v. Medbourne, the 'Bros' v. the 'Blaenaus', the shoemakers v. the drapers, the bachelors v. the married men, the spinsters v. the married women – rather than as the member of a club one had joined voluntarily and where the primary reason for associating was in order to play football. In these folk games, communal identity took precedence over individual identity, the pressure to take part was intense, and the degree of individual choice that players had was, compared with amateur footballers today, relatively small.

Whatever their names, and whether associated with a specific festival or not, the folk antecedents of modern football were openly emotional affairs characterized by physical struggle. Such restraints as they contained were loosely defined and imposed by custom as opposed to elaborate formal regulations which are written down, requiring players to exercise a high degree of self-control, and involving the intervention of external officials when a deliberate foul is committed, a foul occurs accidentally or this self-control breaks down. As a result, the basic game-pattern – the character of these folk games as struggles between groups, the open enjoyment in them of excitement akin to that generated in battle, the riotousness, and the relatively high level of socially tolerated physical violence – was always and everywhere the same. In short, these games were cast in a common mould which transcended differences of names and locally specific traditions of playing.

Folk football in continental Europe

As has been shown, ball games similar to the British folk antecedents of modern football were played in France. Just as in Britain, these folk games were prohibited by royal edict, for example by Philippe V in 1319 and Charles V in 1369 (Marples, 1954: 25). Such attempts were made right up until the Revolution, suggesting that the French authorities were just as unsuccessful at suppressing these games as their British counterparts. Similar edicts were enacted in colonial America showing that the earliest English settlers must have played such games as well (Gardner, 1974: 96).

Although there were a few signs of similar developments simultaneously in England (Dunning and Sheard, 1979: 35), in Italy, as was noted in Chapters 2 and 3, a somewhat more restrained and regulated game, the *gioco del calcio*, had developed by the sixteenth and seventeenth centuries. The participants, we are told, were 'young Cavaliers of good purse', and two teams of twenty-seven members per side played every evening in the Piazza di Santa Croce in Florence from Epiphany to Lent (Marples, 1954: 67). That it remained a rough game is brought out in an English translation, published in London in 1656, of a description by Boccalini. The beginning reads as follows:

> The Noble Florentines plaid the last Tuesday at the calcio in the Phebean field…and though some, to whom it was a new sight to see many of these Florentine gentlemen fall down to right cuffs, said, that that manner of proceeding in that which was but play and sport,

was too harsh, and not severe enough in real combat....[T]he Commonwealth of Florence had done very well in introducing the Calcio among the citizens, to the end that having the satisfaction of giving four or five good round buffets in the face to those to whom they bear ill will, by way of sport, they might the better appease their anger (than by the use of daggers).

(Young, 1968: 88–90)

The presence of pike-carrying soldiers in pictorial representations of the game (Marples, 1954, facing p. 21) suggests that the social control function attributed to *calcio* by Boccalini may not always have been performed. It is reasonable to suppose, as I suggested in Chapter 2, that pikemen were necessary in case the excitement of the struggle led either the young noble players or members of the crowd to get carried away and lose their self-restraint (Guttmann, 1986: 51).

The development of modern soccer

Although *calcio* was known to a handful of English writers and their readers for around a hundred years, they were members of a small elite and it is doubtful whether their knowledge had any direct effects on the British folk antecedents of modern football. (See Chapter 3 for a fuller discussion of the unlikely possibility that soccer may have been modelled on *calcio*.) With or without gentry support, these continued to be widely played by the common people in the traditional manner until the nineteenth century, while as far as one can tell, Florentine *calcio* froze at or around the developmental level reached in the sixteenth and seventeenth centuries. In short, the development of modern football appears to have been a process which occurred autonomously in England. Two processes that took place more or less simultaneously in the eighteenth and nineteenth centuries are of relevance in this connection: (1) the cultural marginalization of folk football, a process that began in the middle of the eighteenth century and gathered pace in the nineteenth; and (2) the development of newer forms of football in the public schools and universities from about the 1840s onwards.

The cultural marginalization of folk football

Regarding the cultural marginalization of folk football, it is enough to note that these forms of playing seem to have fallen foul of the 'civilizing' and 'state-formation' processes as they were experienced in eighteenth- and nineteenth-century Britain. That is, increasing numbers of people came to regard the roughness of folk football with repugnance. At the same time, the formation of the new police in the 1820s and 1830s placed in the hands of the authorities an instrument of social control more efficient than any previously available. The prohibitions which had begun in 1314 could thus be made to stick and 'the bill for maintaining artillery and the debarring of unlawful games' could be removed from the statute book. Another influence may have been at work as well. It is possible that the survival of folk football in the face of centuries of opposition had been predicated in part on support from sections of the aristocracy and gentry. If that is, indeed, a reasonable supposition, then a further reason for the cultural marginalization of these antecedents of modern football may have been connected with the way in which industrialization and state formation involved an augmentation of the power of rising bourgeois groups. As a result, status competition between members of the bourgeoisie and the landed classes grew more intense, leading the latter to grow more status exclusive in their behaviour and withdraw their support from traditional sports. Whatever the degree of adequacy of this hypothesis, it is certainly the case that public schools were the central loci of the development of embryonic forms of soccer and the rival rugby code. In order to see why, it is necessary to delve into aspects of the social history of the public schools in greater detail than I did in Chapter 2.

The development of football in the public schools

Initially formed as charitable institutions for the education of 'poor and needy scholars and clerks' or as local grammar schools, during the eighteenth and early nineteenth centuries the public schools were transformed into boarding schools for fee-paying pupils from the upper and upper middle classes (Dunning and Sheard, 1979: 47–51). At least two consequences followed. The first was that the class discrepancy between masters (teachers) and pupils inherent in the structure of this type of school, where middle-class academics were attempting to cater for the educational needs of boys who mostly came from higher social strata than themselves, meant that masters were unable to prevent the emergence of forms of self-rule by the boys. The second was that this power and status discrepancy between masters and pupils led to a chronic lack of discipline and not infrequent rebellions by the boys. As I showed in Chapter 2, the revolt at Winchester in 1818 could only be quelled by the militia using bayonets and, in 1793, the boys there 'victualled the College for a regular siege, ransacking the shops for provisions'. They also 'provided themselves with swords, guns and bludgeons and…mounted the red cap of liberty and equality'. At Rugby in 1797, the headmaster's classroom door was blown off its hinges, his windows were smashed and his books were thrown onto a bonfire. Order was only restored with military help (Dunning and Sheard, 1979: 51–3).

Youthful bravado probably played a part in these rebellions. Those in the 1790s were undoubtedly affected, at least superficially, by then-contemporary events in France. From a sociological point of view, however, the rebellions were the most obvious surface manifestations of a struggle between masters and boys in which, for a long time, neither party was able to establish effective dominance over the other. The result was the gradual crystallization of a system of dual control which later came to be known as the 'prefect–fagging system'. This was a system in which the rule of masters was granted a degree of recognition in the classroom in return for their reciprocal recognition of the right of 'prefects' – the leaders among the older boys – to exercise dominance as far as extracurricular activities were concerned.

The 'fagging' part of the system emerged as part of the same process. The fact that masters were unable to control the oldest boys meant they were unable to control them in relation to their younger fellows. As a result, there emerged a dominance hierarchy among the boys determined mainly by relativities of age and physical strength: the boys who were older and/or physically stronger 'lorded it' over those who were younger and/or physically weaker. The juniors were forced into the role of 'fags', that is into providing menial, ego-enhancing and possibly sexual services for their seniors. The strongest held sway and, as one would expect of teenage males untrammelled by effective adult control, often exercised their power mercilessly.

The prefect–fagging system was central to the early development of football. At each public school the game was one means by which older boys asserted dominance over juniors. One of the customary duties which developed for fags was that of 'fagging out' at football. This meant they were compelled to play and restricted for the most part to the role of 'keeping goal', that is they were ranged *en masse* along the baselines. Thus it is suggested that, at Westminster in the early nineteenth century, 'the small boys, the duffers and the funk-sticks were the goalkeepers, twelve or fifteen at each end'. 'Douling', the name given to football at Shrewsbury, was the same as they used for 'fagging'. It is reputedly derived from the Greek for 'slave'. At Winchester in the early nineteenth century, fags, one at either end, were even used instead of goal-posts, the ball having to pass between their outstretched legs to score. Fags were also used as a means of boundary demarcation (Dunning and Sheard, 1979: 55).

Just as in the folk antecedents, football in the public schools at this stage was governed by oral rules. This meant that the character of the game varied from school to school, differences being affected by decisions made in relation to the geographic peculiarities of particular playing areas – the game was not yet played on 'pitches' constructed and marked out for purposes of playing football – and by the accretion of locally specific traditions. Despite such differences, however, handling the ball as well as kicking was allowed at *all* the schools.

All forms of public school football at this stage were also rough. In the 'scrimmages' in Charterhouse 'cloisters football', for example, 'shins would be kicked black and blue; jackets and other articles of clothing almost torn into shreds; and fags trampled under foot' (Dunning and Sheard, 1979: 56). At Westminster, 'the enemy tripped, shinned, charged with the shoulder, got you down and sat upon you – in fact, might do anything short of murder to get the ball from you' (Dunning and Sheard, 1979: 55). And in Charterhouse 'field' football, 'there were a good many broken shins, for most of the fellows had iron tips to their very strong shoes and some freely boasted of giving more than they took' (Dunning and Sheard, 1979: 56). Iron-tipped shoes were also used at Rugby where they were called 'navvies'. According to an Old Rugbeian reminiscing in the 1920s, navvies had 'a thick sole, the profile of which at the toe much resembled the ram of an ironclad', that is a battleship (Dunning and Sheard, 1979: 55–7).

The development of written rules and the bifurcation of soccer and rugby

During the 1830s and 1840s, at a point when the cultural marginalization of folk football was beginning to reach its peak, newer forms of the game, more appropriate to the emergent social conditions and values of an urbanizing and industrializing society in which state formation and civilization were correlatively advancing, began to develop in the public schools. Centrally involved in this process were: (1) the committing of the rules to writing; (2) a stricter demarcation and limiting of the size and shape of the playing area; (3) the imposition of stricter limitations on the duration of matches; (4) a reduction in the numbers taking part; (5) an equalization in the size of contending teams; and (6) the imposition of stricter regulations on the kinds of physical force that it was legitimate to use. It was in the course of this incipient modernization that the soccer and rugby ways of playing began recognizably to emerge out of the matrix of locally differentiated public school games. Rugby appears to have been the first to begin to take on its distinctive profile.

It remains widely believed that rugby resulted from a single deviant act by a single individual (Macrory, 1991: 23–52). The individual in question was William Webb Ellis who is said in 1823, 'with a fine disregard for the rules of football' customary at Rugby at that time, to have picked up the ball and run with it. There is no doubt that Webb Ellis was a pupil at Rugby in 1823. What is doubtful is this reductionist explanation of the emergence of the rugby game. It is sociologically more plausible to suppose that rugby and soccer were co-produced. That is, they are best understood as having been produced, not simply within particular public schools in isolation, but within the wider social field formed by *all* the public schools at the particular stage of industrialization, urbanization, civilization and state formation reached in Britain between about 1830 and the 1850s. It was a stage when tensions between the landed classes and the rising bourgeoisie were growing more intense and, it seems reasonable to suppose, these intensifying class and status tensions were reflected in relations among the public schools, playing a part in the development of these in many respects diametrically opposite ways of playing football.

Assuming the extant data provide a reliable guide, it seems that the first public school to commit its football rules to writing was Rugby. According to Marples (1954: 137) and Young (1968: 63), this process took place in 1846. In 1960, however, I came across a set dated 1845. (See Macrory, 1991: 86–90.) These were basically the same as those produced in 1846, except that they were preceded by a set of organizational and disciplinary rules which provide a clue as to why this process of codification may have taken place. The prefect–fagging system at Rugby had recently been reformed by Thomas Arnold, headmaster there from 1828 to 1842. Basically, what Arnold achieved – I am talking about his disciplinary, not academic, achievements – was the transformation of the Rugby variant of the prefect–fagging system from a system of dual control which was conducive to persistent disorder into a system of indirect rule which was conducive to greater harmony both in staff–student relations and in those among the boys. There is, however, no evidence that he was directly involved in the transformation of Rugby football which depended on this development. The rules were not committed to writing until three years after Arnold's death.

A crucial aspect of the reformed prefect–fagging system at Rugby as far as the development of football was concerned consisted of the fact that it permitted the masters to increase their power whilst simultaneously preserving a substantial measure of self-rule for the boys. A system of informal assemblies they called 'levees' grew up, the name presumably taken from the practice of Louis XIV of France of holding meetings whilst rising from bed. Significantly, it was a 'Sixth Form Levee' (an assembly of the senior boys) which produced the written rules of 1845, and the first section was concerned with tightening up and legitimizing the administrative role of prefects in relation to football.

Correlation, of course, does not necessarily imply causation. However, the fact that the available evidence points towards Rugby as having been both the first public school to achieve effective reform of the prefect–fagging system and the first to commit its football rules to writing suggests strongly that these two processes were linked. There is reason, furthermore, to believe that, besides Arnold's qualities as a teacher, the fact that effective disciplinary reform was first achieved at Rugby was connected with that school's relatively recent formation as a public school – it had been a local grammar school until the 1790s – and the fact that its pupils tended to come from lower ranks in the upper and middle classes than those at, say, Eton and Harrow. The status discrepancy between masters and pupils would thus have been lower at Rugby, making that school correspondingly easier to reform (Dunning and Sheard, 1979: 74, 75).

Again, if the surviving evidence is a reliable guide, the second public school to commit its football rules to writing was Eton, located next to Windsor and with associations with the royal court. As I noted in Chapter 2, written rules were produced there in 1847, two years after the Rugbeians had committed their football rules to writing. Evidently the size of teams was customary and taken for granted by Etonians at that time for there is no mention of it in the 1847 rules. However, Young claims that eleven-a-side football was played at Eton as early as 1841 (Young, 1968: 67–8). The fact that matches between limited, equal numbers – fifteen or twenty a side – also began at Rugby in 1839 or 1840, although matches between uneven sides continued to predominate, suggests the possibility that there were forms of communication among the public schools as far as football matters were concerned (Dunning and Sheard, 1979: 90).

Four among the thirty-four rules laid down at Eton in 1847 are of special interest. They are:

8.   The goal sticks are to be seven feet out of the ground: a goal is gained when the ball is kicked between them provided it is not over the level of the top of them.
9.   The space between each goal stick is to be eleven feet.
22. Hands may only be used to stop the ball, or touch it when behind. The ball must not be carried, thrown, or struck by the hand.
29. A player is considered to be sneaking when only three, or less than three, of the opposite side are before him and may not kick the ball.

The first three of these rules were diametrically opposite to their counterparts at Rugby where carrying the ball and scoring by kicking above H-shaped posts were legislated for in the rules of 1845. They can thus be considered as legislating for an embryonic form of soccer. So can rule 29, the rule regarding 'sneaking' (the evocative Eton term for 'offside') even though the Field Game continues today to resemble rugby in that its rules do not allow deliberate forward passing. Use of the term 'sneaking', with its moralistic flavour, is indicative of how strongly the boys at Eton felt at that stage about this particular form of gaining an unfair advantage

Marples (1954: 140) speculated that the first schools where a non-handling game developed were Westminster and Charterhouse. However, the available evidence suggests that he was wrong. For example, writing in 1903, Captain F. Markham, a former Westminster pupil, remembered that 'running with the ball (Rugby fashion)…and "fist-punting" were both allowed in Westminster football until 1851 or 1852' (Dunning and Sheard, 1979: 55). In other words, there seems to have been an interval of four to five years between the abolition of handling at Eton and the outlawing of such a practice at Westminster. Perhaps after a period of experimentally introducing a rugby element into their football, the Westminster boys were following Eton's lead? Similarly, when written rules were produced at Charterhouse for the first time in 1862, stopping the ball with one's hand and catching were allowed (Dunning, 1961:

104). And according to Shearman (1887), the rules at Harrow included four governing the use of hands as late as 1887. It would thus seem that Eton was the first public school to impose an absolute taboo on the use of hands. It follows accordingly that the Eton Field Game was probably the earliest prototype of soccer.

Why should the boys at Eton have wanted to produce such a game? One doubtful possibility is that the Etonians produced an entirely kicking game completely oblivious to what was happening at other public schools. However, they are unlikely to have been such 'cultural dopes'. They considered their school to be the leading public school in all respects. It was the second oldest, only Winchester being able to take pride in a longer pedigree. Having been founded by Henry VI in 1440, Eton was also able to boast about being a royal foundation. Moreover, being located next to Windsor, it continued to have connections with the royal court and to recruit its pupils mainly from the highest social strata. One can easily imagine how the Eton boys would have reacted to the development of a distinctive way of playing football at Rugby, in their eyes at the time an obscure Midlands establishment which catered primarily for parvenues.

Under Arnold, the fame of Rugby School had begun to spread and, with it, the fame of their football. The Rugby boys, it seems reasonable to suppose, were hoping to draw attention to themselves by developing a distinctive game. However, it would seem similarly not unlikely that, by developing a form of football which was equally distinctive but in key respects diametrically opposite to the game at Rugby, the Etonians were deliberately attempting to put the 'upstart' Rugbeians in their place and to 'see off' this challenge to Eton's status as *the* leading public school *in all respects*. As Elias (1994) showed, status competition between upper-class and rising middleclass groups has played an important part in the civilizing processes of Europe. More particularly, in 'phases of colonization' members of the latter would adopt the manners and standards of the former, leading these upper-class groups in 'phases of repulsion' to develop, as means of status demarcation and exclusion, more refined standards involving the imposition of a demand for the exercise of even greater self-control. The hands are among the most important bodily implements of humans and, by placing an absolute taboo on their use in a game, the Etonians were demanding that players should learn to exercise self-control of a very high order. In a soccer-playing society today where children learn to kick the ball and not to use their hands from a young age, this might not seem a particularly difficult demand. However, when it was first introduced, it must have been equivalent to being required to balance peas on the back of one's fork. Indeed, we hear that, when Etonians and others first tried to introduce the non-handling game to members of the working class, the latter were required to play holding a shilling and were allowed to keep it if they succeeded in not using their hands.

The emergence of soccer as a national game

Starting in the 1850s, the embryonic soccer and rugby games spread into the wider society. Two more general social developments underpinned this process: an expansion of the middle classes which occurred correlatively with continuing industrialization, urbanization, state formation and civilization; and an educational transformation usually referred to as the 'public school games cult' (Marples, 1954: 119ff.). There is no need to analyse these wider developments here. It is enough to note that the games cult helped to establish social conditions conducive to the spread of football in its embryonic modern forms, above all playing a part in transforming what were destined to become soccer and rugby into status-enhancing activities for adult 'gentlemen'.

This process of diffusion led to pressure for unified rules. For example, the formation of a 'Football Parliament' was suggested in a letter to *The Daily Telegraph* in September 1863 (Macrory, 1991: 166). Several attempts were made to form a national code but there was no basis for consensus among the participating groups. Or more precisely, there were two: support polarized around the embryo soccer and rugby models but neither camp was able to establish unequivocal dominance. Consequently, the bifurcation of soccer and rugby which appears to have been set in motion by Eton–Rugby rivalry in the 1840s was perpetuated on a national level, leading to the formation of separate ruling bodies, the Football Association (FA) in 1863 and the Rugby Football Union (RFU) in 1871. Only the formation of the FA need concern us here. Two partly autonomous developments are of relevance in this connection: the formation of the earliest independent clubs; and the growth in the importance of football as a leisure activity at Oxford and Cambridge.

The first reliable record of a football club in England comes from Sheffield, Yorkshire, where occasional matches were recorded as early as 1855 and where Sheffield FC issued a constitution and set of rules in 1857 (Young, 1968: 76–8). Another club is recorded in the Sheffield suburb of Hallam in the same year and, by 1862, there were fifteen clubs in the district. Numbers 5 and 8 of the rules formulated by the Sheffield Committee in 1857 show that Sheffield football was modelled on one or more of the embryo soccer games. These rules were:

5. Pushing with the hands is allowed but no hacking or tripping up is fair under any circumstances whatever.
8. The ball may be pushed or hit with the hand, but holding the ball except in the case of a free kick is altogether disallowed.

(Young, 1968: 77)

The extant data suggest, however, that most early clubs were founded in the south of England, particularly in and around London. For example, Forest FC, a club which played at Snaresbrook, Essex, was founded in 1859 by a group of

Old Harrovians, prominent among them C. W. and J. F. Alcock, the sons of a Sunderland Justice of the Peace who were shortly to figure prominently in the formation of the FA. Forest changed its name to Wanderers in 1864 but maintained the Harrow connection. Another club with Harrow associations was N.N. (No Names), Kilburn, but the date of its foundation remains unknown. Other clubs known to have been in existence by 1863 include Blackheath (1858), Richmond (1859) and Harlequins (1859), all three playing variants of rugby. Also founded by that time were the following embryo soccer clubs: Crystal Palace (1860), Notts County (1862) and Barnes (1862).

The significance of the Universities of Oxford and Cambridge for the development of soccer lies principally in the fact that it was at those institutions that young upper- and middle-class adult males began for the first time regularly to play the newer forms of football. These forms began to be engaged in by undergraduates in the 1840s in conjunction with the spread of the 'games cult' to the universities, a fact which is hardly surprising since the majority of students came from public schools. Sport, of course, was already established as a university leisure institution. What happened in conjunction with the games cult was that ball games, together with rowing and track and field, began to replace sports such as hunting at the top of the prestige hierarchy of university sports. It was, in other words, a largely 'civilizing' development in Elias's sense. Cricket and rowing were the first to become established but, from about 1850, devotees of football began to vie for a higher position on the ladder of university sporting prestige for their game. As it gained acceptance, men from different schools, brought up according to different football traditions, were thrown together. Since only relatively small numbers from particular schools found themselves in the same college at any time, in order to secure meaningful contests it was necessary for 'old boys' (former pupils) of different schools to play together. However, the absence of common rules meant that such matches were often full of conflict. For example, we hear that at Trinity College, Cambridge, in 1848, 'the Eton men howled at the Rugby men for handling the ball' (Dunning and Sheard 1979: 104). They evidently regarded it as 'vulgar'. This suggests – not surprisingly if the hypothesis outlined earlier has any substance – that a major axis of tension in Cambridge footballing relations at that time must have been between Old Etonian and Old Rugbeian undergraduates. It was a desire to avoid such tension that led to attempts to construct common rules.

Common rules were produced at Cambridge somewhere between 1837 and 1842, in 1846 and 1848, in about 1856, and in 1863 (Dunning and Sheard, 1979: 104). Only those of 1863 had lasting consequences. That was because, when members of the independent clubs tried in the same year to produce unified rules, they used the Cambridge rules in a way which helped to perpetuate the emergent bifurcation. The 1863 Cambridge rules were produced in October by a committee comprising undergraduates from six schools. Eton, Harrow and Rugby each had two representatives; Marlborough (a rugby-playing school), Shrewsbury and Westminster one apiece. The 6–3 majority on this committee in favour of the embryonic soccer-playing schools led, not surprisingly, to the adoption of the following rules:

13. The ball, when in play, may be stopped by any part of the body, but NOT be held or hit by the hands, arms or shoulders.
14. *All* charging is fair, but holding, pushing with the hands, tripping and shinning are forbidden.

(Dunning and Sheard, 1979: 105)

These rules would probably have remained of local significance only had it not been for a series of meetings held in London towards the end of 1863. These were the inaugural meetings of the FA and deserve detailed consideration.

On the surface, the first three meetings of the new association proceeded smoothly. Draft rules of the game were agreed and printed. However, they embodied significant elements of rugby and, had they been accepted, would have legitimized the closely related practices of 'hacking' and 'carrying' in the new game over which the nascent FA was hoping to preside. The fourth meeting was held on 24 November and the conflict inherent in the incipient bifurcation of soccer and rugby broke into the open. Until that point, it had remained dormant at least as far as officially recorded business was concerned. What happened between the third and fourth meetings was that the 1863 Cambridge rules came to the notice of supporters of the embryonic soccer game and they were impressed, especially by the rules which prohibited 'carrying' and 'hacking'. Encouraged by support from such a prestigious quarter, they attacked. Support also came from the Royal Engineers Club, Chatham, and from W. Chesterman of Sheffield FC. According to Chesterman, the FA's recently printed draft rules were 'directly opposed to football and…more suggestive of wrestling' (Green, 1953: 28). The tide was beginning to run in favour of supporters of the embryonic soccer model.

Shortly after the opening of this fourth meeting, J. F. Alcock, one of the two Old Harrovian brothers, proposed 'that the Cambridge rules appear to be the most desirable for the Association to adopt'. His motion was defeated. So was one by F. W. Campbell of Blackheath to the effect that the Cambridge rules were merely 'worthy of consideration'. Eventually, an amendment was passed stipulating that 'a committee be appointed to enter into communication with the committee of the University to endeavour to induce them to modify some of their rules'. Before the close, however, a motion was carried by a majority of one instructing the Association Committee 'to insist on hacking' in its negotiations with the University. This suggests that, at that stage, some people attending the inaugural FA meetings were still striving to negotiate a truly composite game. It also suggests that, for the moment, neither those in favour of the embryonic soccer code nor those in favour of its rugby rival enjoyed a decisive advantage.

It was thus the fourth meeting of the fledgling FA which witnessed the first open clash between the advocates of what were shortly to become, in Britain, the rival national games and eventually – along with American football which is in any case an offshoot of rugby – the principal forms of football in the world. On 1 December 1863 at the fifth meeting, this conflict was completely revealed. Discussion centred again on the contentious draft rules regarding 'carrying' and 'hacking'. The Secretary-elect, E. C. Morley, said that he did not personally object too strongly to 'hacking' but felt that to retain these rules would seriously inhibit the development of football as an adult game. The President-elect, A. Pember, supported him, referring to a 'fifteen' he had organized for a match: 'I was the only one who had not been at public school,' he said, 'and we were all dead against "hacking".' F. W. Campbell of Blackheath, the principal advocate at the meetings of the rugby code, replied that, in his opinion, 'hacking' was essential if an element of pluck was to be retained in football and threatened that, if 'carrying' and 'hacking' were excluded from the Association game, his club would withdraw. In due course, the contentious rules were struck out and, on 8 December at the sixth and final inaugural meeting, Campbell rose to say that, although his club approved of the FA and its aims, the rules adopted would 'emasculate' football. Blackheath was unwilling to be party to such a game and wished to withdraw. By this action, the Blackheath club paved the way for the final and irrevocable parting of the ways between soccer and rugby.

'Laws' 9 and 10 of the rules adopted by the newly formed FA in 1863 marked the decisive development of soccer away from the rugby practices of 'hacking' and 'carrying'. They were:

Law 9:   No player shall carry the ball.
Law 10:   Neither tripping nor hacking shall be allowed.

The civilizing intent of the drafters of these rules emerges further from Law 14 which reads:

Law 14:   No player shall be allowed to wear projecting nails, iron plates or gutta percha on the soles or heels of his boots.

Nevertheless, that the game at that stage continued to involve a handling component emerges from Law 8, the start of which reads:

Law 8:   If a player makes a fair catch, he shall be entitled to a free kick, providing he claims it by making a mark with his heel at once.

To a late twentieth-century reader, the unquestioned patriarchal assumption that soccer was exclusively a game for males stands out in this formulation. Its final development as a fully non-handling game for outfield players took place during the period 1860 to the 1880s. Crucial in this connection was the formation of the International Board in 1882. One of its first acts was to lay down the following rule:

> No player shall carry, knock-on or handle the ball under any pretence whatever except in the case of the goalkeeper who shall be allowed to use his hands in defence of the goal, either by knocking-on or throwing, but not carrying the ball.
>
> (Green, 1953: 579)

'Carrying' was defined as taking two or more steps when handling the ball. The intention of the law-makers in framing this rule was evidently to prevent even goalkeepers from playing in anything like a rugby fashion.

Since kicking and limited handling games seem to have survived perfectly well at a number of public schools, it is reasonable to suppose that this final development of soccer as a non-handling game did not come about as a result of some 'logic' implied by the rules laid down in 1863. On the contrary, it seems more likely that such a development would have been in large measure occasioned under the impetus of competitive pressure with the still developing rugby game. The rugby clubs had banded together in 1871 to form the RFU and, then as now, the proponents of soccer and rugby were involved more or less consciously in a struggle for adherents.

This competitive struggle must have been more intense in those early days when the FA and the RFU remained in their infancy and when their respective games were still developing towards their modern forms. One of the ways in which the law-makers of the FA sought in that situation to gain a competitive edge was by distinguishing their game as much as possible from rugby. It seems that one of the central stratagems through which they tried to do this was by trying to appeal to a more adult, more 'civilized' clientele. That was implied by the remarks of Secretary-elect Morley at the fifth inaugural meeting and in Chesterman of Sheffield's implication in his letter to the committee that the rugby of those days resembled wrestling. Chesterman's observation is interesting because, from early in the process of bifurcation, the development of soccer has involved not only – for all players except the goalkeeper – the imposition of an absolute taboo on the use of hands as means of propelling and eventually controlling the ball, but also an accretion of prohibitions on the use of hands and arms as means of impeding opposing players, for example by holding them, tugging their shirts, or elbowing them. The use of hands and arms, of course, is not uncontrolled in rugby but in the development of that game it has become central both to moving the ball and tackling. In this sense, soccer can be said to be representative of a higher stage in a 'civilizing process' than rugby. It is not by any means surprising in the context of a competitive and emotionally arousing game that this is the area in which the 'laws' are most frequently breached.

The accretion of taboos around the use of hands was significant for the development of soccer as the game we know today. By the end of the nineteenth century, in fact, soccer had come in all basic respects to assume its modern form. Other significant developments in the laws are listed in Table 4.2.

The spread of soccer

Even before it had achieved a fully recognizable modern form, soccer began to spread, first through the British Isles and later around the world. The introduction of the FA Cup in 1871–2 was initially decisive in this process. Since 1871 was the year in which the RFU was formed, one cannot discount the possibility that competition with rugby may have played a part in the initial introduction of what was destined to become England's most famous soccer competition. As this process of diffusion got under way, public school 'old boy' and other upper- and middle-class clubs first of all reigned supreme. However, the game proved so attractive that soccer soon started to spread rapidly, not only geographically but also downwards in the class hierarchy. As a result, the game gradually came to be more deserving of its current label as 'the people's game'.

As the spread of soccer continued, growing numbers of spectators began to

Table 4.2 Significant developments in Association football laws

Year	Development
1866	Introduction of tapes across the top of goal-posts
1873	Definition of 'offside' as follows: when a player kicks the ball, any one of the same side who, at such a moment of kicking, is nearer to the opponents' goal-line is out of play, and may not touch the ball himself, nor in any way whatever prevent any other player from doing so until the ball has been played, unless there are at least three of his opponents nearer their goal-line. (The number of opponents between the kicker and the opposing goal-line was reduced from three to two in 1925.)
1877	Cross-bars as well as tapes permitted
1880	Referee first mentioned
1891	Referee patrols the field of play. 'Umpires' become linesmen who patrol the sidelines. Introduction of penalty kick. Introduction of goal nets
1895	Replacement of tapes by cross-bar
1897	Dimensions of the field of play fixed at: length 100–130 yards; breadth 50–100 yards

Source: Green (1953)

be attracted, particularly to top-level games, and some clubs began to levy admission charges. In this way, the economic basis for the emergence of professionalism began to be laid down. Professionalism was ratified by the FA in 1885 and, in 1888, a 'Football League' of twelve clubs was formed. They played each other on a home and away basis and competed for the title of 'Champions'. The Second Division was added in 1892, the Third Division (South) in 1920, and the Third Division (North) in 1921. In 1958, the regionalized Third Divisions gave way to national Third and Fourth Divisions, thus ushering in a system which remained basically intact until 1992 when a Premier Division, nominally under the control of the FA, was formed out of the existing First Division clubs, and the Football League was reduced to a lower-status competition of three divisions. As I shall elaborate in Chapter 5, there are reasons to believe that Football League Divisions 2 and 3 are unlikely to survive long into the twenty-first century as national competitions in which full-time professionals are employed.

Simultaneously with these developments soccer began to spread around the world. This, too, was a process which occurred rapidly, indicating that the game met social and psychological needs other than in the country where it was founded. The first German football club was founded in Hannover in 1878. In The Netherlands, the first club was founded in 1879–80, in Italy in about 1890 and in France in 1892 (Elias, 1986b: 128). FAs had been formed in Scotland in 1873, Wales in 1876, and Ireland in 1880 (Green, 1953: 48). The first FAs outside the UK were formed in Denmark and The Netherlands in 1889. Belgium and Switzerland followed in 1895 (Arlott, 1977: 302), Germany in 1900, and Portugal in 1906 (Elias, 1986b: 28). La Fédération Internationale de Football Associations (FIFA) was formed in Paris in 1904 by delegates from Belgium, Denmark, France, The Netherlands, Spain, Sweden and Switzerland, representatives from Britain being noticeable by their absence. Presumably their reasons for remaining aloof were compounded by a mixture of feelings of superiority over having 'invented' the game and fear regarding diminishing control over a 'ludic product' which they regarded as peculiarly their own. (Interestingly, the theme song of 'Euro 96', the European Football Championships which were staged in England in 1996, had as its first line 'Football's Coming Home' thus indicating the persistence of this complex of superiority and inferiority feelings.) The English FA did affiliate with FIFA in 1906. However, it withdrew in 1914, rejoined in 1924, withdrew again in 1928, only permanently joining in 1945 (Green, 1953: 198ff.; Young, 1968: 167).

A good idea of the speed with which the international expansion of soccer took place is provided by Table 4.3. Table 4.4 provides data on participants in and attendances at World Cup Finals and sheds further light on soccer's global spread.

During the twentieth century, soccer emerged as the world's most popular team sport. The reasons for its comparative success are not difficult to find. It does not require much equipment and is comparatively cheap to play. Its

Table 4.3 The growth of FIFA (1904–94)

Year	Number of Associations	Year	Number of Associations
1904	7	1950	73
1914	24	1954	85
1920	20	1959	95
1923	31	1984	150
1930	41	1991	165
1938	51	1994	190★

Source: Adapted from Tomlinson and Whannel (1986: 889)

Note:
★ Added by present author

Table 4.4 World Cup Finals: venues, participants and attendances (1930–90)

Date	Venue	Winner	Attendances	No. of matches
1930	Uruguay	Uruguay	434,500	18
1934	Italy	Italy	395,000	17
1938	France	Italy	483,000	18
1950	Brazil	Uruguay	1,337,000	22
1954	Switzerland	West Germany	943,000	26
1958	Sweden	Brazil	86,000	35
1962	Chile	Brazil	776,000	32
1966	England	England	1,614,677	32
1970	Mexico	Brazil	1,673,975	32
1974	West Germany	West Germany	1,774,022	38
1978	Argentina	Argentina	1,610,215	38
1982	Spain	Italy	1,766,277	52
1986	Mexico	Argentina	2,199,941	52
1990	Italy	West Germany	2,510,686	52

Source: Adapted from Tomlinson and Whannel (1986: 90–1)

rules – apart perhaps from the offside law – are relatively easy to understand. Above all, these rules regularly make for fast, open and fluid play, and for a game which is finely balanced among a number of interdependent polarities such as force and skill, individual and team play, attack and defence (Elias and Dunning, 1986: 191–204). As such, its structure permits the recurrent genera- tion of levels of excitement which are satisfying for players and spectators alike. At the heart of this lies the fact that matches are physical struggles between two groups governed by rules which allow the passions to rise yet keep them – most of the time – in check. To the extent that they are enforced and/or voluntarily obeyed, the rules of soccer also limit the risk of serious injury to players. That is another respect in which it can be said to be a relatively 'civilized' game. Soccer played at top level also has a 'ballet-like' quality and that, together with the colours of the players' clothing, helps further to explain its spectacular appeal.

Of course, other sports possess some of the characteristics listed here but arguably only soccer has them all. That, it is reasonable to believe, is why it has become the world's most popular team sport. In turn, its world-wide popularity and the degree to which fans identify with their teams help to explain why it is the sport most frequently associated with spectator disorder (Dunning *et al.*, 1988; Williams *et al.*, 1989; Murphy *et al.*, 1990). I shall concern myself with this issue – the emergence of soccer hooliganism as a world problem – in Chapter 6. In Chapter 5, I shall examine some of the 'economic aspects' involved in the development of modern sport, again using soccer as a principal example.

5

THE DYNAMICS OF SPORTS CONSUMPTION

Introduction

To speak of the 'consumption' as opposed to the 'playing' and 'watching' of sport involves a recognition of the relationships between sport and 'the economy'.[1] To use such 'economic' language also presupposes that sport is currently undergoing a process of commodification and coming to be more entangled in the contradictions, pressures, opportunities and balances between conflict and consensus characteristic of what it is fashionable to call 'consumer' or 'post-modern' societies.[2]

In this chapter, I shall undertake an exploration of aspects of the commodification of sports from a figurational standpoint in an attempt to see whether, in this manner, new insights can be arrived at. However, because Marxists of various persuasions have so far made the most important contributions to the understanding of this process, I shall begin with a critical appraisal of some Marxist writings. I shall then set forth what I take to be some of the principal similarities and differences between the Marxist and figurational approaches. Finally, I shall sketch out a figurational diagnosis of some key aspects of the development of sport in Britain, paying special attention to what are conventionally called its 'economic' aspects.

Marxist approaches

Probably the first scholar to develop a consistently Marxist approach to sport was Bero Rigauer whose *Sport and Work* was published in German in 1969. In what has justifiably come to be regarded as a classic, Rigauer suggested that modern sports 'are no autonomous system of behaviour; they appear along with numerous other social developments whose origins lie in early-capitalist bourgeois society' (Rigauer, 1981: 1). Sports, Rigauer argued, were initially a type of recreation pursued by elites for their own enjoyment. For the members of these elites, they functioned as a counter to the strains of work but, with the increasing development of industrial capitalism and the correlative spread of sports down the social hierarchy, they have come to take on characteristics which resemble those of work. To the extent that such a process has occurred, it follows, according to Rigauer, that sports must be unable to function as a counter to work.

Particularly germane for present purposes is Rigauer's analysis of the commodification of sports. 'The question is', he asks, 'can top-level sports bring forth values that we can usefully define as commodity-like? Do top-level sports follow the principles of an exchange society?' Rigauer answers in the affirmative. The athletes, he says, are producers, the spectators consumers. The performance of the former has become a commodity which is exchanged in the market for money. That is so whether the producer–athlete is an amateur who nominally only receives expenses or a professional who is paid a salary, because 'the ideal of the pure amateur in top-level sports' became a myth long before the distinction was abolished (Rigauer, 1981: 67–8). This argument is perceptive. According to Rigauer, top-level sport has been commodified and emerged correlatively as a demanding and achievement-orientated area of social life. The belief that it functions as a counter to work remains widespread but this belief, Rigauer suggests, is an ideology which hides from the participants the 'real' function of sport: that of reinforcing in the leisure sphere an ethic of hard work, achievement and group loyalty which is necessary for the reproduction of a capitalist–industrial society. It helps, according to Rigauer, to maintain the status quo and bolsters the dominance of the ruling class.

Rigauer's thesis was developed from the standpoint of 'critical theory', the genre of Marxist sociology initiated by Adorno and Horkheimer at the University of Frankfurt's Institut für Sozialforschung in the 1920s, what became known as 'the Frankfurt School'.[3] Similar conclusions about the structure and functions of modern sport were reached by French scholar Jean-Marie Brohm, writing from an 'Althusserian' standpoint in the 1970s (Brohm, 1978: 175). Sport, Brohm argued, is not 'a transcendent entity, over and above historical periods and modes of production' but, on the contrary, 'the product of a[n] historical turning point'. More specifically, it first appeared in England, 'the birthplace of the capitalist mode of production, at the beginning of the modern industrial epoch'. Brohm's argument is complex but one of his central theses is that sport is an 'ideological state apparatus' as opposed to a 'repressive' one. That is, it functions through persuasion rather than force by instilling in people an illusion of freedom and the belief they can exercise choice. In fact, sport performs a triple function according to Brohm. More particularly, it

> reproduces bourgeois social relations such as selection and hierarchy, subservience, obedience etc;…spreads an organisational ideology… involving competition, records and output; and…transmits on a huge scale the general themes of ruling bourgeois ideology like the myth of the superman, individualism, social advancement, success, efficiency etc.
>
> (Brohm, 1978: 77)

Brohm also put forward 'twenty theses on sport' in which he advanced propositions such as: 'the capitalists of sport appropriate players and athletes who thus become their wage labourers'; there is a class struggle in sport 'between the suppliers of capital and the suppliers of performances'; top-level sportspersons are 'professional performers in the muscle show' and also very often advertising 'sandwich-board men'; mass spectator sport is a highly commercialized enterprise spurred on by competition and the drive for profit; the commercialization of sport operates on four principal levels: (1) the establishment of a sports products, goods and services industry; (2) the development of spectator sport as a base for advertising; (3) the tapping of citizens', especially workers', resources to swell profits; and (4) the sports betting industry, that is racing and the pools.

Other aspects of Brohm's 'twenty theses' hold that: mass spectator sport 'operates as a sort of catharsis machine, an apparatus for transforming aggressive drives' with the consequence that, 'instead of expressing themselves in the class struggle, these drives are absorbed, diverted and neutralized in the sporting spectacle'. In this way, 'sport channels the energies of the masses in the direction of the established order'; that mass spectator sport 'treats the masses as morons', especially via the publication in the mass media of trivial stories; and that, through its rituals, ceremonies, anthems and flag-waving, sport 'contributes to a process of emotional fascistification' (Brohm, 1978: 178–81).

An interesting critique of work such as that by Rigauer and Brohm has been mounted from within the Marxist tradition by John Hargreaves (1986), an adherent to the 'hegemony theory' of Antonio Gramsci. If sport resembles work in its propensity to alienate people, Hargreaves asks,

> why does it, in marked contrast to work, continue to be so popular? If people are so stupefied as to be completely unconscious of their alienation…would compensatory mechanisms like sports spectacles be necessary at all, and would it not be more likely that whatever was imposed on people from above would be accepted without demur anyway?
>
> (Hargreaves, 1986: 42)

Besides hegemony theory, there are according to Hargreaves two types of Marxist approach to sport and related problems: what he calls 'correspondence theory' and 'reproduction theory'. Although it would be wrong to think in terms of totally distinct 'pure types', if I have followed Hargreaves' reasoning, the early work of Rigauer can be said to be an example of the former type, that of Brohm, to contain elements of the latter. Hargreaves describes 'correspondence theory' and 'reproduction theory' thus:

Correspondence theory characterizes sport as a simple reflection of capitalism: its structure and its cultural ethos are completely determined and dominated by capitalist forces and the interests of the ruling class, so that it is a totally alienating activity. Reproduction theory, on the other hand, claims that culture and sport are related to the capitalist mode of production and the dominant social relations in terms of their specificity, that is, their differences and their autonomy; and that it is precisely because of their autonomy that they are enabled to function to reproduce the dominant social relations.

(Hargreaves, 1982: 104–5)

According to Hargreaves, the fundamental weakness of correspondence theory and reproduction theory is that both share 'a one-sided, deterministic and static model of capitalist society'. 'Hegemony theory', by contrast, deals 'with processes, that is, with forms of social life which are historical, and...tightly interwoven' (Hargreaves, 1982: 49). It also conceptualizes sport 'as an object of struggle, control and resistance, that is an arena for the play of power relations' (Hargreaves, 1982: 14). Furthermore, sport is part of 'culture', and 'cultural processes are no less material or real, i.e. no less important a feature of social life than economic and political processes'. There are, Hargreaves suggests, two 'internally linked dimensions' of processes of cultural formation. More specifically, 'culture is both constituted by people consciously making choices' and, because it is inherited as traditions formed through the choices made by people in the past, 'constitutive of choice and action'. Culture thus acts as a powerful but not totally determining constraint (Hargreaves, 1982: 47).

This is reminiscent of Marx's famous statement that people 'make their own history, but they do not make it just as they please; they do not make it under circumstances chosen by themselves, but under circumstances directly found, given and transmitted from the past' (Marx and Engels, 1942: 315). For Hargreaves, it is precisely this balance between freedom and constraint which provides sport as a cultural form with a degree of autonomy. However, in contrast to the position adopted by 'reproduction theorists', Hargreaves suggests that the autonomy of sport does not lead it in a mechanical sense to contribute to the reproduction of 'dominant social relations'. On the contrary, such autonomy is a precondition both for the development of sport's own internal crises and contradictions, and for the 'emancipatory potentialities' which, according to Hargreaves, it enjoys. In saying this, he does not seek to deny that sport can and in some respects does play a part in reproducing the status quo. For example, the progressive incorporation of sport into 'consumer culture' constitutes, for Hargreaves, one of the most important determinants of the relationship between sport and national identity (Hargreaves, 1986: 220). Furthermore, notes Hargreaves, in the present age sport is 'the means of body expression *par excellence*'. As such, it is crucial to the capacity of 'consumer culture' to 'harness and channel bodily needs and desires' (Hargreaves, 1986: 217). At the same time, however, according to Hargreaves, the existence of sport 'as an autonomous means of expression' produces effects which serve to undermine rather than bolster the status quo. He writes:

> The autonomy of sport places limits on its use value, beyond which any legitimizing, accommodating function it may possess tends to be jeopardized and conflict generated instead. The tendency inherent in the commercialisation of sport, to transform it into an entertaining spectacle, runs the continual risk of raising the followers' expectations of excitement etc faster than sport organised along such lines can satisfy them, and therefore of ultimately alienating the audience. Secondly, ruthless sporting competition, whether commercially or politically structured...can have unforeseen, counter-productive effects. The pursuit of success at all costs against the opponent does not necessarily produce the most exciting spectacle, especially when the strategy adopted is the negative one of avoiding defeat. It may also result in systematic rule-breaking on the part of contestants and the organizations behind them which damages participants and alienates supporters. Such consequences make the task of selling sport as an uplifting form of family entertainment and as an exemplification of the national virtues, difficult to sustain. In particular, the ludic element is inherently irreducible to programming for profit and control: the more the desire to play is frustrated and reduced, the less it works as entertainment, and the less efficacious sport is for control purposes....The ritualistic and dramatic character of sport is delicately constructed and does not automatically reproduce social relations. In certain circumstances the sporting occasion that normally solemnizes and celebrates the social order can be transformed, so that the signs are reversed to signal irreverence and disorder. The contest element always makes, not only the outcome of the sporting event itself unpredictable, but also the efficacy of the whole occasion as political ritual unpredictable as well.
>
> (Hargreaves, 1986: 22)

So, according to Hargreaves, it is not enough to characterize 'people's involvement in sporting activity, simply in terms of commodity consumption'. In their sports, they draw on stocks of knowledge which mark out participation as quite different 'from the act of shopping in the local high street'. Going to watch a sport is more comparable with attending the theatre or a festival. The selling of sport as 'exciting entertainment', however, contributes to rising expectations and 'creates tensions between producer and audience, which may at times erupt into violent confrontation'. Indeed, continues Hargreaves, interestingly reversing the standard official line, the attempt to bourgeoisify football is salutary: the more up-market it has moved and the more it has been packaged as 'family entertainment', the greater the propensity for unruly crowd behaviour.

(Hargreaves, 1986: 136)

I have two objections to Hargreaves' arguments here, the first more conceptual, the second more empirical. In the first of these passages, his language could be taken to imply that he conceives of sport as possessing some kind of eternal and unchanging 'essence'.[4] He has a parallel tendency to employ concepts such as 'consumer culture' in a reifying way as well; that is, to use such abstract terms as if they referred to actors who do things. In the second passage, Hargreaves seems erroneously to believe that crowd violence at football is a relatively recent consequence of an attempt to 'bourgeoisify' the game and sell it as 'family entertainment'. This is an issue which I shall deal with in Chapter 6. In the present context, the main point I want to make is that there is much in Hargreaves' overall arguments to commend them from a figurational standpoint. However, there is much to be critical of as well. This is an appropriate point at which to draw up a balance sheet regarding these Marxist contributions and to spell out why figurational sociologists take issue with some of what they say.

A figurational critique

Although they do not constitute a totally united group, no figurational sociologist would seriously disagree with Brohm's critique of the media's trivialization of sport. They might, though, want to take account of the part played in this process by sportspersons themselves and would also perhaps attribute the contribution of sportspersons to the mass media trivialization of sport to the vulnerability which stems from the upward social mobility of most of them and the fact that the shortness of their active careers leads to pressure to 'make hay while the sun shines'. Although they would probably think that more detailed empirical research is necessary in this connection, most figurational sociologists would also accept much of what Brohm and Rigauer have to say about the penetration of sport by capital, the concomitant processes of commodification and the permeation of sport by work-like structures. These processes and, as one of their aspects, the virtual disappearance of amateurism at the highest levels, are widely accepted as matters of empirical fact, so much so, indeed, that it could be argued that there are elements of tautology in the accounts of Rigauer and Brohm. That is, top-level, professional sports are not *like* work: for the performers, they *are* work, however much more extrinsically rewarding and intrinsically enjoyable they may be than many other occupational forms. The point is to explain *how* and *why* processes of professionalization and commodification have taken place in sport, and that Rigauer, Brohm and the other representatives of 'correspondence theory' and 'reproduction theory' have so far failed in any meaningful sense to do. They point usefully to what are widely regarded as some of the failings and problematic features of modern sport but their analyses lack explanatory content and do little more than document descriptively the capitalistic organization, ethos and momentum of many modern sports. Although not itself unproblematic from a figurational standpoint, the work of 'hegemony theorists' such as Hargreaves is more satisfactory in these regards.

Hargreaves hit the nail on the head when he suggested that correspondence theory and reproduction theory involve a 'one-sided, deterministic and static model of capitalist society'. Figurational sociologists share with hegemony theorists a concern with processes, with the structuring of social relationships in space and time. Although they conceptualize such problems differently, they also share the hegemony theorists' concern with the centrality of power, contestation and resistance in social life, and with the fluctuating balance between these polarities and those of co-operation and consensus. Where they begin seriously to depart from scholars like Hargreaves is over questions such as what constitutes a sociological explanation. More particularly, although Hargreaves is rightly critical of the correspondence and reproduction theorists for their 'one-sided, deterministic and static' models, his own approach, while not 'static', cannot entirely escape the charge that it, too, is 'one-sided' and 'deterministic'.

'[R]ecognizing the centrality of culture,' Hargreaves writes, 'does not necessarily deny the effectivity of the mode of production, which can and must be granted the status of exerting crucial pressures and limitations on people's way of life.' Later he continues:

> once economic constraints, i.e. the class power…based on ownership and control of the means of production, is given its due weight, there remains a lot to be explained, and talk about economic determination often turns out to be trivially true with respect to the solution of specific problems.
>
> (Hargreaves, 1986: 48)

A figurational sociologist might want to use different language. He/she would not see economic constraints as reducible solely to class power or class power as reducible solely to ownership and control of the means of production. That said, there is little in these two sentences with which a figurational sociologist would disagree. That is not the case, however, when Hargreaves describes hegemony theory as 'an attempt to give a sense of the primacy of economic relations in social being without reducing the latter to the former' (Hargreaves, 1986: 104–5). Such a formulation may reflect a desire to avoid reductionism but, particularly since Hargreaves fails to tell us what he understands the difference between 'primacy' and 'centrality' to be, it sits uneasily with his reference to the 'centrality of culture'. It is a formulation, too, which arguably involves a form of 'economic determinism'. It does so in the sense of implying a law-like, historically transcendent statement to the effect that economic relations are not just important in social life – a statement with which no sane person could seriously disagree – but that they are always and everywhere more important than anything else.

The objections of figurational sociologists to 'economic determinism' are manifold and complex (Dunning, 1992). Despite the attempts of scholars like Hargreaves to avoid the economic determinism which they see as inherent in other forms of Marxism, these objections apply just as much to hegemony theory as they do to other Marxist positions. In order to illustrate the idea that there are processes which cannot be adequately explained in solely economic terms, it must be enough to point to the emergence of state monopolies of force and processes of pacification under state control. While they obviously have economic aspects such as the establishment of state monopolies on taxation and while they obviously could not occur independently of economic preconditions of various kinds, such processes arguably have their own relatively autonomous dynamics which involve elements other than the economic. They also have ramifications on the economy which are not taken account of adequately in Marxist analyses which reduce everything to the mode of production or which, though seeking in the manner of Hargreaves to avoid reductionism, nevertheless still stress what he calls 'the primacy of economic relations'. Thus, Elias identified what he termed a 'monopoly mechanism' in the social development of West European states, a trend towards the build-up of state monopolies of force and taxation which was, he suggested, involved reciprocally with economic processes in the development of modern capitalism. Centrally at work in this connection, Elias argued, were hegemonial struggles among rival contenders for the 'royal position' which cannot be adequately explained by reference to economic processes alone (Elias, 1994). As I hope to show, such arguments have implications for explaining the development of modern sport which are critical of the sorts of explanations proposed by scholars like Hargreaves, Rigauer and Brohm.

One further aspect of the analysis offered by Hargreaves deserves comment. It is his idea of 'the nature of sport as an autonomous means of expression', of the existence of a 'ludic element' which, as Hargreaves puts it, 'is inherently irreducible to programming for profit and control'. This idea seems to have essentialist undertones, to imply that, in Hargreaves' view, there is a 'play element' inherent in sport, a kind of 'essence' which universally imparts to sport a degree of protective autonomy independently of its social locations, social organization and the patterns of socialization, values, 'habituses' and power ratios of the people involved. Figurational sociologists have a concept of the autonomy of sport as well. However, it is non-essentialist and stresses relative autonomy, not, as could be taken to be implicit in Hargreaves' formulation, autonomy of an absolute kind. Above all, figurational sociologists do not seek to deny that sport – or for that matter anything else – can be programmed for purposes of profit and control. On the contrary, they seek to explain what actually happens in such regards principally by reference to the changing power balances among the groups involved, the location and manner of integration of the sports concerned in the wider developing social framework, and the character and structure, above all the stage of development, of this wider social totality.[5] A figurational analysis of some key aspects of the development of modern sport will illustrate how such an analysis differs from those of Marxists in crucial respects. This analysis will focus on the 'economic' aspects of this process and should be seen as supplementary to the analyses offered in Chapters 2 and 3.

A typology of professional sports

Despite the differences between them, Rigauer, Brohm and Hargreaves share the fact that they trace the origins of modern sport solely to its capitalist roots. From a figurational standpoint, this is not so much a wrong as an over-simplification. It leads these scholars to ignore or underplay the sorts of processes which I discussed in Chapters 2 and 3, for example the relatively independent part played in this process by aristocratic and gentry groups. In this chapter, however, I shall follow a different tack. I suggested earlier that Hargreaves was rightly critical of the 'reproduction theorists' in arguing that the autonomy of sport means that it does not contribute mechanistically to the reproduction of 'dominant social relations'. I also suggested that Hargreaves' own conceptualization is one which arguably has essentialist undertones. Indeed, it is possible to go further and suggest that, by talking about the autonomy of a reified conceptual abstraction, 'sport', rather than about the variable relative autonomy or variable relative power of specific human groups, Hargreaves falls foul of what philosophically orientated sociologists such as Giddens (1984) call the 'agency–structure dilemma'. A concept focused on human beings and their interdependencies lies at the heart of the figurational approach. Not only does it arguably avoid the 'agency–structure' trap (Dunning, 1992), it also implies that autonomy, being a function of relationships, is always relative and never absolute. A brief analysis of some aspects of the history of professional sport in Britain will provide a means of illustrating this approach.

Broadly speaking, the term 'professional sport' can be said to refer to any kind of ludic activity from which people obtain financial gain. Seen in these terms, the following nine types of sports professionalism can be distinguished. They are 'pure', analytically separable types in the sense that many sports at particular stages in their development reveal a mixture of two or more types. The types are distinguishable primarily in terms of two interlocking dimensions: first, the degrees of openness or legitimacy of the professionalism involved; and second, the relationships in them between the producers of the sports performance and the consumers and others who provide the financial support which enables the producers to gain financially from their performances. The first four types involve professionalism of a covert, non-legitimate type. The terms 'shamateurism' or 'sham amateurism' are appropriate for describing these types. The remaining five types involve forms of sports professionalism which are overt and legitimate. The nine types are as follows:

Covert, non-legitimate types of sports professionalism ('shamateurism')

1   A type of sports professionalism in which nominally amateur sports-persons are supported by the state via sinecures in the military, police or civil service. Examples: the former Soviet Union and Eastern Europe before the break-up of the Soviet 'empire'.

2   A type where financial support for sportspersons is provided through jobs, often sinecures, in private commercial and industrial firms or through an administrative/organizational job in the sport *per se*. Examples: Rugby Union until 1995 and English county cricket until the 1960s.

3   A type in which sportspersons are subsidized by means of university scholarships. Example: college football and other sports in the USA. In some ways, the former (?) practice in Oxford and Cambridge colleges of recruiting students more for their sporting prowess than their intellectual abilities approximated closely to the parameters of this type.

4   A type in which nominally amateur sportspersons gain financially by being given 'boot money'; that is, are clandestinely paid from money taken at the gate or from funds provided by rich patrons, the mass media, commercial sponsors or from advertising revenues. Example: Rugby Union in Britain prior to its becoming openly professional in 1995.

Overt, legitimate types of sports professionalism

5   A type of sports professionalism in which financial support is provided by wealthy individual patrons. Example: cricket in eighteenth-century England.

6   A type where financial support is provided from money taken at the gate. Examples: touring/peripatetic sports teams such as William Clarke's 'All England (cricket) XI' in the 1850s; professional soccer in Britain up to the 1960s.

7   A type where financial support is provided by the fund-raising activities of supporters/members. Examples: soccer, Rugby Union and Rugby League in Britain today.

8   A type where financial support is provided by commercial and industrial advertisers and sponsors. Example: soccer in Britain today.

9   A type where financial support is provided by the media in payment for the broadcasting/telecasting of matches and events. Examples: the

contemporary Olympic Games, the soccer World Cup and most top-level sports in the majority of Western countries.

Lack of space precludes anything other than a limited discussion of these types. I shall restrict myself to consideration of three of the overt/legitimate types: eighteenth-century cricket as an example of type 5; soccer and cricket in the late nineteenth/early twentieth centuries as examples of type 6; and present-day soccer as an example involving a changing admixture of all five overt/legitimate types, together with the payment of 'bungs', that is illegitimate payments to managers, players and their agents when the transfer of a player is taking place. My discussion will focus centrally on the changing relative autonomy of the direct sports producers, the patterns of sports consumption involved in the different types, and the changing relative autonomy of the consumers.

Professional cricket in eighteenth-century England was dependent for its structure and ethos largely on the wealth and undisputed social dominance of the aristocracy and gentry. Its emergence was a relatively conflict-free social process. That was the case mainly because of the existence in English society at that stage of a class structure based on the secure dominance of a leisured, landed elite, in which the balance of power between classes involved gross inequalities and in which no effective challenge was possible to the position of the dominant class.

The effectively undisputed power of the aristocracy and gentry in eighteenth-century England gave to members of the landed classes a measure of autonomy sufficient to enable them to structure cricket virtually in their own interests. The type of professionalism which emerged was based on clear subordination of the professional to his patron and almost complete dependency as far as life chances were concerned of the former upon the latter. Members of the aristocracy and gentry hired top-level players, nominally as household servants, as coachmen or to work on their estates, but in reality mainly on account of their cricketing prowess (Brookes, 1978: 60ff.). There were also at that stage small numbers of what Brookes calls 'independent players' who hired out their services on a match-by-match basis (Brookes, 1978: 63). And there were opportunities for entrepreneurs like George Smith, Thomas Lord and James Dark to make money from the ownership and management of grounds (Brookes, 1978: 73). Crowds in excess of 20,000 are estimated as having sometimes attended matches and spectators were charged an entrance fee – twopence – for admittance to London's Artillery Ground in the 1740s (Brookes, 1978: 50)

There were thus some capitalist elements within the overall structure of cricket at that stage but they cannot be said to have determined either that structure or the ethos of the game. Both were fundamentally dependent on the secure power and great wealth of the aristocracy and gentry. That a few lower-class individuals could earn or enhance their livings from their sporting prowess, or by exploiting such commercial opportunities as were beginning to become available in sport, seemed to members of the aristocracy and gentry the simple extension of a 'natural order' in which fate had decreed that they themselves should inherit power, wealth and status. Cricketing aristocrats and gentlemen at that stage were producers and consumers of sports performances, players and organizers as well as watchers. As players, they were involved largely for themselves, reinforcing the pleasure they derived by gambling on the results of matches (Brookes, 1978: 41–4). Their behaviour was orientated not so much towards pecuniary gain as towards the intensification of excitement and augmentation of the prestige gains that could be obtained by demonstrating to their peers that they were above mere questions of financial gain and loss. Although they were not a fully fledged court aristocracy, they were engaging in variants of the prestige-orientated rationality which, Elias suggested, contrasts with the finance-orientated rationality of bourgeois groups (Elias, 1983: 92).

Cricketing aristocrats and gentlemen in eighteenth-century England led their teams onto the field under their own colours. In some ways, they were like feudal warlords leading armies into battle. They were enabled in this manner to act out prestige rivalries with other members of their class that were both specific to cricket and more general. One of the most striking things about this pattern of professional sport, however, is the fact that these aristocrats and gentlemen could play alongside their socially inferior professional employees, change in the same dressing rooms, eat and drink with them during the convivial evenings which followed matches and, even in the presence of large crowds, contemplate with relative equanimity the humiliation of defeat at the hands of social inferiors. Little threat was posed in these regards to their self-image and social status. Nor were they dependent financially or, at least not substantially, for ego enhancement on the crowds who came to watch. For their part, the spectators, the vicarious consumers of cricket at that stage, must have enjoyed watching their social superiors at play, perhaps especially when the latter suffered reverses at the hands of socially inferior professionals. Consumers of cricket must also have derived pleasure from watching exciting matches and from the opportunities for sociability and gambling provided. The level of excitement involved has, of course, to be judged against the relative paucity of organized entertainment available for the lower classes at that time. Indeed, in some ways, watching 'gentlemen' risk humiliation on the cricket field may have had something in common with another popular entertainment at that time: going to watch public hangings.

The professionalization of soccer and rugby contrasted markedly with this pattern. It began in the late nineteenth century at a stage in the development of British society when state formation and industrialization were considerably more advanced and when, in conjunction with these processes, the balance of power between classes had begun to shift. Most obviously of all, a more effective bourgeois challenge to the hegemony of the landed classes had been mounted and there were signs of a proletarian challenge to the increasing dominance of the bourgeoisie. Under the increasingly fluid social conditions that were coming to prevail, class tensions ran higher than had previously been the case and patterns of status-exclusiveness began to replace the comparatively free and easy mixing of social classes on the sports field that had been characteristic of the eighteenth and early nineteenth centuries. The development of professional soccer and rugby reflected this pattern of class tensions and status-exclusiveness. As a consequence, this development was a process accompanied by conflicts of a disruptive character and sometimes resulted in severe dislocations. For example, in 1895 rugby split along class and regional lines into amateur and professional segments. Ten years before, a similar schism had threatened to occur in soccer, and even cricket was subject to severe tensions as forms of organization and career pattern which fitted in with the newly emerging social conditions began to be worked out (Dunning and Sheard, 1979: esp. Chapters 7, 8 and 9).

It was in this period that the amateur–professional dichotomy reached the peak of its development both in relational and value terms. For a while, amateurs and professionals continued to play together but, in the social situation that was coming to prevail, defeat on the sports field at the hands of socially inferior groups became harder for members of the higher classes to tolerate. It came to symbolize for more of them what they feared most in society at large: political and economic defeat at the hands of the working class. There developed, correspondingly, a pattern of segregated sports participation in which amateurs and professionals were, for the most part, kept apart. Where they did continue to play together, it was in a context of ritual and etiquette designed to emphasize the professionals' social inferiority. At the same time, an amateur ethos stressing sport as an 'end in itself' and emphasizing such 'gentlemanly virtues' as 'fair play', 'character-building' and being self-controlled and generous in victory and defeat received its highest development. One of the corollaries of this ethos was the idea that professionalism is the antithesis of 'true sport', that it is, by its nature, destructive of the character of sport as 'play'. In its most extreme form, stress was laid on the idea that direct participation is the only valuable form of sports consumption. Correlatively, spectatorship was puritanically derided as 'idle' and 'morally damaging', and discouraged on that account.

Such a pattern, above all the existence of values according to which professionalism and spectatorship are antitheses of sport, helps in part to explain the notoriously poor facilities provided for spectators at many British sports grounds until the 1990s. It also helps to explain the fact that the legislators of sports such as soccer have traditionally been loath to take the interests and wishes of spectators into account. In part, however, this pattern has had the opposite effect as well, indirectly forcing a limited form of accommodation to spectator interests. More particularly, such a pattern meant that, until recently, professional sports in Britain have been less exposed to commercial, profit-orientated pressures than their counterparts in North America. There, professional sports clubs are usually owned by a corporation or wealthy individual and run as commercial concerns (Gardner, 1974). If gates and profits fall, the club is often moved to another town which, it is believed, will offer a more fruitful market. Such a situation has been inconceivable in Britain up to now. It is reasonable to hypothesize that one of the reasons why has been the persistence of amateur values, albeit in slowly changing and generally speaking weakening forms. For example, when in the late nineteenth century the majority of Football League clubs registered as limited liability companies, the FA was able to prevent them paying their shareholders dividends exceeding 7.5 per cent of profits. A consequence was that local identifications and an interest in the game *per se* tended to outweigh the desire for personal profit in the motives of directors. It also meant that relatively strong and enduring traditions of local support for clubs could be built up. These traditions help to explain why, when profit-orientated tycoons such as Robert Maxwell and David Evans tried in the 1980s to merge and shift the locations of the Reading, Oxford United and Luton Town clubs, not only were such moves widely seen as inconsistent with fundamental English values, but relatively effective protest movements were set in motion.

The motivations for attending soccer matches as spectators rather than players have tended to comprise a mixture of a desire to experience pleasurable, de-routinizing excitement (Elias and Dunning, 1986; see also Chapter 1) and the expression of a degree of identification with the local team and whatever social unit it represents. Unlike the shareholders and directors of clubs who derive their power in the sport from the fact of ownership, however, and unlike professional players who derive a measure of power from their union membership and, more ephemerally, from their skill and hence their 'market value', spectators/fans enjoy relatively little power in a football context other than the ability to 'vote with their feet', to write critical articles and books, to organize local and/or national campaigns, or to behave violently and disruptively at matches. In British soccer, organized supporters clubs began to be formed in the late nineteenth century and a National Federation of Supporters' Clubs was founded in 1926. However, these organizations have remained relatively weak and easy for the authorities and major club shareholders to incorporate and tame. The reasons why are not difficult to find. They include the fact that support for a football club is a leisure commitment, not an occupational one. Unlike the directors with their financial involvement and the players with their career involvement, the majority of fans commit only comparatively small amounts of time and money to their support. These amounts, although they may be large relative to the incomes of the fans, are dwarfed by the thousands and millions invested by directors. Consequently, however strong the emotional bonds of supporters with their clubs, their football involvement is not connected with the production of their basic life chances and this affects the pattern and degree of their involvement. Furthermore, although they regularly talk about the game at work or in the pub, the supporters of a football club only assemble *en masse* for something like two hours a fortnight for eight months a year. That is, whilst this is less true of those who regularly travel to watch their team away, they do not experience the sorts of continuous exposure to common conditions found in many work situations, conditions conducive to the kinds of effective and co-ordinated collective action which Weber described as 'rational', 'societal' action as opposed to what he called 'mass action' of an 'amorphous' type (Weber, 1946: 180–95). Nor do the majority of supporters typically think much beyond the achievement of playing success for their clubs. Finally, while they may be united through their support for football, they are divided by their support for clubs which are rivals in the competition for scarce soccer resources and success. They also often have strong traditions of hatred for particular clubs and their fans. Examples are the mutual hatreds of the fans of Arsenal and Tottenham, Leeds and Manchester United, Leicester City and Nottingham Forest. All this militates against the formation of effective national organizations.

Starting in the 1950s, as wages and leisure opportunities in Britain began to increase in conjunction with the gradual emergence of an economy dependent on and capable of supporting an 'affluent' or 'consumer society', a process the beginnings of which can be traced to the 1930s (Dunning *et al.*, 1988), football spectators began increasingly to vote with their feet, choosing either to watch the game on TV in the comfort of their homes or to avail themselves of various among the other leisure options which were coming to be offered. The consequent decline of revenues from the gate, coupled with the increased outlay on players' wages following the abolition of the maximum wage in 1961, largely as a result of a successful action by the Professional Footballers Association (PFA), meant that clubs were forced to look increasingly for revenue to more affluent groups than had tended to support soccer in the recent past and to sources such as advertising, commercial sponsorship, TV and the fund-raising activities of supporters. In short, soccer in that context began to embrace elements of the fifth, sixth, seventh, eighth and ninth types of sports professionalism distinguished in the typology outlined earlier. As King (1995: 88) has shown, this situation favoured the bigger clubs in the First Division because, since they delivered the biggest audiences to TV, they were more in demand and obtained more frequent TV exposure. British soccer became caught in a double-bind in which power and wealth accrued increasingly to the top clubs whilst simultaneously being drained from the lower divisions.

Writing of declining spectator attendances, Hargreaves suggested that such processes 'may be amplified by sponsorship'. Cases in point, he wrote,

> are the transformation of horse-racing and football into TV spectacles. This coincides with the decline in attendance at the gate, and this in turn has stimulated further demand for sponsorship money to offset

the loss of revenue, which is followed by a further drop in attendance and so on in a vicious downward spiral. Sponsorship in this sense may not be much of a solution as far as the spectator at the event is concerned.

(Hargreaves, 1986: 119)

This was published in 1986. Since then, total attendances at Football League and, since its introduction in 1992, Premier League matches have increased every season. Attendances at Cup matches have increased as well. Since sponsorship revenues increased in line with this process of growth, it is clear that the sort of downward spiral, not unreasonably referred to by Hargreaves in the mid-1980s, is not the only possibility. Much more likely as King again has pointed out is the reduction of professional soccer in England to two national leagues by sometime early in the next century (1995: 531).

Postscript: the commodification of English soccer

As far as what one might call direct consumption by players is concerned, soccer in Britain can be said to be in a fairly 'healthy' state. Because a few figures are readily to hand, I shall use the case of England in order briefly to illustrate this point. In 1991, some 45,000 English soccer clubs were affiliated to the County Football Associations. Between them, these clubs regularly fielded approximately 60,000 teams (FA, 1991: 64). Assuming that each team had a squad of 13–15 players, this means that there were between 780,000 and 900,000 players of organized, FA-affiliated soccer in England at that time. According to the FA, moreover, a 600 per cent increase in affiliated women's and girls' clubs took place between 1971 and 1991. Only 10 per cent of these clubs were reported as having been associated with male counterparts (FA, 1991: 65). Against this, the FA reported a 70 per cent decline in opportunities to play soccer in schools in 1984 and 1985 and, correlatively with this, an increase of approximately 500 per cent in the number of independent, non-school-affiliated clubs catering for the 9–16 age range. According to the FA, 'high parental indiscipline' was associated with the latter clubs (FA, 1991: 64). One encounters here a 'proto-hooligan' constituency which is urgently in need of research.

As far as professional soccer is concerned and despite a general trend towards increasing match attendances and growing revenue from sponsorship and television, the finances of a large number, perhaps even a majority, of British professional clubs remain in a parlous state. In June 1991, the (English) FA published what it called a *Blueprint for the Future of Football* in which a principal recommendation was that a Premier League, formed by the clubs in the old First Division and administered by the FA rather than the Football League, should be formed. Sponsored by a brewing company, Carling, and having struck a lucrative deal with the satellite television company BSkyB, the

121

FA Premier League was inaugurated in 1992. It soon became apparent that one of the main effects of this restructuring was that it was enabling leading English clubs to compete more effectively in the struggle for top players with the giants of Italy and Spain than had been possible in the 1980s.

In that way, the earlier trend for the Football League to become an exporter of stars and, possibly, in conjunction with this 'brawn drain', towards being relegated to the status of a 'feeder league' for the soccer colossi of Southern Europe, appears at least temporarily to have been halted. Indeed, given the signing by English clubs in the years following the inauguration of the Premiership of outstanding continental players such as Bergkamp, Cantona, Ginola, Klinsmann, de Matteo, Vialli and Zola, sometimes in the face of Italian or Spanish competition, the earlier trend may even have been reversed. The return from Italy of English players such as Platt and Gascoigne points in the same direction.

Such a reversal of the 'brawn drain' is likely to be viewed as a positive development by many English fans. However, another probable consequence of the formation of the Premier League is less likely to be viewed by so many in such favourable terms. What I have in mind is a wholesale restructuring of the English professional game, with many clubs in the lower divisions of the Football League being forced to resort to the employment, solely or mainly, of part-time professionals and even in the case of some, being constrained to revert to amateur status. This putative restructuring may also lead to a region-alization of the lower divisions, a return to a situation in some ways comparable with that which prevailed in the 1940s and 1950s when, in order to keep travelling costs to a minimum, there was no national Fourth Division but a Third Division (South) and a Third Division (North). Such a restruc-turing could also lead to some clubs being forced out of the Football League and perhaps even the demise of this organization.

King (1995) argues that the splitting up of the Football League and the formation of the Premier League came about in conjunction with the increasing power in the game (and indeed in the wider society) of what he calls 'the new business class', mainly self-made men who owe their wealth primarily to the 'post-Fordist economy' (Hall and Jacques, 1990) which began to emerge in Britain in the 1980s in response to the collapse of the general 'post-war consensus' and the 'Keynesian welfare state'. Such an economy is based on flexible specialization and orientated increasingly to the production of commodities more for the symbolism they imply than their use value. Entrepreneurs from the new business class were quick to spot the fact that the popularity of football made it, from their standpoint, a virtually ideal arena for advertising and investment. According to King, however, a crucial 'conjunc-ture' (he uses the term in its Gramscian sense) in this process was provided by the government's acceptance of the recommendations of the Taylor Report into the Hillsborough tragedy of 1989,[6] especially that a major programme of stadium renewal and investment should be embarked upon. This was because it forced clubs to search for new sources of revenue and to become more rationally capitalistic (King, 1995: 171), a process which mainly favoured bigger clubs, leading them to believe they had special needs which would be better served in a separate, 'Premier' League. This is a persuasive argument. However, it is arguably too 'natiocentric' and fails to pay sufficient attention to the degree to which these developments in football and the wider society formed a response by powerful groups to globalization, including the increasing globalization of capital.

As far as professional players are concerned, a likely consequence of these developments is a further increase in the polarization of their ranks between the highly paid few and the moderately or poorly paid many. Although there were signs of it at least as early as the 1950s – the sums earned by Denis Compton of Arsenal, Middlesex and England (he was a 'dual international' but more famous for his cricketing than his footballing prowess) from his use in advertising the hair product 'Brylcreem' spring most readily to mind – this process can be traced primarily to the abolition of the maximum wage. Perhaps as many as 50 per cent of the present pool of professional players will be forced by this continuing process to become part-time professionals or into the amateur levels of the game. Of course, this may improve the long-term life chances of some by constraining them to devote more attention to their educations and extra-footballing careers than has traditionally been the practice of the majority of English professionals. Moreover, given the increasing internationalization of the market for sporting labour (Maguire, 1994a), some will undoubtedly find opportunities for playing and coaching abroad. Internationalization, however, is likely to entail an increase in competition in the global marketplace for places in the club teams of particular countries, a process which will have been intensified by the recent judgment of the European Court of Justices in the Bosman case that UEFA's stipulation that clubs can field no more than three non-national and two 'naturalized' players in European matches constitutes a restriction on freedom of movement and violates European Community law.

In and of itself, the Bosman case provides evidence of the degree to which global, in this case specifically European, processes are coming increasingly to play a part in the sporting lives of nations. Interestingly, this has so far sparked at least two seemingly contradictory reactions: on the one hand, the English PFA has taken the lead in seeking to secure a watering down if not the reversal of the Bosman judgment, while, under the leadership of Argentinian Diego Maradona and Frenchman Eric Cantona, an International Players' Union was inaugurated in November 1995. An International Association of Football Agents was launched the following month. If processes of globalization continue at their current pace – and the avoidance of a Third World War and/or a global ecological catastrophe is probably one of the central preconditions for this – it seems likely that these fledgling organizations and their members will be empowered, whilst more established, national organizations such as the PFA whose leaders are trying to halt or reverse the direction of current trends will be increasingly marginalized and remembered in the future as late twentieth-century equivalents of those figures in the nineteenth century who sought to prevent the free movement of 'football labour' from Scotland into England or who argued in favour of only players born in particular towns, cities and countries being allowed to play for the teams which represent these social units (Dunning and Sheard, 1979: 155ff.). Of course, the triumph, on balance, of universalism, cosmopolitanism and achievement-orientation over particularism, localism and ascription is by no means guaranteed. National sentiments remain strong and may well – similarly in some respects to what happened in former Yugoslavia – bring to a halt and then reverse what has been a dominant trend in sport and society for more than a hundred years.

Agreeing with King (1995), I have already suggested that a probable consequence of these developments is a reduction by some time early in the twenty-first century in the number of national leagues in England and Wales from four to two, with teams in the current Second and Third Divisions being forced to field mainly part-time professionals and to play in local or regional leagues. As far as teams in the two remaining national leagues are concerned – perhaps they will come to form the First and Second Divisions of the Premier League? – fans will probably have to pay higher prices to watch football played by increasingly cosmopolitan teams. Together with this, the importance of national leagues will probably diminish as European competitions come increasingly to the fore.

Although complaining about higher prices, the fans of teams in the remaining national leagues who can afford to pay them will probably be reasonably content with their lot. However, an understandable reaction to such possible/probable developments on the part of fans who fear that their clubs may be being forced by this process out of the national spotlight will be to feel angry and to lay the blame for this threatened status-loss on what they see as the greed of the people in charge of the national game and the alienation of the latter from rank-and-file supporters. It is undoubtedly the case that many of the currently most powerful people in English soccer are greedy, status-, wealth- and power-hungry individuals. However, without an adequate sociological diagnosis of why the current restructuring of English football is taking place, it will be difficult for the groups involved, including ordinary fans, to develop appropriate strategies for protecting and securing their interests and for understanding what they can and cannot realistically expect. What would a more adequate diagnosis of the restructuring of football look like?

The first thing worthy of note is that, whilst the main 'proximate cause' of the current restructuring is undoubtedly the financial, power, wealth and prestige striving of the most powerful people in the game, this does not involve an adequate explanation of their behaviour because it is too individualistic and involves abstracting them from the increasingly competitive and increasingly international situation in which they are enmeshed. In other words, although such influences play a part, the restructuring of English soccer cannot be adequately explained either solely in terms of the motives of individuals or natiocentrically by reference to processes and events in England alone. It has to be seen, above all, in the context of the processes of Europeanization and globalization which are currently occurring at an accelerating rate. That this is the case is shown, as I have said already, both by the reversal of the earlier 'brawn drain' and by the Bosman case of 1995 which is having ramifications, not only on the structure and financing of English soccer but also on the structure and financing of soccer in the whole of Europe and beyond. Let me close this chapter with a preliminary diagnosis of the power structure of contemporary English soccer which takes off from what I wrote earlier on this subject and which sets out what this power structure can be taken to mean for the understandings and actions of ordinary fans.

Among the significant developments which took place in English soccer in the 1980s were the foundation of the Football Supporters Association (FSA) and the emergence of the 'fanzine movement', the mushrooming of fan-produced soccer magazines, some of them national but most local and connected with particular clubs. The FSA was formed in the wake of the Heysel tragedy in 1985 and in response to the mainly authoritarian, 'law and order' reactions of the Thatcher government both to Heysel and football hooliganism. Haynes comments on the fanzine movement thus:

> Football fanzines form part of a new affective sensibility and relation-ship to the world…capturing new moods, feelings, and desires through varying degrees of concern and energy for the future of the sport, in both parochial and global senses. Football fanzines are also part of a 'culture of defence' which has developed in opposition to specific modernizing processes within the game (enforced all-seater stadiums, increased commercialization, heightened influence of television comp-anies and sponsors) and specific social and legal regulations (the shelved ID card scheme and the intense media focus and re-representation of football fans).
>
> (Haynes, 1995: 146–7)

As a description of the fanzine movement and the motivations of its personnel, it is difficult to see how Haynes' study could be bettered. However, he is less strong on sociological diagnosis. King (1995: 277) has persuasively argued that

> it is pointless idealizing the role of fanzines as fundamentally opposed to the commercial forces…coursing through football, for, in very real ways, the fanzines are part of these same forces. They are themselves entrepreneurial enterprises which have responded to a niche in the

market. Indeed fanzines are classical post-Fordist productions. They use new computer technology to produce a commodity for a quite precisely defined market.

Furthermore, as Roderick (1996) points out, Haynes fails to enquire into the social origins of those who produce and read fanzines, a crucial first step in attempting to assess their power resources relative to those of others in and relevant to the game. In order to see what these are, it is necessary to locate the personnel of the fanzine movement in social stratificational terms, that is in terms of their wealth, prestige and other forms of cultural capital. However, it is also important to locate them within the wider figurations in which they are involved. That can only be properly done by means of theory-guided research. In the absence of such research – which would be complex, expensive and difficult to fund[7] – all that can be offered in the present context is the following schematic and in some ways overly simple diagnosis of the overall power structure of contemporary English football.

What Clarke (1992) called 'the [English] football figuration' involves at the highest levels the following interlocking groups and organizations: the owners, sales, administrative and other non-playing personnel of clubs; overall controlling organizations such as the FA, the FA Premier League and the Football League; players, managers and coaches; the mass media, increasingly in recent years, television, both terrestrial and satellite; and finally, the fans. In its turn, the English football figuration has to be seen as located both within the wider (and changing) figurations which constitute British society and an international football figuration which is rapidly becoming increasingly global in scope. The club owners, for example, are either directly, or indirectly via sponsorship arrangements, locked increasingly into the global operations of powerful multinational companies.

In these terms, it is easy enough to see that, although they are the most numerous and although the other groups and organizations are dependent on the money and time which fans devote to watching and reading about football and buying football-related products – multinational companies, of course, could soon pull out if, for whatever reasons, they began to perceive sponsoring football as against their interests – fans are, individually, the least powerful persons in the football figuration. The club owners are nearly all rich men whose wealth and ownership rights give them the power to make critical decisions. The leading FA personnel have at their disposal the resources of a powerful organization whose right to arbitrate for the game is backed by law, tradition and the fact that most people in the football figuration accept the legitimacy of the FA's right to rule. Players have the PFA and this, as I suggested earlier, facilitates them in acting collectively, for example by threatening to withdraw their 'labour' or actually doing so. Individually, the power of players, mainly but not solely of top-level stars, is buttressed by their status as media celebrities, by the adulation heaped on them by fans, and increasingly by the agents they employ and who themselves have a representative association. The media, too, are backed by massive resources, especially television companies such as BSkyB which forms part of Australian-born tycoon Rupert Murdoch's transglobal media empire, News Corporation.

These powerful groups are far from united and the tensions and conflicts between them somewhat reduce their power. However, on account of their small size and access to wealth and the media of communication, it is easier for groups of them to act in unison than it is for the large and relatively amorphous mass of fans. As I have already noted, the 1980s did see the formation of the FSA and the emergence of the fanzine movement, adding to already-existing organizations such as the National Federation of Football Supporters' Clubs. The 1980s also witnessed a successful campaign by Charlton fans to keep their club at its long-standing ground, the Valley (Bale, 1993: 88ff.), whilst Northampton Town fans, under the able leadership of Brian Lomax, managed to buy into representation on their club's board. All this marked an increase in the power of football fans. However, whether taken singly or collectively, the power of the organizations and individuals involved remains relatively slight for a number of easily identifiable reasons. For one thing, effective organization on the part of fans on a national scale is impeded by such things as their sheer numbers, their geographic dispersal and the fact that, although they are united by their love of football, they are simultaneously divided by their often passionate support for their clubs and their equally passionate hatred of their rivals. Fans are also divided by such general factors of social demography as class, sex, age, race/ethnicity and region, to say nothing about such political differences among them as whether they are for or against, for example, the recent 'kick racism out of football' campaign. Only by uniting on a national level and threatening to withdraw their support, say for a month or a season and perhaps by actually doing so, or by concertedly refusing to buy merchandise from the club shops on which top clubs have in recent years become dependent for a not insignificant part of their revenue, would football fans stand a chance of effectively combating the powerful actors ranged against them in the football figuration. However, in order to do that, they would have to risk denying themselves access to one of the most important, pleasurable and meaningful things in their lives, namely expressing their support for clubs to which they are passionately attached, and that, under present circumstances, few seem willing to do.

Members of the FSA and the personnel of the fanzine movement regularly express their displeasure over the fact that they have never been directly consulted over the currently occurring process of football *perestroika*. Given their relative powerlessness, they should not be surprised. Nor should they be surprised if, in the currently emerging situation, they are treated even more as mere consumers than they have been in the past and if the game they love continues to be increasingly commodified and treated as a vehicle for commodity promotion. That is the reality of the current balance of power in the English football figuration. A long, hard campaign to draw more supporters into their organizations, and long hard thinking about the kinds of clubs and football they want, will be necessary before the present structure can be altered in a democratizing direction which gives supporters a more effective voice. This situation is one which calls not only for more debate but also for more theorization and research on the production and consumption of soccer than have so far been carried out. If such a programme materializes and if past precedent is anything to go by, it is a fair bet that Marxists and figurational sociologists will be at the forefront in the process.

Post-postscript

On coming to power in 1997, one of the first acts of the 'New Labour' government was to set up a 'Football Task Force' headed by former Conservative Minister David Mellor, and comprising Sports Minister Tony Banks, FA Chief Executive Graham Kelly, two representatives from the Football Trust, and one from the FSA. There is little doubt concerning the sincerity of the Task Force members' desire to secure a better deal for 'ordinary' football fans. However, whether they have the power or vision to achieve anything significant is doubtful. On present evidence, what they seem to be heading towards is the production of some kind of 'Fans' Charter', a football equivalent of the ineffective 'Citizen's Charter' produced under John Major. Nor does their understanding of crucial football-related issues always appear particularly astute. Speaking in Leicester in January 1998, Tony Banks expressed implacable opposition to the reintroduction of limited terracing to Premier League and First Division grounds on the basis of the crudely dichotomising argument that seating is inherently safe and terracing inherently unsafe. It does not seem to have struck him – or the civil servants who advise him – that it is a question of the kinds of seating, the kinds of terracing, the permitted supporter densities and, above all, the behavioural norms which fans adhere to. Fans committed to standing are dangerous to themselves and others in seated accommodation, especially if the latter is only flimsily built!

In Leicester, members of the Task Force expressed strong opposition to racism in football and were equally vehement in their condemnation of clubs for not passing any of the profits obtained from TV back to the fans in the form of lower ticket prices. However, the moral outrage of the Task Force members did not appear to be marked by an adequate sociological diagnosis. Above all, they seemed unaware of the degree to which it is not only clubs but top-level players, managers and their agents who are benefiting, illegally as well as legally, from the exploitation of ordinary fans. Soccer in Britain at the moment – the same is probably true of top-level sport around the world – is locked into a situation of what Durkheim (1964) would have called 'classic anomie'. Given the amounts of money flooding into the game and the accelerating pace of European and global change, the standards by means of which individual greed used to be kept reasonably in check have broken down. It would be helpful if the Task Force could seek to address this issue as a matter of urgency and if the government could seek to remedy the growing social pathology of what is no longer 'merely a game' but a sports industry which has grown to be of great national significance.

6

SOCCER HOOLIGANISM AS A WORLD SOCIAL PROBLEM

Introduction

Soccer hooliganism is alive and – quite literally – kicking. It is alive, not as used to be thought in the 1970s and 1980s as a mainly English problem but as one which is world-wide in the sense of occurring – or as having at some time in the past occurred – in virtually every country where 'soccer' is played. In this chapter, I shall explore this problem sociologically in an attempt to explain it. I shall do so primarily by reference to an analysis of data collected in England but I shall go beyond that and offer a few speculative hypotheses about some of the possibly internationally shared features of soccer hooliganism as a social problem. First of all, however, I want to look at some data.

In the early stages of the research we started in Leicester in the 1970s, we examined a range of English newspapers and recorded items on violent football-related incidents involving fans rather than players which were reported as having occurred outside the United Kingdom. We looked at newspapers from 1890 onwards and ceased recording at the end of 1983. This means that, whilst our figures cover most of the twentieth century, they do not cover the years after 1983. In that sense, they are incomplete. Nevertheless, they are revealing as a rough indication of the world-wide incidence of soccer hooliganism. More particularly, we came across reports of 101 incidents of football-related violence which were said to have occurred in thirty-seven countries between 1908 and 1983. The countries referred to and the numbers of incidents reported are cited in Table 6.1.

Measured in terms of reported deaths and injuries, the most serious of these incidents were as given in Table 6.2.

Compared with some of the figures reported here, the deaths of thirty-nine fans in the Heysel Stadium, Brussels, at the 1985 European Cup Final between Liverpool and Juventus, are placed in a revealing perspective. Since the hooligan-related deaths at Heysel were probably more important than any other single set of events in fixing in world opinion the idea of football hooliganism as the 'English disease', the data in Tables 6.1 and 6.2 provide fairly conclusive evidence that soccer hooliganism is and never has been a problem

130

Table 6.1 World-wide incidence of football-related violence as reported in English newspapers, 1908–83

Country	Year
Argentina	(*c.*)1936, 1965, 1968
Australia	1981
Austria	(*c.*) 1965
Belgium	1974, 1981
Bermuda	1980
Brazil	1982
Canada	1927
China	1979, 1981, 1983
Colombia	1982
Egypt	1966
France	1960, 1975, 1977 (two incidents), 1980
Gabon	1981
Germany★	1931, 1965 (two incidents), 1971, 1978, 1979 (two incidents), 1980, 1981 (three incidents), 1982 (six incidents)
Greece	1980 (two incidents), 1982, 1983
Guatemala	1980
Holland	1974, 1982
Hungary	1908
India	1931, 1982
Ireland★★	1913, 1919, 1920 (three incidents), 1930, 1955, 1970, 1979 (three incidents), 1981
Italy	1920, 1955, 1959, 1963 (two incidents), 1965 (two incidents), 1973, 1975, 1979, 1980, 1981, 1982
Jamaica	1965
Lebanon	1964
Malta	1975, 1980
Mexico	1983
New Zealand	1981
Nigeria	1983
Norway	1981
Peru	1964
Portugal	1970
Romania	1979
Spain	1950, 1980 (two incidents), 1981, 1982
Sweden	1946
Switzerland	1981
Turkey	1964, 1967
USSR	1960, 1982,
USA	1980
Yugoslavia	1955 (two incidents), 1982 (two incidents)

Source: Williams *et al.* (1989)

Notes:

★ Apart from the reported incident in 1931, these incidents were reported as having taken place in the former Federal Republic (West Germany)

★★ Includes incidents reported as having taken place in both Eire and Ulster as well as incidents reported before the partition

Table 6.2 Selected incidents at which serious crowd violence was reported

Country	Year	Match	No. of deaths	No. of injuries
Argentina	1968	River Plate v. Boca Juniors	74	150
Brazil	1982	San Luis v. Fortaleza	3	25
Colombia	1982	Deportivo Cai v. Club Argentina	22	200
Peru	1964	Peru v. Argentina	287–328	500
Turkey	1964	Kayseri v. Sivas	44	600
USSR	1982	Moscow Sparta v. Harlem	69	100

Source: Williams *et al.* (1989)

peculiar to the English. But an apparent paradox has arisen in this connection, namely that, precisely at a time when soccer hooliganism has begun to be reported as having become frequent in countries such as Italy and Brazil, the widespread belief has arisen in England that its own domestic hooliganism problem has either been 'cured' or 'disappeared'. This belief is a myth.

Soccer hooliganism in England: reality and myth

From the late 1960s until around the middle of 1990, the year of the World Cup Finals in Italy, soccer hooliganism was routinely regarded as one of England's major social problems. In the 1990s, however, a different perception came to prevail. Gordon Taylor, Chief Executive of the English PFA, expressed it when he wrote in September 1993 of how, since the nadir represented by Heysel, 'a joint policy between local authorities, police, government and football has dealt successfully with the hooligan problem' (*Guardian*, 30 September 1993). Only the week before Taylor's article appeared, the idea that the English problem of football hooliganism had been 'solved' was proposed by Birna Helgadottir writing in *The European*. Contrasting what she took to be the current English situation with what is happening on the continent, she argued that the 'ugliest habits [of the English hooligans] are being imitated by young hooligans from Greece to Rome....But in Britain the situation is, ironically, quieter than it has been for years' (*The European*, 23 September 1993).

Helgadottir's article was headlined 'Return of the Violent Fans' and premised on the assumption that, while the English hooligans have entered a period of relative quiescence at home, they have, beginning with the 1992 European Championships in Sweden, started regularly to engage in their hooligan activities on the Continent once again, the violence and vandalism of England fans in Amsterdam and Rotterdam in November 1993 being at the time she was writing only the most recent large-scale example. Both aspects of this assumption represent a gross oversimplification of a complex issue. That is, the English hooligans have not 'returned': they have never gone away. And English fans are continuing to engage in hooligan behaviour in both domestic and international contexts as they have done at *varying rates* since the 1970s.

What appears to have happened and been misread by people such as Taylor and Helgadottir is that, since the 1990 World Cup Finals, the English problem of football hooliganism has been 'de-politicized' for a variety of reasons. More particularly it has been de-politicized, first as a result of the Thatcher government's decision to withdraw Part I of its Football Spectators Bill. This was a measure the central provision of which was a demand for computerized entry to matches and it was condemned by Lord Justice Taylor in his report on the Hillsborough tragedy of 1989 where ninety-five people were crushed to death at a football match in Sheffield as likely to *increase* rather than *decrease* the incidence of crowd fatalities (Taylor, 1990).

The issue of soccer hooliganism also began to be de-politicized in England in 1990 as a result of the then Conservative government's decision to withdraw its opposition to the English FA's annual application to UEFA for the re-admission of English clubs to European football following the ban imposed as a result of Heysel. A consequence of these two political decisions was that the occurrence of football hooliganism, especially hooligan incidents involving English fans in domestic contexts, became less 'newsworthy' and hence less frequently reported, particularly by the national media. That is, the British media lost two reasons they had had during the second half of the 1980s for regularly focusing on football crowds and their behaviour: the interest generated in connection with discussions of the Football Spectators Bill; and the interest generated in conjunction with the FA's attempts to get English clubs reaccepted into European competition. Three other factors worked in the same direction: the 'feel-good factor' generated by the England team's better-than-expected performance in 'Italia 90' and the fact that it was awarded FIFA's 'Fair-Play Trophy'; the mood of self-congratulation engendered at the higher levels of English football by the programme of stadium renewal embarked on in the light of the recommendations of the Taylor Report (in this connection, the false idea gained ground that new all-seater stadia would help to 'civilize' the hooligan fans); and probably of equal importance to the de-politicization of hooliganism, an attempt by the football authorities and members of the 'new business class' involved in the ownership of Premiership clubs at 'news management' with the intention of fostering a public image of English football as a 'safe', 'family' game which has managed successfully to put its hooligan past behind it. Agencies of state may also have been involved in this process of image management. They certainly became involved in it in and after 1996 when, in conjunction with the FA, both the Major and Blair governments became involved in trying to bring the 2006 World Cup Finals to England.[1]

Two academic arguments which broadly accept the myth that English soccer hooliganism has disappeared are worthy of consideration. The first is by Ian Taylor. Writing in 1991, he referred to what he called the 'extraordinary absence of hooliganism and other ugly incidents from English football grounds during the 1990–91 season'. 'An astonishing sea-change,' he went on, 'is taking place in the culture of some of [England's] football terraces', and he attributed this process to the conjuncture of the BBC's 'packaging' of 'Italia 90' with the removal of perimeter fences from many grounds in response to the Taylor Report. According to Ian Taylor, the process worked in something like the following way. The removal of 'cages' reduced the frequency of 'animal-like' responses among fans, and this interacted with the packaging of the 1990 World Cup Finals in which, as Taylor put it, 'the opera of Pavarotti would meld ethereally into a poetic display of European football', producing a re-emphasis on 'style'. As a result, Taylor argued, 'hooliganism [became] suddenly decidedly unfashionable, passé, irrelevant' (*Independent on Sunday*, 21 April 1991).

The second academic argument is that of Birger Peitersen. It is his contention that what he calls the 'hooligan period' of football is now a thing of the past. 'Hooliganism fortunately plays a much smaller role today on the football scene,' he says. 'The football supporters have taken over and their activities bind together and stimulate the more enjoyable moments of games of football' (Peitersen, 1996: 52). Peitersen makes use in this connection of Fiske's (1991b) distinction between 'mass culture' – the cultural products of industrial capitalism – and 'popular culture' – the way in which people 'use, abuse, and subvert these products to create their own meanings and messages' (Peitersen, 1996: 52). He does so in order to highlight the ways in which a strong element of carnival has developed among European soccer spectators in recent years. It is one of Peitersen's contentions that the Danish 'roligans' – 'friendly hooligans' – played a central innovative role in this introduction of the 'carnivalesque'. I shall discuss the 'roligan' phenomenon later. For the moment, I want to suggest that the arguments of Peitersen and Taylor are suspect in certain regards. I shall confine my observations to the English football scene.

Significant changes have certainly taken place in English soccer since the 1980s. Attendances at top-level matches have increased regularly since 1986–7, and 1992–3 witnessed the launch of the Premier League. As I noted in Chapter 5, this was associated with a restructuring of the ownership of many top-level clubs and coincided with a move towards all-seater stadia. As part of this, things like American-style dancing girls were introduced as a means of crowd entertainment/crowd control. However, such forms of what Fiske would regard as 'mass culture' were supplemented by independent innovations of a 'popular culture' type. For example, copying Danish and Dutch fans, a growing use of face paints took place, together with the wearing of bizarre forms of dress – for example, males dressing as nuns or wearing animal costumes. All these innovations introduced a distinct element of carnival to the game. At the same time, the 'fanzine' movement signified the emergence of a new, hitherto unprecedented form of football literacy (Jary *et al.*, 1991; King, 1995; Haynes, 1995) and, although still marginalized, the Football Supporters' Association which was founded in 1985 succeeded in gaining a toehold in the higher councils of the English game.

It is easy to see why people like Taylor and Peitersen who are deeply committed to soccer are liable to read such changes as having made a serious dent in the hooligan problem. Nevertheless, the explanation of the supposed decline of soccer hooliganism in terms of a growing concern with 'style' and 'carnival' seems flawed. For one thing, the fact that the 1990 World Cup Finals were associated in England with a hitherto unprecedented form of hooliganism, namely attacks on foreigners by fans who had been watching the Italia 90 matches on television (similar attacks occurred in conjunction with Euro 96 and the 1998 World Cup Finals), shows at the very least that the BBC's 'packaging' of the tournament did not immediately have the effect hypothesized by Taylor. Moreover, the 'soccer casual' movement, the switch of hooligan and other fans in the 1980s from a 'skinhead' to a 'casual' style involving the wearing of actually or apparently expensive 'designer' clothes, clearly shows that an interest in style and an interest in violence are not mutually exclusive. And that carnival and violence are not mutually exclusive either is shown by the European Middle Ages, contemporary South America and the annual jamboree in Notting Hill. Indeed, Peitersen seems not to have noticed how Fiske's analysis of English 'popular culture' in the nineteenth century depends to a large extent on Malcolmson's (1982) demonstration of how seriously violent by present-day standards many elements of that 'popular culture' were (Fiske, 1991b: 70–4).

There is also substantial evidence that the English problem of soccer hooliganism has not been solved. England fans rioted in Sweden in 1992, in Amsterdam in 1993, in Dublin in 1995 and in Marseilles in 1998. Proponents of the 'hooliganism is a thing of the past' thesis can only account for such incidents by tortuously claiming, as Helgadottir did, that the English hooligans have become peaceful at home and only engage in violence abroad. But the evidence is against them. Take the figures in Tables 6.3 and 6.4. Table 6.3 offers a selection of incidents which took place at or in conjunction with Premiership, Football League and other matches during 1992–3. In fact, in that season more than sixty football hooligan incidents took place in England and Wales. Eleven of these were regarded as 'serious' by the police, two allegedly involved murders, and CS gas was used by hooligans on four occasions. Incidents occurred at all levels of the Premier and Football Leagues, as well as in conjunction with an international played at Wembley. Only twenty-six of the incidents, however, involved trouble inside grounds. Hence, in the majority of cases they were not readily visible to the media, and it was partly as a result of this that relatively few were reported, especially at national level. There has also been a media policy of not pointing cameras at incidents inside

Table 6.3 Selected hooligan incidents at or in conjunction with Premiership, Football League, international, pre-season friendly and other matches in England and Wales

Date	Match/fans involved	Type of incident
7 October 1992	Notts. Forest v. Stockport	CS gas used, eight policemen hurt
18 October 1992	Sunderland v. Newcastle	Thirty arrests, 200 ejected
31 October 1992	Leyton Orient v. Swansea	Fights in London (Marble Arch)
31 October 1992	Grimsby v. Portsmouth	Missiles thrown at players
14 November 1992	Darlington v. Hull	Pub fights in city centre and station
16 and 24 November 1992	Stoke v. Port Vale	Fights inside and outside ground/town centre
19 December 1992	Chelsea v. Manchester Utd	CS gas thrown in Covent Garden pub
12 January 1993	Southend v. Millwall	Pitch invasion, pub fights★
16 January 1993	Tranmere	Fan beaten to death (racial more than football related)
19 January 1993	Cardiff v. Swansea	Pitch invasion, pub fights★
30 January 1993	Leicester v. West Ham	Fights outside ground, CS gas thrown in pub
20 February 1993	Tottenham v. Leeds	300 in fight, CS gas thrown in pub★
5 March 1993	Tottenham and Blackpool fans	Fighting in Blackpool prior to Spurs/Man. City match
7 March 1993	Man. City v. Tottenham	Pitch invasion, fighting outside ground★
17 March 1993	England U18 v. Ghana	Attack on police
3 April 1993	Sheffield Wed. v. Sheffield Utd	Fighting, murder★
3 April 1993	Millwall v. Portsmouth	Pub fights, missiles thrown★
24 April 1993	Peterborough v. Leicester	Pitch invasion, arson
28 April 1993	England v. Holland	Pub fights, police attacked
1 May 1993	Reading v. Swansea	Fighting inside/outside ground, pitch invasion★
2 May 1993	Aston Villa v. Oldham	Disturbances in Oldham; riot police used
4 May 1993	Exeter v. Port Vale	Attack by fans on referee
8 May 1993	Millwall v. Bristol Rovers	Pitch invasion, missiles thrown★
8 May 1993	Halifax v. Hereford	Mounted police used. Fighting inside ground
Div. 1 Play-off Semi-final	Portsmouth v. Leicester (at Nottingham's City Ground)	Fights outside the ground
Div. 1 Play-off Final	Swindon v. Leicester City (at Wembley)	Leicester fans ransacked Wembley pub. Disturbances in Swindon

Notes:
These data were provided by Ian Stanier, a Leicester postgraduate student
★ Denotes police judgement of disturbance sufficiently serious to 'stretch' available police resources

Table 6.4 Football–related incidents known to the British Transport Police, 1990–3

	Season	No. of incidents
1990–1991	(21 August 1990 to 5 June 1991; includes end-of-season play-offs)	204
1991–1992	(17 August 1991 to 3 June 1992; includes end-of-season play-offs and one international)	260
1992–1993	(8 August 1992 to 31 May 1993)	127
1993–1994	(24 July 1993 to 22 December 1993; first half of season only)	64
	Total	655

Note:
The remaining twelve incidents known to the BTP took place in conjunction with pre-season matches

grounds, a policy based on the ostrich-like supposition that, if you do not show and directly confront a serious problem, it will somehow go away.

Data provided by the British Transport Police (BTP) for the period 21 August 1990 to 22 December 1993 point in the same direction. More particularly, the BTP recorded a total of 667 incidents in contexts of travel to and from football matches in England between August 1990 and December 1993, a period which covered three and a half football seasons. The seasonal breakdown of these incidents is provided in Table 6.4.

These data from the BTP are not unproblematic. They may even be indicative of a decline of incidents associated with football match travel in 1992–3. However, what they suggest with a relatively high degree of certainty – and they are backed up by the data provided in Table 6.3 – is that, contrary to what has become a widely held belief, soccer hooliganism in England has not disappeared. It may have declined as a publicly recognized problem but hooligan behaviour in football contexts, more often outside than inside stadia, is continuing to occur. Of course, since the national incidence of soccer hooliganism is impossible to measure with precision, and since many hooligans enjoy publicity and revel in their notoriety, this pattern of underreporting since 1990 may have contributed to a factual decline to some degree. All that can be said with certainty is that the problem is continuing to occur and that the figures quoted here provide nowhere near a complete measure of its incidence in 1992 and 1993. Events during 'Euro 96', the European Football Championships held in England in June 1996, point in the same direction. So do events in France during the 1998 World Cup. For purposes of conciseness, I shall deal here solely with Euro 96.

It is widely believed that Euro 96 passed off without the occurrence of hooliganism on a substantial scale. For example, discussing the hopes of the English FA that FIFA will allow England to host the 2006 World Cup, journalist Martin Thorpe wrote of Euro 96 that

UEFA's ability to turn a handsome profit on a tournament in which England matched the best teams on the field and avoided trouble off it will go down well with FIFA when it chooses a venue for the second World Cup of the new century.

(*Guardian*, 12 October 1996)

The England team's standard of play – they reached the semi-finals only to be beaten by Germany in a penalty shoot-out – the standard of football produced in the tournament overall, and the carnival atmosphere generated by the crowds cannot be disputed. What is in doubt is whether trouble was avoided off the field. There is ample evidence that it was widespread. For example, crowds gathered in London's Trafalgar Square following England's game against Spain on 22 June and had to be dispersed by riot police. Disturbances were also reported in Hull, and fights between Englishmen and Spaniards broke out in Fuengirola and Torremolinos on Spain's Costa del Sol (*Independent*, 24 June 1996). By far the most serious rioting occurred, however, following England's defeat by West Germany in the semi-finals when trouble was reported, not only in London, but in Basingstoke, Bedford, Birmingham, Bournemouth, Bradford, Brighton (where a Russian teenager was mistaken for a German, stabbed in the neck and almost killed), Dunstable, Exeter, Haywards Heath, Mansfield, Norwich, Nottingham, Portsmouth, Shropshire and Swindon (*Daily Mail*, 28 June 1996). The events in London's Trafalgar Square were reported in the *Daily Mail* as follows:

> The agonising moment when Gareth Southgate's penalty was saved…was the trigger for a night of sustained hooliganism. Draped in flags and brandishing bottles, thousands spilled out of the pubs and bars…within moments of Germany's victory.…The worst flashpoint came in Trafalgar Square.…[I]t was the centre of…orchestrated rampage.…Up to 2,000 people poured into the square shortly after 10.06 pm.…[T]he situation rapidly deteriorated.…Cars and motorists…found themselves engulfed in the rapidly-escalating violence with German Volkswagens and Mercedes quickly singled out. A hard core of 400 hooligans…burst out of the square and attacked a police patrol car. The two officers inside had to flee for their lives as in less than a minute the car was smashed to pieces. The hooligans surged towards the Thames, shattering windscreens, turning one vehicle over and setting fire to a Japanese sports car.…Between 10.10 pm and midnight, police received 2,500 calls requesting urgent help. Of these 730 were related to violent disturbances.…The final toll around Trafalgar Square was 40 vehicles damaged, six overturned and two set alight. Seven buildings were damaged with 25 police officers and 23 members of the public injured across London, as well as a further 18 casualties, both police and civilians, in Trafalgar Square

itself....Nearly 200 people were arrested across London with 40 held during ugly scenes in Trafalgar Square.

(*Daily Mail*, 28 June 1996)

These events were the most violent among a series, varying in violence and scale, which took place across England during Euro 96. They took place despite a co-ordinated police effort which had been planned for some three years, cost an estimated £20 million (BBC1, 10 July 1996), and involved the well-publicized arrest of 'known hooligans' up and down the country before the tournament. *The Times* sports correspondent John Goodbody realistically concluded that: 'What Wednesday night emphasized is that whenever the English supporters are taking part in an international tournament, it is inevitable that there will be trouble. However careful the preparations, trouble-makers will ensure that there will be confrontations' (*The Times*, 28 June 1996). Events in France, especially Marseilles, in July 1998 proved John Goodbody right.

Explanations of soccer hooliganism

In England, five main popular explanations of soccer hooliganism have been proposed, each espoused by the media and politicians. These explanations – some at least partly contradictory of the others – are that soccer hooliganism is 'caused' by: excessive alcohol consumption; violent incidents on the field of play or biased and incompetent refereeing; unemployment; affluence; and 'permissiveness'. None of them is supported by the available evidence, at least as far as playing a deeper, more enduring role in the generation of soccer hooliganism is concerned. Alcohol consumption cannot be said to be a 'cause' of football hooliganism because not every fan who drinks in a football context fights, not even those who drink heavily. The converse is also true: that is, that not all hooligans drink. For example, in England some hooligan leaders claim they do not drink before fighting because they need a clear head in order to direct operations and avoid being caught unawares by rivals or the police (Dunning *et al.*, 1988). There *is* an *indirect* connection between soccer hooliganism and alcohol consumption, however, in that the masculinity norms of the groups involved tend to stress ability to fight, 'hardness' and ability to 'hold one's ale' as marks of being a 'man'.

Violence on the field of play and refereeing that is or is perceived as biased can similarly be dismissed as lying at the roots of soccer hooliganism. That is because incidents take place before and after as well as during matches, often at considerable distances from grounds. Nor can unemployment – the favoured 'cause' of the political left – be said in some simple sense to produce soccer hooliganism. For example, during the 1930s when unemployment in England was high, the incidence of reported match-related violence was at an all-time low. Similarly, when English football hooliganism began to enter its

139

current phase in the 1960s, the national rate of unemployment was at its lowest ever recorded level. And today, the rate of participation in football hooliganism by the unemployed varies regionally, being higher in areas such as the north of England where unemployment is high and lower in what were, until recently, low-unemployment areas such as London and the South-East. In fact, almost every major English club has its soccer hooligans, independently of the local rate of unemployment, and fans from more affluent areas used in the 1980s regularly to taunt their less fortunate rivals by waving bundles of £5 or £10 notes at them *en masse*, singing (to the tune of 'You'll never walk alone') 'You'll never work again'! However, unemployment can be said to be an indirect cause of soccer hooliganism in the sense of being one among a complex of factors which help to perpetuate the norms of aggressive masculinity which appear to be basically involved.

The fourth popular explanation of soccer hooliganism, namely that 'affluence' rather than unemployment is the principal 'cause', tends to be favoured by the political right. Not only is it in direct contradiction of the explanation by reference to the supposed 'causal' role of unemployment, but it is also sometimes associated with the explanation in terms of 'permissiveness', for example when it is suggested that football hooliganism is an attribute of the 'too much, too soon' generation. However, whatever form it takes, the explanation in terms of 'affluence' is contradicted by the available evidence and seems largely to result from a misreading of the fashion-switch on the part of young British football fans during the 1980s from the 'skinhead' to the 'casual' style. The skinhead style was, of course, openly working class; the casual style, by contrast, is apparently 'classless'. The clothes worn by devotees of the latter style may be but are not necessarily expensive. Sometimes they are stolen and sometimes only apparently expensive, for example when 'designer labels' are sewn onto cheap, sometimes stolen, sweaters. Of course, some soccer hooligans are at least temporarily affluent, either because they have well-paid jobs or prosperous parents or because they make money through black market activities or involvement in crime. But the bulk of the available evidence runs counter to the 'affluence thesis'. Reasonably reliable data on the social origins of football hooligans first began to become available in the 1960s and they have been remarkably consistent since that time, suggesting that, while hooligans come from all levels in the class hierarchy, the majority, some 80–90 per cent, come from the working class, that is mainly from the ranks of manual workers with low levels of formal education (Dunning *et al.*, 1988).

The popular explanation in terms of 'permissiveness' appears similarly deficient. It is superficially plausible in that the advent of the so-called 'permissive society' in Britain in the 1960s coincided with the growing perception of football fan behaviour as problematic by the authorities and the media. However, soccer hooliganism in Britain as a fact if not by name can be traced back to the 1870s and 1880s (Dunning *et al.*, 1988) and the *coup de grâce* for the 'permissive society' argument is given by the fact that, since soccer hooliganism began to be recognized in Britain as a social problem in the 1960s, soccer matches have become more heavily policed and subject to tighter controls; that is, watching British football has become anything other than 'permissive'. Moreover, during the 1980s, the Thatcher government sought explicitly by means of 'authoritarian', 'law and order' policies to reverse what it saw as the generally deleterious 'permissiveness' of the 1960s and 1970s. And yet, soccer hooliganism – and crime in general – continued to grow.

Other than the 'figurational' explanation, four principal academic explanations of English football hooliganism have been offered: the 'anthropological' explanation of Armstrong and Harris (1991) and Armstrong (1998); the Marxist explanations of Taylor (1971, 1982) and Clarke (1978); the 'ethological' explanation advanced by Marsh *et al.* (1978) and Marsh (1978); and the explanation in terms of psychological 'reversal theory' proposed by Kerr (1994). Whilst each of these explanations has its particular strengths, each has its particular deficiencies, too.

The anthropological work on football hooliganism by Armstrong and Harris is based on rich, in-depth descriptions of the behaviour of football fans from Sheffield, a two-club town. It is theoretically eclectic, present-centred and, as is often the case with ethnographic or participant observation research, its principal author (Armstrong) seems insufficiently aware of the limitations which derive from reliance on the unsupported testimony of a single individual. Insufficient attention is also paid to the way in which the dynamics of fan behaviour and relationships may have been affected by the fact that Sheffield is a two-club town; and the need for comparative observation with one-club towns such as Leicester and other two-club towns such as Liverpool and Nottingham was apparently not seen. These limitations are compounded by the author's peremptory dismissal of virtually all research in the field other than his own, a stance which is not conducive to open dialogue and hence to the possibility of publicly establishing the degree to which the – in many ways – rich, deep and dense Sheffield findings confirm or refute the findings of others.

The work of Taylor and Clarke is insightful regarding the ways in which recent developments in English football have been bound up with the capitalist character of the economy. However, neither of these authors carried out systematic in-depth research into soccer hooliganism and both apparently fail to grasp the significance of the fact that the phenomenon principally involves conflict between working-class groups which only regularly become involved in conflict with the football authorities and the police – and less directly with other representatives of the state – as part of an attempt to fight among themselves. In his early work, Taylor even described football hooliganism as a 'working class resistance movement'. Marsh *et al.* do not make such mistakes. However, their work lacks an historical dimension with the consequence that they tend to see hooligan fighting – or what they call 'aggro' – as an unchanging historical constant. Moreover, in their stress on 'aggro' as 'ritual violence', that is violence which is mainly symbolic or metonymic in the sense of involving aggressive posturing but not the completion or 'consummation' of aggressive acts, they fail to see that ritualised aggression can be seriously violent.

Finally, through his use of 'reversal' theory, Kerr seems to do little more than dress up in complex psychological jargon some relatively simple sociological ideas. He writes:

> The metamotivational state combination operative during most types of soccer hooligan activity is paratelic-negativistic-autic-mastery. The paratelic-negativism element within this combination (with accompanying high levels of felt arousal and felt negativism) gives rise to the type of provocative, playful paratelic aggression that characterizes so many examples of soccer hooligan activity. Hooligan behaviour in these circumstances is not necessarily malicious, but is engaged in with the major purpose of generating excitement and the pleasures of release from rules.
>
> (Kerr, 1994: 109)

Kerr seems to think that the soccer hooligans' quest for excitement through violent, deviant and delinquent acts in soccer-related contexts can be explained as a simple 'reversal' from one 'metamotivational state', 'boredom' (Kerr, 1994: 33ff.), to another, 'excitement'. It is difficult to see how what he writes does more than dress up in psychological language what Elias and I had written more than twenty years before (although we wrote about routinization in this connection and not simple boredom), at the same time reducing a complex and graduated socio-behavioural reality to a crude dichotomy. Above all, there is no reference in what he writes to what is also arguably centrally at stake in soccer hooligan fighting, namely norms of masculinity. These figure centrally in the figurational explanation.

The 'figurational' explanation of soccer hooliganism

The Leicester research on soccer hooliganism was carried out within the framework of the 'figurational' paradigm advocated by Norbert Elias. It is one of the distinctive claims of the adherents to this paradigm that it is not so much method as discovery which 'legitimizes' research as 'scientific' (Elias, 1986b: 20). Accordingly, in seeking to add to the understanding of soccer hooliganism, we adopted a rather catholic approach to method, using a combination of direct observation, participant observation and historical study. The historical part of our research was central and mainly took the form of time-series content analysis of official records and newspaper reports.[2] In both cases, data were collected covering the late nineteenth century to the mid-1980s.

Using this combination of methods, we made four principal discoveries in the sense of adding knowledge-based foci to the debate about and research on soccer hooliganism. These discoveries were:

1 that soccer hooliganism is not and never has been a solely English or British phenomenon but is found to varying degrees and in different forms in virtually every country where the game of Association football is played;
2 that forms of crowd violence occur in sports other than soccer as well as in countries other than Britain;
3 that in Britain, there is a history of hooligan behaviour at soccer which was not labelled as such but stretches back beyond the 1960s, the period when the problem is popularly thought to have started;
4 that soccer hooliganism is predominantly an expression of a pattern of male aggressiveness characteristically found, in the English case at least, in the 'rougher' sections of the working class and that one of the principal ways in which it is produced and reproduced is by the experience of living towards the bottom of the social scale. A type of community structure which approximates in greater or lesser degree to what Suttles (1968) called 'ordered segmentation' is often, though not always, involved in this connection. It is a type of community structure which leads to the recurrent formation of gangs which fight.

I have already reviewed the data on the first of our 'discoveries' so there is no need to repeat them. The second discovery provides strong evidence against a version of the theory of catharsis which is sometimes proposed. What this version holds is that soccer is more regularly associated with crowd violence than other sports because, as a more 'civilized' and less violent game, it provides fewer opportunities than, for example, boxing, rugby or American football for spectators to work out their frustrations vicariously by identifying with violent actors on the field of play. This theory is falsified by the simple fact that crowd violence *is* associated with sports such as boxing, rugby and American football. Holt (1981), for example, showed that fighting between opposing fans is a regular occurrence at Rugby Union matches in the South of France, while a pattern of what one might call 'celebratory rioting' is a frequent accompaniment of 'gridiron' football and other top-level sports in the USA (see Chapter 7). A more straightforward explanation of the relatively greater frequency of crowd violence in conjunction with soccer is that Association football is the world's most popular team sport and that a large proportion of its spectators are drawn from towards the bottom of the social scale in the countries where it is played. This relatively greater factual frequency of fighting and disorder is also often magnified perceptually by the media exposure which the game attracts; that is, although in England in the 1990s the reverse has tended to occur, the problem of crowd violence in soccer can be made to appear greater than is in fact the case by the frequency of newspaper, radio and TV coverage. This kind of exposure can, under certain conditions, positively affect the 'real' incidence of soccer-related crowd trouble by attracting to the game people who want to fight.

Our third main finding is that crowd violence has occurred in conjunction with professional soccer matches in Britain in every decade since the game emerged in a recognizably modern form in the 1870s and 1880s. However, the reported incidence of such violence – in the form of newspaper reports and the reports of match officials to the FA – has not been constant decade by decade but has roughly taken the form of a U-shaped curve. More particularly, the reported incidence was relatively high before the First World War; fell between the wars in England, though not in Scotland; remained low after the Second World War but started rising in the mid-1950s, slowly at first but then more rapidly in and around the mid-1960s. Every form of what is labelled 'football hooliganism' by the authorities and media today – missile throwing, pitch invasions, attacks on players and match officials, and fights between fan groups – is observable throughout this period of more than 100 years. However, attacks on players and officials tended to predominate before the First World War, while fights between fan groups have tended to predominate since the 1960s (Dunning et al., 1988).

The pattern of soccer hooliganism which began to emerge in the 1960s seems, in part, to have been predicated upon the greater frequency with which fans were travelling to away matches. This, in turn, was clearly a consequence of greater affluence, developments in the sphere of transport and communications, and the emergence nationally of a distinctive, largely male-orientated and male-dominated youth culture. As far specifically as soccer hooliganism is concerned, the playing of the World Cup Finals in England in 1966 seems to have acted as a catalyst. Before that event, the principal working-class 'folk devils' in Britain – 'teddy boys', 'mods' and 'rockers' – were not noted for regularly fighting at football. However, for their successors, the 'skinheads' who first became active in 1967, football was a principal theatre of operations. In part, this seems to have come about in conjunction with the media reporting of football immediately prior to the World Cup Finals.

I have already suggested that the incidence of soccer-related disorderliness in Britain had begun to climb in the mid-1950s. This slow rise continued into the 1960s and seems to have contributed to a media-generated panic in which newspapers began to report relatively minor soccer disturbances in sensational terms. That the World Cup Finals were about to be played in England appears to have been crucial in this regard. In November 1965, for example, a Millwall fan threw a 'dead' hand grenade onto the pitch during his team's away 'local derby' against London rivals Brentford. This was reported as follows in the *Sun* under the headline 'Soccer Marches to War':

The Football Association have acted to stamp out this increasing mob violence within 48 hours of the blackest day in British soccer – the grenade day that showed that British supporters can rival anything the South Americans can do.

The World Cup is now less than nine months away. That is all the time we have left to try and restore the once good sporting name of this country. Soccer is sick at the moment. Or better, its crowds seem to have contracted some disease which causes them to break out in fury.

(*Sun*, 8 November 1965)

There *was* fighting at this match both inside and outside the ground, and one Millwall fan sustained a broken jaw (*Sun*, 27 September 1965). However, the *Sun* chose to concentrate on the symbolic violence of the hand grenade and implicitly equated this incident with the full-scale riot which had taken place in Lima, Peru, in 1964 (see p. 132).

Commenting in April 1966 on disturbances which took place at a match between Liverpool and Celtic, the editor of the *Sun* wrote:

> It may be only a handful of hooligans who are involved at the throwing end, but if this sort of behaviour is repeated in July, the world will conclude that all the British are hooligans....Either the drift to violence must be checked or soccer will be destroyed as an entertainment. What an advertisement for the British sporting spirit if we end with football pitches enclosed in protective wire cages.

> (*Sun*, 21 April 1966)

Elements of self-fulfilling prophecy were involved in this account in two respects: first, the combination of football hooliganism *per se* and the public reaction to it did lead 'the world to conclude' over the next couple of decades that many Britons, especially the English, 'are football hooligans'; and second, football pitches in England did become enclosed in 'protective wire cages', in that way contributing to the Hillsborough tragedy in 1989 when ninety-five Liverpool fans were crushed to death on just such a wire-caged terrace. (A ninety-sixth fan died in hospital later.) A more immediate effect of this kind of sensationalistic reporting, though, was unintentionally to advertise soccer grounds as contexts where exciting and, in the traditional sense of that term, 'masculine' action takes place, hence helping to draw into football (mainly) young men most of whom had started dressing in the skinhead style and for whom fighting was at least as important as football.

A few verbatim quotations from English football hooligans will shed light on their characteristic motives and values. The four quotations which follow are from statements made by soccer hooligans in or about the 1960s, 1970s and 1980s. Reminiscing about the emotions he experienced during his days of hooligan involvement in the 1960s, E. Taylor wrote in 1984 that the excitement of battle, the danger, the heightened activity of body and mind as the adrenaline raced, the fear and the triumph of over-coming it. To this day, when trouble starts at a game I come alive and close to getting involved. I may not forget the dangers of physical injury and criminal proceedings but I do ignore them.

(*Guardian*, 28 March 1984)

Similar sentiments were expressed by a 26-year-old lorry driver interviewed in conjunction with the 1974 Cardiff City v. Manchester United game, a match where serious trouble had been anticipated. He said:

> I go to a match for one reason only: the aggro. It's an obsession. I can't give it up. I get so much pleasure when I'm having aggro that I nearly wet my pants....I go all over the country looking for it....[E]very night during the week we go round looking respectable....[T]hen if we see someone who looks like the enemy we ask him the time; if he answers in a foreign accent, we do him over; and if he's got any money on him, we'll roll him as well.

(Harrison, 1974: 602–4)

Here is how one of our Leicester informants put it in 1981. His words illus-trate the sort of rationality which tends to be involved:

> If you can baffle the coppers, you'll win. You've just gotta think how they're gonna think. And you know, half the time you know what they're gonna do 'cos they're gonna take the same route every week, week in, week out. If you can figure out a way to beat 'em, you're fuckin' laughin': you'll have a good fuckin' raut. ['Raut' is Leicester slang for a fight.]

Finally, when interviewed in 1984–5 for the Thames TV programme *Hooligan*, a member of West Ham United's 'Inter City Firm' (ICF), England's most notorious football hooligan gang at the time, said:

> We don't – we don't go – well, we *do* go with the intention of fighting, you know what I mean....We look forward to it.... It's great. You know, if you've got, say, 500 kids coming for you, like, and you know they're going to be waiting for you, it's – it's good to know, like. Like being a tennis player, you know. You get all geed up to play, like. We get geed up to fight....I think I fight, like, so I can make a name for meself and that, you know. Hope people, like, respect me for what I did, like.

Despite the fact that they cover a period of more than twenty years, these statements are consistent. What they reveal is that, for the young men involved, football hooligan fighting is basically about masculinity, territorial struggle and excitement. For them, fighting is a central source of meaning, status or 'reputation' and pleasurable arousal. Thus Taylor spoke of 'battle excitement' and 'the adrenaline racing'; the ICF member referred not only to the excitement generated in fighting but also to the respect among his peers that he hoped his involvement would bring; and the lorry driver spoke of 'aggro' as a pleasurable, almost erotically arousing, obsession. This latter point received confirmation when Jay Allan, a leading member of 'the Aberdeen Casuals', a Scottish football hooligan 'firm', wrote of fighting at football as being even more pleasurable than sex (Allan, 1989). It receives further confirmation from the fact that members of the ICF referred to football hooligan fighting as ''avin' it off'', a London expression which is more usually used for sex. That the statement by Allan is not the only example of a non-English expression of this kind of sentiment is suggested by the fact that a 17-year-old Brazilian *torcida* is reported as having told the Rio newspaper *Journal Do Brasil* in 1994 that: 'For me fighting is fun. I feel a great emotion when the other guy screams in pain. I don't care about how other people feel, as long as I'm happy' (*The Australian*, 15 December 1994). Bill Buford expressed the same idea in more literary terms when he wrote:

> [The hooligans] talk about the crack, the buzz and the fix. They talk about having to have it, of being unable to forget it when they do, of not wanting to forget it – ever....They talk about it with the pride of the privileged....They talk about it in the way that another generation talked about drugs and drink. One lad, a publican, talks about it as though it were a chemical thing...once it's in the air, once an act of violence has been committed, other acts will follow inevitably – necessarily....Violence is one of the most intensely lived experiences and, for those capable of giving themselves over to it, one of the most intense pleasures...crowd violence was their drug.
>
> (Buford, 1991: 206–7)

Sociologically, the point is to explain why some people obtain intense pleasure from participating in war-like violence and why football has been chosen as an arena – it is far from being the only one – for enacting these violent rituals. The figurational hypothesis we developed in the 1970s and 1980s is concerned with addressing these issues and can be summarized as follows.

A quest for pleasurable excitement is a common feature of leisure activities in all societies. Particularly in industrial societies, what is involved is a search for a counter to the emotional staleness which tends to be engendered by the routines of non-leisure life (see Chapter 1). Furthermore, present-day England is a patriarchal society in which males generally are expected under certain circumstances to fight, and high status is legitimately conferred on good fighters in particular occupational contexts, for example the military and the police. However, the dominant norms in English society demand that males should not be the initiators of fights and require them to confine their fighting to self-defence, defence of their families and loved ones, defence of 'the realm', and sports such as boxing. The 'core' soccer hooligans, those who engage in soccer hooliganism most regularly, seeking out confrontations with opposing fans rather than being drawn into fighting by the exigencies of particular situations, contravene these socially dominant norms. They are liable to initiate and plan attacks and to fight publicly in situations where, according to the dominant norms, fighting is taboo. For them, a quest for status as 'hard men' and the 'pleasurable battle-excitement' engendered in hooligan confrontations forms a central life interest. Sociologically, the point is to explain why. Who are the 'core' soccer hooligans and what in their social circumstances, personality, habitus and experiences explains their deep commitment to fighting and the fact that they deviate from the dominant norms in this regard? This question brings me to the fourth 'discovery' of the Leicester research. It involves reference, not to some kind of inborn pattern of behaviour, to an 'aggressive instinct', but to a learned behaviour pattern which appears to be recurrently generated in specific social figurations. Soccer is a context where this behaviour is expressed and reinforced but it is not a context where the primary generation takes place.

The currently available data on the social origins of English soccer hooligans are relatively scanty. Such as they are they suggest that, while soccer hooligans come from *all* levels of the class hierarchy, the overwhelming majority (80–90 per cent) come from the working class. That is, the majority have relatively low levels of formal education and work in manual occupations. The data also suggest that, with one possible exception, this sort of distribution has remained stable since the 1960s when English soccer hooliganism first began to attract public concern. More particularly the data of Harrington (1968) on the 1960s, of Trivizas (1980) on the 1970s, and of the Leicester group (1988) and Armstrong (1998) on the 1980s, all suggest that the majority of English soccer hooligans come from the lower reaches of the social scale. A smaller, relatively stable proportion is recruited from around the middle, and an even smaller, equally stable proportion from at or near the top. The exception is a possible increase in the participation of skilled relative to semi-skilled and unskilled males in the 1980s as compared with the 1960s and 1970s. This change corresponded with the abandonment of the 'skinhead' style. The principal problem sociologically is to explain why the working-class bulk of English soccer hooligans behave as they do.[3]

As Suttles (1968) notes, one of the dominant features of many working-class communities is the single-sex, male peer group or 'street corner gang'.[4] Suttles coined the term 'ordered segmentation' to describe the structure of communities of this sort and suggested that gangs tend to develop out of the high levels of age-group segregation and segregation of the sexes (sometimes, but not invariably, also accompanied by racial and/or ethnic segregation) which tend to be found in communities of this type. The formation of gangs is reinforced by the strong, narrow bonds of local and kin identification often formed by working-class people, especially those lower down in the working-class hierarchy of prestige. This tends to work according to some variation or another of the following pattern. Age segregation tends to involve a pattern of sending children onto the streets to play, unsupervised by adults, at an early age. Such a pattern can be exacerbated and reinforced by poverty, cramped living conditions and a variety of domestic pressures. For its part, sex segregation is conducive to a higher than usual level of objectification mutually by men and women, particularly by the males. It also involves a tendency for mothers to occupy a central position in the family and for girls, by adolescence, to be drawn into the home. One of the consequences of this overall pattern is that adolescent males are left largely to their own devices. As a result, they tend to band into groups which are determined, on the one hand, by ties of kinship and close or common residence, and on the other by the threat posed by the development of parallel 'gangs' in adjacent communities. But why do such gangs fight and what part do they play in the production and reproduction of aggressive masculinity?

One of the crucial social structural determinants of the aggressive masculinity of these rougher sections of the working class – and by 'rough', I am referring to the violent norms they adhere to, not to their levels of material deprivation – appears to be the comparative freedom from adult control experienced by such working-class children and adolescents. The fact that so much of their early socialization takes place on the streets in the company mainly of their age peers means that such children and adolescents tend to interact roughly with each other and to develop dominance hierarchies in which age, strength and physical prowess are crucial determinants. Such a pattern seems to emerge, in part, because children generally depend on adult control for the chance to develop stable internalized restraints over aggression. Where adult control is lacking or applied only intermittently, inconsistently and violently, there are few direct and immediate checks on the emergence of dominance hierarchies of this kind. Indeed, to the extent that adult control involves the use of physical (and verbal) violence, such hierarchies tend to be reinforced.

The relatively low levels of formal education of most members of the working class are conducive to a greater degree of violence and aggressiveness, too. For many, school is an alien environment and relatively few learn in that setting to defer gratification and to strive continuously to reach long-term goals. Their values tend to be inimical to education and characterized by what one might call 'present-centred fatalism'. As a result, they experience formal organizations such as schools as threatening and hostile. The contrast between the relative freedom of the streets and the restrictive controls and regulations of the school is particularly significant in this regard. They also react against schools on account of the educational stress on the abstract and intellectual as opposed to the immediate, concrete and physical, regarding the former as 'effeminate' and only the latter as in strict conformity with the ideas of masculinity they espouse.

Assuming they are able to find work, such tendencies are reinforced by the macho cultures of the workplaces where many working-class males tend to be employed. In fact, the physical strength of their males as workers and fighters is one of the few power resources available to the working class, especially to people at its lower levels. Their macho tendencies are further reinforced by the pattern of male–female segregation and general male dominance in all areas except the immediate family which tends to characterize working-class communities, again especially those which are lower down the social scale. Under such conditions, males are not systematically subjected to 'softening' female pressure. Indeed, to the extent that working-class females grow up to be relatively violent themselves and to expect such behaviour from men, the violent tendencies of the latter tend to be reinforced. Further reinforcement comes from the relative frequency, especially in lower-working-class areas, of feuds and vendettas between families, neighbourhoods and street corner gangs. The people who grow up in communities of this sort tend to have close and narrow bonds of identification with kin, neighbours and their gangs. They also tend to be intolerant of people who are different from them-selves; that is they tend to be racist, sexist and nationalistic in a chauvinistic sort of way. However, their rigidities in these regards tend to go hand in hand with a degree of flexibility as far as bonding in fight situations is concerned. Here, they tend to form temporary *ad hoc* allegiances according to what anthropologists call 'the Bedouin syndrome'. This is based on the following principles: a friend of a friend is a friend; the enemy of a friend is an enemy; the enemy of an enemy is a friend; and the friend of an enemy is an enemy. As a result of bonding in terms of these principles, working-class males are able in a football context, like the Bedouins in their tribal wars, to put quite large 'armies' into the field with little or no formal organization and central control (Cohen and Robins, 1978).

On the Leicester working-class estate where our fieldwork was carried out, there were in the early 1980s three discernible gangs each of which corresponded mainly to a territorial segment of the wider community. These gangs regularly fought each other but tended to unite if one was challenged by or came into conflict with a group from a neighbouring community. On a Saturday, however, groups from all over Leicester and its environs united under the banner of Leicester City FC to 'see off' the challenge represented by the 'invasion' of the city by visiting fans, the core group coming over time to call themselves 'the Baby Squad'. Similarly, fans from the north of England united in the face of an 'invasion' by fans supporting a southern team and, vice versa, southern fans united in the face of an 'invasion' from the north.

Exceptions to this rule are provided by the mutual rivalry of northern teams such as Manchester United and Leeds (which come respectively from Lancashire and Yorkshire with their traditional 'Wars of the Roses' rivalry), and southern teams such as Tottenham and Arsenal (where the principal source of the rivalry appears to be geographical propinquity). Midlands rivalries such as that between Leicester City and Nottingham Forest appear to fall into this category, too. This fluid pattern of unification in conflict, operating through a series of levels, is characteristic of 'ordered segmentation'. At the highest level of segmentation as far as English soccer is concerned, fans from all over the country unite in opposition to some foreign 'foe'. In a sense, this sort of unifying pattern where club and regional ties are sunk momentarily through identification with the national team is typical of football fans more generally and perhaps of non-sports-related patterns of national identification as well. As far as core soccer hooligans are concerned, however, their central interest lies in inflicting physical defeat on common enemies at all the varying levels of segmentation, establishing momentary control over their enemies' territories or repulsing them from their own, and not simply in securing vicarious pleasure from watching their team win the 'mock battle' on the field of play. Some core hooligans are more interested in fighting than football and others are not interested in the game at all, being drawn into confrontations by the reputation and perceived threat posed by particular groups of visiting fans. They are anxious to play their part in defending the honour of their city or town.

Writing of soccer hooliganism among Protestant working-class males in Northern Ireland and making it clear that not all such males engage in violence, Bairner (1995: 17) has written that:

> It is clear that many Protestant working-class communities in Northern Ireland, particularly in Belfast are characterized by segmental bonding. This may help to explain why young men from these communities, when faced with problems emanating from the outside world, react with displays of aggressive behaviour, for example at soccer matches.

This provides support for the Leicester hypothesis. It is important, though, to note that this hypothesis is figurational and does not involve reference to a crude 'segmental–non-segmental dichotomy' but rather to the idea of *degrees* of segmentation which range from the sort of tightly knit forms of sectarian-based community found in Belfast and perhaps in cities such as Glasgow, to the more fluid, open and impersonal forms of bonding which, although these cities contain highly segmented pockets, predominate in larger cities such as London. Nor does the hypothesis depend on the idea that the sorts of estate and other locale-based patterns of hooliganism we discovered in Leicester in the early 1980s were either set in stone or universal. In fact, in the course of the 1980s, the primarily estate-based pattern in Leicester gave way to an extent to a more city-centre-based formation which called itself 'the Baby Squad' and many of whose members met initially in pubs, clubs or the football ground itself.

Nor does the Leicester hypothesis involve the idea that, in some simple, direct and immediate sense, 'ordered segmentation' is a 'cause' and certainly not *the* 'cause' of soccer hooliganism. The contention is rather that such structures appear to play a part in the sociogenesis and reproduction of male adolescent street gangs and a 'violent masculine style', but that, in patriarchal societies, such a style can be generated, reinforced and reproduced in other contexts, too, for example the military, the police and some branches of sport such as boxing and Rugby League. Of course, not all males who grow up in segmented communities become violent, only the dominant ones and their followers. And some of these violent males express their violence in contexts other than football. Furthermore, the presence in an area of communities which approximate closely to ordered segmentation will have effects which radiate out from their immediate vicinity, affecting the culture of local schools and local youth culture more generally, leading even males from middle-class backgrounds – for example, for defensive reasons in schools, pubs, clubs and other public spaces – to take on some of the characteristics of a 'violent masculine style'. One could speak of these effects radiating through a 'figurational field'.

Starting in the 1960s when football hooliganism in England first began to be defined as a 'social problem' in relation to which remedial action was required, the football authorities and the state responded primarily via 'law and order' measures, that is by means of punishments and controls. Such an approach received a substantial measure of media support. However, the consequences of these policies have not been to eradicate soccer hooliganism as intended but mainly unanticipated in at least four ways. More particularly, such policies have tended: (1) to displace the more serious forms of hooligan behaviour outside grounds; (2) to increase the solidarity of hooligan fans; (3) to increase the recruitment into watching football of 'hard men' who want to fight; and (4) to increase the organization and sophistication of these violent males as far as fighting in soccer-related contexts is concerned.

The displacement of soccer hooliganism away from grounds has been neither a simple nor a direct and unilinear process. Each phase in the process has been followed by a widening of controls, first to the immediate vicinities of grounds and then to the major points of entry into the towns and cities where matches are played, for example motorway exits, railway and bus stations. Around the beginning of the 1980s, the core soccer hooligans caught the authorities 'on the hop'. Up until that point, the controls inside grounds had been focused primarily on the 'terraced', standing areas. Starting in about 1980, however, groups such as West Ham United's ICF began to occupy the seated areas of grounds, engaging in hooligan behaviour where the authorities least expected it. The authorities responded by introducing membership schemes of various kinds, leading, once more, to the displacement of hooliganism outside grounds. Expressing it sociologically, one can say that, in the absence of attempts to tackle soccer hooliganism at its *social roots*, that is attempting to transform the forms of masculinity involved in a restraining and civilizing direction, the principal consequence of the imposition and reimposition of punishments and controls was to displace the problem into areas where the controls were, or were perceived by the hooligans as being, weak or non-existent.

It is not unreasonable to suppose that it was partly in conjunction with the end of the first phase of this cycle of displacement, that is in the early and middle 1970s, that English hooligans first began to 'export' their behaviour to continental countries. At that stage, the relative laxity of controls in soccer-related contexts in continental Europe contrasted markedly with the tight and extensive mesh which was being established in England. So did the ready availability of alcohol which was, in most cases, by English standards, cheap. This served to consolidate the English hooligans in their pattern of engaging in soccer hooliganism abroad. However, this 'export' was double edged in the sense that growing numbers of youths in continental countries, perhaps motivated in part by a desire for revenge for defeats inflicted by the English, began to adopt the latter as role models. In this way, soccer hooliganism 'English style' began to be added to the various domestic products of continental countries, coming to form a problem that is increasingly Europe-wide.

The suggestion that, during the 1980s, English hooligans began to act as role models for their counterparts in continental countries should not be taken to imply that the process of modelling was entirely one way. There is reason to believe that the fashion-switch on the English terraces in the 1980s from the 'skinhead' to the 'casual' style was partly based on an attempt to imitate continental, particularly Italian, fashions, a process in which the fans of English – and Scottish – clubs whose teams played most frequently in Europe probably took the lead, namely, in England, clubs such as Arsenal, Manchester United, Tottenham and Liverpool, and in Scotland, clubs such as Glasgow Rangers, Celtic and Aberdeen. Ironically, that the wearing of Barbour jackets seems to be *de rigeur* for the latest wave of Italian hooligans is indicative of Italian fans modelling their behaviour on an English style.

Preliminary theoretical reflections on soccer hooliganism as a world-wide problem

In order to develop a cross-nationally adequate theory of soccer hooliganism what would ideally be required would be a systematic, in-depth cross-national study carried out by an international team of sociologists in terms of a standardized set of concepts and methods and directed towards testing an agreed-on theory or set of theoretical propositions. Such a study would be difficult to set up and administer, expensive to carry out and, given the currently existing lack of paradigmatic unity in sociology, probably difficult if not impossible to arrange. In the absence of any such study, the following hypotheses derived from the Leicester research are offered as a preliminary contribution.

The first thing worthy of note is that much of what I have said in this chapter about English soccer hooliganism is itself based on a set of generalizations. That is, there are local variations within the general English pattern which I have not taken into account and which are produced *inter alia* by such temporally and spatially variable structural sources as: the relative prosperity of particular towns and cities; changes over time in this regard; the demography and peculiar occupational structures of different towns and cities; and their particular traditions and histories, including their particular traditions and histories as far as football and football rivalries are concerned. Such particularities constitute an area which is rich in possibilities for research by social historians and anthropologists who are ideographically inclined. However, and this is a crucial point, a body of studies of that kind will be mainly descriptive and constitute an addition to knowledge merely in a low-level, aggregative sense. They will not make a higher-level contribution to knowledge unless they are tied to a theory.

The need for a combination of theory and observation in order to advance explanatory understanding was recognized by Comte as early as the 1830s (Andreski, 1974: 21–2). Elias (1987), too, stressed the need for the constant cross-fertilization of the theoretical and empirical in research. Of course, what is true of the need for a balance between particularizing and generalizing studies in a single country is multiply compounded when the focus of attention is turned to the world-wide aspects of a phenomenon. That is, an aggregate of merely descriptive studies of hooliganism in particular countries will not constitute much of an increment to knowledge unless such studies are related explicitly to a theory. It is in the hope of contributing to a debate focused towards the production of an agreed-on set of theoretical propositions about soccer hooliganism as an international phenomenon that my concluding remarks in this chapter are addressed. I shall start by discussing what I take to be two dimensions of the problem which one can say with a fair degree of confidence are likely to be internationally shared.

The first of these dimensions of soccer hooliganism which are probably internationally shared is connected with the fact that soccer everywhere, whilst it is work for the professional players and those otherwise occupationally involved, is, for spectators, a leisure pursuit, one of the principal *raisons d'être* of which is the generation of excitement. Whenever a large crowd turns up to watch an exciting leisure event the probability is high that some of its members will abandon their self-controls and behave in disorderly and sometimes violent ways. Ignoring for present purposes the question of the specific situational 'triggers' at sports events which spark violence, it can be said that the seriousness of the violence which takes place is likely to vary between countries and their constituent classes and other subgroups according to their specific trajectories and levels of civilization (and de-civilization). The probability of spectator violence in soccer contexts is also likely to be exacerbated by the degree to which spectators identify with the contending teams and the strength of their emotional investment in and commitment to the victory of the teams they support. Many English fans, for example, claim to be 'passionate' about their teams. In turn, the strength of spectators' emotional investment in the victory of their sides is liable to be a function of the centrality and significance of football in their lives; that is, of whether it is one among a number of sources of meaning and satisfaction for them or just the only one. Spectators for whom identification and emotional involvement with a soccer team are the central source of meaning in their lives are, it is reasonable to suppose, likely, *ceteris paribus*, to be among those most likely to lose their self-control and behave in a disorderly manner in soccer contexts. Further to this, the centrality of soccer in people's lives is likely to differ, *inter alia*, in terms of such variables as their degrees of sexual satisfaction, whether they have a regular partner or are married and, if so, how happily, their levels of education, the degrees to which they are able to obtain satisfaction from their occupational work, and, indeed, whether they are able to find employment at all. However, the people who fight at football for these sorts of reasons are not the 'core' soccer hooligans.

The second dimension of soccer hooliganism which is probably internationally shared relates more directly to the fighting dimensions. It is the fact that, although there are differences between and within countries in this regard, for example between social classes, regional and ethnic groups, and although feminists in some countries have succeeded in denting it to a greater or lesser extent, all societies in the world today are characterized by general forms of male dominance, especially in the public sphere, and hence are permeated by patriarchal values and institutions. Although there are stylistic differences between, for example, Hispanic ideals of *machismo* and North European and North American masculine ideals, a general characteristic of patriarchy is the expectation that males will be aggressive and fight, that an ability and willingness to fight in specific situations, for example for one's country in a war or for one's wife and children if they are attacked, constitutes a key mark of what it means to be a 'man'. Football is a context which is conducive to eliciting patriarchal fighting behaviour because the game itself is a mock fight and because, despite the success of women's football around the world in recent years, the game originated as a male preserve and continues to this day to be permeated by patriarchal values. Of course, this is true not just of soccer but sport in general. Indeed, it is more true of sports such as boxing. But let me return to soccer. What my general argument means is that, whenever large numbers of males, especially males divided by passionate support of rival teams, assemble in the context of an exciting leisure event such as a soccer match, fighting among some of them is a not improbable outcome.

So far in these concluding remarks, I have focused on the regular, *ad hoc* generation of disorderliness and violence in soccer contexts which results from the character and structure of top-level, professional soccer as a type of leisure event. Forms of soccer hooliganism, however, are also generated through the way in which soccer is embedded in wider social contexts. One of the consequences which follow from this is that more or less organized groups of fans – 'firms', 'crews', 'ultras', *torcidas* – sometimes attend matches with the *intention* of fighting other fans and perhaps also the police. Such people can be called 'core' soccer hooligans. It has even been suggested that, in some countries, for example Portugal, club owners sometimes incite and even pay their fans to fight opposing fans. In all these cases, the violence is *premeditated*. The Leicester research suggests that, in England, fans who go to matches intending to fight, that is those who are not satisfied simply with vicariously experiencing 'battle excitement' by watching the 'mock fight' on the field of play, first began to be drawn to the game in substantial numbers in the 1960s. The Leicester research also suggests that the unintentional 'advertising' of the game by the media as a context where exciting and, above all, violent action regularly takes place played an important part in attracting fans of this kind to soccer. This suggests that the forms and extent of media coverage of soccer in particular countries will be one of the influences on their patterns of soccer hooliganism. Highly publicized fighting in soccer contexts also means that soccer can become a context which is attractive to extreme right-wing groups as a place for recruiting street fighters and engaging in a kind of terrorist activity to gain publicity for their cause. Evidence points to a group called 'Combat 18' – combat on behalf of Adolf Hitler (1 = A, 8 = H) – as being involved in the disturbances sparked by English fans in Dublin and Bruges in 1995. There is also evidence of extreme right-wing involvement in soccer hooliganism in Belgium, Germany, Italy and Spain. And in some countries, for example England and Germany, left-wing groups have begun to organize to fight the fascists/racists in soccer contexts.

The Danish, and to some extent, the Scottish experiences of soccer hooliganism provide an instructive contrast. In Denmark towards the end of the 1970s, concern began to be expressed about a growing soccer hooligan problem. However, in direct contradistinction to the punitive 'law and order' approach which was then dominant in England, the Danish authorities responded mainly by means of a strategy of incorporation. More particularly, the hooligans were embraced by officialdom and the media who defined them as 'roligans', a Danish term which translates as 'friendly hooligans' (Peitersen and Holm-Kristensen, 1988). The Danish 'roligans' tend to drink heavily, sometimes to excess, but are proud of their reputation as 'friendly' and have developed mechanisms of self-policing in order to maintain it. The work of Giulianotti (1991) indicates that something similar operates with Scottish fans abroad, though not in domestic contexts. Scottish fans who follow their national side abroad are shown by Giulianotti to be proud of their reputation as boisterous, heavy drinking and peaceful, particularly the fact that it contrasts with the hooligan image of the English. In turn, this Janus-headed character of Scottish fans, that is the violence differential between their behaviour in domestic and international contexts, suggests that one of the preconditions for the relative success of the 'roligan strategy' in Denmark may have been the smallness and relative unity of Danish society, that is the lack of divisions there of a kind that are liable to be productive of variants of 'ordered segmentation' such as those approximated in the divisions in Scotland, particularly Glasgow, between Protestants and Catholics, and in Great Britain between the Scots and the English. These differences are worthy of systematic research. The contrast between Northern Ireland, where sectarian-based football holiganism is a regular occurrence, and the Irish Republic, where fan fights take place more at soccer, rugby and the Gaelic games, is also worthy of closer investigation.

I have shown how the Leicester research suggests that a majority of, if by no means all, English soccer hooligans are working class. Research in Scotland, Belgium, the Netherlands and Italy points in the same direction. More particularly, a study of Scottish soccer 'casuals' found that

> all the evidence points to the fact that 'football casuals' come predominantly from the lower levels of the social scale and are basically working class youths. (In the Edinburgh survey, 75 per cent of the 'casuals' arrested fell into the 'unskilled manual' or 'unemployed' category. None came within the 'managerial-professional' category.)
>
> (Harper, 1989–90)

Similarly, a study of soccer hooliganism in Leuven concluded that 'most of [Belgium's] "hard core" football hooligans...had a short and frustrating school career. Most...come from unstable working-class families. Almost none...have a regular job....Their material situation is poor, the casuals get their expensive clothes by theft' (Van Limbergen et al., 1987: 8). According to the research of Van der Brug in Holland, typical Dutch hooligans tend to resent and resist formal education; are more likely than non-hooligans to be unemployed; have parents who display a relatively tolerant attitude towards the use of violence and aggression; and gain prestige and status from fighting and generally displaying macho characteristics (Van der Brug, 1986). Finally, on the basis of a survey of Bologna 'ultras', Roversi concluded that

> the majority of the young 'ultras' are from the working class. The group in employment contains 169 males and 46 females. In this group the skilled and unskilled blue-collar workers visibly predominate, both compared to workers of other kinds and within the sample as a whole; they represent 80.3% and 51.9% respectively. They are warehousemen, porters, shop-assistants, bricklayers, carpenters but

above all shop-floor workers....It must be emphasized that only 3.9% of the entire sample admitted to being unemployed.

(Roversi, 1994: 359–81)

Despite differences of theoretical orientation and in the categories used, there is substantial consistency between these Scottish, Belgian, Dutch and Italian findings and those of the Leicester research. It would be interesting to discover whether research into soccer hooliganism in other countries reports similar findings.

It is important by way of conclusion to stress that it is unlikely that the phenomenon of soccer hooliganism will be found everywhere to derive from identical social roots. As a basis for further research, it is reasonable to hypothesize that the problem will be fuelled and contoured, *ceteris paribus*, by what one might call the major 'fault-lines' of particular countries. In England that means social class and regional inequalities; in Scotland (at least in Glasgow) and Northern Ireland, religious sectarianism; in Spain, the linguistic subnationalism of the Catalans, Castilians, Gallegos and Basques; in Italy city-based particularism and perhaps the division between north and south as expressed in the formation of 'the Northern League'; and in Germany, the relations between East and West and political groups of the left and right. Religious, ethnic and city-based particularism may well draw in more people from higher up the social scale than tends to be the case in England. Arguably, however, a shared characteristic of all these 'fault-lines' – and, of course, each can overlap and interact with others in a variety of complex ways – is that they are liable to produce structural approximations to 'ordered segmentation' or better, to express it in Elias's terms, 'established-outsider' figurations in which intense 'we-group' bonds and correspondingly intense antagonism towards 'they-groups' or 'outsiders' are liable to develop (Elias, 1994). However, let me make myself perfectly clear. I do not consider this as having the status of anything other than a working hypothesis. It needs to subjected to public discussion and above all tested by means of systematic, theory-guided, cross-national empirical research, and doubtless in that context it will need to be modified, revised and expanded in numerous ways and perhaps even rejected altogether.

7

SPORTS CROWD VIOLENCE IN NORTH AMERICA

Introduction

An idea which remains popular in Britain is that, even though the USA is the most violent of all present-day industrial countries (Gurr, 1989), it nevertheless has sports spectators who are almost uniformly peaceful. This judgement surfaces perhaps most frequently when comparisons are made with soccer spectators in Western Europe, especially the English. In this chapter, I shall endeavour to show by reference to data from Canada as well as the USA that this popular idea is a myth and that North American sports fan behaviour, far from contradicting American 'exceptionalism' in this regard, is fully consistent with the generally greater violence of the USA. I shall also undertake a preliminary exploration of whether sport and society in North America can be said to have undergone a civilizing process in Elias's sense. In order to obtain some purchase on this complex subject, I shall start with an examination of the work of a scholar who is, to my knowledge, one of the few who has attempted to explain American violence in theoretical terms, psychologist Peter Marsh (Marsh et al., 1978; Marsh, 1978).

The theory of ritual aggression

According to Marsh, what he calls 'aggro' is a human, socio-cultural equivalent of the ritualized fights of non-human animals.[1] Such fights are 'intra-specific', and held by ethologists (e.g. Huxley, 1969; Lorenz, 1966; Tinbergen, 1953) to involve inborn restraints. It was Huxley who first used the term 'ritualization' in connection with fighting of this kind, defining it as 'the adaptive formalization or canalization of emotionally motivated behaviour under the telenomic pressure of natural selection' (Huxley, cited in Marsh et al., 1978: 127). Huxley's use of the term 'telenomic' – 'goal-directed' – and its seemingly uncritical embrace by Marsh et al. is possibly indicative of teleology on their part, of their adherence to an 'evolutionistic' as opposed to an 'evolutionary' position in Toulmin's (1972) sense. It is thus a possible indication of a failure on their part to conceptualize biological evolution non-teleologically, that is as a 'blind process' in the manner of Dawkins (1986) and Elias (1994). However, that is less relevant for present purposes than the Marsh group's adaptation to humans of a body of ethological theory which holds that forms of intra-specific conflict which are ceremonial in character have evolved within many species of non-human animals – Lorenz referred to them as 'tournaments'. These are exclusively male and involve trials of strength over territory, access to receptive females and dominance within the group. They are crucially held to be restrained by inborn mechanisms which serve to minimize physical damage, especially the occurrence of death. Marsh comments on the ritualization of aggression as follows, suggesting that football hooliganism is a human equivalent:

> Virtually all species of animal are aggressive...for reasons which appear ...very sound. Firstly, aggression allows for the establishment and maintenance of relatively stable patterns of dominance and submission. Secondly, the process is involved in territorial defence, resulting in optimum dispersal of animals in relation to the resources available in their environment. Some species have more rigidly structured dominance hierarchies than others and there is also great variation in the extent to which animals are territorial. But aggression is common to all and it is one of the things which keeps them in the survival game. At the same time, however, it presents a problem because of its destructive potential. Rivals need to be subdued and trespassers repelled. But if such activities regularly resulted in death and serious wounding a species would soon find itself on the verge of extinction. Not only would the population decline as a result of the increased fatality rate but the basic dominance networks would rapidly fall apart. You can't very well dominate another male if you have killed him. And if, in the process, you have also been seriously wounded then an easy task is presented for ambitious rivals....The solution here is ritualization. By turning the whole conflict business into aggressive ritual, fights became stylized games and displays – things which bear an uncanny resemblance to the events...at the football ground.
>
> (Marsh, 1978: 33–4)

Despite the teleology involved in the repeated use of terms like 'reason' and 'need', Marsh and his colleagues do not fall into the trap of biological reductionism. On the contrary, they make it clear that, 'whilst animals may rely on instinctive patterns of motor co-ordination to direct their ritual displays of threat and submission, [humans] develop social systems which rely on culture for their transmission. But the end result is the same – order' (Marsh *et al.*, 1978: 128).

There is a lot to be said in favour of this line of research. Humans do share with other animals specific physiological processes which are triggered in fight/

160

flight situations. Humans also lack 'instinctive patterns of motor co-ordination to direct their ritual displays of threat and submission'. Beyond this, however, the work of Marsh *et al.* enters murky waters. They are, for example, too dependent on the ideas of Huxley and Lorenz regarding the rareness of intra-species killing among non-human animals. Huntingford and Turner (1987: 46) conclude that 'in spite of the widely accepted picture of animal aggression as a harmless exchange of signals, fierce fighting, injury and killing are quite common features of conflict among members of the same species'. And although they partially accept the picture offered by Huxley and Lorenz, on the basis of their research into chimpanzees Wrangham and Peterson suggested: 'that chimpanzees and humans kill members of neighbouring groups of their own species is…a startling exception to the normal rule for animals' (1997: 63). Marsh and his colleagues also jump too quickly from their discussion of ethological data to soccer hooliganism in order to illustrate their ideas on human forms of ritualized aggression. Strangely, they ignore in this connection Lorenz's (1966: 241–2) suggestion that sport *per se* 'can be defined as a specifically human form of non-hostile combat, governed by the strictest of culturally developed rules'. They thus miss one of the prime sites where the ritualization of aggression can be studied as a social process and muddy their case by focusing on a form of sports deviance, soccer hooliganism, rather than its 'normal' forms.[2] Marsh *et al.* also fail to see that human ritualized fighting, for example the earliest knightly tournaments in Europe (Barber, 1974; Guttmann, 1986), can be exceedingly bloody. This suggests that violence and ritual among humans are not mutually exclusive in the way Marsh *et al.* seem to believe (Dunning *et al.*, 1988). Above all, Marsh and his colleagues fail to see the need to study empirically the ways in which the fighting rituals of humans in sport and elsewhere develop over time and the conditions under which they may be conducive to greater degrees of violence and those under which violent impulses are kept under stricter control. Nowhere is this lack of specifically *sociological* understanding revealed more clearly than in Marsh's solo attempt to deal with the issue of violence in the USA.

Aggro in the USA

According to Marsh, a tradition of ritualized and socially constructive fighting has failed to develop in the USA. He writes:

> Looking for aggro in American history is like looking for the proverbial needle in an equally proverbial haystack. Even today, Americans find the concept difficult to handle. They have little experience of it and little in their past to give any idea of the principles on which it is based. All of which might go some way towards explaining why the USA is in such a violent mess.
>
> (Marsh, 1978: 81)

Implicit in this argument is a possible explanation for the absence of direct equivalents of soccer hooliganism in the USA. That is the case because, according to Marsh, soccer hooliganism is one of Britain's principal forms of aggro. If it is true that there is an absence of aggro traditions in the USA – and there is a wealth of evidence which suggests that Marsh is wrong on this score – then it is reasonable to deduce from Marsh's arguments that it is unlikely that phenomena such as soccer hooliganism could or ever will develop there. In other words, contrary to a common American perception, if Marsh is right, soccer hooliganism in Britain and other European countries does not by itself provide evidence of a process of 'decivilization'. On the contrary, the logic of Marsh's case seems to be that, since they usually only involve violence of a ritualized and socially constructive kind, aggro in general and soccer hooliganism in particular are evidence of the more 'civilized' character of European countries. It is the USA, because it lacks traditions of aggro, which is *really* 'uncivilized', which, in Marsh's words, is in a *really* 'violent mess'. This argument is implausible. What evidence and reasoning led Marsh to conclude that there are no equivalents of aggro in the USA?

It is Marsh's contention that America is unique regarding its levels of violence. He sets forth his reasons for reaching this judgement in the following terms: 'The history of violence in America,' he says, 'is quite unlike the history of violence elsewhere in the world. It reflects what can happen when men set out to radically reshape their modes of living and attempt to create new worlds from scratch' (Marsh, 1978: 82). In other words, according to Marsh 'American exceptionalism' in relation to violence is an unintended consequence of the USA being what he regards as a 'socially engineered' society, one born of social protest, migration, and subsequently colonial revolt, in which an attempt was made to create a social order which would not reproduce what Americans saw as the iniquities of European life. Marsh also argues that the pioneers did not migrate to the 'New World' as tribes or communities but as individuals fired by personal ambitions and Utopian dreams. 'They came,' he suggests, 'without social order and, from very early on, the order of nature was devalued by the fact that guns were in the hand of every man and boy' (Marsh, 1978: 82). In that context, what Marsh calls 'unstructured mob violence' tended to develop – he fails to see that, although disorderly, it is far from lacking structure in the sense of regularity – and the only means available for combating it was the almost equally (in Marsh's unsociological sense) 'unstructured' vigilante tradition. In Marsh's words once more:

> The makeshift response to violence within the early American communities was to throw up...bands of vigilantes...charged with the unenviable job of trying to introduce some sense of order.... But if anything, they probably made the situation worse. In fact, Americans now suffer not only from the frontier tradition but also

from the vigilante tradition which still finds its expression in the outrageous thuggery of groups such as the Ku Klux Klan.

(Marsh, 1978: 82)

Another salient feature of American history, according to Marsh, is that the European upper-class tradition of ritualized duelling did not spread there. In order to support this contention, he cites Baldick's (1965) quotation of de Tocqueville who wrote in 1831 that:

> In Europe one hardly ever fights a duel except in order to say that one has done so; the offence is generally a sort of moral stain which one wishes to wash away, and which most often is washed away at little expense. In America one only fights to kill; one fights because one sees no hope of getting one's adversary condemned to death. There are very few duels, but they almost always end fatally.
>
> (Baldick, cited in Marsh, 1978: 81)

De Tocqueville, of course, could not possibly have foreseen that, whilst in countries such as Britain and France the upper-class tradition of duelling increasingly declined with the rise of the middle class, in Germany social development followed a different course. More particularly, in Germany in the last quarter of the nineteenth century duelling of a highly ritualized and barbaric kind increased in frequency and significance, playing an important part in integrating the rising middle class into what Elias called the *satisfaktionsfähig* establishment of the Wilhelmine empire (Elias, 1996: 50ff.). This was an establishment orientated around a code of honour in which duelling and the demanding and giving of 'satisfaction' occupied pride of place. The fact that Marsh failed to take this development into account is testimony to the historical and sociological weakness of the argument he constructs.

This is not to say that Marsh's argument is entirely without merit but rather that it is weak on balance. There are sociological reasons for thinking that he may be right in believing that, at the present level of knowledge, attempts to impose 'Utopias' can misfire. This is suggested by aspects of the history not only of the USA but also of other countries where revolution played a key part, for example China and Russia. There is also reason to believe that attempts to purge human relations of violence can unintentionally have the opposite effect. That is perhaps especially the case at the present level of knowledge when practitioners of the human sciences lack a degree of agreed-on understanding sufficient to enable them to persuade powerful groups that measures based largely on punishments and controls are more likely to increase than reduce violence (Dunning *et al.*, 1988; Murphy *et al.*, 1990). This argument is not inconsistent with Marsh's theory. However, Marsh's overall argument about violence in the USA seems to depend on overgeneralization in two respects: first, on the basis of a rather inadequate theory; and second, on the basis of sketchy data. Where, for example, is his evidence that the USA is unique regarding violence? Would one not expect it to display certain similarities in this regard to other societies colonized by Europeans, such as Australia, Canada, New Zealand and South Africa, to say nothing of the Hispano-Catholic and also originally colonial societies in South and Central America? What about the part played by slavery and the mass migration of different national and ethnic groups in contributing to the USA's patterns of violence? And perhaps more importantly from a method-ological standpoint, is it sociologically meaningful to compare American history since the seventeenth century with the histories of European societies over exactly the same stretch of time? Since the latter are considerably older, would it not be more a case of comparing 'like with like' to compare American history and development since the seventeenth century with European history over a longer time? Furthermore – and this is implicit in de Toqueville's remarks about duelling and Marsh's discussion of the vigilante tradition in the USA – would it not be sociologically more revealing to focus upon trajectories of state formation? If one does that it becomes clear, even at the present level of knowledge, that in the seventeenth, eighteenth and nine-teenth centuries what became the USA was a society experiencing stages of state formation more comparable with the stages experienced in Western Europe in the Middle Ages. There, too, states were initially weak (Elias, 1994) and it was common for people to carry arms. Medieval Europe also experi-enced recurrent blood feuds and the regular formation of 'mobs' and vigilante gangs. Unlike the USA, however, the medieval societies of Western Europe were ruled by warriors (and priests) and experienced frequent bloody wars. By contrast, even though the higher echelons of the American military have come in the course of the twentieth century, as Mills (1956) has shown, to be incorporated into the national 'power elite', the USA has never been subject to anything so closely approximating exclusive military rule with the conse-quence that relatively peaceful, relatively secular and relatively democratic political processes have tended to prevail.

Similarly, the relatively early achievement of dominance in the USA by bourgeois groups helps to explain the hegemony in the USA of *laissez-faire* values. That, in turn, together with the temporally contracted occurrence of state formation, helps to explain why the federal state has failed to penetrate so deeply into the American social fabric as has been generally the case in Western Europe and why groups who campaign for the rights of individual citizens to carry arms remain considerably more powerful than their European counterparts. However, perhaps the central weakness of this appli-cation by Marsh of his theory of 'aggro' to the USA is that he fails to consider the elements of 'aggro' that have been documented in the behaviour of American street gangs.[3] Marsh briefly notes this possibility but dismisses it peremptorily on account of the racialization of gang warfare (Marsh, 1978: 101). Given his equation of ritualization with the diminution of serious violence, perhaps the greater levels of violence that American street gangs are known recurrently to engage in led him to fail to take them into account since to have done so would have rapidly brought him face to face with his theory's contradictions? Nor – and this is perhaps even more surprising – does he follow the lead of Lorenz (1967) and consider the development of American sports as forms of 'aggro', that is as arenas within which aggressive behaviour can, usually within controlled limits, be expressed in a socially tolerated and constructive way.

It thus appears that, even though he does not fall into the trap of biological reductionism, Marsh's application of an a priori theory modelled on the, in part, dated findings of ethologists is not very helpful for illuminating the balance of similarities and differences between the forms and levels of sports crowd violence and their history in Europe and the USA. A critical examination of his application of this theory does, though, suggest that differences in the processes and trajectories of state formation on either side of the Atlantic, particularly the degree to which state formation in the USA has been, comparatively speaking, temporally compressed, may offer clues in this regard.

The history of sports crowd violence in the USA

The account which follows is not based on primary research. It has been pieced together from secondary sources and supplemented by reference, first, to such newspaper material as has come to my attention and, second, to suggestions made by North American colleagues. It is offered in the hope of stimulating North American sociologists and historians to carry out research into long-term trends in sports crowd violence in Canada and the USA which probes the issues involved more deeply than I have been able to do and which avoids the mistakes which I, as an Englishman writing about their countries, am bound to make.

In 1968, Goodhart and Chataway wrote: 'In America which is so often characterized as a land bubbling with violence, sporting hooliganism, apart from racial disturbances, seems to be largely unknown' (Goodhart and Chataway, 1968: 144). The 'racial disturbances' they were referring to were the fights between black and white youths which accompanied the Civil Rights struggle and led to the banning of high-school 'night matches' in many parts of the USA (Guttmann, 1978: 132). Apart from these, they argued, crowd troubles at American sports events were few and far between. However, in 1977, less than ten years after Goodhart and Chataway made their pronouncement, an American journalist went so far as to claim that 'Fear and loathing in the stands is certainly not a new phenomenon, but mass recreational violence has never been so rampant in the sports arenas of America' (Greenberg, 1977). This judgement was backed by sociologists. For example, Edwards and Rackages suggested, also in 1977, that 'sport-related violence flourishes today in crisis proportions...violence has indeed increased and become more malicious – particularly over the last three years' (Edwards and Rackages, 1977: 222). And Yiannakis *et al.* reported in 1978 that:

> During the past few years, crowd and player violence in sport has increased to such an extent that it has drawn the attention of the mass media, school officials and academicians and resulted in considerable debate regarding its antecedents and consequences. A specific type of violence, namely player violence, has even been taken up by American courts. This burgeoning of violence has also prompted the formation of special commissions at both local and national level to investigate its causes.
>
> (Yiannakis *et al.*, 1979: 216)

That none of these authors was referring simply to a short-term trend is suggested by Young who wrote in 1988 of an 'emergent', newly perceived 'social problem'. He was referring to the 'evidence of a growing spectrum of forms and frequencies of sports crowd disorder in [the North American] context' (Young, 1988: 383).[4] Let me examine some of this evidence.

The earliest reference to disorderly behaviour by an American sports crowd I have come across dates from 4 July 1900. The events described in the following account are reported as having taken place in Chicago at a baseball match between the Chicago Cubs and the Philadelphia Phillies:

> Thousands of gunslinging Chicago Cubs fans turned a Fourth of July doubleheader into a shoot-out at the OK Corral, endangering the lives of players and fellow spectators. Bullets sang, darted, and whizzed over the players' heads as the rambunctious fans fired round after round whenever the Cubs scored against the gun-shy Philadelphia Phillies. The visiting team was so intimidated it lost both games of the twin bill at Chicago's West Side Grounds.
>
> In the sixth inning of the opener, the Cubs triggered an explosive six-run rally as guns and firecrackers blasted away from all sides of the ball park. When the inning finally ended, the shell-shocked Philly outfielders emerged from a haze of gunpowder smoke that hung over the field like a battleground pall.
>
> In the second game, the Cubs tied the score in the bottom of the ninth as the fans cheered them on with a blaze of gunfire. First, the left field bleachers let loose with a salvo. Then the right field bleachers responded. Hundreds of spectators in the grandstand were so happy they began shooting holes in the roof, causing flying splinters to shower down on their heads.
>
> By the bottom of the twelfth inning, ammunition was running short for many fans, so they pounded their seats with the butts of their guns. But others, who were still well-supplied with bullets, fired

a fuselage to rattle Phils hurler Al Orth and his team-mates. The barrage worked. Philadelphia misplayed two balls for an error and an infield hit. The strain began to show on Orth. Barry McCormick laid down a sacrifice bunt but that was fielded by Orth. But the nettled Orth threw wildly past first, allowing the winning run to score.

When the Cubs won, one armed-to-the-teeth fan stood up and shouted to his cohorts, 'Load! Load at will! Fire!' and they did. The last remaining ammo was spent in one booming volley. Said *The Daily Inter Ocean…*: 'The actions of the spectators and the noise of the revolver shots reminded one of a pleasant little afternoon – at a lynching bee'.

(Nash and Zullo, 1986: 133–4)

Assuming this to be an accurate report, I would surmise that what was being described was a pre-arranged action by Chicago fans designed to intimidate the opposing team and enhance their own team's chances of winning. We are not told whether there were any injuries and, if so, how many and how serious they were. It would seem unlikely that the use of guns on such a scale could have passed off with no injuries at all. More germane for present purposes, however, is that the kind of behaviour reported here, especially the use of guns, is consistent with the picture of the USA as a relatively violent society. Nevertheless there is evidence which points to the occurrence of a civilizing process in American sport.

The development of American sport as a civilizing process

To my knowledge, the sorts of research into the development of sport in North America which would be necessary properly to test the theory of civilizing processes in that context have not been carried out. Indeed, the popularity in the USA and Canada of sports such as 'gridiron' football could be taken as evidence for the view that North American society remains very violent and in that sense 'uncivilized'. However, although neither the violence of American society nor the violence of some of its sports can be seriously denied, the evidence suggests that the present-day gridiron game has grown out of antecedents which were more violent. In the 1890s, for example, not only tackling and blocking but also 'slugging' – the punching of opponents – were apparently accepted as legitimate. As a player of that time is reported to have said: 'Mostly [the players] stood bolt upright and fought it out hammer and tongs, tooth and nail, fists and feet', adding that 'arguments followed almost every decision that the referee made' (Gardner, 1974: 99). Methodically thought-out 'mass plays' such as the 'flying wedge' also formed part of American football then. This tactic involved two lines of players joined to form a V, each player except the foremost hanging on to the one in front and all of them charging at full speed with the ball-carrier protected in their midst. Hapless opponents were supposed to bounce off the flying wedge or be flattened when they tried to halt its progress. In 1905 alone, it seems, no fewer than eighteen college players were killed and a further 159 seriously injured as a result of tactics of this kind. President Roosevelt was apparently so concerned that he convened a meeting of representatives from Harvard, Princeton and Yale, admonishing them that 'brutality and foul play should receive the same summary treatment as the man who cheats at cards' (Gardner, 1974: 100). Having apparently seen a photograph of a player injured in a Pennsylvania–Swarthmore match, he also threatened to prohibit the game by federal decree (Riesman and Denney, 1971: 167).

The response to Roosevelt's intervention and the more general climate of growing concern was the legitimization of the forward pass, an innovation which marked a decisive break in the development of American football away from its roots in English rugby – a game in which only backwards passing is allowed – and which simultaneously opened up the game and eliminated what Gardner called 'the ponderous bulldozing of the mass plays' (Gardner, 1974: 100). It was also around this time, it seems, that players began to wear the sorts of protective equipment characteristic of American football today. Such a line of development can be said to have been 'civilizing' in that it afforded greater protection for the players. However, it also permitted the retention of a physically violent game whilst at the same time introducing the possibility of new forms of injury – for example, from the clash of helmeted heads.

Changes in interracial behaviour as black Americans have become increasingly integrated into major professional sports also seem broadly consistent with the occurrence of a civilizing process, more particularly with the view that a decrease in the incidence of violent behaviour in and around American sports has taken place as the twentieth century has progressed. Take the case of boxing. When Jack Johnson defeated James Jeffries in Reno, Nevada, in 1910 to become the first black world heavyweight champion, the response in many parts of the USA was extremely violent. According to Guttmann:

> In Houston, Charles Williams openly celebrated Johnson's triumph and a white man 'slashed his throat from ear to ear'; in Little Rock, two blacks were killed by a group of whites after an argument about the fight in a streetcar; in Roanoke, Virginia, a gang of white sailors injured several blacks; in Wilmington, Delaware, a group of blacks attacked a white and whites retaliated with a 'lynching bee'; in Atlanta a black ran amok with a knife; in Washington...two whites were fatally stabbed by blacks; in New York, one black was beaten to death and scores were injured; in Pueblo, Colorado, thirty people were injured in a race riot; in Shreveport, Louisiana, three blacks were killed by white assailants. Other murders or injuries were

reported in New Orleans, Baltimore, Cincinnati, St. Joseph, Los Angeles, Chattanooga, and many other smaller cities and towns.

(Guttmann, 1986: 119)

Interracial violence – on the part of players – was also apparently common in the early history of American baseball. For example, it seems that the practice of deliberately 'spiking' the legs of basemen with the 'feet first slide' was introduced in the late nineteenth century in an attempt to cripple black players as part of a more general attempt to remove them from the game (Boyle, 1971: 261; see also Chapter 8 of the present volume). In the meantime, as one might expect in a former slave society in which racial prejudice and inequality remain deeply rooted, interracial violence has not disappeared from American sport. There were, for example, interracial disturbances in 1937 when Joe Louis became world heavyweight champion by defeating the German, Max Schmeling (Guttman, 1986: 132). Evidently common pride as Americans and hostility towards a representative of Nazi Germany were not sufficiently strong to overcome the anti-black feelings of the whites involved. And as I noted earlier, a spate of interracial fighting at high-school night matches accompanied the black push for greater equality in the 1960s (Guttmann, 1978: 132). It appears, however, that interracial violence in an American sports context has never recurred on the same nation-wide scale or with such ferocity as in 1910, and it accordingly seems reasonable to suppose that a greater number of white Americans are now willing to a degree to tolerate, not only more racially integrated sports, but also black supremacy in such contexts. They also seem more willing to countenance the individual and collective expression by blacks of pride in black sporting achievements. In short, there seems to have taken place a moderate civilizing of black–white relations in the sphere of American sports.

To speak of a limited civilizing process as possibly having taken place in the context of American sports is not to deny the continuing and perhaps growing problem there of player and spectator violence pointed to by Young (1988). In 1983, for example, the Miller Lite survey on 'American Attitudes Towards Sports' reported that:

Three out of every five Americans believe that violence is a serious problem in sports today, while half say fights between players lessen their enjoyment of the game. Seventy per cent believe that sports violence is harmful to young viewers.

(Coakley, 1990: 140)

The reference here to 'sports today' seems to be indicative of a widespread belief that American sports were less violent in the past. However, to my knowledge, research designed to establish whether that was the case has not been carried out. Nor has an attempt been made to ascertain whether such a belief is, in part, a consequence of a civilizing shift in people's threshold of repugnance regarding violence and hence of a lowering in their tolerance towards forms of behaviour such as fist-fights which previously would have been more widely regarded as acceptable. What is certain is that spectator violence continues to occur on a substantial scale in the USA and that, consequently, the European belief that American sports spectators are invariably orderly and peaceful is a myth.

Sports spectator violence in North America today

In 1975, Lewis collated the number of 'riots' at sports events reported in six American newspapers in the years 1960–72. He discovered that a total of 313 'riots', involving seventeen deaths, were reported in that period, an average of twenty-six 'riots' per year. The sport-by-sport breakdown was: baseball, 97; (gridiron) football, 66; basketball, 55; (ice) hockey 39; boxing, 19; horse-racing, 11; motorcycle and car racing, 10; golf, 4; soccer, 3; wrestling, 3; athletics, 2; tennis, 2; and air sports, 2 (Guttmann, 1986: 162). Lewis was not crystal clear in his definition of a 'riot' or in the criteria used in the construction of his breakdown. It is accordingly impossible to reach judgements on the scale and seriousness of the events he reported. Nor did he cite newspaper descriptions detailing what reporters perceived as having taken place in particular cases. However, the sorts of violent crowd disturbances that take place at sports events in the USA are illustrated by the following report of what transpired at a gridiron match at the Schaefer Stadium, Foxboro, Massachusetts, on 18 October 1977:

> The game started at 9 pm…but the fans began drinking their dinners hours earlier *en route* to Schaefer Stadium and in the parking lots outside the Foxboro, Massachusetts, sport complex. By game time, all the participants – the New England Patriots, the New York Jets, the ABC Monday Night Football Crew and the crowd – were primed for action. There was plenty of it. While the Patriots were routing the Jets, 41–7, the jubilant fans turned on each other, on the cops and out onto the field. The game was interrupted half a dozen times as eleven rowdies, chased by security guards, tried out the Astro-Turf. Twenty-one fans were arrested for disorderly conduct, eighteen were taken into protective custody for public intoxication, two were booked for throwing missiles, two for assault and battery and one for possession of a dangerous weapon. One fan stole another's wheelchair and was arrested for larceny. Thirty spectators were taken to hospital with cuts and bruises, one was stabbed and two died of heart attacks. Foxboro policeman, Tom Blaisdell, sustained a dislocated jaw and a concussion, and while a local sheriff was administering mouth-to-mouth resuscitation to a coronary victim in the stands, a drunken fan

urinated on them both. 'It was a tough game', said Foxboro police chief, John Gaudett as he reviewed that night's blotter. 'But I've seen even worse.'

(Greenberg, 1977: 217)

It may not be without significance that the Foxboro police chief claimed to have seen 'even worse' incidents. Moreover, since the behaviour of the disorderly fans in this case seems to have been related to the victory of the local side, it seems reasonable to conclude that this was an example of what one might call a 'celebratory riot'.

That sports-related disorders in the USA do not take place solely in the immediate context of matches is suggested by the events described in *The Times* as having taken place in Pittsburgh, Pennsylvania, in 1971 following the triumph of the Pittsburgh Pirates in the final of that year's baseball 'World Series':

> An extraordinary orgy of destruction, looting and sexual excess took hold of Pittsburgh, Pennsylvania…following the unexpected victory of the Pittsburgh Pirates baseball team….During nearly ten hours of wild, drunken celebration around the city, men and women indulged in public love-making and nudity. More than 100 people were injured and about 100 others arrested. Some 30 shops were looted and another 30 damaged. Two incidents of sexual assault occurred in full view of hundreds of celebrating fans who, according to eye-witness reports, cheered the assailants and made no attempt to help the victims. There was scattered gunfire during the rampage and one of those admitted to hospital was a middle-aged man suffering from a gunshot wound.
>
> (*The Times*, 19 October 1971)

Young refers to such disorders as 'post-event riots'. The following list (supplied by Kevin Young) gives an idea of the frequency and geographical spread of their occurrence since the late 1960s: October 1968, Detroit; October 1971, Pittsburgh; January 1975, Pittsburgh; November 1983, Toronto; October 1984, Detroit; May 1986, Montreal; November 1986, Hamilton, Ontario; June 1990, Detroit; June 1992, Chicago; February 1993, Dallas; June 1993, Montreal; June 1993, Chicago; and June 1994, Vancouver. The sports involved were baseball, basketball, (ice) hockey, and (gridiron) football. There was one death in Detroit in 1984, eight in the same city in 1990, two in Chicago in 1993 and one in Vancouver in 1994. There were over a thousand arrests in Chicago in 1992 and two police officers were shot and fourteen fires were started.

The Vancouver riot in 1994 is worth exploring in greater detail. It is estimated that some 70,000 persons were involved. However, according to police

171

and media estimates, only one-half of 1 per cent of this total took part directly in the trouble. The mean age of the troublemakers was 19.7 years. Over 80 per cent were male and about half those charged were unemployed. Further research would be necessary to ascertain whether such a social profile is typical of the participants in North American celebratory riots in general.

The reported occurrence of twelve deaths in conjunction with this selection of North American riots is dwarfed by the larger number of soccer-related deaths which occurred at Heysel (thirty-nine) and Bradford (fifty-five) in 1985 and at Hillsborough (ninety-six) in 1989. Of these, however, only the Heysel tragedy was directly related to hooliganism and, even in that case, the collapse of a defective wall was a major contributory factor to the deaths.[5] And despite the extreme male chauvinism and sexism of many of the fans involved, rape and sexual assault are not usually reported as accompaniments of soccer hooliganism in Europe.

A study of the 'Grey Cup' festivities undertaken by Listiak *et al.* in Hamilton, Ontario, in 1976 sheds light on aspects of what one might call the North American tradition of 'celebratory rioting'. Although US teams sometimes take part in it, the Grey Cup is the Canadian equivalent of the 'Super Bowl'. Listiak and his co-workers compared the behaviour they observed in a number of middle-class 'lounges' with what they saw in lower-class 'bars' in Hamilton when that city hosted the Grey Cup game. They describe behaviour in the middle-class 'lounges' as follows:

> The atmosphere of these establishments was super-charged with a high degree of gregarious behaviour and boisterous conduct, and the level of this legitimate deviance continued to rise as the evening and the drinks flowed on. Spontaneous shouts and yells and horn-blowing emanated from various parts of the bar, competing with each other in…volume.…Males engaged in spirited camaraderie and backslapping types of behaviour. Sporadically spirited fights would break out.
>
> (Listiak *et al.*, 1976: 416)

By contrast, 'the whole lower-class bar scene could be described as "business as usual"'. That is, more serious 'fights broke out every hour or so'. Guttmann comments on this difference thus:

> The fights…in the lounge were unusual events associated with a special kind of celebration while the brawls in the bar were 'business as usual'.…[I]t is likely that the disadvantaged members of every society tend to express their frustrations in direct forms of deviance while the advantaged make greater use of the Saturnalia-like opportunities of the institutionalized 'time-out'. Since football combines primitive elements with a sophisticated complex of teamwork and

172

strategy, it seems especially well suited for its dual function as a model of modern social organization and…an occasion for atavistic release.

(Guttmann, 1978: 135)

This conceptualization is perceptive but sociologically problematic. It is doubtful whether the owners and workers in the middle-class lounges would have regarded the 'spirited fights' and presumably also the broken glasses which regularly accompany boisterous behaviour of this kind as 'legitimate'. Given that, a term such as 'tolerated deviance', the idea that boisterous behaviour is acceptable on certain occasions as long as it does not exceed certain bounds, is more adequate for describing the form of middle-class behaviour described here. (My guess is that the 'spirited fights', assuming they were 'real' and not 'mock fights', would, in all probability, have been regarded as breaking those bounds.) These authors also fail to stress that what was observed in both lounges and bars were class variations on a common theme – patriarchal norms of masculinity which continue to operate in North America despite the limited success of feminists in challenging them and the fact that proportionately more females attend major (i.e. male) sports events in North America than characteristically happens in Europe. They also failed to see that, independently of social class, playing with, testing and in that sense deviating from norms seems to be a common ingredient of many forms of leisure sociability (see Chapter 1). More importantly still, Guttmann's behaviouristic idea that deviance stems solely from frustration misses the fact that, again independently of class, a hedonistic quest for enjoyable excitement is often expressed in social deviance. That certainly appears to be the case as far as European soccer hooliganism is concerned. It is with a comparison of North American forms of sports spectator violence and soccer hooliganism that I shall conclude this chapter.

A comparison of North American sports crowd violence with soccer hooliganism

Forms of sports fan violence which stem basically from frustration are observable at soccer and other sports in Britain. Examples are disorders triggered by a team losing an important match where the atmosphere is highly charged or because fans are dissatisfied with the way their club is run. The latter happens in North America, too. A recent example occurred in December 1995, when Cleveland Browns fans, upset over the announcement by owner, Art Modell, that he was moving the club to Baltimore, ripped up banks of seating in the 'bleachers' and hurled them onto the pitch (*Independent*, 19 December 1995). Celebratory riots are observable in Britain as well, though they are usually smaller in scale. In Britain, disorders of this kind do not usually involve much more than an incursion onto the field of play which is not usually violent in intent, although violence can occur if the authorities overreact. However, soccer hooliganism in Europe typically does not take either of these forms. Rather, it involves groups of young adult and adolescent males who have chosen soccer as a context in which to fight. For them, ability and willingness to fight, the expression of courage, toughness and physical prowess in a confrontation, usually but not always with similarly motivated and consenting fans who support the other side, together with the display of loyalty towards their 'mates' are sources of emotional arousal and ego-enhancing prestige and hence enjoyable. In seeking out and initiating fights, such males contravene the dominant norms of masculinity which stress that one should be able 'to defend oneself' if attacked but not start a fight.

The generally macho climate of English soccer appears to be a reason why such males have come to use the game in this country as an arena for their 'war-games'(see Chapter 6). Also, the frequency of away-match travel since the 1950s regularly brings despised and hated rivals into one's town, hence providing a target for attack. Reciprocally, away travel to support one's side regularly provides opportunities to 'invade' another city or town. For these fans, spice is added to the occasion by the element of risk involved in the confrontation with rival supporters. It is also added by the fact that their activities are socially disapproved of and illegal and hence draw down the attentions of the police. The quest for pleasurable excitement and ego-enhancing prestige in a soccer context – many such males receive positive pleasure and reinforcement from being defined by the media and other representatives of 'respectable' society as 'folk devils', as reviled and feared 'outsiders' – help to explain why they are deeply committed to hooligan activities in a soccer context and why they are difficult to dislodge. Fighting in match-related contexts acts for them as a stimulant and is high up in their value-scale.

Basic to the habitus and values of these males is their attachment to an 'aggressive masculine style'. Their habitus, norms and values appear similar in many ways to those of the street gangs in the USA described in that rich body of sociological literature which started most significantly with Thrasher (1936) and the Chicago School. Indeed, the behaviour of English soccer hooligans seems to conform in many ways to the present-centred hedonism described by Cohen (1955). In short, soccer hooliganism can be understood in part as involving the usurpation of a major professional sport by structurally generated equivalents of street gangs. The government, those who own and control the clubs, and the people in charge of English soccer nationally have so far proved unsuccessful in their attempts to eliminate the 'hooligan challenge'. The same is true of Europe generally. The authorities may have more of less succeeded, by means of a massive police presence on match days and a battery of stifling controls, in making it difficult – though by no means impossible – for hooligans to fight inside stadia. However, they have failed to dislodge them from the total context of the game. Would it be stretching the point too far to suggest of English soccer hooliganism that it is as if the street gangs of, say, Los Angeles, Chicago or New York had chosen American football or baseball as a context in which to fight and usurped large sections of the physical and social space occupied by these sports?

That gangs in the USA have occasionally been involved in sports-related violence is suggested by the public inquiry which took place into the riots which occurred in Detroit following the final of the 1984 World Series and which found that the trouble had been caused, not by baseball fans, but by what the report called 'street kids' (Williams, 1986: 8). Since the inquiry did not mention the 'street kids' as seeking out opposing fans or, indeed, as having attended the match, it would seem that the Detroit riots of 1984 only resembled 'English-style' soccer hooliganism superficially. The 'street kids' were presumably taking advantage of a 'celebratory riot' in order to pilfer, loot and mug.

That looting is a common feature of these North American sports-related disorders is suggested by what Mayor Daley said in commenting on the Chicago disorders of June 1992: 'When you celebrate something in America, you break a window and grab something. When people have an excuse to loot, they loot' (*Chicago Herald*, 16 June 1992). That a degree of premeditation, co-ordination and planning is also sometimes involved is indicated by a report on the 1993 Montreal disorders which referred to 'organized groups of looters us[ing] the Stanley Cup celebration as a screen for their activities' (*Globe and Mail*, 12 October 1993). Commenting on the Vancouver riot in 1994, a reporter in the same newspaper wrote: 'Police officials confirm that the busiest looters carried cellular telephones to alert each other to the best pickings but deny the chaos was masterminded by criminals' (*Globe and Mail*, 3 November 1994). This provides confirmation of the degree of organization involved in such rioting but suggests, contrary to what is presumably a widespread North American belief, that criminal conspiracy is not involved in these events. Looting is also a common accompaniment of soccer hooliganism in England. However, the similarities between it and North American celebratory riots appear to end there. It is worth enquiring why soccer-hooligan-type spectator disorders have not emerged in top-level North American sports on any significant scale.

In common with other Western industrial societies, the USA and Canada have highly publicized mass spectator sports, some of which, especially baseball, (gridiron) football and (ice) hockey, have a pronounced macho emphasis. The USA also has a long-established tradition of street gangs, and the dominant norms of masculinity – the 'John Wayne' image – lay stress on fighting and ability to 'handle oneself'. Why, then, have forms of sports crowd disorderliness more akin to soccer hooliganism not developed? Only systematic research could provide a definitive answer to this question. It is nevertheless possible to speculate about conceivable reasons. Some clues appear to be provided by Listiak *et al.*'s research.

Listiak *et al.* reported a highly charged atmosphere in the middle-class bars in Hamilton which he studied on the occasion of the 1976 Grey Cup game.

By contrast, the atmosphere he and his colleagues observed in their sample of lower-class bars was more low key. This suggests a level of interest in the match among these lower-class Canadians that was lower than among their middle-class counterparts. Perhaps it stretched as far as watching the game on the bar TV but not as far as attending the stadium. This suggests that the lower classes in Canada and the USA may be more excluded, for example on financial grounds, and self-excluding from national sports, particularly as attending spectators, than their counterparts in Britain. As far specifically as blacks are concerned, the high profile achieved by black stars in recent years, together with the opportunities for college attendance which are provided by college coaches targeting ghetto high schools as rich sources of likely recruits, may to some extent have countered this, helping to foster the myth that, for blacks, sport forms an avenue of upward social mobility of substantial proportions, not just for a few. However, assuming that it can be substantiated empirically, such a pattern of exclusion and self-exclusion from national sports by groups other than blacks may be connected with the peculiarities of state formation in the USA. More particularly, the more highly developed welfare state in Britain, coupled with the tradition of state intervention to compensate for the vagaries of the 'free market' – both of which survive, although they have been severely dented by the application of 'Thatcherite' (and 'New Labour'?) poli-cies since 1979 – may have helped to integrate more sections of the working class into the overall national consensus, thereby incorporating more of them more fully into sports such as soccer. In the USA by contrast, federal and state policies based to a greater degree on *laissez-faire* values may have resulted in a greater proportion of the lower classes being less incorporated into dominant values and, consequently, less integrated into national sports. In its turn, a consequence of this may have been to insulate American professional sports to a greater degree from lower-class patterns of fighting.

What is more certain is that the high cost of tickets for major sports in North America will act as a deterrent to lower-class attendance. Then again, the longer distances between teams and the cities they represent seem likely to inhibit fans travelling away (Coakley, 1998). In any event, regular away-match travel does not seem to be such a central part of the culture of sports spectatorship in North America as it has become in Britain and continental Europe. As a result, opposing fans – a ready-made, usually highly visible, group of 'outsiders', a readily identifiable 'enemy' or 'target' – are not so frequently in evidence at matches. Finally, as Young (1988: 371) has suggested, the *relative* lack of a national press in the USA and Canada[6] and the fact that there are more major crimes for reporting on TV mean that violent sports-related inci-dents tend to be reported only locally, hence helping, on the one hand, to sustain a public perception of the sports context as largely trouble-free and, on the other, from the standpoint of potential 'hooligans' to devalue sports as a site for 'exciting action'.

However, there are indications which suggest that, should a tradition of travelling regularly to away matches become firmly established in North American sports and should, in that context, minor incidents be blown up by sensational media coverage, a pattern of fighting more directly comparable with soccer hooliganism could easily become institutionalized. As I noted in Chapter 6, in England during the 1980s fans from the more prosperous south would often taunt rivals from the less prosperous north by waving bundles of £5 and £10 notes and singing: 'You'll never work again'. Similarly, at high-school football matches in Texas, parents supporting 'white' teams regularly taunt the players and supporters of teams of Mexican descent by chanting: 'You're going to work for us' (communication from Roger Rees, Adelphi University). It is not difficult to imagine such a pattern being transposed into the context of major professional sports should an appropriate target regularly present itself.

I have also been told that, in North American contexts where travel to support one's team away is possible because the distances involved are relatively small, for example in cases such as the Green Bay Packers v. the Minnesota Vikings, pre-match fighting is a regular occurrence. However, the best example of regular fighting in a North American sports context I have come across was provided by Hunter S. Thompson (1979). Comparing American football in the 1960s and 1970s, he wrote:

> Pro football in America is over the hump. Ten years ago it was a very hip and private kind of vice to be into. I remember going to my first 49er game in 1965 with 15 beers in a plastic cooler and a Dr. Grabow pipe full of bad hash. The 49ers were still playing in Kezar stadium then, an old grey hulk at the western end of Haight Street in Golden Gate Park. There were never any sell-outs, but the 30,000 regulars were extremely heavy drinkers, and at least 10,000 of them were out there for no other reason except to get involved in serious violence....By half time the place was a drunken madhouse, and anybody who couldn't get it on anywhere else could always go underneath the stands and try to get into the long trough of a 'Men's Room' through the 'Out' door; there were always a few mean drunks lurking around to punch anyone who tried that...and by the end of the third quarter of any game, regardless of the score, there were always two or three huge brawls that would require the cops to clear out whole sections of the grandstand.
>
> (Thompson, 1979: 84)

Interestingly, Thompson describes this pattern as coming to an end when, on the 49ers moving to Candlestick Park, prices were doubled and the crowd came to consist of 'a sort of half-rich mob of nervous doctors, lawyers and bank officers who would sit through the whole game without ever making a sound' (Thompson, 1979: *loc. cit.*). Whether or not a deliberate policy was involved, this seems similar to the less successful attempt made in English soccer, especially since the 'new business class' (King, 1995) assumed control of the higher reaches of the game in the 1980s, to deal with the problem of soccer hooliganism by taking the game 'upmarket'. However, whether that is so or not, Thompson's example points towards the existence of a 'hooligan-type constituency' at sports in the USA, suggesting that, given an increase in away-match travel and/or the sensational reporting of spectator behaviour, a more direct equivalent of soccer hooliganism could easily emerge.

In this chapter, I have reviewed what I have been able to discover from secondary sources regarding patterns of sports spectator violence in the USA and Canada. I am sure that my lack of familiarity with these North American societies and their sporting cultures will mean that I have made mistakes. To say this is not to imply that I think I do not make mistakes writing about sport in England. It is simply to underscore the fact that I think it would be an interesting exercise to undertake comparative research on patterns of sports crowd violence in the USA, Canada, Britain and other European countries. The arguments I have put forward in this chapter are intended to provide a skeletal framework for such research. If I am right, Elias's theory of civilizing processes will offer better leads in this regard than Marsh's theory of aggro.

8

SPORT IN THE PROCESS OF RACIAL STRATIFICATION

The case of the USA

Introduction

Writing in 1989, Susan Birrell drew attention to what she called 'the atheoretical approach to racial relations that has characterized the work of sports studies scholars'. She also noted a corresponding lack of 'any sophisticated, critical analysis of racial relations', states of affairs which she detected both within sports studies and the parent disciplines (Birrell, 1989: 223, 213). I agree with Birrell's diagnosis and, in this chapter, I shall strive to make a contribution towards remedying the deficiency. More particularly I shall try to lay the foundations for a figurational/process-sociological understanding of the part played by sport in 'race relations' and, reciprocally, of some of the ways in which sport has been shaped by inequalities and struggles between so-called 'racial' groups. Such an analysis will involve undertaking two basic tasks: first, a conceptualization of race relations as fundamentally involving questions of power; and second, an exploration of the social conditions under which sporting prowess can become a power resource. I shall illustrate this conceptualization mainly by means of an historical/developmental analysis of race and sport in the USA.

According to Birrell, the dominant stress in studies of 'race' in the sociology of sport to date has been on studies of 'Black male athletes' (Birrell, 1989: 213). Among the limitations this produces, she contends, is the fact that 'class is almost completely obscured through our practice of reading "race" as "race/class" and letting the analysis go at that. Thus we produce an image of race and sport as homogenous and undifferentiated' (Birrell, 1989: 214). Whilst recognizing their strength, Birrell goes on to criticize the predominance in the field of studies of 'centrality' and 'stacking'. She writes:

> we continue to produce studies on centrality and stacking, not because of their theoretical significance but because the data are there. Twenty years ago such studies provided major insight into stratification by race, and it is startling to know that such patterns persist today, but

there is no theoretical news in this tradition. We need to move to more powerful questions.

In the past, our approach has been to assert that race exists and to ask what effect membership in a particular race or ethnic group has on sport involvement. A more profound approach is to conceive of race as a culturally produced marker of a particular relationship of power, to see racial identity as contested, and to ask how racial relations are produced and reproduced through sport.

(Birrell, 1989: 214)

I agree with Birrell regarding the originality and value of work in the 'centrality/stacking' tradition.[1] However, I would go beyond the criticisms which constitute her central thrust and suggest that, because of its overriding emphasis on sports structures *per se* rather than on the interrelationships between sports and the wider social contexts in which they are organized, watched and played, such work has tended to take these wider contexts for granted. As a result, work on 'centrality' and 'stacking' has arguably left unexamined both the often profound ways in which these wider contexts have become 'racialized' over time (Small, 1994)[2] and the conditions under which processes of at least partial 'de-racialization' can occur. I also agree with Birrell regarding race and power. In what follows, although I, too, will focus primarily on black male athletes in the USA, I shall conceptualize 'race' as a specific form of power relations. I shall also try to move beyond Birrell by conceptualizing sporting prowess as itself a power resource under specific conditions and by trying to follow through empirically some of the repercussions of such a conceptualization. In order to reach that point, I shall first of all offer a few generally critical comments on what may be regarded as some old-fashioned approaches to race and race relations, namely the work of: Lockwood (1970); Warner (1949); Warner's associates, Alison Davis and the Gardners (1941); and that of Frazier (1962). I have chosen to focus on these authors because their work will hopefully enable me to bring some recently neglected aspects of race relations into the discussion.

Because, among the older approaches, it is the most sophisticated theoretically, I shall start with a critique of Lockwood's contribution. As I shall try to show, he shares my view concerning the inapplicability of class and stratification theories to problems of race. However, whereas Lockwood focuses solely on the possibility that this may stem from the specificity or uniqueness of race relations, what I want to suggest is that, in many ways, the specificity of race relations is apparent rather than real, an artefact of the inadequacy of stratification theories in their current forms rather than of the total uniqueness of racial inequality as a form of stratification. In the context of this discussion, I shall introduce aspects of Durkheim's theory of the division of labour, more specifically his concept of 'mechanical solidarity' (Durkheim, 1964), and I shall use it, in part, as a means of reintroducing the concept of caste. After that, I shall review: (1) Elias and Scotson's theory of 'established-outsider figurations' (Elias and Scotson, 1994); (2) Elias's concept of power as a polymorphous, figurationally generated property of social interdependencies (Elias, 1978); and (3) Elias's theory of 'functional democratization' (Elias, 1978). Then I shall seek to apply this body of theory empirically in an attempt to illustrate: (1) how the development of American society in the eighteenth and nineteenth centuries involved the emergence of a figuration which facilitated the perpetuation of extreme dominance of whites over blacks, together with the internalization at a deep level of their habitus by large numbers if not a majority of the latter, of their own 'group disgrace' and, as a corollary, of white people's 'group charisma'; (2) how, even in the context of slavery, sporting prowess came to be one of the few power resources available to blacks; (3) how the development of American society in the twentieth century contributed to a slight but nonetheless detectable shift in the balance of power between these socially produced racial groups away from whites and towards blacks, leading to a correlative change in the habitus of growing numbers of the latter in the direction of greater self-confidence and 'racial pride'. It was, I shall suggest, such a figurationally generated change in the balance of racial power that led American blacks in growing numbers to begin to reject their stigmatization by whites – at the levels of their habitus and personality as well as in their more outward social relations – and to fight more openly, systematically and self-confidently against white dominance, contributing in the process to the racial violence and sporting protests which flared up in the 1960s. Further to this, I shall seek to show (4) how the sporting prowess of blacks, which was first manifested on the slave plantations and during 'reconstruction', continued to form a power resource which contributed over time to the expansion of the 'black bourgeoisie'. And, finally, I shall examine (5) how – characteristically of the formation of the American black bourgeoisie more generally – the sporting aspects of this overall social process may not have been wholly beneficial as far as the majority of blacks are concerned.

Some older theories of racial stratification revisited

In the late 1960s, largely following the widely acknowledged failure of earlier sociological approaches, especially the 'normative' functionalism of Parsons (Lockwood, 1964), to predict the American racial explosion, an attempt was made to delineate precisely the nature of race relations as an area of sociological problems. The discussion focused centrally on the degree to which race relations can be considered to be similar to other types of social stratification. Many Americans, whether of a functionalist (Kahl, 1961), Weberian (Marx, 1969) or more Marxist persuasion (Blauner, 1972), more or less explicitly accepted that race relations are a form of class and status relations. However, Lockwood raised doubts about the definitional consensus among these 'strange bedfellows', suggesting that there are limits to the analysis of race relations in class and stratification terms. That, he said, is partly because class inequalities stem from the division of labour but racial inequalities do not (Lockwood, 1970: 57); partly because racialism in a society leads to specific forms of intra-class tension and the alignment, within groups socially defined as races, of protest movements which involve patterns of group identification and unification across class lines; and partly because specific moral, aesthetic and sexual connotations of colour are built into language (Lockwood, 1970: 59). I shall concern myself here with the first and second of these issues.[3] They are inter-related in clear-cut ways.

The first of Lockwood's arguments arguably involves a failure to appreciate aspects of Durkheim's theory of the division of labour, more specifically its developmental focus. Thus, whilst the main thrust of Durkheim's argument is that division of labour is conducive to the emergence of 'organic solidarity' based on 'bonds of interdependence' (Durkheim, 1964),[4] he also held that such a process takes place only in the longer term, leading in the first instance to types of solidarity in which mechanical and organic forms are mixed. In addition, he argued, there has been a historical tendency for advancing division of labour to be correlated with the decline of 'caste' (Durkheim, 1964: 378). I do not think that Durkheim said so explicitly, but one form of social arrangement in which mechanical and organic solidarity can be said to be mixed occurs where a society is divided into 'racial castes'. That is because racial alignments are based on specific 'similitudes' which are either natural (e.g. skin colour) or socially constructed (e.g. Hindu caste marks, 'Stars of David' in Nazi Germany) rather than on bonds of interdependence established through a division of labour. Hence they are mechanical in Durkheim's sense.

This suggests that the degree to which 'racial' alignments occur in modern, urban–industrial societies can be said to be an index of the fact that such societies remain mechanically integrated in part. It also follows that, to the degree that the social experiences of some groups in such societies lead their members to form bonds which approximate to an ideal type of mechanical solidarity, that is for them to bond entirely or almost entirely with 'their own kind', such groups will be liable to develop extreme forms of racist identification and belief. Poor whites in racially mixed rural or mainly rural communities, the poorest sections of the urban–industrial working class in 'multi-ethnic' countries, and lower-middle- and downwardly mobile middle-class individuals in such societies who find it difficult to cope with status ambiguity and failure (Elias, 1996), are examples. Such people tend to have narrow life experiences, low levels of education and feelings of frustration regarding what they have achieved in life relative to their expectations, and this makes them prone to bond with people who are like themselves and to be intolerant of newcomers and strangers, 'others' whom they perceive as different and hence threatening, contributing to a double-bind process (Elias, 1987) or 'vicious circle' through which the narrowness of their experiences is reinforced, hence intensifying their intolerance, and so on. This suggests that it is not, as is commonly supposed, only the status ambiguity of such groups, that is their high caste/low or falling class status which contributes to their proneness to racist identifications and beliefs, but their mechanical – or perhaps better, their 'segmental' – solidarity, too, that is their bonding primarily in terms of 'similitudes'. Such a line of analysis does not find it difficult to cope with the propensity of such groups to intra-class conflict, that is towards conflict with racially different members of the same class. It follows as a corollary of the degree to which they are segmentally (mechanically) bonded. Nor does it find it difficult to cope with racial identifications across class lines. Such identifications follow from the degree to which the members of different classes are constrained by the strength of racial alignments in the wider society into identifying with other members of their own racial segment and into realizing that they have shared as well as conflicting interests with the latter. Let me expand on my use of the concept of caste.

Use of the concept of caste to describe a racially divided society is a tradition which goes back to Weber who suggested that 'caste is…the normal form in which ethnic communities…live side by side in a "societalized" manner' (Weber, 1946). This tradition was criticized by Leach (1962) but, if Berreman (1960) was correct, on grounds which are arguably spurious. I do not wish to reopen the controversy over the cross-cultural applicability of this concept but reference to its usage in the work of Warner (1949) and Davis and the Gardners (1941) will serve a useful purpose. The latter depicted the structure of caste and class in what they regarded as a typical southern American town as in Figure 8.1.

The fact that the 'caste', 'race' or 'colour' line depicted here does not follow the horizontal axis but is skewed towards the vertical represents a social structural fact of some significance. According to Warner (1949), it must have been closer to the horizontal at the end of the Civil War, that is immediately after the emancipation of the slaves. Since that time, it has skewed towards the vertical largely on account of the internal stratification of the 'black' or 'negro' caste; that is, because of the differentiation of blacks into upper, middle and lower classes. The significance of this process, more particularly of the emergence of what Frazier (1962) called the 'black bourgeoisie', lies primarily in the fact that it has involved the emergence of socially marginal upper and middle classes, that is classes of high class but low caste status. That, of course, has been commonly observed (Davis et al., 1941; Warner, 1949; Kahl, 1961). Nevertheless aspects of its significance have arguably tended to go unnoticed, especially the fact that it has involved the emergence of upper and middle classes, segments of which have forms of politically radical potential, more specifically, of upper- and middle-class groupings which, although the majority of their members may not be radical in terms of their general political allegiances and beliefs, do tend to be radical in terms of their implications for the structure and dynamics of racial stratification. For example, whilst not all members of the black bourgeoisie in the USA join racial protest organizations

Figure 8.1 Class and race lines in the American South

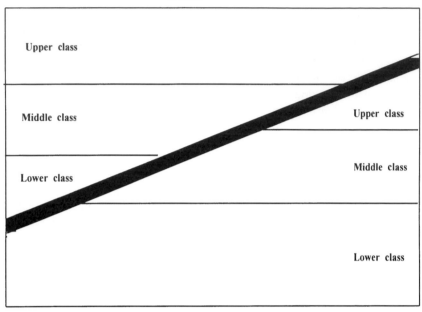

Whites

Blacks

Source: Adapted from Davis *et al.* (1941: 10)

such as the National Association for the Advancement of Colored People (NAACP), most such organizations were founded by members of the black bourgeoisie (together, of course, with sympathetic whites). Similarly, a majority of members of black protest organizations in the USA are black bourgeois, and it is from that source (again together with some white 'liberals' and 'philanthropists') that the bulk of the leadership, funds, organizational, legal and political expertise of such organizations derives. Furthermore, to the degree that members of the black bourgeoisie come to perform roles in the 'front regions' (Goffman, 1959) of racially integrated institutions such as banks, for example as managers and tellers, whites find themselves structurally constrained regularly to interact as equals with and not infrequently as subordinates to blacks. That is, they are constrained into 'organic' or, more precisely, 'functional bonding' with blacks, a fact which signifies a substantial alteration in the structure of stratification in terms of racial castes. I shall argue later that the formation of the black bourgeoisie has been one of the principal sources of the changing power ratio (Elias, 1978: 74ff.) of blacks and whites in the USA. More specifically, it reflects and has arguably been a principal source for facilitating the occurrence of a degree of what Elias (1978) called 'functional democratization' in race relations in that country. As I shall attempt to show, it has also been important in transforming the racially contoured structure of American sport.

There are at least two reasons why the significance of this structural transformation may have been overlooked. It could derive from the prominence of nominalist, individual-centred paradigms and assumptions among American sociologists and from the correlative fact that, whilst they have been sensitized to the consequences of this emergent status-inconsistency for intercaste *behaviour*, for example to the anomalies which arise when low caste, high class blacks interact with high caste, low class whites (Kahl, 1961: 246–7), they have been blinded to its consequences for the *dynamics of racial stratification*, that is as a source for the sociogenesis of structural change. Alternatively, it could derive from the tendency of sociologists generally to expect the upper and middle classes to be politically conservative and the lower classes, or at least sections of them, to be politically radical, an expectation which stems from the Marxist and similar paradigms and which tends perhaps to be especially confounded when class and caste hierarchies intersect, for, in such cases, there is arguably a tendency towards the generation of distinct types of upper- and middle-class radicalism and lower-class conservatism. Frazier rightly stressed the tendency for the black upper and middle classes to engage in status-conscious attempts to imitate their white counterparts (Frazier, 1962: 112–26) and the fact that the class hierarchy of blacks in the USA is itself, in part, a colour-caste hierarchy, that is that there is an inverse correlation among American blacks between class position and degrees of skin pigmentation, thus providing testimony to the extent to which they have internalized the values of the dominant whites (Frazier. 1962: 23–4). Yet, whilst Frazier was correct to emphasize these facts, it is reasonable to suppose that his 'insider' perspective may have contributed to his underestimating the simultaneously radical propensities and implications for change that are structurally generated by the marginal status of the black bourgeoisie. Status consciousness and the internalization of white values may seem *logically* inconsistent with radical potential but they are not necessarily *structurally* incompatible with it. Frazier admitted that predominantly black bourgeois organizations such as the NAACP are characterized by 'racial radicalism' (Frazier, 1962: 89), that is by a belief in the equality of blacks and whites, but he was blinded, for example by the anti-communist stance of the NAACP in the 1950s (Frazier, 1962: 91) and the commitment to dominant values which this implied, into underestimating the consequences of such organizations for the long-term dynamics of race relations. In short, he seems to have fallen into the not uncommon trap of believing that a radical ideology and posture are prerequisites for the contribution by a group or organization to the sociogenesis of structural change. Let me turn now to the relevant aspects of Elias's approach.

'Established–outsider' figurations and Elias's theory of power

Elias and Scotson's *The Established and the Outsiders* (1965, 1994) reports a study, carried out in the late 1950s and early 1960s, of a dominance–subordination figuration formed by two working-class groups in a suburb of Leicester, a town in the English East Midlands. According to Elias, these groups were identical in terms of all conventional indices of social stratification, differing only in the fact that the 'established' group had lived in the community for several generations, whilst the 'outsiders' were relative newcomers. Yet a whole constellation of symptoms normally associated with class and social oppression was detectable in the relations between them. This led Elias to ask:

> What…induced the people who formed the first of the two groups to set themselves up as…higher and better…? What resources of power enabled them to assert their superiority and to cast a slur on the others as [people] of a lesser breed? As a rule one encounters this kind of figuration in connection with ethnic, national and group differences (such as those between classes)….But here in Winston Parva the full armoury of group superiority and group contempt was mobilized in the relations between two groups who were different only with regard to the duration of their residence….Here one could see that 'oldness' of association…was, on its own, able to create the degree of group cohesion, the collective identification, the commonality of norms, which are apt to induce the gratifying euphoria that goes with the consciousness of belonging to a group of higher value and with the complementary contempt for other groups.
>
> At the same time one could see here the limitations of any theory which explains power differentials only in terms of a monopolistic possession of non-human objects such as weapons or means of production and disregards the figurational aspects of power differentials due purely to differences in the degree of organization of the human beings concerned….[T]he latter, especially differentials in the degree of internal cohesion and communal control, can play a decisive part in the greater power ratio of one group in relation to that of another….[In the small community of Winston Parva], the power-superiority of the old-established group was to a large extent of this type. It was based on the high degree of cohesion of families who had known each other for two or three generations, in contrast to the newcomers who were strangers in relation not only to the old residents but also to each other. It was thanks to their greater potential for cohesion and its activation by social control that the old residents were able to reserve offices in their local organizations…for people of their own kind and firmly to exclude from them people

186

who lived in the other part and who, as a group, lacked cohesion.... Exclusion and stigmatization of the outsiders by the established group, thus, were powerful weapons used by the latter to maintain their identity, to assert their superiority, keeping the others firmly in their place.

(Elias, 1994: xvii–xviii)

The power of the established group in Winston Parva depended, according to Elias, on the fact that the 'oldness' of their association enabled them to develop greater cohesion relative to the outsiders, many of whom started as strangers to each other, and this, in turn, enabled them to monopolize official positions in local associations. That, the greater cohesion of established relative to outsider groups, he suggests, is a common, 'purely figurational' aspect of dominance–subordination relations. The criticism implied here of the Marxian and similar approaches is later taken up by Elias explicitly. He recognizes the sociological value of what he calls Marx's 'great discovery' but is critical of what he regards as the tendency in some sociological circles – it was probably strongest in the 1960s and 1970s – 'to see in it the end of the road of discovery about human societies. One might', he adds, 'rather regard it as one manifestation of a beginning' (Elias, 1994: xxxii). Elias continues:

> Marx...uncovered an important 'truth' when he pointed to the uneven distribution of the means of production and thus to the uneven distribution of the means for satisfying people's material needs. But it was a half-truth. He presented as the root-source of the goal-clash between power-superior and -inferior groups the clash over 'economic' goals such as that of securing a sufficient food supply. And to this day the pursuit of 'economic' goals, elastic and ambiguous as this use of the term 'economic' is, appears to many people as the 'real', the basic goal of human groups by comparison with which others appear to be less 'real', whatever that may mean.
>
> (Elias, 1994: xxxiii)

Elias would not have sought to deny that Marx's theory of class formation deals with the generation of a particular sort of social cohesion, namely that involved in the transformation of 'classes in themselves' into 'classes for themselves' (Bendix, 1953: 30). What he would have denied is that such processes are universally to be understood solely intra-societally and in relation to modes of production. 'Economic' forms are socially structured and structuring but, Elias contended, they are not alone in that respect: other aspects of figurations which, especially in an age of increasing globalization, have to be understood inter-societally and not simply intra-societally such as state formation, the length and density of interdependency chains, and the relative cohesion of and balance of power between groups are equally structured and determining and no less 'real'. Under specific circumstances, these other aspects enjoy degrees of autonomy in relation to and even dominance over the mode of production. That is, in this as in other aspects of his work, Elias rejected the notion of universal 'law-like' relationships between 'social parts' (Elias, 1974). Consistently with this he suggested that the degree to which 'economic' conflicts are paramount in a society is partly a function of the balance of power between groups. He wrote:

> the supremacy of the economic aspects of established–outsider conflicts is most pronounced where the balance of power between the contenders is most uneven....The less that is the case, the more recognizable become other, non-economic aspects of the tensions and conflicts. Where outsider groups have to live at a subsistence level, the size of their earnings outweighs all their other requirements in importance. The higher they rise above the subsistence level, the more does even their income...serve as a means of satisfying...requirements other than that of stilling their most elementary animalic or 'material' needs; the more keenly are groups in that situation liable to feel the...inferiority of power and status from which they suffer. And it is in that situation that the struggle between established and outsiders gradually ceases to be, on the part of the latter, simply a struggle for stilling their hunger, for the means of physical survival, and becomes a struggle for the satisfaction of other human requirements as well
>
> (Elias, 1994: xxxii)

As I shall argue later, this analysis is particularly apt regarding the status and power struggles of the 'black' bourgeoisie.

'Racial' inequality as an 'established–outsider' figuration

As far as race is concerned, Elias shows that race relations are not unique as a type of social stratification or, in his terms, 'established–outsider figuration'. He singles out four features as common to intra-class established–outsider relationships of the kind investigated in 'Winston Parva' and to interclass, interethnic/'racial' and international dominance–subordination relationships as well, namely: (1) the tendency for members of established groups to perceive outsiders as 'law-breakers' and 'status-violators', that is as 'anomic' (Elias and Scotson, 1994: 177–81); (2) the tendency for the established to judge outsiders in terms of the 'minority of the worst', that is in terms of the minority of outsiders who actually do break the law and violate standards; (3) the tendency for outsiders to accept the established group's stigmatization of them, that is to internalize the 'group charisma' of the dominant group and their own 'group disgrace'; and (4) the tendency for the established to view the outsiders as in some way 'unclean' (Elias, 1994: xixff.). It is on the fourth of these common features that I shall focus here.

Elias and Scotson showed that the established group in Winston Parva believed that the houses of the outsiders, especially their kitchens, were less than clean. That is similar, Elias suggested, to the tradition which gained currency in Britain from about the 1830s of referring to the 'lower orders' as 'the great unwashed' (Elias, 1994: xxvii). It is also similar to the notions of 'uncleanliness' and 'pollution' in the Indian caste system; to the fact that the Burakumin, a minority in Japan, are stigmatized by the label 'Eta' which means 'full of filth'; and to the fact that comparable notions are generally associated with established–outsider relations based on 'real', that is phenotypical and usually readily observable racial differences such as skin colour, as well as with racial differences which are 'supposed' rather than 'real', for example the difference between 'Aryans' and Jews in Nazi Germany which had to be enforced by making the latter wear a Star of David. Thus it is (or was) a common belief of American whites that blacks are 'personally unclean, diseased, smell bad [and] are physically unpleasant to associate with' (Allport, 1954: 258). The notion of 'supposed' as opposed to 'real' racial differences (i.e. differences which have a partly biological base) can be illustrated through Elias's discussion of the Burakumin or 'Eta' of Japan.

Elias suggests that a common property of established–outsider figurations is the generation of collective fantasies by the dominant about the subordinate group. Although there are no detectable genetic differences between them, one of the collective fantasies of the dominant Japanese about the minority Burakumin – the latter appear to be descendants of low-ranking, caste-like groups associated occupationally with death, childbirth and animal slaughter (Elias, 1994: xxix) – is the idea that the latter are born with a bluish birth mark under each arm. In that way, the social stigma attached by the established to the outsider group is reified, transformed in their imagination into a material stigma. 'It appears,' says Elias,

> as objective, something implanted upon the outsiders by nature or the gods. In this way the stigmatizing group is exculpated from any blame: it is not we, such a fantasy implies, who have put a stigma on these people, but the powers that made the world – they have put a sign on these people to mark them off as inferior or bad people.
>
> (Elias, 1994: xxxiv–xxxv)

And he concludes:

> terms like 'racial' or 'ethnic'...used in this context...in sociology and...society at large are symptomatic of an ideological avoidance action. By using them, one singles out for attention what is peripheral to these relationships (eg, differences of skin colour) and turns

the eye away from what is central (eg, differences in power ratio and the exclusion of a power inferior group from positions with a higher power potential). Whether or not the groups to which one refers when speaking of 'race relations' or 'racial prejudice' differ in their racial descent and appearance, the salient aspect of their relationship is that they are bonded together in a manner which endows one of them with very much greater power resources than the other and enables that group to exclude members of the other group from access to the centre of these resources and from closer contact with its own members, thus relegating them to the position of outsiders. Therefore, even where differences in physical appearance and other biological aspects to which we refer as 'racial' exist in these cases, the socio-dynamics of the relationship between groups bonded to each other as established and outsiders are determined by the manner of their bonding, not by any of the characteristics possessed by the groups conceived independently of it.

(Elias, 1994: xxx–xxxi)

The erroneous belief that blacks are innately intellectually inferior to whites but correlatively innately superior in 'physical' spheres such as sports is a variant of the sorts of collective fantasies Elias had in mind. It differs marginally from most beliefs of this kind in that the fantasy of the intellectual inferiority of blacks is, as is typical, based on popular speculation about and pseudo-scientific observation of a 'minority of the worst', whilst the belief in their innate sporting superiority is based on popular speculation about and pseudo-scientific observation of a 'minority of the best', that is top-level athletes. However, as far as I can tell, this variation does not detract from the applicability of Elias's insights to the field of race and sport. Accordingly I want to use these insights as a tool for exploring the manner in which, starting from a situation characterized by virtually total dominance of whites over blacks in which sporting prowess was one of the few power resources available to the latter, the long-term dynamics of American social develop- ment led, especially in the course of the twentieth century, to the emergence of a societal figuration in which a slight but nonetheless detectable shift in the balance of racial power occurred, a shift which is more publicly apparent in the field of sport than in many other spheres of American life. Before I do this, however, it is necessary to undertake a discussion of Elias's concepts of power and functional democratization.

Power as a sociological concept

To date, the two dominant sociological conceptions of power have been those of the Marxists and the Weberians. It is on the latter that I will concentrate in what follows. According to Weber, 'we understand by "power" the chance of a man or a number of men to realize their own will in a communal action even against the resistance of others' (Weber, 1946: 180). Elsewhere, he offered the following variation on this: 'power means any chance within a social relationship to realize one's own will, even in the face of resistance, regardless of the basis on which this chance rests' (Weber, 1972: 28; my translation from original German). It was this idea of the relational character of power that was seized on by Elias. Thus he wrote of 'balances' or 'power-ratios' and suggested that:

> From the day of its birth, a baby has power over its parents, not just the parents over the baby. At least the baby has power over them as long as they attach any kind of value to it. If not, it loses its power....Equally bi-polar is the balance of power between a slave and his master. The master has power over his slave, but the slave also has power over his master, in proportion to his function for his master – his master's dependence on him. In relationships between parents and infants, master and slave, power chances are distributed very unevenly. But whether the power differentials are large or small, balances of power are always present wherever there is functional interdependence between people....Power is not an amulet possessed by one person and not by another; it is a structural characteristic of human relationships – of *all* human relationships.
>
> (Elias, 1978: 74)

Elias went on to tie the concept of power explicitly to that of interdependence. A solution to the problems of power more adequate than those on offer in sociology so far, he suggested,

> depends on power being understood unequivocally as a structural characteristic of a relationship....We depend on others; others depend on us. In so far as we are more dependent on others than they are on us, more directed by others than they are by us, they have power over us, whether we have become dependent on them by their use of naked force or by our need to be loved, our need for money, healing, status, a career or simply for excitement.
>
> (Elias, 1978: 93)

Since one cannot direct others without having the power to do so in the first place, the reference here to 'being directed by others' is tautological.[5] Otherwise, this diagnosis is sociologically profound. What Elias is suggesting is twofold: (1) that power is 'polymorphous' and inherent in all human relationships; and (2) that the key to understanding power lies in the interdependency of people. The examples Elias gives in the selections I have quoted all refer to 'bi-polar' or 'two-person' relationships, but he was clear that power balances in the wider society and in the relationships between societies are always multi-polar; that is, they involve complex configurations of interdependent individuals and groups. Elias might have added that, in a society where sport is highly valued, sporting prowess is a positive power resource and that, under specific circumstances, it can be used to a greater or lesser degree to offset the disadvantages of racial stigmatization, even slavery. Another way of putting it would be to say that, in a society where sport is valued, sporting prowess can be a form of 'embodied power', part of a person's habitus which gives them what Bourdieu (1984) calls 'cultural capital'.

Elias's theory of functional democratization is inherent in his concept of power as deriving from interdependence. He contends that the social transformation usually referred to by terms denoting specific aspects such as 'industrialization' or 'economic growth' in fact involves a transformation of the total social structure (Elias, 1978: 63ff.). And, he suggests, one of the most significant aspects of this total transformation consists in the emergence of longer, more differentiated and denser 'chains of interdependence' (Elias, 1994). Concomitantly with this, according to Elias, there occurs a change in the direction of generally decreasing power differentials within and among groups, more specifically an equalizing change to some degree in the balance of power between rulers and ruled, social classes, men and women, the generations, parents and children (Elias, 1978: 65ff.). At the most general level, Elias maintains, such a process of 'functional democratization' occurs when increasing specialization takes place. That is because the incumbents of specialized roles gain from their specializations chances of exerting varying degrees of reciprocal influence and control.[6] The power chances of specialized groups are further enhanced if they manage to organize since then they become able by collective action to disrupt the wider chains of interdependence on which a modern society depends. It is in ways such as these, according to Elias, that increasing division of labour and the emergence of longer chains of interdependence lead to greater, more even forms of reciprocal dependency and, hence, to patterns of multi-polar influence and control within and among groups. It is important to stress that I have said here '*more even* forms of reciprocal dependency', not '*even*' forms. The comparative is significant. Our hypothesis is about empirically demonstrable processes of equalization but is not intended to deny the great inequalities which still remain or which have increased in certain respects in recent years. I have now reached a point at which it is appropriate to apply this body of theory to the development of American race relations and some of the complex ways in which sport has been implicated in that process.

Sport in the process of racial stratification in the USA

A figurational account of the genesis and subsequent modification of the pattern of 'established–outsider' relations which emerged between blacks and whites in the USA and which focuses on the part played by sport in that process must seek to accomplish at least three things. More specifically, it has to show:

1   how the relations between blacks and whites came to involve the concentration of power chances in the hands of whites, leading blacks in large numbers: (a) to be readily exploitable; (b) at first in large numbers to accept their stigmatization as inferior – of course, there have always been notable exceptions such as Frederick Douglas – and (c) to be unable, in many cases as a result of the internalization of the group charisma of whites and their own group disgrace at a deep level of their habitus, to offer effective resistance to white rule;

2   how the long-term development of the USA, more specifically its gradual emergence in the nineteenth and twentieth centuries as the world's most powerful nation, led, principally via struggles connected with processes of functional democratization, to a slight but not insignificant shift in the balance of racial power, enabling blacks increasingly to shed their negative group image and fight more effectively and self-confidently against white dominance and their own internalization of the idea of the whites' group charisma;

3   finally, how, under specific conditions, sporting prowess, the partly individually inherited, partly socially conditioned bodily (including 'mental') ability to excel in activities which are socially recognized as 'sports', becomes a power resource which enables some individuals to gain prestige, privilege and – sometimes but not always – money wealth, conferring on them a capacity to negate to a greater or lesser degree the power disadvantages which stem from being defined as members of a supposedly inferior and factually exploited racial group.

Stages in the development of black–white relations in the USA

Black–white relations in the USA can be said to have passed through three overlapping stages: a stage of plantation slavery; a stage of colour castes; and a stage of urban ghettos. During the second stage the pattern of extreme white dominance and acceptance by numbers of blacks – often at deep levels of their habitus – of their stigmatization by whites as 'inferior', a pattern which first developed on the slave plantations, continued to exist. However, in the modified figuration which developed following the abolition of slavery (although its roots, too, can be traced back in part to social relations on the slave plantations) there began to take place the formation of an embryonic 'black bourgeoisie' or black middle class. In this way, a slight shift in the power ratios of blacks and whites was set in motion. However, it was at the stage of urban ghettos that there occurred the most significant long-term change in the balance of racial power in the USA that has taken place so far. The expansion of the black bourgeoisie and, as part of it, the occurrence of functional democratization, were centrally implicated in this process. As I hope to show, at every stage in the development of American black–white relations, the exploitation of their sporting talents by athletically gifted blacks played a part of some importance, mainly by adding to the ranks of the black bourgeoisie.

Race relations at the stage of plantation slavery

One source of the relative powerlessness of blacks in the first stage of white dominance in the USA was the fact that they had been forcibly transplanted to the country as slaves. Both on the slave ships and the plantations, their power chances were often further reduced by the deliberate stratagem of keeping the members of particular tribal and language groups apart, thus making difficult that degree of communication which is one of the preconditions for effective group resistance (Elkins, 1959). The power chances of recently arrived slaves were further reduced by the fact of their transportation to an alien and unfamiliar cultural context and – although this varied between states and, within states, between plantations (Blassingame 1972) – by the systematic resort to physical violence by the plantation owners and their agents. Whippings, use of the stocks and, on the larger plantations, imprisonment in the plantation jail were not uncommon. Runaways were hunted with dogs – a variant of the English 'hue and cry' and apparently a favourite leisure activity in some parts of the Old South – and, when caught, clapped in irons and sometimes branded or castrated. Ill-treatment was limited by the fact that slaves were valuable 'property' in which considerable money had been invested and because they had to be fit enough to work either on the plantation or in the master's house. Furthermore, physical damage could reduce their resale price and, in the case of house slaves, their value for purposes of display. Against this, recalcitrant slaves were more expendable, especially on the larger plantations where punishment in public could serve as an effective means of social control. To say this is not to deny that masters sometimes developed genuine bonds of affection and concern for their slaves, with the proviso, of course, that the latter did not become 'uppity' and showed themselves willing 'to keep their place' (Adams, N., 1854; quoted in McKitrick, 1963: 148–61).

From the standpoint of the slaves, the plantation figuration approximated closely to what Goffman (1959) called a 'total institution'. The plantations were 'closed systems' in the sense that slaves were not usually allowed to leave their confines except in the company of their master or, in the case of slaves considered trustworthy, with a pass or letter which showed they were not runaways but transacting their master's business. They were also subjected to the ritual degradation of being publicly bought and sold. Sometimes slaves were allowed to tend their own gardens and livestock as a means of supplementing their rations but, otherwise, they worked solely for their masters, not themselves, Moreover, most were kept to a large extent outside direct involvement in the money economy in at least three senses: (1) the necessities of life were, for the most part, purchased or otherwise provided by their masters; (2) they were not paid a money wage; and (3) the produce of their labour was marketed by their masters and the revenue obtained pocketed by the latter. As I shall show later, however, sporting prowess and gambling were sources of money for some slaves. Moreover, masters sometimes paid small sums for the sexual favours of female slaves (Haley, 1976).

In some parts of the South, the numerical predominance of blacks led whites to fear slave rebellions, a fear reinforced by occasional bloody uprisings and the occurrence of revolutions in countries such as Haiti (Elkins, 1959; Aptheker, 1943). In general, however, the overall figuration of the South made the dominance of whites, especially of the plantation owners, relatively secure. State formation in colonial and early post-colonial America was in its early stages and the 'planter aristocracy', the owners of the largest plantations and the bulk of the slaves, controlled each Southern state. 'Poor whites' formed a numerical majority among the whites but most of them were small farmers or landless and illiterate agricultural labourers. Moreover, they were ecologically scattered and difficult to organize as a class. As a result, the planter aristocracy were subject to effective pressure from neither above nor below. This meant they were able to control the state apparatus and the plantations and exploit in their own interests, virtually untrammelled by external constraints, the human capital on which they were so heavily dependent.

Some Southerners justified slavery by means of an attack on capitalism and free labour which was in some ways reminiscent of the cruder forms of Marxist critique (Genovese, 1969). Slaves, they argued, were better treated than the industrial labourers of the North since the latter were left entirely at the mercy of 'market forces'. Prominent among those who argued in this vein were Henry Hughes (1829–62) and George Fitzhugh (1806–81). Interestingly, in 1854 Hughes became the first American to use Auguste Comte's recently coined word 'sociology' (McKitrick, 1963: 51). He wrote a book called *A Treatise on Sociology* and, later the same year, Fitzhugh published his *Sociology for the South: or the Failure of Free Society*. Lyman (1990: 192) has called their group 'the Southern Comteans'. Central to their supposedly sociological arguments were that humankind is 'naturally' divided into the strong and the weak, and that slavery is the best means for getting the former to protect the latter.

It is hardly surprising, in the context of such an overall figuration, that many blacks came to develop a habitus which betrayed great dependency on their masters and to internalize both the 'group charisma' of the latter and their own 'group disgrace'. Elkins (1959) wrote of the 'infantilization' of the majority of slaves. Such a term is too reminiscent of the collective fantasies of the dominant whites but there may be something in what Elkins said. The

195

slave plantations did, as he suggested, have some similarities to the Nazi concentration camps and may well have produced in some ways similar effects on the habitus and personality of some of their victims, for example extreme dependency patterns, identification with the oppressor and a degree of 'infantilization' in the sense that, like infants, their dependency was very great. However, unlike infants, in the case of the majority of slaves dependency was permanent and ultimately maintained by the state-sanctioned right for masters to exercise life and death power over the slaves. Moreover, unlike the Nazi concentration camps, some of which also exploited slave labour, the plantations of the American South were not orientated towards genocide. That would not have been in the interests of the planter aristocracy. Genocide was not in the economic interests of the Nazis either but they were acting in terms of a fervently held belief that Jews constituted a threat to the 'Aryan master race' (Elias, 1996). Similar ideas took root in the South but not on a scale of much significance until after slavery had been abolished. For example, Senator Benjamin Tillman of South Carolina seriously proposed the killing of 30,000 blacks in his home state, and a popular book of the time was entitled *The Negro: a Beast* (Boyle, 1971: 260–1).

There were other differences between the plantations and the concentration camps, above all the fact that aspects of the plantation figuration meant that slaves had a greater degree of autonomy in relation to their masters than the concentration camp inmates had in relation to theirs. For example, the larger plantations could not be effectively policed at night and the slaves were thus afforded the chance for relatively independent activities, for example religious gatherings in the slave quarters or on other parts of the plantation (Genovese, 1974). They would hold parties or attend them on neighbouring plantations, sometimes with their masters' permission and with liquor provided by the latter. In some cases, masters and mistresses would watch the festivities and occasionally even join in (Wiggins, 1977). In addition, slaves who developed a degree of expertise in specific fields could increase their masters' dependency on them, in that way reducing somewhat the degree of asymmetry which was otherwise inherent in the pattern of master–slave interdependence. Sporting prowess was one such form of expertise.

Black participation in sport on the slave plantations

Birrell has written of sport and slavery that

> in their discussion of the resistance of racial groups to their total subordination, Omi and Winant (1988) give the example of blacks under slavery in the United States who 'developed cultures of resistance based on music, religion, African traditions, and family ties' (p.73). Noticeably absent from this account is sport. We should explore why, not just to uncover examples of Black sporting traditions but in

order to explore the place of sport in this particular culture of resistance. Was sport absent, and if so, why? Was the ideology of sport constructed in such a way that sport as constituted could not serve resistant ends? Or were the sport activities of slaves not comprehended as sport within dominant definitions?

(Birrell, 1989: 221)

These are important questions. However, Birrell was evidently unfamiliar with the pioneering work of Sammons, Wiggins and others on sport among the slaves of the *ante bellum* South. Whilst this work remains in its infancy, what it suggests is that the slaves had as rich a tradition of engaging in sport as one would have expected to emerge under the limiting conditions of the slave plantations. Ex-slave, Frederick Douglass, for example, saw sport as used by the masters for purposes of social control, writing that 'sports and merriments' were among the most effective ways of 'keeping down the spirit of insurrection' (cited in Sammons, 1994: 216). Relying on the work of Genovese, Wiggins (1977) partly disagrees. However, Sammons has posed a series of pertinent questions through which he attempts to strike a middle course. 'What role,' he asks, 'did slaves have in shaping and controlling their games? Did they use sport and amusement to get back at masters? Or were these activities less transgressive and more strategic devices for simulating, if not imitating the dominant culture?' (Sammons, 1994: 255). My reading of the available evidence is that, despite the well-established tradition among blacks of getting back at the dominant whites in those limited social spaces in which they could escape surveillance – as described by Ralph Ellison, for example, in *The Invisible Man* – sport was unlike music, religion and dance in the sense that slaves took on and for the most part did not add to, innovate in or otherwise independently develop the sporting traditions of the planter aristocracy. For that reason, whilst sporting prowess could constitute a power resource for individual slaves in relation to their masters, the sporting traditions of the slaves in general cannot be construed as having contributed much to a collective 'culture of resistance'. But, of course, such cultures are just as often sources of undesirable unintended consequences as they are of 'progressive' social change. Let me attempt to demonstrate how that was so.

The main sports in question were prize-fighting, wrestling, horse-racing and cock-fighting which were, apart from fox-hunting 'English-style' (Martin, 1995), the principal sports of the *ante bellum* South. Slaves also took part in foot-races and ball games (Wiggins, 1977: 273) but I shall not consider them here since they do not appear to have been favoured by the planter class to the same extent, and hence prowess at them, whilst it may have constituted a source of pleasurable excitement for the slaves in such leisure hours as they were allowed and enabled them to rank themselves against one another, would not have been a potential power resource of any significance in relation to their masters.

As far as prize-fighting/boxing is concerned, Sammons has written that:

> Although there is debate on the subject, most written accounts indicate that the first black boxers were slaves. Owners allegedly pitted their finest physical specimens against one another in 'no-holds-barred' matches for the glory of the plantation and sizeable wagers. Boxing historian Elliot Gorn maintains this practice was rare because it violated business sense; he argues that it was mostly the stuff of myth.
>
> (Sammons, 1990: 31)

Gorn may have been projecting modern capitalist norms of economic rationality such as were developing in the American North onto the plantation owners of the Old South. The latter were members of an early post-colonial, pre-industrial, pre-capitalist, even in many ways anti-capitalist society (Hughes, 1854; Fitzhugh, 1854) and sought to model themselves on the English aristocracy and gentry. As such, conspicuous competitive display, including conspicuous competitive display of the boxing prowess of their slaves, probably figured as high in their scale of values as capital accumulation and a desire to protect their human 'property'. Furthermore, some of them may have derived sadistic pleasure from forcing their slaves to fight, together with re-inforcement of their sense of power. In any case, that boxing did take place regularly on the plantations is a fact about which there is little doubt. Douglass mentions it in his autobiography (1968: 84–9) and Wiggins writes that

> planters would frequently organize formal boxing contests and pit their slave champions against other slave champions of the community. Many times more money was won on wagers during these fights than on the horses. Legend has it that extremely good 'boxer slaves', after earning fortunes in bets for their masters, were given their freedom and moved away from the South so that they could ply their fistic trade to better financial advantage to themselves.
>
> (Wiggins, 1977: 273)

It would be interesting to probe in greater detail the degree to which this idea of boxing being a route to manumission was, as Wiggins has it, legend or fact. Ann Malone's research into wrestling is possibly of relevance in this connection. She shows that wrestling 'was fairly common among slaves in Louisiana and Texas', and that slave owners would pay 'a premium for wrestlers because of their potential value in garnering gambling stakes' (cited in Sammons, 1990: 265n.). It seems likely that the same would have applied to boxing and that some slaves may have earned sufficient money for their masters to persuade the latter to grant their freedom.

That some slaves did obtain manumission at least partly on account of boxing skill is suggested by the career of Tom Molineaux. Believed to have been born on a cotton plantation in Virginia, Molineaux came to England in 1809 and fought twice against Tom Cribb, Champion of England, 1807–11, on the first occasion nearly defeating him (Wignall, 1923: 85ff.). Molineaux was trained by William Richmond, also a black American and prominent boxer in England. Richmond was discovered during the American War of Independence on Sturton Island by General Earl Percy, later Duke of Northumberland, and taken to England in 1777 (Wignall, 1923: 251). The available sources do not suggest whether Richmond was a freedman or slave but they do indicate that he trained a number of other black boxers, among them Johnson, Wharton, Kendrick, Sutton and Robinson (Wignall, 1923: 253). It would be interesting to discover more about these men and the degree to which boxing prowess could serve as a power resource through which racial prejudice and slave status could be partially negated, leading in some cases to manumission. What is certain is that planters in the Old South did not fear their slaves learning boxing skills to the same extent as they feared them learning to read or write (Douglass, 1968). Boxing skill also fitted in with the white collective fantasy of blacks as 'savage' and 'inferior' beings who were closer than whites 'to the jungle'.

Slaves also took part in horse-races, both of an informal kind on the plantations to which they belonged and of a formal kind on race tracks. According to Wiggins, they also often accompanied their masters to the race track and numbers served as trainers. Two slave jockeys were William Greene and Jacob Stroyer, the latter having been first employed as a trainer (Wiggins, 1977: 273–4). Again, it would be interesting to discover whether ability as a trainer or jockey served as a power resource for slaves in relation to their masters as boxing seems to have done.

According to Wiggins, gambling was another favourite leisure occupation of the slaves. 'Despite strict laws forbidding slaves from gambling they would lay a wager with white men at horse races and cock fights' (Wiggins, 1977: 274). Powell provided confirmation of this when he wrote that: 'slaves engaged in cock-fighting among themselves and attended public matches with the gentry and middling sort' (1993: 370). He went on to quote the diary of a Virginian planter, Philip V. Fithian, who recorded that Easter Monday 1774 was 'a general holiday; Negroes now are all disbanded and are at Cock Fights through the County'. The following Sunday, Fithian said he had observed 'slaves fighting cocks near the stable, as was the custom on their one day of discretionary activities' (Powell, 1993: 371). And a revealing advertisement regarding a runaway slave published in Virginia in 1774 warned that a man 'remarkable for cock-fighting, card-playing and many other Games was about to attempt to escape the colony by passing as a freeman' (Powell, 1993: 371). This suggests that slaves did participate directly in the money economy of the South to some extent and is consistent with the hypothesis that skill in training fighting cocks and gambling could serve as power resources.

Let me conclude this section with the observation that, although in its infancy, the study of sport and slavery provides revealing evidence on the character of the Southern slave plantations as social institutions. It shows, for example, that, despite some similarities, they were very different from the Nazi concentration camps. It also provides a telling indication of the significance of sport for a full understanding of social relations.

Emancipation and changing race relations after the Civil War

The emancipation of the slaves in the American South did not occur as a result of a figurationally generated change in the balance of power between whites and blacks but in conjunction with the Civil War; that is, a struggle of a type which is common in post-colonial figurations where the divisive (centrifugal) pressures inherent in the social structure had hitherto been masked by common opposition to the colonial power. Viewed retrospectively, it was a war connected with the formation of the USA as a capitalist urban–industrial nation-state and with the correlative rise of the bourgeoisie to national dominance. In short, it was connected with struggles among the dominant whites in which blacks were little more than pawns. It is, accordingly, not surprising that emancipation did not lead, in the short run, to significant changes in the social position of the latter.

Although a few managed to gain seats in Southern legislatures during the reconstruction era, blacks as a whole were not sufficiently powerful to have been able to compel whites to take their interests into account. They were scattered, either in small rural settlements or in the 'coloured quarters' of what were essentially market towns tied mainly to the cotton monoculture. The ecological fragmentation of their mode of existence was not conducive to communication or organization based on recognition of the common interests they shared as a group in opposition to the dominant whites. By keeping most of them out of full involvement in the money economy, moreover, slavery had not permitted the occurrence of even those forms of capital accumulation which are usual among peasants. Hence, no equivalent of a 'kulak' class could form among them and the majority of blacks remained poor, having to devote most of their energies simply to keeping alive. Such forms of consolidation of their powerlessness relative to whites meant that slavery was replaced by a dominance system in which blacks, although nominally free, continued to be subject to multiple subordination and exploitation by whites. Economically, this took the form of 'sharecropping' and 'debt peonage' (forms of indebtedness to plantation owners which kept blacks virtually enslaved) and use of the law to supply cheap labour, for example by arresting blacks on trumped-up charges and freeing them on bail to plantation owners in return for a promise to work at pitiful wage rates.

Yet, whilst emancipation did not significantly alter the material position of blacks, it did alter the overall figuration of the South in at least one respect: it made blacks more directly subject to the vicissitudes of the markets for land and labour. This brought them into *direct* competition with poor whites, leading the latter, along with whites who were socially marginal (e.g. members of the lower middle classes and those who were downwardly mobile) and former slave owners who were resentful at having been deprived of 'the peculiar institution' by 'interfering Northerners' – men such as Fitzhugh who had expressed what appeared to be genuinely paternalistic sentiments towards blacks before the Civil War, became rabid racists after it (Genovese, 1969) – to develop exaggerated fantasies about the threat of 'black domination'. Partly on account of these beliefs and partly on account of the 'segmental solidarity' of such groups, that is the fact that they formed bonds across class lines around the shared similarity of their 'whiteness' and their shared hostility to others who were different, such as blacks, the dominant response of these whites tended to be violent and racist. For example, they established or joined virulently racist organizations such as the Ku Klux Klan. Organizations of this type operated mainly clandestinely during reconstruction but came more into the open once federal troops started to be withdrawn from the South.

A central consequence of the movement of groups like the Ku Klux Klan more into the open was that the rate of lynching blacks grew annually from about 1870 to about 1890. It started to decline around the turn of the century because that period marked the legal consolidation of the caste-like figuration involving white dominance and black subordination which had begun to emerge as soon as slavery was abolished. This process of legal consolidation was symbolised by a series of decisions made by the United States Supreme Court between 1873 and 1898 (Wiggins, 1986: 108), notable among them the declaration as constitutional in 1896 in the case of *Plessy v. Ferguson* of an act passed in Louisiana in 1890 which legalized the segregation of railway carriages. This was a crucial decision since, under the distorting ideology that 'separate' could mean 'equal', it gave federal backing to the constitutions which were established in all Southern states whereby not only transport, but also education, employment, residential areas, eating establishments and public facilities such as parks were increasingly segregated by law. This legally buttressed segregation – it was similar to South African 'apartheid' in many ways – and the caste-like system of white dominance which underlay it secured important gains for whites of all classes. For the white upper and middle classes, it secured a permanent supply of cheap, readily exploitable labour and removed the threat of a racially united working class. For poor whites, it limited black competition in the field of employment in two main ways: first, through the creation of 'job ceilings' which made it difficult for blacks to rise above the ranks of unskilled and semi-skilled labour; and second, by the permanent restriction of blacks to 'pariah' occupations. At the same time, it provided poor, insecure and socially marginal whites with an important psychological gain for which they did not have to work by ensuring that, even though they stood at or near the bottom of the white social hierarchy, they did not stand at the bottom of the *overall* social order of the South. In order to secure the implementation of this gain, interracial contact was forced to take a ritual form in which deference to all whites was demanded from all blacks. For example, depending on their age, black males were addressed by whites as 'uncle' or 'boy' and forced to call all white males 'sir'. Breaches of the rules of interracial etiquette were swiftly and severely punished, nowhere more than in the case of violation of the sexual aspects of the code, for example if a black man was held even so much as to have glanced at a white woman. This is indicative of a further gain for whites, namely that white males had available to them two classes of women, black as well as white. Blacks and women were the losers. Neither group was sufficiently powerful to resist these and other encroachments into their lives by dominant white males.[7]

It would be wrong to conclude that the abolition of slavery and its eventual succession by a colour-caste figuration had no long-term effects on American race relations. One critical long-term consequence was the further consolidation of the embryonic black bourgeoisie. This process began under slavery where it grew, for example, from the distinction between 'field slaves' and 'house slaves', many of the latter becoming 'gentrified' relative to their counterparts whose work was restricted to the fields and who thus did not come regularly into close contact with the dominant whites in domestic social settings. Freed slaves, an at present unknown proportion of them probably owing their manumission largely to their sporting prowess, were another source of social stratification among American blacks. Some 'freedmen' became slave owners themselves (Koger, 1995). However, the development of the black upper and middle classes was mainly implicit in the formation of colour castes *per se* since this implied that a number of crucial tasks, for example hairdressing, teaching, the provision of legal, medical and funeral services, had, given the existence of an inflexible pattern of racial segregation, to be performed independently by blacks, hence offering the chance of capital accumulation to those who monopolized the provision of such services. Although not much is known about it at the moment, it seems likely that, just as had been the case under slavery, the possession of sporting prowess – the ability to provide sporting 'services', if you like – played a part of some significance in this consolidation of the embryonic black bourgeoisie. The likelihood of that being the case is intensified by the fact that this process of internal stratification of the 'black caste' coincided temporally with the early development in the USA of the modern forms of organized and commercialized professional sport (Ingham and Beamish, 1993).

Sport and the black bourgeoisie under 'colour-caste' segregation

Although research in this area has hardly begun, present indications are that, just as under slavery, blacks with exceptional sporting talent were able in the context of the gradual replacement of 'the peculiar institution' by segregated colour castes to use their sporting prowess as a means of enhancing their power chances. At this stage, however, it did not enhance their chances of obtaining manumission – they were 'free' in a legal sense already – but of increasing their earning power and social status and hence their chances of obtaining admission to the ranks of the embryonic black bourgeoisie. The jockey, Isaac Murphy, was a prominent example.

Murphy – that was his mother's father's name – was born Isaac Burns in Kentucky in 1861. He died in 1896 at the age of 35. He was the first jockey to win three Kentucky Derbies. He also won the American Derby four times and the Latonia Derby five times. In his overall career, his winning percentage was 44 per cent; more particularly, he was victorious on 628 of 1,412 mounts (Wiggins, 1979: 16). At the height of his career, at a time when other top jockeys were earning around $5,000 a year, Murphy's annual earnings are reported to have been between $15,000 and $20,000 (Wiggins, 1979: 17). Such earnings clearly qualified Murphy for black bourgeois status. As Wiggins expressed it:

> Murphy's financial standing afforded him many opportunities and privileges denied other blacks of the period. While most members of his race were barely able to carve out a living, Murphy was purchasing lavish clothing and being accompanied by a personal valet during the racing season. He owned property in some highly desirable white neighbourhoods in Lexington and as far away as Chicago. He owned his own stable of horses which he rode in local races around Lexington. Murphy and his wife also organized elaborate social entertainments. In fact, it was said that Murphy entertained more often than 'any black man in the South, if not in the whole country'.
>
> (Wiggins, 1979: 17)

Isaac Murphy was not an isolated exception but one of a larger number of black jockeys in the USA after the Civil War. For example, according to Wiggins 'fourteen of the fifteen jockeys in the first Kentucky Derby in 1875 were blacks' (Wiggins, 1979: 15). It would be interesting to establish how Murphy and other members of the black bourgeoisie who owed their social position solely or largely to their sporting prowess were viewed by more established members of that embryonic class, for example by doctors, lawyers, clergymen and other professionals. It would also be interesting to establish whether the sporting route into the black bourgeoisie differed between sports (being affected by different sports cultures, for example) and whether it was conducive to upward mobility of a relatively stable, secure and permanent kind which could be passed on to future generations. In Murphy's case, since he owned a stable and property in Lexington and Chicago, presumably it did.

Horse-racing was not the only sport in which American blacks participated at the top level in the second half of the nineteenth century. For the most part, they played on a segregated basis but, as Wiggins has established, 'black pugilists boxed white fighters [and] black baseball players frequently competed with white athletes' (Wiggins, 1979: 15). According to Boyle, Bud Fowler in the 1860s was the first black to play professional baseball (Boyle, 1971: 260). Sammons cites James W. Johnson who claimed in 1930 that, during the 1880s, every major city in the South had a black baseball team which was 'invariably better than its white counterpart' (Sammons, 1994: 218). Black baseball players, we are told, were also 'loudly applauded in such cities as Louisville, Baltimore and Washington DC'. And two blacks, Moses 'Fleetwood' Walker and his brother, Welday, both played major league baseball with the Toledo Mudhens of the American Association in the 1880s (Wiggins, 1986: 104). According to Gwendolyn Captain, the Walker brothers had also played in the major leagues in the 1870s (Captain, 1991: 90). In addition, in 1887 some twenty blacks were playing for teams in the minor leagues (Wiggins, 1986: 104).

In the same period, a small number of blacks competed in sports at prestigious universities outside the South. These included Moses Walker, the baseball player, who went to Oberlin; William Washington, another Oberlin alumnus; George A. Flippin of Nebraska; George M. Chadwell of Williams College; William Tecumseh Sherman Jackson of Amherst; and William Henry Lewis who attended both Amherst and Harvard. Lewis was selected for Walter Camp's 'All-American (football) Teams' in 1892 and 1893, and went on to become a prominent lawyer (Wiggins, 1991: 165). It seems likely that none of these college athletes would have owed their social mobility solely or largely to their sporting prowess but would have been born into the emerging black bourgeoisie. It is, however, reasonable to suppose that, in the context of American universities at the end of the nineteenth and beginning of the twentieth centuries, their abilities as sportsmen may have helped to some extent to offset the difficulties they would have faced as pioneering members of a racialized minority in what were overwhelmingly white institutions.

The experiences of black sportsmen such as Lewis ran counter to what was the dominant trend in American sports as the nineteenth century drew to a close. This was a tendency for sport which had hitherto been characterized by a degree of racial integration to become increasingly segregated along the lines of colour caste. Wiggins has interestingly suggested that, in the decades immediately following the Civil War, the career of jockey had been stigmatized as 'nigger work' but that, in the 1890s, whites formed 'anti-coloured unions' in order to drive blacks from the tracks (Wiggins, 1979: 31). Captain has similarly discussed how blacks were forced out of top-level baseball, presumably in part in order to enable whites to monopolize what was becoming an increasingly lucrative career (Captain, 1991: 90). However, deeper motives may have been at work as well. Thus it seems possible that racist whites would have experienced playing sports like baseball with blacks as 'polluting', perhaps especially sharing the same changing, dining, travelling and hotel facilities with them.

This trend towards increasing racial segregation in sport was also a consequence of growing racial intolerance in American society at large as indexed by the growing prominence of organizations such as the Ku Klux Klan, the increasing incidence of racial lynchings, and the granting of legitimacy to racist constitutions in the South by the US Supreme Court in 1896. It is hardly surprising in such a social context that violent means were sometimes used in order to drive blacks out of professional sports. The following story appeared in *Sporting Life* in 1891:

The Discovery of the Slide

The Feet-First Slide Due to a Desire to Cripple Coloured Players

'No', said Ed Williamson, the once great shortstop...to a reporter, 'ball players do not burn with a desire to have coloured men on the team'. It is, in fact, the deep-seated objection that most of them have for an Afro-American professional player that gave rise to the 'feet-first' slide. You may have noticed in a close play that the base-runner will launch himself into the air and take chances on landing on the bag. Some go head first, others with the feet in advance. Those who adopt the latter method are principally old-timers and served in the dark days prior to 1880. They learned the trick in the East. The Buffaloes...had a Negro for second base. He was...one of the best players in the old Eastern League. The haughty Caucasians...were willing to permit him to carry water...or guard the bat bag, but it made them sore to have...one on the batting list. They made a cabal against this man.... The players of opposing teams made it their special business in life to 'spike' this brunette Buffalo. They would tarry at second...just to toy with the sensitive shins of the second baseman. The poor man played in two games out of five perhaps; the rest of the time he was on crutches. To give the frequent spiking of the darky an appearance of accident the 'feet-first' slide was practised. The Negro got wooden armour for his legs and went into the field with the appearance of a man wearing nail kegs for stockings. The enthusiasm of opposition players would not let them take a bluff. They filed their spikes and the first man at second generally split the wooden half cylinders. The coloured man seldom lasted beyond the fifth inning, as the base-runners became more expert. The practice survived long after the second baseman made his last trip to hospital.

(Boyle, 1971: 261)

Seven years earlier, Moses and Welday Walker had been forced out of the Toledo team by the threat of mob violence in Richmond, Virginia (Boyle, 1971: 260). Violence was also used against blacks in a Northern college context. For example, Paul Robeson – later world famous as a singer and actor – who was selected when a student at Rutgers for Walter Camp's 'All-American' teams in 1917 and 1918, had his nose broken, his shoulder dislocated and his body lacerated with cuts and bruises by his Rutgers team-mates on his first day of training (Wiggins, 1991: 166–7). If sporting prowess did aid integration in those contexts, it evidently did not do so immediately or universally.

According to Wiggins, 'black athletes were virtually eliminated from white organized sport by the last decade of the nineteenth century' (Wiggins, 1986: 110) and forced to compete in clubs and leagues of their own. Examples were baseball teams like the Cuban Giants of New York, the Columbia Giants of Chicago and the Philadelphia Giants (Captain, 1991: 90). However, boxing formed a partial exception to this trend. George Dixon, a black, held the US bantamweight title from 1890 to 1892 and the featherweight title from 1892 to 1900. Joe Walcott, another black, won the welterweight title in 1901 and held it to 1906. And Joe Gans held the lightweight title from 1902 to 1908 (Sammons, 1990: 33–4). However, the most famous black boxer of that period was Jack Johnson, the so-called 'Black Menace', who won the world heavyweight title by defeating James J. Jeffries in 1910. According to Sammons, on the day following the fight there were many deaths and injuries from racial conflicts throughout the country (Sammons, 1990: 39; see also Chapter 7 of the present volume). Jeffries articulated the extremely tense racial dimension which was perceived as inhering in this fight when he claimed that, in agreeing to it, he was responding to 'that portion of the white race that has been looking for me to defend its athletic superiority' (Sammons, 1990: 37). Sammons hypothesizes that boxing did not undergo the trend towards virtually complete racial segregation to the extent experienced in other sports because 'it is, and always has been, a sport of confrontation and combat, a weaponless war, individualized; thus fighting between blacks and whites did not indicate comradeship or social acceptance' (Sammons, 1990: 34). This hypothesis is plausible. However, another plausible reason why boxing was not drawn fully into the overall trend may be that generally held white stereotypes of boxers gelled with their generally accepted stereotypes of race. That is, both boxers and blacks were widely believed by whites to be 'animalic' and 'unintelligent'. Hence, little threat was perceived in allowing black–white fights to continue. Moreover, allowing blacks and whites to continue to compete directly in boxing provided whites such as Jeffries for a while with an opportunity to demonstrate the 'athletic superiority' and 'superior intelligence' of the 'white race' over the members of 'a race' whom they widely believed had been equipped for boxing by 'nature'. This was a period before the ideology of the 'athletic superiority' of blacks had developed.

The partial demise of the colour-caste figuration and the 'ghettoization' of blacks

The seeds of the disintegration of the colour-caste figuration which had grown up in the USA in the second half of the nineteenth century were present even as it first began to be consolidated. The position of the USA in the growing system of international interdependencies had been crucial to the initial establishment of white dominance in that country. The power of the colonizing British made it possible for them (the British) to dominate, and later to abolish, the slave trade, and Britain's industrialization, more specifically the development of the cotton industry, had facilitated the emergence of the cotton monoculture in the post-colonial South. International contingencies were similarly implicated in the downfall of that system and the transformation of the wider figuration with which it was intertwined. The emergence of countries such as Egypt and China as producers of cotton for the world market led, together with the increasing manufacture of artificial fibres, to a decline in the profitability and competitive capacity of the American South and subsequently to the decline of the cotton monoculture and the colour-caste figuration which had grown up in conjunction with it. As a result, blacks and poor whites were forced in large numbers to leave the South. They were simultaneously attracted to the North and West by the employment opportunities which were being opened up by industrial expansion, a process which was speeded up during the First World War, slowed down during the depression of the 1930s, and speeded up once again during the Second World War and the period of American world dominance which was achieved during and after it. The strict immigration legislation enacted in the face of mounting prejudice against immigrants from Southern and Eastern Europe (which paralleled the growth of prejudice against blacks), led to a drastic decline in the capacity of American industry to recruit cheap labour from abroad. It was forced to rely increasingly on domestic sources, and blacks and poor whites from the South came to form a chief means of filling the gap.

The effects of this migration on the social situation of blacks were dramatic. In 1900, some 90 per cent lived in the South. By 1960, only just above one-half remained there. The migration was not simply a move out of the South but from rural to urban areas. A comparable rural–urban migration occurred in the South as well, as, latterly, an urban–industrial mode of living began to take root there. Again by 1960, blacks had come to constitute between 14 per cent and 54 per cent of the populations of major American cities. This representation of blacks in the American urban population did not reflect their proportional membership of the population as a whole – about one-tenth – but the fact that their movement to the cities coincided with, and was in part the stimulus for, an exodus of whites to the suburbs. In that way, the urbanization of American blacks was a process of 'ghettoization'.

At first, this process involved the virtual reconstitution in an urban context of the colour-caste figuration which had developed in the pre-industrial South. The emergent system of ghetto-dwelling urban racial castes was more impersonal but the fact that it was based fundamentally on overt physical marks of difference meant that it was relatively easy to reconstitute in urban settings. The deep-rooted anti-black feelings of large numbers of Northerners and Westerners – 'Jim Crow' legislation had been enacted in some Northern states before the Civil War, long before such legislation was felt necessary by whites in the South – provided the motive. In the longer term, however, ghettoization had important consequences for the balance of power between blacks and whites, contributing to a slight but nonetheless detectable increase in the power of the former relative to the latter, to the internalization of a more positive self- and group image as part of the habitus of increasing numbers of blacks, that is to a growing shedding by blacks of feelings of the 'group charisma' of whites and of their own 'group disgrace', and simultaneously to an increasing willingness of blacks to struggle individually and collectively for the right to equal status and equal treatment which they saw as embodied in the US Constitution. This long-term process was complex. Although they were interdependent and interreacted, I shall conclude this penultimate part of the chapter by singling out for discussion what seem to have been its principal components. They were as follows:

1   The fact that the ghettoization of blacks and their incorporation into a caste-like urban figuration facilitated more effective communication, perception of the common interests which they shared in opposition to whites and hence organization on their part than had been possible given the relatively high ecological scattering of their situation in the rural South. In short, this process was conducive to the incipient formation of blacks as what Marx (Bendix, 1953) might have called a 'class', or more properly, a 'caste', 'racial' or 'ethnic' group 'for themselves'.

2   The fact that urban concentration facilitated rioting. Whites grew increasingly fearful of the black ghettos, coming to see them as a powder keg ready to explode. This, together with the race riots which have recurred in the USA since the early 1960s, provides a further measure of the power increment gained by blacks under urban conditions. Even though they have typically been sparked by real or perceived injustices at the hands of the police, directed at non-black-owned small businesses in the ghettos, and have served as a vehicle for looting as well as political

protest, the riots have nevertheless tended to be perceived by whites as posing a more general threat, for example to their residential areas and capital concentrations such as factories, power plants, office blocks and political, judicial and administrative buildings. It would be wrong to see the threat posed in this connection as simply 'economic'. Such capital concentrations are an index of the complex networks of human interdependence which grow up in urban–industrial societies and it is the operation of these networks which is threatened by rioting just as much as the capital concentrations *per se*. It is also threatened by sabotage and urban guerrilla warfare which exist as possibilities in such a situation. Indeed, in the 1960s these tactics began to be used on a small scale by the most militant blacks. All of this constituted a power increment to blacks because it helped to force their social situation to the forefront of the national political agenda. Unlike in the days of slavery and immediately after the Civil War, whatever their political persuasions whites had to take the interests of blacks more into account. And blacks themselves ceased increasingly to be relatively passive victims and came in greater numbers to be more politically active in the determination of their fates.

3   The integration of blacks in growing numbers into the urban–industrial occupational structure – principally at lower levels in the stratification hierarchy and with lesser rates of job security and higher rates of unemployment than whites – also began to increase their power chances, especially where they formed trade unions or managed to secure the desegregation of 'white' ones. Such an effect is a principal source of 'functional democratization' in Elias's (1978) sense. It follows generally as a result of occupational differentiation since specialist groups, when their members become conscious of their common interests and begin to organize on that basis, can, by withdrawing their labour, effect a greater or lesser breakdown in wider networks of interdependence.

4   The integration of increasing numbers of blacks into the money economy as wage-earners as opposed to mainly subsistence farmers and 'debt peons' – itself an index of their growing integration into the developing nation-wide network of interdependency chains – had among its consequences the fact that the organized withdrawal of their purchasing power enabled them to hurt firms which refused to employ black labour or practised other forms of discrimination. Simultaneously, the increase of black purchasing power increased the dependency of business generally on the 'Afro-American' market, a fact which became reflected in the growing use of blacks – sportspersons prominent among them – in advertising. This, too, contributed to the growth of more positive self- and group images on the part of growing numbers of blacks.

5   Although white 'liberals' also played a part in their formation, the internal stratification of the urban black caste, especially the gradual emergence of a well-educated and comparatively affluent black bourgeoisie, began to be

central in providing leadership, funds, organizational expertise, legal and political 'nous' for the setting up of rationally orientated, non-violent protest organizations such as the NAACP, the Urban League, and the Southern Christian Leadership Conference (SCLC). Although there were, and still are, many conflicts between them which have tended to lessen their impact, these organizations began to pursue long-term strategies through which the gradually changing balance of power between blacks and whites which has been inherent in the increasing incorporation of the former into an urban–industrial nation-state figuration has been made increasingly manifest. A crucial moment in this regard came in 1954 when the US Supreme Court overturned the 'separate but equal' doctrine which it had declared legitimate in 1896. A long-term legal battle orchestrated and largely financed by the NAACP played an important part in securing that reversal. It was, perhaps more than anything else, the single most important signal for the overt, nation-wide civil rights struggle of the 1950s and 1960s to begin.

Arguably at the root of the motivations of members of the black bourgeoisie in supporting organizations like the NAACP lay the frustration engendered by the ambiguities and anomalies inherent in their position as the dominant, 'established' group in a subordinate, 'outsider' caste. Their comparative affluence meant that questions of status could take precedence in their lives over simple bread and butter issues, whilst their widespread rejection by whites of objectively comparable socio-economic standing constrained them into an ambivalent identification with the poorer members of their caste. On the one hand, because in the wider society – despite the light skin pigmentation of many of them – their 'blackness' was the principal criterion in terms of which they were socially defined and judged, they were led to identify with poorer blacks and to perceive themselves as sharing common 'racial' interests with the latter. On the other, many were repelled by the poverty, low levels of education and 'culture', and what they regarded as the 'uncivilized' living conditions, manners, etiquette and language of many poorer blacks. Once the dynamics of the protest movement thus set in motion had got under way, the stage was set for the movement of more militant and radical black protest groups such as, in the 1960s, the Student Non-Violent Co-ordinating Committee (SNCC), the 'Black Muslims' and 'Black Panthers' to enter the arena. (A notable sports-related event in this connection occurred at the 1968 Olympics in Mexico, when medal winners Tommie Smith and John Carlos gave the 'black power' salute instead of saluting the American flag when on the medal winners rostrum.) Even as far as groups such as the SNCC, the 'Muslims' and the 'Panthers' were concerned, however, many of their members and quite a few of their leaders came from the ranks of the black bourgeoisie, principally from among its younger age groups, especially from blacks at university. That only serves to underline the fundamental dependency of the American civil rights movement on the internal stratification of the black caste which occured correlatively with the increasing absorption of blacks into the developing urban–industrial figuration of American society as a whole

Especially at the universities, many whites identified with and came actively to support the struggle of their black fellow students. Not only were they angered at the ways in which racial discrimination runs counter to the dominant tenets of 'the American Creed' but, through mixing with blacks at college, they were able to see how superficial and literally only 'skin deep' were the differences which separated them from their black fellow students. In a word, mixing at close quarters with black students who principally came from the assimilated black bourgeoisie provided many white students with strong experiential proof of how false the dominant racial ideologies were. Such experiences provided a counter to the media-promoted images of blacks, particularly during riots, as violent and disorderly, a superficial reading of which could support the collective racist fantasies of uneducated whites. During the 1960s, the civil rights movement began to succeed in obtaining better employment opportunities for blacks, in securing voting rights for blacks in the South, in forcing the desegregation of public facilities and in pressing the federal and state governments to place the issue of racial discrimi-nation at the forefront of the political agenda. They also triggered a 'white backlash' but I shall not consider that in this context. Rather, I shall explore sociologically the part played by sport and sportspersons in the continuing formation of the black bourgeoisie and the civil rights movement in which members of that class (caste) fraction were principal activists.

Sport and the black struggle for civil rights

From the end of the nineteenth century until after the Second World War – with notable exceptions such as boxing, track and field, and sport in college contexts outside the South – sport in the USA was characterized by extreme forms of racial segregation. Today, with the end of the twentieth century rapidly approaching, blacks are strongly represented – as far as participation though not as far as management and ownership are concerned – at the top levels of major American sports. In short, a process of racial desegregation at the top levels of American sport is under way. In an attempt to explain this process, Coakley suggests that

> it is clear that financial motives have been primary in the desegrega-tion of sport. If black athletes had not improved winning records and increased profits for those who controlled sports, the racist policies that had restricted black participation for so long would not have changed as rapidly or as completely as they did in certain sports. In sports where it is not possible to make money there has been much less interest in recruiting blacks or in communicating to the black

community that opportunities are available. And blacks have not been blind to opportunities in sports.

(Coakley, 1990: 210)

This argument is persuasive but incomplete. It cannot explain why the process of desegregation started overtly to occur in 1946 when owner Branch Rickey signed black baseball player Jackie Robinson for the Brooklyn Dodgers. Rickey could not possibly have foreseen the profits which would eventually be made by employing blacks. Nor can Coakley's argument explain why, earlier in the century, the owners of major league baseball clubs and their counterparts in other sports were apparently unaware of the profits seemingly to be obtained from including blacks in their teams. In order to move towards a more complete explanation, it is necessary to contextualize the growing desegregation of top-level American sports in relation to the wider development of race relations.

If asked to explain Jackie Robinson's breakthrough into major league baseball, many Americans would probably attribute it to individual characteristics such as Robinson's superior playing skills or Rickey's political beliefs and financial perspicacity. In other words, they would explain it reductively. However, the available evidence points to Robinson's breakthrough marking a decisive early moment in a process, the roots of which can be traced to before 1946. In fact, the evidence suggests that men such as Robinson and Rickey were merely prominent actors in a wider development in which the continuing emergence of the black bourgeoisie played a crucial part. One of the most overt symptoms of this development was a media campaign against segregated baseball.

It seems that 'liberal' white journalists began the campaign. Westbrook Pegler of the *Chicago Tribune* started the ball rolling in 1931, receiving support from fellow journalists Heywood Broun and Jimmy Powers, who made pro-desegregation speeches at the baseball writers' annual dinner in 1933 (Wiggins, 1983: 6, 7). This served as a stimulus for black newspapers to enter the fray. According to Wiggins, central among them was the *Pittsburgh Courier Journal*, the largest and perhaps most radical black newspaper in the USA at the time (Wiggins, 1983: 5). It first added its voice in 1933, a leading role in its campaign subsequently being played by Wendell Smith who became its sports editor in 1938. Smith fought on behalf of racially integrated baseball, coming later to act as mediator between stars of the segregated black leagues and owners such as Rickey.

Other members of the sports staff of the *Courier Journal*, most notably Chester Washington, Alvin Moses and Rollo Wilson, played a part in the campaign, too. As journalists, it is reasonable to suppose, they were members of the emerging black bourgeoisie. Smith, for example, had been educated at West Virginia State College where he graduated with a Bachelor of Education degree in 1937 (Wiggins, 1983: 10). As writers, principal among the power resources available to these men were logic, rhetoric, factual evidence and persuasion, resources which would then have been in short supply among the relatively uneducated majority of blacks. Smith and his fellow writers were also able to take the longer view. What centrally concerned them was the effects on the group image and individual self-confidence of blacks of being excluded from the top level of the American major national sport, a sport deeply imprinted in the habitus and psyche of a majority of Americans. The existence of segregated leagues, they contended, implied that blacks were less than full citizens and, during the late 1930s and early 1940s, they were able to make telling use of the fact that there were uncomfortable parallels between the social situation of black Americans and the treatment of minorities, especially Jews, in Nazi Germany (Wiggins, 1983: 11).

A crucial moment in the *Courier Journal's* campaign came in December 1943 when Smith managed to persuade baseball commissioner Judge Landis to meet with a delegation from the Black Newspaper Publishers Association (Wiggins, 1983: 21). This, in itself, provides testimony to the growing power of blacks. If Landis had not seen them as people 'who mattered', at least to a degree, he could simply have refused to meet them. Among those present at the meeting were: John Sengstacke of the *Chicago Defender*, President of the Publishers Association; Ira Lewis, President of the *Courier Journal*; Howard H. Murphy, business manager of the *Baltimore Afro-American*; and Paul Robeson, the actor, singer and former college sports star (Wiggins, 1983: 20–3). Using material from interviews conducted by Smith, Lewis was able to claim that most baseball managers and players were no longer opposed to an integrated game, and that Americans generally (influenced by the world success of stars like Joe Lewis and Jesse Owens) accepted black participation in boxing and college track and field (Wiggins, 1983: 21–2). Asked at the end of the meeting whether they had any questions for the publishers, the forty-four baseball officials present remained silent. However, afterwards they issued the following statement: 'Each club is entirely free to employ Negro players to any and all extents it pleases. The matter is solely for each club's decision, without restriction whatsoever' (Wiggins, 1983: 22–3).

This was mere rhetoric. At that point, none of the owners of major league clubs had any intention of signing black players but sought, instead, to uphold the *de facto* white monopoly at baseball's highest levels. Nor can the possibility be discounted that many regarded the prospect of integrated baseball as potentially 'polluting' for whites and thought, via the projection of their own feelings, that racist beliefs remained widespread among managers, players and spectators. Many owners of clubs in the segregated black leagues, too, were either opposed to or ambivalent regarding the prospects of a racially integrated game and refused to provide active support for Smith's campaign. Like their white counterparts, they were conservative on the issue and fearful of social change. The leaders of black baseball, said J. B. Martin, President of the Black American League in 1943, could not 'force big league owners to admit

Negro players' (Wiggins, 1983: 20). As often happens when changes in the direction of a higher level of social integration are afoot, leaders on the lower level were fearful that they would lose in terms of power, influence, finance and prestige. The black club owners appear to have been no exception. There is reason, however, to believe that Martin and his fellow black owners had underestimated the growing power of blacks and the changes which were beginning correlatively to occur in black–white relations in American society at large.

Smith continued to argue in favour of racially integrated baseball. He also sought to secure trials ('tryouts') for black players with major league clubs, eventually playing a part in persuading Rickey to sign Robinson for the Brooklyn Dodgers. This took place in October 1945. That it was only one manifestation of a wider process which was being propelled by the growing power of the black bourgeoisie and facilitated by the anti-racist climate fostered in the context of the war against the Nazis is suggested by the fact that, in May the same year, Rickey and Larry McPhail, President of the New York Yankees, had been selected by their representative leagues to head a committee charged with examining whether blacks should be integrated into the game. Around the same time, Vico Marcantonio, a US Congressman for New York State, demanded a congressional investigation into racial discrimination in baseball, and Mayor La Guardia of New York City appointed Rickey as part of a ten-man committee to look into the issue. In November 1945, one month after Rickey had signed Robinson, the committee strongly recommended the acceptance of blacks in major league baseball (Wiggins, 1983: 27–8). It is reasonable to suppose that an important part in this process had been played by the campaign fought by Wendell Smith and his associates, and that this campaign, in turn, had been to a considerable extent predicated on the growth in the numbers of well-educated and articulate blacks which occurred as part of the emergence of the black bourgeoisie of which Smith and his colleagues formed part.

By 1959, fifty-seven of the 400 or so players of major league baseball in the USA were black, around 12 per cent (Boyle, 1971: 259). Table 8.1 charts the growth of black representation in top-level baseball, (gridiron) football and basketball between 1954 and 1989.

Over the same period, a comparable expansion of black representation occurred at the top levels of other sports in the USA as well, most notably boxing and track and field. According to Frazier, 'the Negro ball players have become symbols of achievement, symbols of Negro participation in a white world, and with their high incomes and conspicuous consumption…are an important part of the bourgeois elite' (quoted in Boyle, 1971: 275–6). In other words, the desegregation of top-level American sport, a process which appears to have depended substantially on the black bourgeoisie for its sociogenesis and continuing momentum, contributed to the further expansion of that class.

Table 8.1 The percentages of black athletes in the three major professional team sports from the 1950s to the present*

Baseball**		Football		Basketball	
Year	%	Year	%	Year	%
1954	7	1956	14	1954	5
1967	11	1968	28	1962	30
1978	17	1975	42	1970	56
1980	28	1982	49	1980	75
1985	20	1985	54	1985	75
1988	21	1988	57	1989	73***

Source: Coakley (1990: 208)

Notes:
*   Data were not available for the same years in each sport
**   These percentages were computed by dividing the number of black players into the *total* number of players listed on team rosters, including pitchers. Some studies give different figures for these years because computations were made without including pitchers in the analysis. Since pitchers make up over 40 per cent of the team rosters in major league baseball, and since there are few black pitchers, these other studies give higher percentages that those given here
***   This figure excludes 'rookies' (newly recruited players)

That also seems to have been true of the civil rights movement generally. The reasons why were inherent in the deep structure of the social process through which that movement was generated. Since it was initially mainly a product of ghetto life, in particular of the fact that segregation forced blacks to perform virtually all service and professional (including sports) functions for themselves, the power and influence of the black bourgeoisie were, at first, restricted almost solely to the 'coloured quarters' of Southern towns and, later on, to the ghettos. As a result, the overall pressures of functional democratization tended initially to be caste specific, that is, operative mainly among whites, to a lesser extent among blacks and hardly at all in the relations between blacks and whites. From the 1960s, however, blacks began to be elected as mayors, and larger numbers than before began to work in racially integrated contexts, for example for the federal government, in managerial and front-line positions in department stores, schools and banks, and most significantly for present purposes, in top-level sports. That meant in contexts where the pressures of functional democratization could operate *between*, rather than as had tended previously to be the case, simply *within*, racial castes. And that meant, in its turn, that for such groups, the gains of the civil rights movement could be more easily consolidated and enhanced.

However, for the vast mass of poorer blacks, the egalitarian rhetoric of the civil rights movement served merely to kindle aspirations which, especially in a period of declining employment opportunities for unskilled and poorly educated workers, could not be satisfied in the short run and which contributed correspondingly to the riots of the mid-1960s and later. The effects of these riots and of black protest more generally on the dynamics of racial stratification in the USA have been complex. In part, they led younger black activists, many from black bourgeois backgrounds, to become disillusioned with moderate leaders, to press for 'black power' and, in some cases, at least in the 1960s, increasingly to reject non-violent tactics as means of goal achievement. This, in turn, served to split the moderate leadership, pushing some into a more radical stance. It also served to intensify the 'white backlash' which had been beginning to grow ever since the changing balance of power between blacks and whites began to be translated into organized protest and meet with a measure of success. It was partly for this reason that the civil rights movement only managed to make a comparatively small dent in the power of the dominant whites and that its principal long-term effect, apart from leading the black bourgeoisie to grow larger, has been to exacerbate and polarize the class division of blacks which began most significantly to occur with the formation of colour castes and the process of ghettoization.

To an extent, black professional sports stars have unintentionally contributed to this process of intra-caste class polarization. As top-level sports in the USA came to be increasingly desegregated in and after the 1940s, black sports stars began in growing numbers to become high earners and integrated, as Frazier said, increasingly into the black bourgeoisie, making a small but by no means insignificant addition to its overall size. However, one of the effects of their success, as Edwards (1973), Cashmore (1990) and, more recently and controversially, Hoberman (1997) have shown, has been to signal to poorer young blacks that sport represents a means of escape from ghetto poverty, leading many to concentrate on sport at the expense of education and other means of increasing upward mobility chances. Some have been 'aided' in this regard by teachers who accept the myth of the genetically determined athletic superiority of blacks, being pushed by them to channel their energies into sport (Cashmore, 1990: 88ff.). However, as Leonard and Reyman, using data from the 1980 US census, have shown: 'The opportunities for upward social mobility in sport are highly restricted − for females 4/1,000,000 (.004%); for males, 7/1,000,000 (.007)' (quoted in McKay, 1995: 195). McKay summarizes the currently dominant sociological position on this issue thus:

> the handful of athletes (most of whom are men) who go 'from rags to riches', are rare exceptions to the obdurate American class structure. Although a small number of black men obtain athletic scholarships, this has little effect on their career prospects. Gates claims that about 75% of black male athletes never graduate; Lapchick reports that around 80% of black football and basketball players at NCAA Division 1 schools fail to graduate; [and] between

1983 and 1987, 44 major NCAA universities failed to graduate any of their black basketball players who started as freshmen.

(McKay, 1995: 194–5)

McKay's figures highlight the continuing exploitation of American blacks by the 'athletic superiority, intellectual inferiority' myth. However, an additional – NB: not alternative – interpretation can be placed on the figures supplied by Gates and Lapchick, namely that between 20 and 25 per cent of blacks who secure athletic scholarships *do* manage to graduate. It would be interesting to establish what proportion manage subsequently to consolidate themselves, via their sporting prowess and/or educational qualifications, at some level in the black bourgeoisie. Whatever that proportion turns out to be it is clear that, whilst sporting prowess and success may be an individual power resource, they are not necessarily always a collective one.

As a counter to the exploitation of the majority of American blacks via the medium of sport, Gates (1991) has called for 'professional black athletes to contribute a share of their income to the United Negro College Fund, and to publicize the value of obtaining an education among young blacks'. Edwards (1969) made similar suggestions (both quoted in McKay, 1995: 198). Writing in the 1960s, Boyle argued that black baseball players tended to be 'race men'; that is, despite their own upward mobility, they continued to identify with other members of their caste, including those who were poorer. This was expressed through membership of and financial support for the NAACP (Boyle, 1971: 277). Similar levels of race consciousness in sport were expressed by the black power demonstrations of Smith and Carlos at the 1968 Olympics and in the organization of black dissidence in American sport in the 1960s in which Harry Edwards played a leading role (Edwards, 1969). However, black American sports stars in the 1990s appear to be more commercially orientated and self-interested and less concerned with the plight of the black majority than their counterparts in the 1960s. As McKay, citing Wenner (1994), recently reminded us, Michael Jordan and his black fellow members of basketball's gold medal winning 'Dream Team' at the Barcelona Olympics in 1992 also staged a protest on the victory podium. However, it was not a political protest but one related to a conflict of interests between their sponsors, Nike, and the official Olympic sponsors, Reebok. They had been supplied with warm-up suits displaying the Reebok logo and what they did was to obscure this during the award ceremony. As Charles Barkley is reported to have said: 'Us Nike guys are loyal to Nike because they pay us a lot of money. I have two million reasons not to wear Reebok' (McKay, 1995: 199).

Conclusion

It is reasonable to suppose that the emergence of a not insubstantial black bourgeoisie in the USA can be interpreted sociologically as representing a

217

change in a civilizing direction within the context of the overall balance between civilizing and decivilizing trends in that country. Correspondingly, the entrapment of the vast majority of blacks in inner-city ghettos with bleak life prospects and problems such as growing drug dependency and criminal, often drug-related gangs can be construed as representing a 'barbarizing' development of even more massive proportions. If the arguments presented in this chapter have any substance, black sports stars could play a useful, perhaps pivotal, role in the development and application of policies designed to redress the de-civilizing aspects of these trends. They could, for example, take up Gates's suggestion and use their star status in an attempt to persuade poor black males to take formal education more seriously and sport less seriously, and by campaigning for the devotion of funds to the improvement of inner-city schools. Of course, to the extent that they prove successful in these regards, a decrease in the intense competitive pressure for sporting success which fuels black superiority in specific sports would probably result and, with it, a decline in that superiority *per se*.

In the short term, this might be perceived as depriving blacks of opportunities in one of the few areas in which they have managed to achieve pre-eminence and hence provoke resentment (Cashmore, 1990: 88). In the longer term, however, to the extent that they proved successful, such policies would lead to a significant equalization of opportunities for blacks across the board and simultaneously remove a central precondition involved in the sociogenesis and persistence of the myth of black sporting superiority and intellectual inferiority. It remains to be seen, however, whether today's black sports stars remain 'race men' (Boyle, 1971) who can be persuaded to play a leading role in political campaigns, or whether the vast sums they earn and the climate of commercialism and hyper-individualization which has become predominant in sport in the contemporary West are conducive to them anomically believing that 'money whitens', helping to counteract the status ambiguity which earlier led members of the black bourgeoisie to identify with their less fortunate fellows.

9

SPORT, GENDER AND CIVILIZATION

Introduction

This chapter grows out of my earlier work on sport as a male preserve (Sheard and Dunning, 1973; Dunning, 1986) and soccer hooliganism (Dunning *et al.*, 1988). However, while in that work one of the principal issues addressed was that of sport and sports-related contexts as sites – whether socially approved or not – for the production and reproduction of masculine habituses, identities and behaviour, in the present chapter I shall extend my focus and explore, in a preliminary way, not simply sport and masculinity but aspects of sport and femininity as well. I shall also look at some of the relationships between femininity and masculinity, particularly as they are expressed through sport.[1]

This broadening of focus does not represent a sudden switch to the area of gender relations. It may not have been widely perceived as such but, as a figurational sociologist who employs a dynamic and relational perspective focused on the study of social processes over time, that is on the emergence, reproduction, development and breakdown of interdependency networks ('figurations'), a concern with gender relations has been one of the central foci of my work since the 1970s. This was recognized by Birrell in 1988 when she wrote:

> Sheard and…Dunning's 1973 article, 'The Rugby Club as a Type of Male Preserve', gained respect as a subcultural study, but because it focused so clearly on males, it was not fully recognized for its importance to feminist scholarship until gender relations was recognized as the proper focus of the field.
>
> (Birrell, 1988: 481)

My previous work thus focused on aspects of male habitus and behaviour in changing contexts of gender power relations. In the present chapter, I shall seek to incorporate into the equation more aspects of the female side, especially those connected with the direct involvement of females in sport.

219

The sociological marginalization of sport and the study of gender

Probably in large part as a consequence of its marginalization as a subject of sociological theorizing and research (see the introduction to the present volume), sport does not figure centrally in many of the recently published mainstream texts that deal with gender (Oakley, 1985; Walby, 1990; Davis *et al.*, 1991).[2] Even where it is mentioned, sport is usually only considered in passing rather than as an important site in the production and expression of gender identities (Hearn, 1987; Brittan, 1989). Since sport remains to this day a largely male-dominated affair, this may not be particularly surprising in female-orientated texts. It is, however, surprising in the growing number of mainstream books which have the social production of masculinity as their principal focus (Seidler, 1992; Morgan, 1992).[3]

Clues as to why sport may have been marginalized in attempts to come to grips with the social production of masculinity are provided by the way in which Brittan approaches the subject. In *Masculinity and Power* he writes:

> Perhaps the most popular image of masculinity in everyday consciousness is that of man-the-hero, the hunter, the competitor, the conqueror. Certainly it is the image celebrated in Western literature, art and in the media.
>
> In a sense, the belief in man-the-hunter, or hero, would seem to have no foundation in the everyday world that most men inhabit. There are very few occasions available for men to be heroes, except as a hobby or for sport. Man-the-hunter has been transformed into man-the-breadwinner. Opportunities for heroism only arise in the sporting field, not in the forest in hot pursuit of food for the tribe.
>
> (Brittan, 1989: 77)

Brittan here correctly identifies sport as a source of the 'hero image' for men. However, by bracketing it with 'hobbies' and conceptualizing it as separate from 'the everyday world', he relegates it to a peripheral status compared with what he evidently regards as the principal locus for the production and reproduction of masculinity in present-day societies: the role of 'man-the breadwinner', that is work. This has at least two negative consequences: first, it means that Brittan anachronistically fails to take account of the recent increase in Western countries of long-term male unemployment and the growing number of females who, through choice, compulsion or some combination of the two, are 'breadwinners'; second – and for present purposes more importantly – it means that Brittan precludes himself from exploring what is arguably one of the most important sites in modern societies for the production and reproduction of masculinity in its more traditional forms, namely sport. (As I shall argue later, sport is simultaneously one of the most significant sites of resistance against and challenge to those forms.) Brittan, of course, is by no means alone in tracing contemporary patterns of masculinity principally to the world of work. Economistic thinking of this kind appears to enjoy something approaching hegemonic status in contemporary sociological theory and research. It is widely taken for granted, enjoying a status close to that of a sociological orthodoxy.

In saying this, it is not my intention to deny the *importance* of work and the economy in perpetuating an andrarchal sexual division of labour (Elias, 1986a)[4] – and as sites for the inculcation, expression, perpetuation and sometimes challenge and change in both males and females of andrarchal habituses, personality structures, behaviour, ideologies and values. It is simply that I question the assertion that economic processes are the *only* ones *centrally* involved in these regards. I think, moreover, that the marginalization of sport as a subject of enquiry in mainstream sociology may have unnecessarily restricted the range of research as far as issues of gender relations are concerned. Indeed, viewed from a non-economistic perspective, there are grounds for believing that sport is one of the key sites in contemporary societies in this regard.

Sport as a site for the production and reproduction of gender habituses and identities

The simple fact that sport is today a central interest in the lives of many people suggests that the empirical study and theorizing of it ought to occupy a more central place in mainstream ('malestream') sociology than they have done up to now. There are also reasons for believing that sport is more than a mere 'hobby', 'pastime', 'recreation' or 'leisure activity'. In fact one can say that, along with religion and war, sport represents one of the most successful means of collective mobilization humans have so far devised. That appears to be the case because of the combination of representational and excitement-generating function that sport can perform (Goodger, 1985; Goodger and Goodger, 1989; Murphy *et al.*, 1990). Indeed, as I suggested in the introduction, sport can even be said in certain respects to be functionally homologous with religion and war. That is, sport can: (1) provide a source of meaning in life; (2) act as a focus of social identification; and (3) offer experiences which are analogous to the excitement and emotional arousal generated in war and other 'serious' situations like 'being in love'. Indeed, many sports fans develop 'love-like' attachments to the teams they support, sometimes even to the detriment of their 'real' love relations whether of a heterosexual, bisexual or homosexual kind.

It is the inherently conflictful character of sport that enables it to be readily adapted to the formation and expression of 'in-group/out-group' or perhaps better, 'we-group/they-group' identifications (Elias, 1991a), though, of course, as I attempted to establish in Chapters 1 and 2, the success of sport in these regards appears to be in large part dependent on the fact that, in its modern forms, the physical dangers inherent in any group mobilization for purposes of conflict have been to a greater or lesser extent reduced via the internaliza-tion of personal controls (*Selbstzwänge*, Elias, 1994) and the institutionalization of social controls (*Fremdzwänge*, Elias, 1994). Another way of putting it would be to say that sport in its modern, more 'civilized' forms involves a usually relatively effective resolution of the antimony between rivalry and friendship. It involves, that is, forms of 'friendly rivalry'. But, of course, in human affairs these things are never permanent. Under specific conditions, such develop-ments are liable to go into reverse. Indeed, there is reason to believe that top-level sports in many countries are being threatened at the moment by the overly serious involvement of players and spectators (Dunning, 1986).

Except for people who are professionally involved, sport, of course, is a leisure activity but, if my argument so far has any substance, it appears to be one which is of considerable importance in the identity formation and habitus, particularly of males (Dunning, 1986). Indeed, such is the pressure to participate in sport – from the media, in schools, from their age peers and, of course, their parents, especially their fathers – that British males, virtually independently of social class though not perhaps of religious and ethnic affili-ations to the same degree, are forced to develop an internalized adjustment to it. That appears to be the case whether they conform and follow a sporting route in their leisure and perhaps their occupational lives, whether they deviate or resist and identify with the forms of 'anti-sports' subcultures which have grown up in British society (Marples, 1954: 130ff.) or whether they take a course which is intermediate between these poles.

Also worthy of note is the fact that, in many parts of British society, perhaps especially in all-male schools, 'deviant' males who, for whatever reasons, opt to follow an 'anti-sports' course are liable to be categorized as 'effeminate', perhaps even as 'homosexual', by their peers. This goes hand in hand with a parallel tendency for sportswomen to be categorized as 'lesbian' or 'butch', an antimony which, in and of itself, is suggestive of the fact that sport poses interesting problems for sociological research. That is the case independently of whether the labelled individuals 'really' are, through some degree of choice, heterosexual, homosexual or bisexual, or whether they are pushed into heterosexual or homoerotic attachments biologically, by a labelling process or by some combination of the two. That the USA experiences similar patterns has been shown by Nelson (1994). In our still heavily andrar-chal world, they are probably experienced in most other countries, too. Let me explore the issue further by endeavouring to ascertain whether Elias's theory of civilizing processes can be of help in teasing out some of the connections between sport and gender.

Sport and gender in the civilizing processes of the West

In her seminal essay, 'Discourses on the Gender/Sport Relationship: From Women in Sport to Gender Relations', Susan Birrell wrote in 1988 that two

British articles published in the 1970s – Ken Sheard's and my 'The Rugby Football Club as a Type of Male Preserve' (1973) and Paul Willis's 'Performance and Meaning' (1974) – 'were apparently so far advanced for American audiences that they lay almost unnoticed for about ten years' (Birrell, 1988: 481). British research in this area may have been more advanced some twenty years ago but, although it has tended to remain 'ghettoized' within the ramparts of the sociology of sport and, in Britain at least, not accorded due recognition in the subject's mainstream, there took place in the USA in the 1980s a creative application by men of 'critical feminist perspectives' to the sociological study of sport, producing a body of literature far in advance of most of what is currently available in Britain. Among the leading figures in this creative process have been Donald Sabo (1985), Alan Klein (1990) and Michael Messner. Writing in 1987, Messner had this to say on the functions of sport in the production of male identities:

> How do we begin to understand the intensity of the sense of identification that many males get from their status as athletes? First, since men have not at all times and all places related to sports the way they do currently, it is important to examine this reality through a historical prism. In the first two decades of this century, men feared that the closing of the frontier and the changes in the workplace, family, and schools were feminizing society. The Boy Scouts of America was founded in 1910 to provide a sphere of life where true manliness could be instilled in boys by *men*. The contemporaneous rapid rise in organized sports can be attributed largely to the same phenomenon. As socio-economic and familial changes eroded traditional bases of male identity and privilege, sport became an increasingly important cultural expression of traditional male values – organized sport became a primary masculinity-validating experience.
>
> In the post-World War II era, the bureaucratization and rationalization of work, along with the decline of the family wage and women's gradual movement into the labour force, further undermined the breadwinner role as the basis for male identity, resulting in a defensive insecurity among men. Both on a personal/existential level for athletes and on a symbolic/ideological level for spectators and fans, sport has become one of the last bastions of male power and superiority over – and separation from – the feminization of society. The rise of football as America's number-one game is likely the result of the comforting clarity it provides between the polarities of traditional male power, strength and violence and the contemporary fears of social feminization.
>
> (Messner, 1987)

Messner's views are similar to my own regarding the limitations of approaches to the formation of male identities of authors such as Brittan. Nevertheless, Messner's arguments appear unnecessarily restricted to an American context. After all, organized sports, for example cricket and boxing, started to develop in Britain in the eighteenth century, somewhat earlier than they did in the USA. The Boy Scouts movement also developed in Britain first. In fact, in England concern about 'social feminization' was expressed at least as early as the writings of Charles Kingsley in the 1840s and 1850s, and appears to have played a part in the development of 'Muscular Christianity' (Sheard, 1972; Maguire, 1986; Bloomfield, 1994). This suggests that a more general process may have been at work, possibly involving two-way diffusion back and forth across the Atlantic. Nelson implicitly recognizes this when she writes that: 'British and American proponents of a "muscular Christianity" movement equated stoicism, courage, tolerance for pain, and quick thinking under pressure with manhood' (Nelson, 1994: 19). This suggests, in turn, that a more general, less specifically American explanatory model than Messner uses may be needed in order more adequately to explain developments of this kind. Ideally, such a model ought also to throw a light onto an issue which Messner did not discuss in the article from which I quoted: the sociogenesis and social consequences of female entry into sports, a range of activities which, in the still predominantly andrarchal societies of the West, started out as virtually exclusive male preserves.

Implicit in Messner's paper are two clues which suggest that Elias's theory of civilizing processes may offer – not all the answers: figurational sociologists are careful never to make grandiose claims of that kind[5] – at least some clues which may be of help regarding the construction of such a theory. More particularly, there is reason to believe: (1) that, by placing constraints on the violent behaviour of dominant males, the closing of the frontier may have marked a stage in the development of American society which was in some ways similar to the processes in European contexts which Elias described as 'the courtization of the warriors' (*die Verhöflichung der Krieger*, Elias, 1994), that is the significant civilizing shift in European social development in which the ruling classes began to undergo the transformation from relatively independent warriors into relatively dependent courtiers;[6] and (2) that what was experienced as growing 'feminization' in the developing USA – and probably Canada, too – may well have been a North American variant of what is a common experience in societies which undergo the twin processes of state formation and increasing pacification under state control, that is two of the key structural features of a civilizing process according to Elias.

Jennifer Hargreaves has perceptively observed that

> because the whole history of modern sports has been based on gender divisions, even radical accounts of women's sports tend to focus on

perceived *differences* between men and women, rather than on the less obvious *relations* of power between them.

(Hargreaves, 1994: 8)

In my view understandably but rather less perceptively, Hargreaves is dismissive of the theory of civilizing processes as a potential means for shedding light on this area and even casts doubt on whether such a process can be said to have empirically occurred in the time-frame focused on by Elias (i.e. between the Middle Ages and the 1930s), especially as far as women are concerned (Hargreaves, 1992: 161–82). Other authors, however, are less dismissive. Whitson, for example, refers to figurational work on gender relations as 'astute' (Whitson, 1990: 24–5) and Crosset acknowledges our suggestion that 'manly rituals associated with sport are related to the power struggle between the sexes' (Crosset, 1990: 48). And although they find it inconsistent with the theory of civilizing processes, Gruneau and Whitson write in this connection that

> Dunning has suggested in a convincing way some possible effects of sport in the evolution of gender relations. First, he suggests that the power of men in any society is reinforced to the extent that important institutions in that society sanction and indeed celebrate the use of force. Conversely, the power of men is weakened whenever rules against the use of force are exercised to an extent that force becomes widely seen as taboo. Second, he suggests that the power of men is strengthened to the extent that men have their own institutions (male preserves) that are honoured in the public sphere; and that male power in society is weakened when these institutions are integrated.

> (Gruneau and Whitson, 1993: 180)

Similarly, when referring to Sheard's and my 1973 paper on rugby clubs as 'male preserves', Birrell adds in this connection that:

> In a recent revision of that paper, Dunning argues the almost biological necessity for the preservation of such spaces, particularly during times of encroachment by women into traditional male worlds and privileges. Thus the changing relations between the sexes and the ensuing civilizing of society lead men to stake out clearly demarcated male turf.

> (Birrell, 1988: 483; Dunning, 1986)

There is, of course, nothing 'biologically necessary' about it. There are also males who identify more or less strongly with women and more or less actively oppose or refuse to participate in such male preserves. Nevertheless, Birrell has grasped here what I take to be some of the connections between civilizing processes and struggles against 'andrarchy'. She can also be read as suggesting that the hypotheses offered by figurational sociologists in this regard receive a degree of support in the writings of Lenskyj (1986), Peiss (1986), Willis (1982) and, surprisingly enough, Jennifer Hargreaves (1994)!

The figurational analysis of gender and gender relations

It seems to me that there are five main ways in which the theory of civilizing processes may be of use for the exploration of problems of sport and gender. More particularly, by looking at such issues relationally and processually, it can arguably provide the beginnings of an explanation of: (1) the meaning/signifi-cance of sport for males who remain committed to variants of traditional male identities and roles; (2) the relative empowerment of females to an extent suffi-cient to allow them to challenge with increasing success for entry into what started out as an exclusive male preserve; (3) the corresponding changes at an ideological and value level regarding what constitute socially acceptable 'femi-nine' habituses and behaviour; (4) the reactions of males who feel threatened by the increasing 'encroachment' of females into this former male preserve; and (5) the motivational sources which lead growing numbers of females to want to take up sport and their reaction to men – and women – who seek more or less consciously to block their entry. In order to show how that is so, it is necessary to spell out some of the core figurational assumptions regarding gender and gender relations.

The first core figurational assumption in relation to gender is the idea that, like all other social relations, the relations between males and females are fundamentally affected by the character and overall structure of the society in which they are lived. The form of the economy, for example whether it takes one or another variant of the capitalist or socialist types, together with the society's level of economic development are clearly of significance in this regard. So is the position of the society in relation to others and the degree to which its intersocietal relations are war-like or peaceful. Generally speaking, war (including civil war and revolution) tends to favour males, peace to favour females. Arguably just as crucial, though, is whether a society has a state and, if so, the degree to which its state has managed to secure an effective monopoly of physical force and correlatively, of taxation, the major means of ruling in societies above a given level of complexity and crucial to their degrees of internal pacification. In other words, if Elias's work was on the right lines, the specific character of gender relations and gender identities in a society, together with its specific values and ideologies regarding gender and gender relations, will be in part a function of the specific trajectory of that society's civilizing process and the level reached in that connection.

The second core assumption is that, although the current level of knowl-edge regarding the 'nature–nurture' interface remains rudimentary, gender relations and identities are built on and around a partly determining biological substratum. One implication of this is that males and females are radically interdependent because they need each other for reproductive purposes and because any society which did not rank reproduction at least relatively highly in its value-scale, whatever mix between heterosexuality, homosexuality and bisexuality its dominant norms allowed, would soon experience severe population problems and perhaps die out. Males and females need each other sexually as individuals too, though, of course, variable numbers of each sex develop homoerotic tendencies. (As an aside, it is worth noting that the degree of tolerance accorded to 'gays', bisexuals, transsexuals and non-violent sexual 'deviants' generally can be counted as one mark of a society's level of civilization.) In short, our second core assumption holds that the relations between males and females are characterized by a fundamental interdependence which derives in part from bio-psychological roots as well as from roots which are socio-cultural in character. In other words, while we do not deny the *crucial* significance of culture and learning in this regard as stressed, for example, by Gagnon and Simon (1973) and Plummer (1975), it is our view that their perspective reflects a variant of what Wrong (1961) called 'the oversocialized conception of man' (*sic!*).

The third core figurational assumption regarding gender is that, again like other human interdependencies, the interdependence of males and females is best conceptualized as involving at a fundamental level a 'balance of power' or 'power ratio' (Elias, 1978). The term 'balance' is not used in the static sense of 'equality' or 'equilibrium' but to signify, via the analogy with a set of scales, the fundamentally dynamic, relational and relative character of power. The fourth core assumption is that, at the heart of the dynamic balance of power between the sexes in any society lies not only the relative capacities of males and females to control economic, political and symbolic/ideological resources, but also their relative capacities to use violence and bestow sexual favours on each other or withhold them.

Connected with this constellation of core assumptions are at least two ostensible facts:

1   that although (a) there is obviously a degree of overlap between the sexes in this regard, (b) some people are born neither unambiguously male nor unambiguously female, and (c) the size differences of men and women are a function not simply of biology but also of social processes connected, for example, with the sexual division of labour and levels of economic development and therefore of the social construction of bodies (Durkheim, 1964; Shorter, 1982; Maguire, 1993a), males have tended in all known societies up to now to be bigger, physically stronger and faster than females and therefore better equipped as potential fighters.
2   menstruation, but, above all, pregnancy and the nursing of infants tend to incapacitate women, among other ways as far as fighting and participating in warfare are concerned.

Of course, modern weapons technology implies a potential for offsetting and perhaps removing altogether the in-built fighting advantages of males. Similarly, invention of the tampon has reduced the inconvenience associated with menstruation, modern birth-control techniques have reduced the proportion of their life-course spent by women in pregnancy, and bottle feeding has made it possible for men to nurse infants. In other words, the power chances derived by men from their strength and capacity for warfare and fighting – there is a long tradition which sees in this one of the principal sources of andrarchy (Sayers, 1982: 65–83; Brownmiller, 1976) – tend to vary inversely with scientific and technological development; that is, they tend to be greater in societies where levels of scientific and technological development are low and vice versa. However, it is reasonable to suppose that the level of state formation of a society, in particular the degree to which its state is capable of maintaining effective monopoly control over the use of physical force, is likely to be a significant influence within it on the developing balance of power between the sexes.[7]

Sport and gender in the civilizing process

Many sports involve forms of fighting, and both fighting and sport appear to derive in complex ways from the same or similar psychological and socio-cultural roots. This is most obviously the case for combat sports like boxing, wrestling and fencing which are, quite literally, socially sanctioned forms of fighting. But it also appears to hold for such contact sports as soccer, rugby, 'field' hockey, 'ice' hockey and American football which can be described as basically involving 'mock battles' between teams. The second thing worthy of note is that Western civilizing processes have involved, on the normative level, an accumulation of controls and taboos, for example against males striking females (Elias, 1986a) and, at the level of the habitus of a majority of males, an advance in the threshold of shame and repugnance regarding violence and aggression (Elias, 1994). As a result, to the extent that it has involved males in being deprived of the right (whether legally sanctioned or not) to use violence in relation to females, it will have led to the increasing privatization of such violence, to the pushing of it increasingly 'behind the scenes' of social life, to its confinement increasingly to domestic social settings. Even there, it is increasingly subject to control. According to Walby, for example:

> The de-legitimating of private male violence against women has reduced, but not removed, one of the forms of power that men have over women. Husbands are no longer the sole arbiters of the accept-able level of violence which is now also regulated by the state.
>
> (Walby, 1990: 149)[8]

Correspondingly, although there are complex class-related, 'race'-related and age-related differences in this connection which I cannot explore in this context, it will have led to increased moral opprobrium being aroused by the idea of males striking females and a correspondingly stronger public reaction when the dominant norms in this regard are breached. Perhaps more importantly, to the extent that it has involved males in being deprived not only of the public right to use violence in relation to females, but – connected with a deeply internalized belief that such violence is wrong – of the psychological capacity and desire to do so except under circumstances of extreme stress, such a process will have played a part in increasing – however marginally – the power of females relative to males. That is, it will have increased the ability of females to pursue their desires and what they perceive as their interests relatively free of the fear that acting thus will produce a physically violent response from males. Many men, however, will feel their masculinity compromised, constrained and threatened, on the one hand by this civilizing process *per se* which they will experience as 'emasculating', and on the other by the correlative growth of female power. Assuming Elias's theory to be sound, it is this twin process which appears to lie at the roots of the fear of 'feminization' discussed by Messner (1987) and which, if I am right, is by no means confined to the USA.

Taking the argument one step further, in the context of relatively pacified and, in that sense, relatively 'civilized' societies, some fields of sport – along with such occupations as the military and the police – will come to represent an enclave for the legitimate expression of masculine aggression and the production and reproduction of traditional male habituses involving the use and display of physical prowess and power. It will come, that is, to represent a primary vehicle for the masculinity-validating experience.

American football and soccer as less and more civilized variants of the sport–masculinity equation?

There are substantial differences between sports and societies as far as the use of sport as a masculinity-validating experience is concerned. For example, it is perhaps reasonable to describe soccer as an intrinsically more 'civilized' and 'civilizing' game than American football, at least when played according to the rules. That is, while it, too, is a mock battle played with a ball, in soccer the war-like element is less obvious, more muted and usually more controlled. For one thing, soccer is a more open game in the sense that scrimmages and mêlées are not central. For another, the smaller number and greater simplicity of its rules make it easier to control.[9] Nor is tackling players who are not in possession of the ball a legitimate tactic. And the players do not dress up in a form of armour in some ways reminiscent of that worn by medieval knights. The protective clothing of 'gridiron' players is even referred to as 'armament' in a book describing American football for British TV viewers (Wurman,

229

1982: 2–9). Finally, although some forms of illegitimate soccer violence are perhaps difficult for match officials to detect and control – for example, the use of elbows when climbing to head the ball or the apparently accidental trip – they are fewer in number than those available to gridiron players. At least that appears to be the case if one takes account of the following repertoire of violent practices which are, or at least once were, apparently legitimate in American football: 'blind-side hitting'; 'chop-blocking'; 'clubbing' or 'bouncer's wallop'; 'crackback block'; 'ear-holing'; 'head-butting'; 'leg-whipping'; 'rake-blocking'; and 'spearing'.[10] In short, it seems reasonable to suppose that soccer is not so intrinsically expressive, supportive and reinforcing of an ethos of extreme male aggressiveness as the 'gridiron' game. That is, even though a fairly extreme form of aggressive masculinity came to be operative in English soccer in the 1980s as demonstrated, perhaps above all, by the play of Wimbledon FC, the basic rules of the game are less dependent on that fact. By contrast, American football is essentially an embodiment and display of male aggressiveness and power. It is also marketed as such. In Messner's words, it provides 'comforting clarity…between the polarities of traditional male power, strength and violence and the contemporary fears of social feminization' (Messner, 1987).

Of course, with its emphasis on the precise measurement of time, distance and the quantifiable aspects of individual performance, American football is also reflective of the high level of rationalization reached by capitalism and sport in the USA. Nevertheless, it also seems reasonable to suppose that grid-iron football is a game which could only have grown up and taken root in a society where there is considerable support for ideals of masculinity which celebrate or at least tolerate a greater amount of overt physical violence than is considered desirable by dominant groups in the societies of Western Europe. This is consistent with the research of Sipes who found that the popularity of the 'combative' sports of football and hunting rose in the USA during its de-civilizing involvement in the Second World War, the Korean War and the Vietnam War, whilst the popularity of baseball, defined by Sipes as a 'non-combative' sport, declined (Sipes, 1973: 64–86). It is also consistent with the fact that the sexual assault, including the rape, of females by top-level male athletes seems to occur more frequently in the USA than in the societies of Western Europe. Nelson is able to devote a whole chapter of *The Stronger Women Get, the More Men Love Football* to this issue. She entitles it 'Sexual Assault as a Spectator Sport' (Nelson, 1994: 127–58). So far as I am aware, no such chapter could be written for a European text, though, of course, that may reflect less a lower factual level of such violence than the fact that violence against females by sportsmen/athletes has not yet been raised to the level of an issue in European countries.

Civilizing processes and female sports involvement

The status of sport as a primary locus for the enactment of 'masculinity-validating' experiences will be threatened to the extent that the growing power and, correlatively, self-confidence, assertiveness and independence of women at the levels of their habitus and in organizational terms help them to mount a successful challenge against traditional andrarchal ideas and institutions and enter sport themselves. From the outset, women have had to struggle to secure a foothold in the world of sport and, as can be seen, for example, from the still male-dominated prestige hierarchy of sports and the correspondingly relatively low exposure of female sports in the mass media, the relatively low rewards which accrue to top-level sportswomen as opposed to those which accrue to men, and the relatively low participation of females in events such as the Olympics (Hargreaves, 1994), their status in this regard remains marginal, if not any longer so seriously insecure. Powerful ideologies questioning their femininity and sexual orientations, and predicting physical and medical damage, continue to be mobilized against them (McCrone, 1988; Vertinsky, 1990, 1994). Over time, however, in conjunction with the slowly changing balance of power between the sexes – which is, of course, a complex, multi-faceted and not simply linear process and one which, under specific conditions, could be reversed – and facilitated by such related developments as the introduction of modern forms of birth control, the related lowering of family size, inventions such as the tampon and modern forms of household technology, increasing numbers of women have succeeded in gaining entry to a greater range of sports. They have presumably been motivated in this connection by such things as: (1) an interest in obtaining the sorts of 'mimetic', 'sociability' and 'motility' satisfactions that can be obtained from sports by men (Elias and Dunning, 1986; see also Chapter 1 of the present volume), together with the sorts of gains regarding identity, self-concept, self-assurance and habitus (e.g. greater feelings of security in public spaces and greater ability to defend themselves against physical attack) which can accrue in that connection; and (2) a desire for equality with men as a result of frustrations experienced over the constraints and limitations traditionally placed on female roles.

Women are currently making strides even in what Snyder and Spreitzer (1989) call 'categorically unacceptable' sports such as soccer, rugby and boxing, that is sports which are still widely regarded as inappropriate for females. Such sports are combat/body-contact events which involve a stress on combinations of power, strength, aggressiveness and speed. As such, they come most strongly and directly into contradiction with the still dominant notions of 'femininity', ideals regularly portrayed in advertising and the media and still widely taken for granted by women and not just men. There are, however, one or two anomalies in this connection which deserve to be considered. 'Field' hockey is perhaps the prime example. In England, it became established as a game for females in the 1880s and 1890s. Writing in the *Badminton Magazine* in 1890, an Edwardian author claimed:

> [For women]…beauty of face and form is one of the chief essentials but unlimited indulgence in violent outdoor sports, cricket, bicycling, beagling, otter hunting, paper-chasing, and – most odious of all games for a woman – hockey, cannot but have an unwomanly effect on a young girl's mind, no less than her appearance.…Let young girls ride, skate, dance and play lawn tennis and other games in modera- tion, but let them leave field sports and rough outdoor pastimes to those for whom they are naturally intended – men.
>
> (quoted in Dobbs, 1973: 177)

Such forms of teleological biological reductionism – the idea that 'nature' is not a complex of blindly occurring processes but has 'intentions' – were common at the time. However, claims that hockey is not acceptable for females were not put forward just by men. McCrone cites two females, the first who

> asserted that 'only the few square, squat, and burly outdoor porter type of girls should play…[the] rough, competitive game of hockey', which 'with its muddy field, rush and excitement, for the unformed, untrained or nervous girl is surely unadulterated lunacy'.

And the second, a schoolgirl who observed that

> hockey made women 'mannish' and neglectful of their domestic duties and just the 'detestable' sort likely to become suffragettes.
>
> (McCrone, 1988: 135)

McCrone accounts for the apparently anomalous development of hockey as a game for females by suggesting that:

> At public schools hockey was often regarded as effeminate and fit only for malingerers, so it never acquired the grandeur or overt masculinity of cricket and football. Thus when women took it up, they were not perceived necessarily as trespassing on a sacred male preserve.
>
> (McCrone, 1988: 128)

This is a powerful argument, consistent with the fact that, in Britain, hockey remained widely regarded in male circles as 'effeminate' at least until the 1950s. However, McCrone fails to offer direct historical evidence on this score and my suspicion is that such a male public school belief may have originated in conjunction with the emergence of hockey as a game for females. Accordingly,

McCrone may have been projecting a more recent value onto the past. Whether that is so or not, her reference to the schoolgirl who argued that female hockey players were likely to become suffragettes suggests that a politically conscious element may have been involved in the emergence of hockey as a game for females. More particularly, females who chose to play hockey in the late nineteenth century were probably fully aware of the then-dominant belief in its 'masculinizing' implications and, whether they became suffragettes or not, were probably deliberately setting their stall out against then-contemporary ideals of femininity and female habitus.

The dominant suffragette view, however, seems to have been less radical. That is, they appear by and large to have accepted dominant views regarding sport and focused their energies more into securing such things as the vote. However, the evidence does suggest that, in the context of a society where legitimate violence had been monopolized by the state and in which sport had become one of the principal arenas for the legitimate inculcation and expression of relatively unreconstructed masculine values, sport came to form one of the main targets of feminist protest. In the words of Brian Dobbs:

> because sport was such an outpost of male chauvinism and something of a masculine symbol, when the women's suffrage movement had failed with every democratic attempt to get this voice, it was sport which had to bear the brunt of the suffragettes' turn to militancy and violence. Throughout 1913, bowling greens, golf clubs, cricket grounds and football grounds had their turf torn up and damaged and their buildings burnt down, all over the country.
>
> (Dobbs, 1973: 178)

Not only did sport come to serve as target for direct feminist protest but growing numbers of women struggled simultaneously to combat the idea that sport is legitimately only a male preserve. In the USA, they received support in this regard from some powerful men. For example, James Naismith, who had invented basketball in 1891 as a winter sport for football players, proclaimed it an 'ideal sport for women' (Nelson, 1994: 14). Nelson suggests in this connection that:

> The first college women's game featured Naismith's original nine-player, one-point-per-basket format. Because female sweat was deemed indelicate, men were not allowed to watch, but five hundred boisterous women packed the stands of San Francisco's Armory hall. 'The fighting was hard and the playing was good', the *San Francisco Examiner* reported. 'The girls jumped, scrambled, and fell over one another on the floor, but they didn't mind it. They were up as quick as a flash, chasing after the ball again'.
>
> (Nelson, 1994: 14)

Although a form of sexual segregation was involved here, this suggests the possibility that, partly on account of a degree of male support, the sporting involvement of females may have been somewhat easier to accomplish in the USA than Britain. To say this is not, of course, to deny the fact that, in addition to the questioning of their sex and sexual orientations, American sportswomen have had to face severe problems regarding their sports involvements that are not typically faced by men. Such problems arise in all societies that are andrarchic. For example, it is well known that, despite the move in Western societies in recent years in the direction of a greater sharing of what were formerly more rigidly segregated conjugal roles (Bott, 1957), wives and partners who work outside the home still tend to be expected – and in many cases still expect themselves – to perform the lion's share of domestic tasks. Working women athletes with a stable partner or husband, however, often experience not a two-way but a severe three-way conflict in this regard. As a British female athlete expressed it in 1981:

> trying to be a wife and mother, to keep a career and training going and trying to keep an interest in sport causes tremendous conflicts and there is never enough time to go round. There is always the feeling that you are never achieving your optimum in any of the varied roles you are trying to perform. This raises great problems for women about guilt and this is one of society's subtle devices. When a woman is training she feels she should be looking after her children or her husband; if she is marking her essays she ought to be doing her training and so on. So there is a great deal of conflict.
>
> (Payne, 1981: 49)

The same sportswoman went on to criticize what she described as women's 'servicing role' for sport. She said:

> I can remember…my mother many years ago always washing my brother's rugby strip and even at the age of 10, I was asked to clean his boots, which I resented, even if he was playing in the First XV.
>
> (Payne, 1981: 49)

This suggests that a great deal of male sport depends on the exploitation of unpaid female labour, thus adding to the motivation of many males to resist greater gender equality and attempts by females to become actively involved in what they (such males) consider to be their own exclusive preserve. It is also arguably the case that the use by males of sporting contexts as sites for the ritual and symbolic vilification and demeaning of females has grown as the power of women has increased (Sheard and Dunning, 1973; Dunning, 1986; Nelson, 1994).

In Britain, the symbolic vilification of women in sports contexts – itself a form of symbolic violence – tends to take place behind closed doors in Rugby Union and more openly in soccer. This is largely a consequence of the social class differences of those who play and watch the different football codes, more particularly of the fact that Rugby Union is predominantly middle class, whilst soccer and the associated culture are predominantly working class. Since rugby football as a male preserve has been dealt with elsewhere (Sheard and Dunning, 1973; Dunning, 1986; Donnelly and Young, 1985; White and Vagi, 1990), let me briefly explore this issue by reference to soccer.

Writing in 1988, Vulliamy offered the following as part of a description of a group of England fans in Stuttgart where they were attending the European Football Championships. They were, he said,

> assembled at the Bierfässle Bar…in shorts and tee shirts, calculating beer prices, scratching their testicles and singing 'Get yer tits out for the lads' whenever a young woman walked by.
>
> (*Guardian*, 13 June 1988)

In the 1980s, another standard part of the repertoire of many hooligan and fringe-hooligan groups of English soccer fans when they travelled away to support their teams involved chanting or singing the following refrain: 'Leicester (Newcastle, Liverpool, Tottenham, etc.) boys, we are here. Fuck your women and drink your beer.' This signalled a predatory intent towards local males but it also symbolized a crude objectification of females and a view of them as 'male property'. As one can imagine, large numbers of females are deterred from attending soccer by such displays. They are deterred in less obvious but no less demeaning ways as well. A prime example is provided by the fact that females are barred from entering the boardrooms of many English soccer clubs, even the female friends and relatives of directors when the latter are using the boardroom to entertain guests.

A more blatant example was provided in 1993 by a BBC TV documentary about women and football. In it, a Stockport County fan – Stockport is a town adjacent to Manchester – described his technique for dissuading a woman who had expressed a desire to watch soccer from attending more than once. Here is a paraphrase of what he said:

> If she insists on going, by all means take her but take her to the worst part of the ground, somewhere in the open where she's bound to get wet. She won't want to go again in a hurry and things will be as they should be once more. Football is a game for men.

This is remarkably similar to what a former Secretary of the FA said at a meeting in 1988. His name was Ted Croker and here, again, is a paraphrase of his words:

Football is a game of hard, physical contact, a form of combat. It is, and must remain, a man's game. Women have no place in it except to cheer on their men, wash and iron their kit, and prepare and serve refreshments.

Massey offers an interesting comment on how many females respond to the male dominance of public space which results from andrarchal values of this kind. She writes:

On the way into town we would cross the wide shallow valley of the River Mersey, and my memory is of dank, muddy fields spreading away into a cold, misty distance. And all of it – all of these acres of Manchester – was divided up into football pitches and rugby pitches. And on Saturdays…the whole vast area would be covered with hundreds of…people, all running round after balls, as far as the eye could see!…I remember all this very sharply. And I remember, too, it striking me very clearly – even then as a puzzled, slightly thoughtful little girl – that all this huge stretch of the Mersey flood plain had been entirely given over to boys.

I did not go to those playing fields – they seemed barred, another world (though today, with more nerve and some consciousness of being a space-invader, I do stand on the football terraces – and love it). But there were other places to which I did go, and yet where I still felt they were not mine, or at least that they were designed to, or had the effect of, firmly letting me know my conventional subordination.

(Massey, 1994: 183)

In societies such as Britain, it is not only gender but class and race as well which induce such a sense of exclusion and subordination. In other words, it is not only females who have such feelings but many male members of subordinate, outsider groups as well, though, of course, many female members of such groups tend to be doubly, even trebly disadvantaged. This caveat notwithstanding, Massey's observations on some of the continuing connections between 'sport, place and gender' are perceptive regarding the limited degree to which gender equalization has occurred in modern Britain whether in sport or other spheres.

Conclusion

I have argued in this chapter that modern sport emerged as part of a civilizing process and is best understood as having come to represent what is for large numbers of males a principal locus for the inculcation and public expression of traditional standards of masculinity. In short, modern sport emerged as a

236

male preserve, a fact which helps to account for the strength of male resistance to attempts by females to enter it or develop sporting enclaves of their own. However, another key aspect of Western civilizing processes has involved to some degree a shift in the balance of power between the sexes in a gynarchic (matriarchal) direction. Since this is an aspect of my case that writers such as Hargreaves (1992: 12–16) find difficult to accept, let me spell out in greater detail what I mean.

The civilizing transformation I am hypothesizing seems to have had such an effect in at least two ways, the first connected with the image of ideal masculine and ideal feminine roles embodied in the form of andrarchal nuclear family which became the norm among the expanding middle classes in the second half of the nineteenth century. Contrary to what used to be a widespread feminist view, this form of family seems, in one respect at least, to have represented a shift towards the equalization of power chances between the sexes. That is because it arguably tied more males more firmly into a more egalitarian form of family than had been the case before – diminishing the Victorian role of *pater familias*, for example – thus subjecting the males involved to the possibility of greater and more regular female influence. If Shorter is correct, in that context more men would have begun to become more attached to and identify more with their wives as persons rather than simply as objects for sexual gratification and producing (especially male) offspring (Shorter, 1982: 294–6).

Second, by imposing a complex of internal and external restraints on the expression of aggression by men, for example via the code of 'gentlemanly' conduct with its simultaneous placing of women 'on a pedestal' and the deeming of it as 'ungentlemanly' to strike them, this overall civilizing transformation may also have been conducive to a degree of equalization of the power chances of the sexes. It would have been so by restricting the opportunities for men to use one of their principal power advantages relative to women – their generally greater physical strength and superiority as fighters. This, in turn, may have increased the chances for women to engage in unified political action, for example by making them feel freer to organize and take part in demonstrations. If this speculative hypothesis has any substance, such a civilizing transformation may have had this effect by reducing the likelihood that demonstrations of nascent female unity, self-confidence, assertiveness and power would be responded to violently by men, including husbands and fathers in a domestic context. More particularly, to the extent that a relatively non-violent response from men to such political involvements and acts by women could be expected, the fears of women would have been reduced and their confidence correspondingly enhanced to go ahead with the struggle for what increasing numbers of women, supported by a small but also growing number of men, were coming to believe were their rights.

In short, it seems reasonable to suppose that the relatively slight but nevertheless significant shift in the balance of power between men and women that first received public expression in the suffragettes movement may have been at least partly a consequence of the 'civilizing spurt' which accompanied Britain's emergence as an urban–industrial nation-state. But let me make it crystal clear: to say this is *not* to imply that the state or general public response to the suffragettes was non-violent. What I am suggesting, rather, is that, although the level of police and public violence against them escalated as the suffragettes themselves felt constrained to adopt more direct and disruptive tactics: (1) the levels and types of violence used against them would have differed, perhaps only marginally, from those used against men; and (2) that *one* of the preconditions for the suffragettes movement *may* have been the renunciation of violence towards women on the part of many of the men to whom individual suffragettes were most closely bonded. This hypothesis does not imply a denial of the continuing occurrence of male violence towards females. I have simply sought to suggest: (1) that violence against females tended from the second half of the nineteenth century onwards to decrease *in public*;[11] (2) that feelings of outrage regarding breaches of the dominant norms in this regard tended in that time-frame to increase; and (3) that, in so far as it continues to occur in societies such as modern Britain, male violence against females *tends* to predominate in the least 'incorporated', socio-economically lowest social strata (Dunning *et al.*, 1988). Indeed, males from these strata are not liable to experience serious feelings of guilt if they behave violently towards females, and women members of such 'communities' tend to expect violent behaviour from their men, thus reinforcing their violent tendencies.

Whilst large numbers of women have tended so far to accept the hegemonic definition of sport as a predominantly male preserve, this shift in the balance of power between the sexes, whilst not by any stretch of the imagination very great, has arguably continued to occur following the initial spadework of the suffragettes. If nothing else, it has clearly been sufficient to make it impossible for traditionally inclined males to prevent females from entering this erstwhile male bastion in growing numbers. The barriers erected against them have been strongest in the combat/contact sports but, in recent years, more and more women have taken up sports such as soccer and even rugby and boxing. Indeed, in the USA this process appears to have gone further than in Britain at least as far as soccer is concerned. Thus the Association form of football has been rapidly accepted as an appropriate sport for females in the USA, a process marked among other ways by the success of the US women's team in winning the Women's World Cup in 1992. Its level of civilization relative to American football and rugby may have played a part in its widespread acceptance by American females.

The growing direct involvement of females in sport represents, in and of itself, an equalizing trend. Nevertheless, this growing female participation in what started as an exclusive male preserve has tended to involve two specific sets of penalties for sportswomen which show that modern sport and society still remain predominantly andrarchic. On the one hand, in contrast to the confirmation of their masculinity through participation in sport by males, the femininity of sportswomen tends to be compromised in the eyes of others, especially as a result of their participation in combat/contact sports. In some cases, it tends to be compromised in their own eyes, too, a reaction which is typical of 'outsider' groups to the extent that they have internalized the 'group charisma' of those who are more established, in this case males (Elias and Scotson, 1994). A possible example is provided by what Wheatley calls the 'subcultural subversions' represented in the mimicking – with an anti-male and pro-lesbian focus – by, for example, female rugby players, of the anti-female, anti-homosexual culture associated with male Rugby Union (Wheatley, 1994: 193–211).[12] On the other hand, females face numerous obstacles with respect to participation in sport which are not experienced by males. As part of the same overall equation, however, male sports are, at the same time, dependent in many ways on 'servicing' by women. Such services may, in some cases, be 'voluntarily' given. Nevertheless, to the extent that 'servicing' of this kind is based more on internalization of the group charisma of males and less freely given and fully reciprocated (i.e. by the provision of comparable services by males), it can be accurately described in neo-Marxist terms as involving the exploitation of unpaid female labour. If I am right, such exploitation, much of it at a taken-for-granted and not fully conscious level on the part of many males as well as many females, constitutes just one of the many sources of inequality in the sphere of sports involvement in the 'late barbarian' societies of today (Elias, 1991b).

CONCLUSION

In this book, I have outlined some of the tenets of figurational or process sociology and attempted to show via a series of theoretical–empirical case studies how a figurational approach is potentially fruitful as a means of adding to the stock of common knowledge about sport as a 'collective invention' or 'social product'. How far I have succeeded must be for others to judge.

It would probably be more usual nowadays to use the term 'social construct' rather than 'collective invention' or 'social product' to describe the fundamentally social character of sport. I have eschewed the common usage because it would be too rationalistic and might convey the wish-fulfilment idea that people at our currently relatively primitive level of understanding of ourselves and the societies we form – even some sociologists are apt to forget that what Comte called 'theological' and 'metaphysical' modes of thinking remain powerful if not perhaps dominant in everyday social thought – are able to exercise greater choice and control over their actions in the context of and in relation to collective inventions such as sports and over social relations more generally than is yet the case. The figurational approach, specifically in this instance to the study of sport, is concerned precisely with adding to the social fund of knowledge in this regard in the belief that greater under-standing will enhance our capacity to exercise control in the increasingly important sport and leisure sphere.

Figurational sociologists share with the adherents to most other schools of sociological thought the belief that greater knowledge will be of assistance in helping people to avoid the in many ways violent, exploitative, neurotic, power-, status- and fantasy-driven social forms, including forms of sport, which have predominated in most societies up to now and to replace them with forms – I understand by 'forms' in this connection the wider social and institutional contexts of sports as well as the sports *per se* – that will be more conducive to advancing the sum of human happiness, contentment and well-being. Our primary stress, however, is on the need for knowledge. We do not believe that, at the moment, our social fund of knowledge about ourselves is great enough to point to forms of action which will skew the balance between intended and unintended consequences with relative certainty in favour of the former. The idea of unintended consequences is, of course, in some ways fairly old. The poet, Robert Burns, for example, wrote that 'the best laid plans o' mice and men gang aft aglae'. American sociologist Robert Merton (1957) spoke of 'the unintended consequences of intended social actions', and Norbert Elias (1994), thinking more of larger collectivities and aggregates and of the longer term, wrote of how 'blind' or 'unplanned' processes which result from the interplay of myriads of individual acts have dominated human history up to now, unintentionally leading not only to 'civilizational advances' such as the emergence of modern sports ('advances' which, especially until recently, have tended mainly to benefit narrow, ruling groups) but also to recurrent wars and economic, racial/ethnic, gender, environmental and other kinds of crises. Assuming that processes such as globalization and technological change continue to occur at something like their current rate, it seems more likely that we will experience an exacerbation rather than an amelioration of crises such as these in the earliest centuries of the new millennium. In that context, if sport can be made to conform more closely than has so far been the case to the ideology that it is conducive to peace and good international relations, it could turn out to be an institution of even greater human significance than it has been up to now.

The figurational/process-sociological approach derives from foundations laid down by Norbert Elias. Elias is coming increasingly to be regarded as one of the greatest sociologists of the twentieth century, if not *the* greatest. I like to think of him as a sociological equivalent of Copernicus.[1] (I have said 'a sociological equivalent' because I am sure there must be others.) In his work, Elias established theoretically and empirically both the quintessentially social character of individual human animals[2] and the fact that the societies we form are 'societies of individuals'.[3] Such anti-Kantian conceptualizations represent what Elias would have called a 'breakthrough'. Although the physical and human/social sciences deal with subject matters that are vastly different, these advances are arguably equivalent to Copernicus's breakthrough in the sense that, just as Copernicus played a key part in the development of modern science by rejecting the old earth-centred (geocentric) view of the solar system and replacing it with a sun-centred (heliocentric view),[4] so Elias can be seen as having established some of the preconditions for the emergence of sociology as a science by correcting what he called the *Homo clausus*, or closed individual, view of humans and replacing it with an orientation towards *Homines aperti*, pluralities of open people each with a blend of inborn and socially learned yet still embodied tendencies to bond with others. Elias (1978) referred to these bonding tendencies as 'open and unattached valencies'. Sexual drives and feelings are perhaps the most obvious among them. The breakthroughs by Copernicus and Elias both involved a process of 'decentring' or 'distanciation': in the case of Copernicus, a decentring from humanity's primary anthropocentrism or centredness on themselves; in that of Elias, a distanciation from the Englightenment/Judaeo-Christian/Kantian/

neo-Kantian view of humans as 'rational' beings who stand 'above' nature and other animals in a world that was created specifically for them.

Also centrally involved in Elias's breakthrough is a stress on the observable fact that each human individual is a process and that humans are bound by ties of interdependence which vary in terms of (1) their degrees of fluidity; (2) the balance between conflict and co-operation they involve; and (3) the balance they contain between centripetal and centrifugal pressures. To express it in simple terms, humans form dynamic (con)figurations with each other (Elias, 1978). Through this formulation, Elias arguably succeeded in circumventing what philosophically orientated sociologists call the 'agency–structure dilemma' (Giddens, 1984), the difficulty philosophers and sociologists have had for centuries in coming up with formulations of the 'individual–society' relationship which avoid reductionism and reification whilst simultaneously doing justice to both the individual and the social sides of the equation. I hope I have provided enough examples of the fruitfulness of such 'Eliasian' conceptualizations in this book.

The concept of figurations can be applied to the interdependency ties within and between 'dyads' and 'triads', within and between institutions such as sports clubs, universities, business firms and political parties, as well as to those within and between classes, 'racial'/ethnic groups and 'survival groups' (Elias, 1978), for example tribes, feudal states and nations. In this way, Elias's formulation can be said to point towards a bridging of the gap between 'micro-', 'meso-' and 'macro-sociological' perspectives.[5] In addition, Elias succeeded in developing formulations which avoid the *Homo clausus* tendency to dichotomize 'body' and 'mind', formulations which, together with his observation of the large numbers of people who are involved in it in various capacities, helped him to grasp the sociological significance of studying sport. Elias conceptualized humans as a species which evolved as symbol-forming, symbol-using animals who are bodily equipped with capacities to 'feel' as well as 'think', and to 'play' as well as 'work'. Humans also depend less than other animals on inherited instincts and more on the social learning and moulding of inborn capacities (Elias, 1978, 1991b). Finally, Elias fruitfully employed the social metaphors of dances and games – as opposed, for example, to such non-social metaphors as machines, organisms and cybernetic systems – in order to illuminate, for example, the complexities of power relations (Elias, 1978). He also formulated a series of concepts such as 'survival' or 'attack-and-defence' units, the 'triad of basic controls', and 'double-bind figurations' which are of considerable potential use in comparative and developmental studies. Several of them have been employed throughout this book.

Another mark of the originality of Elias's contribution is the fact that, with the partial exception of Theodor Adorno,[6] he was, to my knowledge, the only founder of a sociological 'school' who grasped the social significance of sport and made substantial contributions to the sociological study of it (Elias, in Elias and Dunning, 1986). There are, though, aspects of Elias's contribution and that of figurational sociologists more generally which remain controversial and are repeatedly misconstrued in the sociology of sport and elsewhere. Central in this connection are the idea of 'involvement and detachment', and the concept/theory of civilizing processes. A good way of bringing this book to a close will be to respond to some recent arguments on this score, especially those of the Gramscian feminist Jennifer Hargreaves. She has offered a series of trenchant criticisms which, although they fall in most cases wide of the mark, deserve to be taken very seriously indeed.

The belief that the study of social processes is best approached by means of a 'detour via detachment' in which the researcher/theorist attempts to hold his/her passions and emotions momentarily in check in order to maximize the chances that he/she will be able to develop as 'realistic', or better, as 'reality-congruent' a picture as possible of the process or processes in question, forms a key aspect of the figurational canon. Such an approach, we believe, maximizes the chances of obtaining secure knowledge which can act as a guide to effective action. Figurational sociologists consider themselves to be social *scientists* and Elias described the task of scientists thus:

> In the exploration of nature...scientists have learned that any direct encroachment upon their work by short-term interests or needs of specific persons or groups is liable to jeopardize the usefulness which their work may have in the end for themselves or for their own group. The problems which they formulate and, by means of their theories, try to solve, have in relation to personal or social problems of the day a high degree of autonomy; so have the sets of values which they use; their work is not 'value-free', but it is, in contrast to that of many social scientists, protected by firmly established professional standards and other institutional safeguards against the intrusion of heteronomous evaluations.
>
> (Elias, 1987: 6)

Elias was here urging sociologists to strive for greater autonomy both within the academy and in relation to powerful outsider groups such as governments, party establishments, and the providers of research funds. He urged this because natural scientists have discovered solutions to problems which demonstrably work. This contrasts markedly with the mainly ideology-derived 'solutions' on which we remain reliant in the social sciences and which, when applied, frequently result in pernicious, disastrous and destructive unintended consequences. To this end, Elias advocated the development in sociology of standards, institutions and modes of proceeding similar to those of the more successful natural sciences, but moulded to the specific properties of humans and human societies. Adding to the social fund of knowledge, *per se*, he argued, should be paramount over short-term interests and concerns both in theory building and research. But Elias was *crystal clear* that, in striving to achieve these aims, sociologists *cannot* and *should not* abandon their political interests and concerns. On the contrary, these are vital ingredients of successful sociological theorizing and research. As Elias expressed it:

> The problem confronting [social scientists] is not simply to discard [their more involved, political] role in favour of...[a more detached scientific one]. They cannot cease to take part in, and to be affected by, the social and political affairs of their group and their time. Their own participation and involvement, moreover, is itself one of the conditions for comprehending the problems they try to solve as scientists. For while one need not know, in order to understand the structure of molecules, what it feels like to be one of its atoms – in order to understand the functioning of human groups one needs to know, as it were, from the inside how human beings experience their own and other groups, and one cannot know without active participation and involvement.
>
> The problem confronting those who study one or the other aspects of human groups is how to keep their two roles as participant and enquirer clearly and consistently apart and, as a professional group, to establish in their work the undisputed dominance of the latter.
>
> (Elias, 1987: 16)

What is clearly and unambiguously being recommended here is that sociologists should strive in their work to strike a balance between a necessary detachment and an equally necessary involvement. Such a stance, we argue, is conducive to the reduction of the fantasy content of people's thinking – for example, the idea that a Utopia could be produced by means of a violent revolution or that sport could be a realm of 'pure freedom' – and the maximization of its reality orientation. In 1985, Chris Rojek suggested quite fairly that, up until that time, figurational sociologists had produced 'no rules, no drill to accomplish self-distancing from the object of study' (see also Rojek, 1989, 1992). Such a criticism was constructive and led me to formulate a few of the rules which can be said to have been implicit in Elias's teaching and research practice (Dunning, in Dunning and Rojek, 1992: 252). However, how is one to respond to a writer such as Jennifer Hargreaves who, despite the substantial body of written evidence to the contrary,[7] persists in asserting that we advocate 'a methodology of detachment' which 'claims to be objective and uncritical'. This is a travesty of our position on several counts. More particularly:

1   Elias did not simply advocate detachment but urged sociologists to strive for a balance between involvement and detachment, a balance in which both poles are important, involvement for motivation and detailed knowledge, detachment for the wider picture and as a means of minimizing perceptual distortion both of data and the views, concept and theories of others.

2   The concept of 'objectivity' does not appear in the vocabulary of figurational sociologists except as a term which we critique. We see the task of
sociologists as concerned with increasing the 'reality congruence' of
concepts and theories about societies, that is with making our mental
representations of the observable social world approximate as closely as
possible to the properties of that observable world *per se*. It is not a question of striving for 'objectivity' or 'the truth' but of adding to the reality
congruence of the existing stock of knowledge. For example, one could
say that because they involve a focus on how the human species survives
in the material world, Marx's theories represented a development in the
direction of greater reality congruence relative to those of Hegel. Similarly
it is our contention that there is a need today to surpass the degree of
reality congruence achieved by Marx (and Weber, Durkheim and Gramsci,
etc.) and that Norbert Elias is one of the people to have successfully taken
some steps in that direction.

3   Although Elias's sociological stance was not overtly critical in the party
political/ideological sense meant by Jennifer Hargreaves, he did argue in his
teaching that sociological diagnoses which are relatively reality congruent
constitute effective forms of critique to the extent that they expose for
what they are, the corruption and exploitation which have been common
features of most societies up to now.

Jennifer Hargreaves' own recommendation is for a sociology based on what
she calls 'passionate objectivity'.[8] However, if I understand it, this contention,
too, is arguably based on a misapprehension. Jennifer Hargreaves is undoubtedly 'passionately committed' to advancing the cause of female participation
in sport, just as I and other figurational sociologists are 'passionately
committed' to the goal of adding to knowledge as a means of hopefully
contributing to the improvement of the lot of men and women world-wide
and, in the last instance, of helping humanity to survive. However, this does
not mean that Jennifer Hargreaves, any more than we figurational sociologists,
carries out her research and writes her articles and books in a state of high
emotional involvement, let alone having abandoned herself to her passions.
That would be impossible. Researching and writing is, in fact, classical detour
behaviour. They involve striving momentarily to keep one's passions in check.
As I suggested in the introduction, Karl Marx may have written that 'philosophers have *interpreted* the world in various ways; the point however is to *change*
it', but the fact that he devoted his life to laying the foundations for a 'scientific socialism' in which political action would be based on an empirically
substantiated theory of social structure and social change is a good illustration
of such detour behaviour. Marx's life and work is also a good illustration of
how politically committed people can contribute to knowledge. We have been
accused by Jennifer Hargreaves and others[9] of espousing 'value-neutrality', but
it is difficult to see how a person who was 'value-neutral' – supposing that

were possible for anyone other than a dead person or a schizophrenic – would be able to contribute to sociological knowledge or would even want to become a sociologist in the first place!

As part of their quest for knowledge, figurational sociologists are also passionately committed to the idea that, at the moment, the subject stands in urgent need of a synthesis or syntheses in order to counteract the destructive effects of paradigm rivalry. Rivalry can be constructive up to a point but if it prevents sociologists from acting in unison in relation to the providers of funds, politicians, the general public and the representatives of other subjects, its overall effect will be to weaken them. At the moment, the signs in the sociology of sport and the subject more generally are that the destructive effects of paradigm rivalry are beginning to outweigh its beneficial, constructive consequences. The kind of synthesis which, we think, will help to counter these centrifugal pressures is one in which the work of Marx and Marxists (including Gramsci) will have to figure centrally. But so will figures such as Comte, Durkheim, Weber, Simmel, Mannheim and Elias. Admittedly none of these figures is a female but I am personally convinced that figures such as Susan Birrell, Cheryl Cole, Nancy Theberge, Patricia Vertinsky and, despite her stubborn and to me puzzling misconstrual of key aspects of what figurational sociologists have written, Jennifer Hargreaves, will deservedly have aspects of their work integrated into any emerging synthesis in the sociology of sport.

The theory of civilizing processes and a discussion of the development of modern sport in that context ought to figure centrally in any such emerging synthesis, too. A precondition for that to occur, however, is that these issues will have to be approached by the protagonists of rival paradigms in a fairer, more open-minded and, dare I say, detached spirit than has often been displayed so far. Jennifer Hargreaves writes: 'The problem for figurational sociology is not that many of us have *misunderstood* the theory...but that we disagree with its claims and find the Marxist tradition of sports sociology more fruitful for understanding the social world of sports' (1994: 16). I do not for one moment dispute the fruitfulness of 'the Marxist tradition of sports sociology'. What I insist upon, however, is that, *pace* her disavowals, Jennifer Hargreaves *most certainly has* misunderstood the theory of civilizing processes and that she has done so because she wrongly assimilates it with nineteenth-century evolutionary theories in which metaphysical ideas of necessary, unilinear and irreversible 'progress' are posited.

Jennifer Hargreaves reinforces my conviction that she has misunderstood the theory of civilizing processes by misconstruing my statement that it would not 'necessarily be inconsistent with the theory if a rise in violence against women...were currently occurring' (Dunning, in Dunning and Rojek, 1992: 257; Hargreaves, 1994: 16). A key word in this sentence, of course, is 'necessarily'. A long-term increase in violence against women which occurred in the context of a society characterized by a secure state monopoly on violence and taxation and in which a lengthening of interdependency chains and func-

tional democratization were taking place would certainly create severe difficulties for the theory. However, a short-term rise in such violence might not
do so. For example, such an increase might occur as a consequence of immigration from a more violent country. Moreover, in a context of functional
democratization a violent response to the demands for change made by
increasingly powerful females might be expected from socially and psycholog-
ically insecure and immature males in the 'late barbarian' stage of social
development at which we currently stand. Under conditions where a secure
state monopoly was being maintained, however, only if violence towards
females increased in the longer term would the theory be refuted. That would
be the case because the predicted increase in mutual identification among
growing numbers of males and females would have failed to occur. However,
an increase in violence against women which occurred in *the context of a
decline in the tax and violence monopoly of a state* would actually *confirm* the
theory of civilizing processes. Events in former Yugoslavia provide an opportunity to test this proposition. The point is that these are exceedingly complex
and sensitive issues which need to be researched carefully and in detail and
calmly and constructively debated by male as well as female sociologists and
not just arbitrarily and rhetorically dismissed.

Let me conclude by raising one more issue. I may have given the impression
throughout this book that there is complete unanimity among figurational
sociologists. There is certainly a high degree of consensus among us but, more
recently, there have been signs of growing division as well. For example, Dutch
sociologists such as Fred Spier of the University of Amsterdam have suggested
that, because of the recurrent misconstruals, figurational sociologists should
abandon the term 'civilization' in favour of a term such as 'regime'. My view
is that this is profoundly mistaken for a number of reasons: first, because it is
difficult to think of an adequate process-version of regime (I suppose 'regime
formation' might do but 'regimentation' would be clearly inadequate); second,
because it wrongly assumes that 'civilization' (which can be statically understood) rather than 'civilizing process' (which cannot) is the key term in the
figurational conceptual armoury; and third, because if one (a) starts out as
Elias did to construct the outlines of a theory on the basis of a scientifically
grounded view of humans as social beings with bodies and emotions as well
as an (embodied) intellect, (b) studies human social development in the longer
term, and (c) builds twentieth-century scientific ideas on the relationships
between determination and contingency, constraint and freedom into one's
work as Elias did, one is almost bound to come up with a theory much like
the theory of civilizing processes. In any case, as I hope I have shown in this
book, few of the objections so far raised by the doubters withstand scrutiny if
one is careful to take note of what Elias actually wrote.

As one can see from this book, a central theme in Elias's work on sport
involved a focus on problems of aggression, violence and violence control. As
I have tried to show especially in Chapter 2, his position on the balance

between 'nature' and 'nurture' in the production of human violence was very different from the nowadays standard positions of Lorenz (1967), Freud (1939) and their followers who posit an aggressive instinct. In fact, the very occurrence of civilizing processes provides a counter to the idea that humans are 'innately aggressive'. Lorenz believed that the canalization of this 'aggressive instinct' into sport represented one of the few hopes that humanity has in a nuclear age of avoiding self-destruction. He was evidently unaware of the civilizing processes involved in the development of modern sport and that sports themselves can be the sites of serious violence as is shown by the escalation of soccer hooliganism since the mid-1960s. Using the phrase which I introduced at the beginning of this conclusion, modern sports are what Elias would have called a useful 'collective invention'. They are not, however, a panacea. The degree of violence they entail is fundamentally dependent on the habitus and personality structure of the people who play, watch, organize and control them, and these, in their turn, are dependent on the stage in a civilizing or de-civilizing process or the balance between them at which their society stands. As I have noted in this book on several occasions, Elias (1991a) speculated that, in the future – assuming that our overall civilizing processes continue in a broadly 'progressive' direction and that humanity is not wiped out through nuclear war, ecological catastrophe or the collision of the earth with a large asteroid – historians may well look back on even the most civilizationally advanced people of the twentieth century as 'late barbarians'. Perhaps it is the fact that we are 'late barbarians' which accounts for the fact that modern sport is not only a social enclave for the socially legitimate and valuable 'controlled de-controlling of emotional controls' (see Chapter 1) but also a site for the inculcation, expression and preservation of some of the more extreme forms of masculine *machismo* (see Chapter 6). It has also been subject for more than a century to processes of commodification and commercialization, processes which have been accelerating as the twentieth century draws to a close and the consequences of which for sport and violence and, indeed for the very preservation of sport in its modern forms, seem at present indeterminate. (As I wrote this sentence, Murdoch's BSkyB had just paid £625 million to buy Manchester United and Carlton were involved in negotiations with Arsenal.) One thing that can be said with certainty in this connection, though, is that Norbert Elias made significant contributions to the sociology of sport as he did to so many other areas of the subject. It is thus perhaps appropriate to finish this book by paraphrasing Elias's quotation from Holbach at the end of *The Civilizing Process*: 'La civilisation et le sport ne sont pas encore terminées'. It is my hope that, in *Sport Matters*, I have carried the torch a little further from where Elias left off and helped to push the sociological study of sport to a position in the prestige hierarchy of sociological topics which is at least a little higher than the position it has occupied up to now.

NOTES

INTRODUCTION: SPORT AS A FIELD OF SOCIOLOGICAL ENQUIRY

1 I have used quote marks around the terms 'social' and 'economic' in order to indicate the fact that this customary distinction can be misleading if it leads people to ignore the fact that the 'economy' and the 'economic' are social phenomena.

2 Elias and Foucault both saw power as a general phenomenon in human societies. However, while Foucault's conception of a 'microphysics of power' has been legitimately criticized as metaphysical, it is difficult to see how such a charge can be levelled at Elias because, for him, power is a function of interdependency; that is, if A is more dependent on B than B is on A, then, whatever the source of the dependency, B has power over A.

3 In a review article (*Leisure Studies* (1988), 7: 201–8), Chas Critcher dismissed this idea of a 'sparetime spectrum' as 'excessively formal' and then proceeded to make the statement that 'the functionalist notion of social equilibrium is at the centre of the (figurational) view of society'. No textual evidence is given for this assertion other than the unsupportable statement that, 'in many of the essays (in *Quest for Excitement*), especially those by Elias, "function" is the most recurrent term'. It is to me puzzling that a scholar of Chas Critcher's stature can make assertions of this kind without taking the trouble to examine Elias's detailed exposition of how his concept of functions differs from that of 'functionalists'. For an exposition of Elias's discussion of this issue, see Elias (1978). See also pp. 17 and 18 of the present volume.

4 For illuminating critiques of the undue reliance of some sociologists on philosophical work, see Richard Kilminster (1987), 'Sociology and the Professional Culture of the Philosophers', and Nicos P. Mouzelis (1991) *Back to Sociological Theory: The Construction of Social Orders*.

5 For an excellent review of the literature on the social formation of personality which comes down basically on the side of the figurational view, see Ian Burkitt (1991), *Social Selves: Theories of the Social Formation of Personality*.

6 This, of course, was one of the basic arguments of Durkheim in *The Division of Labour in Society* (1964). It is denied, most specifically in relation to Elias, by Giddens in *The Constitution of Society* (1984).

7 For a detailed exposition and attempted rebuttal of some of the most frequent misconstruals, see my 'Figurational Sociology and the Sociology of Sport', in Dunning and Rojek, 1992, pp. 221–84.

8 Elias (1978), pp. 34–157, 'Human Interdependencies – Problems of Social Bonds'.

9 Elias (1978), esp. pp. 15, 22, 30, 37ff., 64, 74ff., 80ff., 92–4, 116, 139ff., 155, 168ff., 172, 175.

249

10 Elias (1978), pp. 158ff., 'The Problem of the "Inevitability" of Social Development'.

1 ON PROBLEMS OF THE EMOTIONS IN SPORT AND LEISURE

1 To have been fully up to date with the latest sociological fashion, I should perhaps have referred here to 'embodied emotions'. However, from a figurational stand-point, use of the adjective 'embodied' would be redundant. That is because, partly on account of the fact that it incorporates the medical as well as the philosophical and sociological training of its founder, Norbert Elias, the figurational perspective is concerned with the relations between human beings considered 'in the round' or, to express it metaphorically, 'body and soul'. It is concerned, that is, with emotions as psycho-physiological processes which are socially as well as psycho-physiologically generated. Given this emphasis, figurational sociologists welcome the recent emergence of specialized sociologies of the emotions and the body, although we regret what we regard as the tendency to see them as separate and unrelated specialisms.
2 Moorhouse has in mind here Stanley Parker (1976), *The Sociology of Leisure*; John Clarke and Chas Critcher (1985), *The Devil Makes Work: Leisure in Capitalist Britain*; and Rosemary Deem (1986), *All Work and No Play*.
3 Elias (1994: 443–524) discusses these issues in some detail in Part Two of *State-Formation and Civilization*, under the heading 'Synopsis: Towards a Theory of Civilizing Processes'.
4 Different forms and levels of routinization are, of course, involved in the life of the 'advanced' and relatively 'civilized' societies of the modern West as compared with the more grinding routinization involved in the daily struggle of, for example, the urban poor in South Africa and countries in Central and South America who are not faced, relatively speaking, by imminent starvation, warfare or violent civil strife. Comparison of the different forms of, for example, soccer support in these contexts would make an interesting research topic.

2 SPORT IN THE WESTERN CIVILIZING PROCESS

1 A reductionist argument which has gained currency recently is the explanation of aggressiveness, especially the aggressiveness of males, by reference to the male hormone testosterone. My suspicion is that, since not all males are equally aggres-sive, it is not testosterone *per se* which is a cause of aggressiveness but the frustration of the male sex drive, a frustration which can be canalized into sport and career pursuits as well as into aggressiveness and crime. It may also be the case that testosterone and 'sexual' arousal may play a part in the enjoyable character of violence.
2 The subtitle of the English translation of Volume I is 'The History of Manners'. It was imposed by Urizen, the first publishers of the translation, because they thought it would help sales. Elias resisted this subtitle strongly because his German subtitle, 'Wandlungen des Verhaltens in den weltlichen Oberschichten des Abendlands' – changes in the behaviour of the secular upper classes in the West – is a more accurate reflection of what the book is about.
3 An example of a 'reverse civilizing process', that is of a 'de-civilizing' or 'barbarizing' process', is provided by former Yugoslavia where the disintegration of a formerly unified state resulted in a power shift towards warlords and their polit-ical cronies.

4 The first of these 'basic controls' is considered by Elias in *Involvement and Detachment* (1987) and *The Symbol Theory* (1991b).

5 Elias's use of the term 'blind process' is reminiscent of Richard Dawkins' usage in *The Blind Watchmaker* (1986). Just as Dawkins uses the term 'blind' in an attempt to produce a non-teleological theory of biological evolution, so Elias uses it in order to lay the foundation for a non-teleological theory of social development.

6 Elias's concept of the means of ruling is a direct parallel to the Marxian concept of the means of production.

7 Marxist writers, for example Anderson (1974), argue that the more highly central-ized dynastic or 'absolutist' states of Western Europe were forms of feudal state. In his *The Nation-State and Violence* (1985), Giddens parallels Elias in arguing that they constitute a distinct stage. Since Giddens was a lecturer at the University of Leicester for some eight years during the 1960s, and Elias, too, was at Leicester in those years, it is difficult to believe that Giddens was not influenced by Elias in reaching this conclusion.

8 The fact that citizens have not been disarmed to the same extent in the USA suggests that the USA, in this regard at least, is technically speaking a less civilized society than the societies of Western Europe.

9 The concept of 'sociogenesis', literally 'social generation', is preferable to the term 'causes' because it helps to avoid an overly simple, mechanistic idea of social deter-mination.

10 Because they were so different from modern sports, Elias coined the term 'agonistic game contests' as a label for describing the 'sports' of Ancient Greece.

11 McIntosh's work is representative of this idealizing tendency because he attempts arbitrarily to impose the modern idea of 'fairness' on the Ancient Greeks. It is undoubtedly the case that there were relatively crude equalizing rules – 'standard-izing' would be a better term – in the sports of Ancient Greece, but it is highly implausible that an equivalent of the modern idea of 'fair play' could have devel-oped in warrior, slave-based societies.

12 It was one of Elias's contentions that a fundamental power resource of males rela-tive to females is their generally superior capacity to use physical violence. It follows that the 'taming' of the European warrior class – the 'knights' through their incorporation into royal courts involved a decrease in their power and an increase in that of female members of their class. For an elaboration of this see Chapter 9.

13 The 1847 Eton rules were discovered by Graham Curry, a Leicester postgraduate student.

14 For a lengthier discussion of this issue, see Eric Dunning, 'Sport in the Civilizing Process: Aspects of the Development of Modern Sport', in Dunning *et al.* (1993).

3 SPORT IN SPACE AND TIME: TRAJECTORIES OF STATE FORMATION AND THE EARLY DEVELOPMENT OF MODERN SPORT

1 It was Frank Kew who pointed out that this is a polarity that Norbert Elias and I had overlooked.

5 THE DYNAMICS OF SPORTS CONSUMPTION

1 It is probably fair to say that many sociologists take concepts such as 'the economy' and 'the economic' for granted. Figurational sociologists, however, investigate the social origins of such terms and attempt to delineate precisely the

nexus(es) of social functions they refer to in societies of different types. It seems possible that one of the reasons why 'hegemony theorists' and 'cultural studies' Marxists experience difficulty with figurational/process-sociological analyses of such matters may be that they take conventional categories like 'the economy' too much for granted. If that is the case, it sits uneasily with their professed claim to be unmaskers *par excellence* of taken-for-granted categories and assumptions.

2 Earlier terms which had in some respects the same meaning were 'mass society' and 'affluent society'. Just as is the case with some 'post-modernist' discussions of 'consumer societies' today, authors who used such terms often spoke and wrote as if they were referring to social formations entirely lacking precedents in the past. Then, as now, the trick in this connection – and it is not easy to perform – is to establish empirically the precise balance between continuity and change which was and is involved.

3 'Critical theory', the work originally of 'the Frankfurt School', is, of course, well known. It is not so well known that Norbert Elias was assistant to Karl Mannheim in the Department of Sociology at the University of Frankfurt at the same time and had close contact with the 'Frankfurt Schüler', Adorno prominent among them.

4 Some American Marxist scholars also adhere to a view of sport as 'transcendental'; see especially William J. Morgan (1985). Assuming that they are accepted as having some validity, the criticisms I have offered of Hargreaves apply, *ipso facto*, to this aspect of Morgan's otherwise insightful work.

5 I am using the term 'stage' here without evolutionary connotations to refer to steps or moments in a developmental sequence that has been established retrospectively.

6 *The Hillsborough Stadium Disaster: 15 April 1989* (1990) Inquiry by the Rt. Hon. Lord Justice Taylor, London: HMSO.

7 In the early 1980s, Patrick Murphy and I put together a proposal for a comprehensive study of patterns of ownership and control in English professional soccer. However, on the advice of the late Sir Norman Chester, we did not submit it to a funding body. It was, in his opinion, too radical and unlikely to have been supported.

6 SOCCER HOOLIGANISM AS A WORLD SOCIAL PROBLEM

1 If it remains true to its principles, the 'New Labour' government ought to seek to bring these Championships, not to England, but to the United Kingdom. Sharing matches with Scotland, Wales and Northern Ireland – and the Republic, too? – would surely represent a positive and imaginative step towards reducing the centripetal, subnationalist pressures which result more than anything else from the taken-for-granted and often arrogant dominance of the English.

2 These historical parts of our work were carried out by Eric Dunning, Patrick Murphy and Joseph Maguire.

3 For a hypothetical discussion of this issue, see Eric Dunning *et al.*, *The Roots of Football Hooliganism* (1988), *op. cit.*; and Eric Dunning, 'The Social Roots of Football Hooliganism: A Reply to the Critics of the 'Leicester School'', in Giulianotti *et al.*, *Football, Violence and Social Identity* (1994), *op. cit.*.

4 Suttles (1968, 1972). The analysis presented here involves a modification and development in some respects of Suttles' original model.

7 SPORTS CROWD VIOLENCE IN NORTH AMERICA

1 'Aggro' is a corruption of 'aggravation' and was used in the 1960s by skinheads to describe their fighting. London skinheads also spoke of 'bovver', a Cockney corruption of 'bother'.

2 This partial support of Lorenz should not be taken as implying support for his view of a human 'aggressive instinct'. People who engage voluntarily in violent sports do so largely because they have learned to see them as meaningful and enjoyable. Although it cannot be described as 'inborn' or instinctive', there is, of course, a physiological base to this enjoyment.

3 The sociological literature on this subject is so vast that it would be pointless to attempt to document it here. It is enough just to say that it stems, more than anything else, from the work of the Chicago School. The work of Suttles (1968; 1972) seems to me to represent one of the best recent developments of that socio-logical tradition.

4 It is impossible to do justice here to the subtlety and complexity of Young's (1988) work. It uses a number of methodological approaches in order to stress the difficulties of measuring a fluid and hitherto to largely unresearched phenomenon such as sports crowd disorder. In particular, Young imaginatively uses a semiotic approach in order to highlight the ways in which perceptions, representations and significations interact with crowd behaviour *per se* in determining the public recognition of such behaviour as problematic.

5 The Hillsborough tragedy was indirectly related to hooliganism in the sense that the attempt of suffering fans to escape from the Leppings Lane pen was at first interpreted by the police as a pitch invasion. Moreover, without the introduction of penning as a means of containing hooliganism, such a tragedy could not have occurred.

6 *USA Today* has emerged, to some extent, as a national paper in the USA in recent years, whilst the *Globe and Mail* claims such a status for Canada. However, neither has such a long tradition of national status as, for example, *The Times*, *Daily Telegraph*, *Daily Express* and *Daily Mail* in England.

8 SPORT IN THE PROCESS OF RACIAL STRATIFICATION: THE CASE OF THE USA

1 For an insightful exploration from a figurational standpoint of the issues of 'centrality' and 'stacking' in English cricket, see Malcolm (1997a; 1997b).

2 Stephen Small's *Racialized Barriers: The Black Experience in the United States and England in the 1980s* (1994) is one of the few general studies of race in which the significance of sport in racial stratification is recognized.

3 Lockwood failed to see that there are moral, aesthetic and perhaps sexual conno-tations built into the description of some jobs as 'dirty' or 'unclean'. Such connotations are also built into popular understandings of the distinction between manual and non-manual labour.

4 Durkheim (1964) used the concept of interdependence in a harmonistic way. It is not used in that sense by figurationalists who focus on the balance between conflict and co-operation, tension and harmony in *all* human relationships.

5 This tautology does not appear in the German text where the words Elias uses are 'mehr auf andere angewiesen sind als sie auf uns' which means 'more reliant on others than they are on us' (Elias, 1970: 97).

6 For example, if you are a student and depend on me for learning sociology, I have power over you. It derives from my specialist knowledge; something that you want. I can give you low marks (grades) or even fail you. However, you have a

degree of control over me as well because you can, for example, give me low marks in your course assessment.

7 Black women were, of course, subjected to triple subordination, that is subordination to white men, white women and black men. See Sammons (1994) and Captain (1991) for a discussion of the prevalence of sexist attitudes and behaviour among black American males.

9 SPORT, GENDER AND CIVILIZATION

1 This chapter is an elaboration of some of the key ideas proposed in 'Process-Sociological Notes on Sport, Gender Relations and Violence Control' which I wrote with Joe Maguire. It appeared in the *International Review for the Sociology of Sport* (1996), 31: 295–321.

2 An exception is provided by Judith Lorber in her *Paradoxes of Gender* (1994), pp. 41–4.

3 This is, of course, not true of the sociology of sport literature where the pioneering work of scholars like Klein, Messner and Sabo is making important contributions to the understanding of the social production and reproduction of masculinity not just in sports but more generally as well.

4 The term 'andrarchy' – which means 'male rule' – is arguably preferable to 'patriarchy' because, while the latter derives from Greek and Latin roots, the roots of the former are solely Greek. 'Patriarchy' also literally means 'rule of the father' rather than 'rule by men'

5 The reason why is that figurational sociologists are acutely aware of the fact that knowledge is developmental; that is, that all of us are dependent on the 'social fund of knowledge' available in particular societies at particular points in time. As far, specifically, as sociology is concerned, it is our position that sociological knowledge at the moment is far less advanced than that in areas such as physics, chemistry and biology.

6 There were, of course, variations within and between European societies within this general process.

7 This balance tends to vary, for example, in the life-course of individuals. Zurcher and Meadow provide a revealing example in their 'On Bullfights and Baseball' (1971: 178), when they write of the Mexican family that: 'The wife and daughters seem to develop a solidly female "mutual protection society", adopt a passively controlling "martyr" role, and wait patiently to seize control whenever the father's dominance falters'.

8 Walby goes on to qualify this contention by suggesting that: 'The infrequency of state intervention, and the humiliation meted out to those women who seek it, indicates that this is more a shift in the locus of control and legitimation of violence than its elimination' (Walby, 1990: 149). If this is right – and it seems that Walby was thinking here more of rape than of male violence against females generally – it suggests that changes at the level of habitus and personality are more important in this regard than changes at the level of legislation.

9 According to Wurman (1982: 20), a veteran NFL referee described his duties as 'trying to maintain order during a legalized gang brawl involving 80 toughs with a little whistle, a hanky and a ton of prayer'.

10 These practices are defined by Wurman (1982: 13) as follows:

Blind-side hit   used on quarterbacks in the act of completing a throw – and on a tailback receiving an option play pass from the quarterback and unable to see the onrushing tackler.

Chop-blocking	vicious blocking down to the knees when a man is held by a team-mate and is in a rigid or off-balance position.
Clubbing or bouncer's wallop	illegal jawbreaker delivered via a smash of arm and fists to the neck. Use of it against receiver Lynn Swann of Pittsburgh led coach Chuck Nell to charge that a 'criminal element' was loose in the sport.
Crackback block	illegal since 1976 in college play and since 1979 in NFL play, this is a clip delivered at or near the scrimmage line by an end slanting back in from the outside.
Earholing	aiming the crown of the head at a player's ear with devastating result.
Head-butting	illegal since 1979 but still common. Grabbing jersey, pulling forward and following with a sharp blow to the head.
Leg-whipping	offensive lineman, having failed on a block, reaches back with his legs and flails them across a man's shins.
Rake-blocking	ramming opponent's chest, then whipping the face mask up to the chin.
Spearing	outlawed by colleges in 1970. This is the deliberate use of the helmet to punish a man, whether stopped or not. Example: in a notorious 1978 incident, Jack 'Black Death' Tatum (Oakland) stuck it to Darryl Stingley (New England receiver). Stingley was left permanently paralysed.

11 The evidence is that, since the 1970s, violence in Britain has been tending to increase (Dunning *et al.*, 1987). It seems highly likely that violence by males against females will have tended to increase correlatively. If that is established and if it is shown that such an increase of male violence against females is largely connected with the growing impoverishment and 'disincorporation' ('alienation') of the lowest social strata, it will confirm rather than disconfirm one of the central tenets of the theory of civilizing processes. For a more extended discussion of this, see Dunning *et al.* (1988), especially Chapter 9 and the conclusion.

12 By understandably engaging in behaviour of this kind, these women arguably give legitimacy to the homophobic behaviour of their male counterparts, thereby undermining the expression of 'civilizing' tolerance towards 'gays'.

CONCLUSION

1 Because in *The Civilizing Process* he outlined in considerable empirical detail a central line in the development of West European societies since the Middle Ages and provided a non-teleological explanation of this development, one might also argue that Elias is a sociological equivalent of Darwin. Such an argument is plausible but I prefer the analogy with Copernicus because it seems to me to be more in keeping with an idea that Elias himself frequently articulated, namely that, despite the advances made in recent centuries in our understanding of the physical and to a lesser extent the biological world, humans remain massively ignorant of the structure and dynamics of the social world that they collectively form and hence prone to distorting magical–mythical and common-sense beliefs about it.

2 For an excellent recent discussion of Elias's contribution on this score, see Farhad Dalal (1998) *Taking the Group Seriously: Towards a Post-Foulkesian Group Analytic Theory*.

3 This is the title of one of Elias's books. See Bibliography.

4 Aristarchus of Samos came up with such a view in the Ancient World; however, it did not catch on. Along with other developments in the direction of a scientific world view in that context, it came, as Elias put it, 'to drown in a sea of Christianity'. These words were spoken by Elias at a Conference at Balliol College, Oxford, in 1981.

5 Elias's own life probably helped him in forming this bridging conceptualization. He was delayed in going to university by the outbreak of the First World War in which he served in a non-combatant capacity – he was part of a telegraphic unit – on both the Eastern and the Western fronts. His studies were interrupted again in 1923 when his father, Hermann, was ruined by the hyperinflation and, of course, the rise to power of the Nazis in 1933 forced him to flee Germany.

6 Adorno supervised the work on sport of Heinz Risse whose *Soziologie des Sports* (1921) was, so far as I know, the first time that this subdiscipline was explicitly named. Adorno also supervised the work of Bero Rigauer which resulted in *Sport und Arbeit* (Sport and Work) (1969).

7 I am thinking of Elias's *Involvement and Detachment* (1987), the discussions in Stephen Mennell (1989, 1992), *Norbert Elias: An Introduction*, and by me in the final chapter of Dunning and Rojek (1992) *Sport and Leisure in the Civilizing Process*.

8 In his 'Play Up: Rethinking Power and Resistance in Sport', *Journal of Sport and Social Issues* (1988), 22(3): 241–51, David Rowe similarly urges a 'sociology with passion'. Interestingly, in an aside on figurational sociology (p. 242), Rowe refers to what he calls 'the grand narrative of the civilizing process', suggesting that he too wrongly regards it as an obsolete nineteenth-century-type 'progress' theory.

9 See, for example, John Horne and David Jary (1987), 'The Figurational Sociology of Sport and Leisure of Elias and Dunning: An Exposition and Critique', in *Sport, Leisure and Social Relations*.

BIBLIOGRAPHY

Abrams, P. (1982) *Historical Sociology*, Wells, Somerset: Open Books.
Albonico, R. and Pfister-Binz, K. (1972) *Sociology of Sport: Theoretical Foundations and Research Methods*, Basle: Magglinger Symposium.
Allan, J. (1989) *Bloody Casuals*, Glasgow: Famedram.
Allport, G. W. (1954) *The Nature of Prejudice*, New York: Doubleday.
Anderson, P. (1974) *Lineages of the Absolute State*, London: New Left Books.
Andreski, S. (1974) *The Essential Comte*, London: Croom Helm.
Aptheker, H. (1943) *American Negro Slave Revolts*, New York.
Arlott, J. (1977) *The Oxford Companion to Sports and Games*, London: Paladin.
Armstrong, G. (1998) *Football Hooligans: Knowing the Score*, Oxford: Berg.
Armstrong, G. and Harris, R. (1991) 'Football Hooligans: Theory and Evidence', *Sociological Review* 39(3): 427–58.
Atyeo, D. (1979) *Blood and Guts: Violence in Sports*, London: Paddington.
Auguet, R. (1972) *Cruelty and Civilization: The Roman Games*, London: Allen and Unwin.
Bairner, A. (1995) 'Soccer, Masculinity and Violence in Northern Ireland: Between Hooliganism and Terrorism', Paper given at the Annual NASSS Conference, Sacramento, California.
Bale, J. (1993) *Sport, Space and the City*, London: Routledge.
Barber, R. (1974) *The Knight and Chivalry*, Ipswich: Boydell.
Bauman, Z. (1977) 'The Phenomenon of Norbert Elias', *Sociology* 13. 117–35.
Bendix, R. (1953) 'Karl Marx's Theory of Social Classes', in R. Bendix and S. M. Lipset (eds) *Class, Status and Power*, Glencoe: Free Press.
Berreman, G. I. (1960) 'Caste in India and the United States', *American Journal of Sociology* 66: 120–7.
Birrell, S. J. (1988) 'Discourses on the Gender/Sport Relationship: From Women in Sport to Gender Relations', *Exercise and Sports Sciences Reviews* 16: 459–502.
Birrell, S. J. (1989) 'Racial Relations Theories and Sport: Suggestions for a More Critical Analysis', *Sociology of Sport Journal* 6: 212–27.
Blassingame, J. W. (1972) *The Slave Community*, New York: Oxford University Press.
Blauner, R. (1972) *Racial Oppression in America*, London: Harper and Row.
Bloomfield, A. (1994) 'Muscular Christian or Mystic? Charles Kingsley Re-Appraised', *International Journal of the History of Sport* 11(2): 172–90.
Bott, E. (1957) *Family and Social Network*, London: Tavistock.

Bourdieu, P. (1984) *Distinction: A Social Critique of the Judgement of Taste*, London: Routledge.

Boyle, R. H. (1971) 'Negroes in Baseball', in E. Dunning (ed.) *The Sociology of Sport: A Selection of Readings*, London: Cass.

Brailsford, D. (1991) *Sport, Time and Society: The British at Play*, London: Routledge.

Bredekamp, H. (1993) *Florentiner Fussball: die Renaissance der Spiele*, Frankfurt/ M: Campus.

Brittan, A. (1989) *Masculinity and Power*, Oxford: Blackwell.

Brohm, J. M. (1978) *Sport: A Prison of Measured Time*, London: Ink Links.

Brookes, C. (1978) *English Cricket*, London: Weidenfeld and Nicholson.

Brooks, D. and Althouse, R. (eds) (1994) *Racism in College Athletics*, Morgantown, WV: Fitness Information Technology.

Brownmiller, S. (1976) *Against Our Will: Men, Women and Rape*, Harmondsworth: Penguin.

Buford, B. (1991) *Among the Thugs*, London: Secker and Warburg.

Burkitt, I. (1991) *Social Selves: Theories of the Social Formation of Personality*, London: Sage.

Cameron, A. (1976) *Circus Factions*, Oxford: Clarendon Press.

Captain, G. (1991) 'Enter Ladies and Gentlemen of Colour', *Journal of Sport History* 18(1): 81–102.

Carew, Sir Richard (1602) *The Survey of Cornwall*, London.

Cashmore, E. (1990) *Making Sense of Sport*, London: Routledge.

Clarke, A. (1992) 'Figuring a Brighter Future', in E. Dunning and C. Rojek (eds) *Sport and Leisure in the Civilizing Process: Critique and Counter-Critique*, London: Macmillan.

Clarke, J. (1978) 'Football and Working Class Fans: Tradition and Change', in R. Ingham (ed.) *Football Hooliganism: The Wider Context*, London: Inter-Action Imprint.

Clarke, J. and Critcher, C. (1985) *The Devil Makes Work: Leisure in Capitalist Britain*, London: Macmillan.

Coakley, J. (1990) *Sport in Society: Issues and Controversies*, St Louis: Times Mirror/Mosby.

Cohen, A. K. (1955) *Delinquent Boys: The Culture of the Gang*, Glencoe, IL: Free Press.

Cohen, P. and Robins, D. (1978) *Knuckle Sandwich*, Harmondsworth: Penguin.

Coles, R. (1975) 'Football as a Surrogate Religion', in M. Hill (ed.) *A Sociological Yearbook of Religion in Britain*, No. 3.

Critcher, C. (1988) Review article on N. Elias and E. Dunning, *Quest for Excitement*, in *Leisure Studies* 7: 201–8.

Crosset, T. (1990) 'Masculinity, Sexuality and the Development of Early Modern Sport', in M. A. Messner and D. F. Sabo (eds) *Sport, Men and the Gender Order: Critical Feminist Perspectives*, Champaign, IL: Human Kinetics.

Csikzentmihalyi, M. (1975) *Beyond Boredom and Anxiety: The Experience of Play in Work*, San Francisco: Jossey-Bass.

Curtis, J. (1986) 'Isn't it Difficult to Support Some Notions of "the Civilizing Process?"', in C. R. Rees and A. W. Miracle (eds) *Sport and Social Theory*, Champaign, IL: Human Kinetics.

Dahrendorf, R. (1959) *Class and Class Conflict in Industrial Society*, Stanford, CA: Stanford University Press.

Dalal, Farhad (1998) *Taking the Group Seriously: Towards a Post-Foulkesian Group Analytic Theory*, London and Philadelphia: Jessica Kingsley.

Davis, A., Gardner, B. B. and Gardner, M. R. (1941) *Deep South*, Chicago: University of Chicago Press.

Davis, K. *et al.* (1991) *The Gender of Power*, London: Sage.

Dawkins, R. (1986) *The Blind Watchmaker*, Harmondsworth: Penguin.

Deem, R. (1986) *All Work and No Play*, Milton Keynes: Open University Press.

Diem, C. (1971) *Weltgeschichte des Sports*, Stuttgart: Cotta.

Dobbs, B. (1973) *Edwardians at Play: Sport 1890–1914*, London: Pelham.

Donnelly, P. (1993) 'Subcultures in Sport: Resilience and Transformation', in A. G. Ingham and J. W. Loy (eds) *Sport in Social Development*, Champaign, IL: Human Kinetics.

Donnelly, P. and Young, K. (1985) 'Reproduction and Transformation of Cultural Forms in Sport: A Contextual Analysis of Rugby', *International Review for the Sociology of Sport* 20(1): 19–38.

Douglass, F. (1968) *Narrative of the Life of Frederick Douglass*, New York: Signet.

Dunning, E. (1961) 'The Development of Football as an Organized Game', unpublished MA thesis, University of Leicester.

Dunning, E. (ed.) (1971) *The Sociology of Sport: A Selection of Readings*, London: Cass.

Dunning, E. (1972) 'Some Conceptual Dilemmas in the Sociology of Sport', in R. Albonico and K. Pfister-Binz (eds) *Sociology of Sport: Theoretical Foundations and Research Methods*, Basle: Magglinger Symposium.

Dunning, E. (1979) 'The Figurational Dynamics of Modern Sport: Notes on the Sociogenesis of Achievement Striving and the Social Significance of Sport', *Sportwissenschaft* 9(4).

Dunning, E. (1986) 'Sport as a Male Preserve: Notes on the Social Sources of Masculine Identity and its Transformations', in N. Elias and E. Dunning (eds) *Quest for Excitement: Sport and Leisure in the Civilizing Process*, Oxford: Blackwell, pp. 267–83.

Dunning, E. (1992) 'Figurational Sociology and the Sociology of Sport', in E. Dunning and C. Rojek (eds) *Sport and Leisure in the Civilizing Process: Critique and Counter-Critique*, London: Macmillan, and Toronto: University of Toronto Press.

Dunning, E. and Maguire, J. (1996) 'Process-Sociological Notes on Sport, Gender Relations and Violence Control', *International Review for the Sociology of Sport* 31(3): 295–321.

Dunning, E. and Mennell, S. (1998) 'Elias on Germany, Nazism and the Holocaust: On the Balance Between "Civilizing" and "De-civilizing" Trends in the Social Development of Western Europe', *British Journal of Sociology* 49(3): 339–57.

Dunning, E. and Rojek, C. (eds) (1992) *Sport and Leisure in the Civilizing Process: Critique and Counter-Critique*, London: Macmillan.

Dunning, E. and Sheard, K. (1973) 'The Rugby Football Club as a Type of Male Preserve', *International Review of Sport Sociology* 8:5–24.

Dunning, E. and Sheard, K. (1979) *Barbarians, Gentlemen and Players: A Sociological Study of the Development of Rugby Football*, Oxford: Martin Robertson.

Dunning, E., Murphy, P., Newburn, W. and Waddington, I. (1987) 'Violent Disorders in Twentieth Century Britain', in G. Gaskell and R. Benewick (eds) *The Crowd in Contemporary Britain*, London: Sage.

Dunning, E., Murphy, P. and Williams, J. (1988) *The Roots of Football Hooliganism*, London: Routledge.

Dunning, E., Maguire, J. and Pearton, R. (1993) *The Sports Process: a Comparative and Developmental Approach*, Champaign, IL: Human Kinetics.

Durkheim, E. (1938) *The Rules of Sociological Method*, Chicago: University of Chicago Press.

Durkheim, E. (1964) *The Division of Labour in Society*, New York: Free Press.

Durkheim, E. (1976) *The Elementary Forms of the Religious Life*, London: Allen and Unwin.

Edwards, H. (1969) *The Revolt of the Black Athlete*, New York: Free Press.

Edwards, H. (1973) *The Sociology of Sport*, Homewood, IL: Dorsey Press.

Edwards, H. and Rackages, V. (1977) 'The Dynamics of Violence in American Sport', *Journal of Sport and Social Issues* 7(2): 3–31.

Eisenberg, C. (1990) 'The Middle Class and Competition: Some Considerations of the Beginnings of Modern Sport in England and Germany', *International Review of the History of Sport* 7(2).

Elias, N. (1950) 'Studies in the Genesis of the Naval Profession', *British Journal of Sociology* 1(4): 291–309.

Elias, N. (1970) *Was ist Soziologie?*, Munich: Juventa.

Elias, N. (1974) 'The Sciences: Towards a Theory', in R. Whitley (ed.) *Social Processes of Scientific Development*, London: Routledge.

Elias, N. (1978) *What is Sociology?*, London: Hutchinson.

Elias, N. (1983) *The Court Society*, Oxford: Blackwell.

Elias, N. (1986a) 'The Changing Balance of Power Between the Sexes in the History of Civilization', *Theory, Culture and Society* 4(2–3): 287–316.

Elias, N. (1986b) 'The Genesis of Sport as a Sociological Problem', in N. Elias and E. Dunning (eds) *Quest for Excitement: Sport and Leisure in the Civilizing Process*, Oxford: Blackwell.

Elias, N. (1987) *Involvement and Detachment*, Oxford: Blackwell.

Elias, N. (1988) 'Violence and Civilization', in J. Keane (ed.) *Civil Society and the State: New European Perspectives*, London: Verso.

Elias, N. (1991a) *The Society of Individuals*, Oxford: Blackwell.

Elias, N. (1991b) *The Symbol Theory*, London: Sage.

Elias, N. (1992) *Time: An Essay*, Oxford: Blackwell.

Elias, N. (1994) *The Civilizing Process: The History of Manners and State-Formation and Civilization* (single integrated edition), Oxford: Blackwell.

Elias, N. (1996) *The Germans: Studies of Power Struggles and the Development of Habitus in the Nineteenth and Twentieth Centuries*, Oxford: Polity (trans. with a preface by E. Dunning and S. Mennell).

Elias, N. (n.d.) 'The Development of Sport as a Sociological Problem, Part 2', unpublished paper.

Elias, N. and Dunning, E. (1966) 'Dynamics of Sport Groups with Special Reference to Football', *British Journal of Sociology* XVII(4).

Elias, N. and Dunning, E. (1969) 'The Quest for Excitement in Leisure', *Society and Leisure* No. 2: December.

Elias, N. and Dunning, E. (1970) 'The Quest for Excitement in Unexciting Societies', in G. Lüschen (ed.) *The Cross-Cultural Analysis of Sport and Games*, Champaign, IL: Sipes.

Elias, N. and Dunning, E. (1972) 'Leisure in the Sparetime Spectrum', in R. Albonico and K. Pfister-Binz (eds) *Sociology of Sport: Theoretical Foundations and Research Methods* Basle: Magglinger Symposium.

Elias, N. and Dunning, E. (1986) *Quest for Excitement: Sport and Leisure in the Civilizing Process*, Oxford: Blackwell.

Elias, N. and Scotson, J. L. (1994) *The Established and the Outsiders*, 2nd edn, with a new introduction by Norbert Elias, London: Sage. (First published 1965.)

Elkins, S. (1959) *Slavery: A Problem in American Institutional Life*, New York: Grosset and Dunlap.

Ellison, R. (1965) *The Invisible Man*, London: Penguin.

Engels, F. (1942) [1890] 'Letter to Joseph Bloch', in V. Adoratsky (ed.) *Karl Marx Selected Works*, Vol. 1, London: Lawrence and Wishart.

Evans, J. (ed.) (1993) *Equality, Education and Physical Education*, London: Falmer Press.

Eysenck, H. H. and Nias, D. K. B. (1978) *Sex, Violence and the Media*, London: Maurice Temple-Smith.

Finley, M. and Pleket, H. (1976) *The Olympic Games*, London: Chatto and Windus.

Fiske, J. (1991a) 'Bodies of Knowledge, Panopticism and Spectatorship', unpublished paper delivered at the 1991 NASSS Conference, Milwaukee.

Fiske, J. (1991b) *Understanding Popular Culture*, London: Routledge.

Fitzhugh, G. (1854) *Sociology for the South*, Richmond: A. Morris.

Football Association (1991) *Blueprint for the Future of Football*, London: FA.

Franklin, J. H. and Moss A. A. Jr (1994) *From Slavery to Freedom*, New York: McGraw-Hill.

Frazier, E. F. (1962) *Black Bourgeoisie*, New York: Collier.

Freud, S. (1939) *Civilization and its Discontents*, Harmondsworth: Penguin.

Fromm, E. (1977) *The Anatomy of Human Destructiveness*, Harmondsworth: Penguin.

Gagnon, J. H. and Simon W. (1973) *Sexual Conduct: The Social Sources of Human Sexuality*, Chicago: Aldine.

Gardner, P. (1974) *Nice Guys Finish Last*, London: Allen Lane.

Gates, H. L. (1991) 'Delusions of Grandeur', *Sports Illustrated* 19 August.

Genovese, E. (1969) *The World the Slaveholders Made*, London: Allen Lane.

Genovese, E. (1974) *Roll Jordan Roll: The World the Slaves Made*, New York: Pantheon.

Gerth, H. H. and Mills, C. W. (1946) *From Max Weber*, New York: Oxford University Press.

Giddens, A. (1984) *The Constitution of Society*, Cambridge: Polity.

Giddens, A. (1985) *The Nation-State and Violence*, Oxford: Polity.

Giulianotti, R. (1991) 'Scotland's Tartan Army in Italy: The Case for the Carnivalesque', *Sociological Review* 39(3): 503–30.

Giulianotti, R. and Williams, J. (eds) (1994) *Game Without Frontiers: Football, Identity and Modernity*, Aldershot: Arena.

Giulianotti, R., Bonney, N. and Hepworth, M. (eds) (1994) *Football, Violence and Social Identity*, London: Routledge.

Glanville, B. (1969) *Soccer – A Panorama*, London: Eyre and Spottiswoode.

Glanville, B. (1980) *The History of the World Cup*, London: Faber and Faber.

Goffman, E. (1959) *Asylums*, New York: Doubleday Anchor.

Golesworthy, M. (1960) *Encyclopedia of Boxing*, London: Robert Hale.

Goodger, J. M. (1985) 'Collective Representations and the Sacred in Sport', *International Review for the Sociology of Sport* 20(3): 179–88.

Goodger, J. M. and Goodger, B. C. (1989) 'Excitement and Representation: Toward a Sociological Explanation of the Significance of Sport in Modern Society', *Quest* 41(3): 257–72.

Goodhart, P. and Chataway, C. (1968) *War Without Weapons*, London: W. H. Allen.

Goudsblom, J. (1977) *Sociology in the Balance*, Oxford: Blackwell.

Green, G. (1953) *The History of the Football Association*, London: Naldrett.

Greenberg, P. S. (1977) 'Wild in the Stands', *New Times* 9(10): 25–7.

Gruneau, R. and Whitson, D. (1993) *Hockey Night in Canada: Sport, Identities and Cultural Politics*, Toronto: Garamond Press.

Gurr, T. R. (1989) *Violence in America: The History of Crime*, London: Sage.

Guttmann, A. (1978) *From Ritual to Record*, New York: Columbia University Press.

Guttmann, A. (1986) *Sports Spectators*, New York: Columbia University Press.

Guttmann, A. (1992) 'Chariot Races, Tournaments and the Civilizing Process', in E. Dunning and C. Rojek (eds) *Sport and Leisure in the Civilizing Process: Critique and Counter-Critique*, London: Macmillan, pp. 137–60.

Hahn, E. *et al.* (1988) *Fanverhalten, Massenmedien und Gewalt im Sport*, Schorndorf: Karl Hoffman.

Haley, A. (1976) *Roots*, London: Vintage.

Hall, S. and Jacques, M. (eds) (1990) *New Times*, London: Lawrence and Wishart.

Hargreaves, Jennifer (1992) 'Sex, Gender and the Body in Sport: Has There Been a Civilizing Process?', in E. Dunning and C. Rojek (eds) *Sport and Leisure in the Civilizing Process: Critique and Counter-Critique*, London: Macmillan, and Toronto: University of Toronto Press.

Hargreaves, Jennifer (1994) *Sporting Females: Critical Issues in the History and Sociology of Women's Sports*, London: Routledge.

Hargreaves, John (1982) 'Sport and Hegemony: Some Theoretical Problems', in H. Cantelon and R. Gruneau (eds) *Sport, Culture and the Modern State*, Toronto: University of Toronto Press.

Hargreaves, John (1986) *Sport, Power and Culture*, Oxford: Polity.

Harper, C. (1989–1990) 'A Study of Football Crowd Behaviour', Lothian and Borders Police, Mimeo.

Harrington, J. A. (1968) *Soccer Hooliganism*, Bristol: John Wright.

Harrison, P. (1974) 'Soccer's Tribal Wars', *New Society* 29:602.

Haynes, R. (1995) *The Football Imagination: The Rise of the Football Fanzine Culture*, Aldershot: Arena.

Hearn, J. (1987) *The Gender of Oppression: Men, Masculinity and the Critique of Marxism*, Brighton: Wheatsheaf.

Heinemann, K. (1993) 'Sport in Developing Countries', in E. Dunning, J. Maguire and R. Pearton (eds) *The Sports Process: A Comparative and Developmental Approach*, Champaign, IL: Human Kinetics.

Hobbs, D. and Robins, D. (1991) 'The Boy Done Good: Football Violence, Changes and Continuities', *The Sociological Review* 39(3): 551–79.

Hoberman, J. (1992) *Mortal Engines*, New York: Free Press.

Hoberman, J. (1997) *Darwin's Athletes*, New York: Houghton Mifflin.

Hoch, P. (1972) *Rip Off the Big Game*, Garden City, NY: Anchor Books.

Holt, R. (1981) *Sport and Society in Modern France*, London: Macmillan.

Horne, J. and Jary, D. (1987) 'The Figurational Sociology of Sport and Leisure of Elias and Dunning: An Exposition and Critique', in J. Horne, D. Jary and A. Tomlinson (eds) *Sport, Leisure and Social Relations*, London: Routledge.

Huizinga, J. (1971) 'The Play Element in Contemporary Sport', in E. Dunning (ed.) *The Sociology of Sport: A Selection of Readings*, London: Cass.

Huntingford, F. and Turner, A. (1987) *Animal Conflict*, London: Chapman and Hall.

Huxley, J. (1969) 'Ritualization of Behaviour in Animals and Man', *Proceedings of the Royal Zoological Society* Series B.

Ingham, A. and Beamish, R. (1993) 'The Industrialization of the United States and the "Bourgeoisification" of American Sport', in E. Dunning, J. Maguire and R. Pearton (eds) *The Sports Process: A Comparative and Developmental Approach*, Champaign, IL: Human Kinetics.

Jary, D. *et al.* (1991) 'Fanzines and Football Culture', *Sociological Review* 39(3): 581–97.

Kahl, J. A. (1961) *The American Class Structure*, New York: Holt, Rinehart and Winston.

Kerr, J. H. (1994) *Understanding Soccer Hooliganism*, Philadelphia: Open University Press.

Kilminster, R. (1987) 'Sociology and the Professional Culture of the Philosophers', Paper delivered at the Annual Conference of the German Sociological Association, Bremen.

Kilminster, R. (1991) 'Editor's Introduction' to Norbert Elias, *The Symbol Theory* London: Sage.

Kimmel, M. S. (ed.) (1987) *Changing Men*, London: Sage.

King, A. (1995) 'The Premier League and the New Consumption of Football', unpublished PhD thesis, University of Salford.

Klein, A. M. (1990) 'Little Big Man: Hustling, Gender Narcissism and Bodybuilding Subculture', in M. A. Messner and D. F. Sabo (eds) *Sport, Men and the Gender Order: Critical Feminist Perspectives*, Champaign, IL: Human Kinetics.

Koger, L. (1995) *Black Slaveowners*, Columbia, SC: University of South Carolina Press.

Leach, E. (1962) *Aspects of Caste in South India, Ceylon and North West Pakistan*, Cambridge: Cambridge University Press.

Lenskyj, H. (1986) *Out of Bounds: Sport and Sexuality*, Toronto: Women's Press.

Lenskyj, H. (1988) 'Measured Time: Women, Sport and Leisure', *Leisure Studies* 7: 233–40.

Listiak, A. *et al.* (1976) 'Legitimate" Deviance and Social Class', in R. Gruneau and J. Allison (eds) *Canadian Sport*, Don Mills, Ontario: Addison-Wesley.

Lockwood, D. (1964) 'Social Integration and System Integration', in G. K. Zollschan and W. Hirsch (eds) *Explorations in Social Change*, London: Routledge and Kegan Paul.

Lockwood, D. (1970) 'Race, Conflict and Plural Society', in S. Zubaida (ed.) *Race and Racialism*, London: Tavistock.

Lorber, J. (1994) *Paradoxes of Gender*, New Haven, CT, and London: Yale University Press.

Lorenz, K. (1966) *On Aggression*, London: Methuen.

Lüschen, G. (ed.) (1970) *The Cross-Cultural Analysis of Sport and Games*, Champaign, IL: Sipes.

Lüschen, G. and Sage, G. (eds) (1981) *Handbook of Social Sciences of Sport*, Champaign, IL: Sipes.

Lyman, S. (1990) *Civilization*, London and Fayetville, AR: University of Arkansas Press.

Macrory, J. (1991) *Running with the Ball*, London: Colins Willow.

Magoun, F. P. (1938) *A History of Football from the Beginnings to 1871*, Cologne: Änglistische Arbeite.

Maguire, J. (1986) 'Images of Manliness and Competing Ways of Living in Late Victorian and Edwardian England', *British Journal of Sport History* 3(3): 265–87.

Maguire, J. (1990) 'More than a Sporting "Touchdown": The Making of American Football in Britain 1982–1989', *Sociology of Sport Journal* 7(3): 213–37.

Maguire, J. (1991) 'The Media-Sport Production Complex: the Emergence of American Sports in European Culture', *European Journal of Communication* 6(3): 315–36.

Maguire, J. (1992) 'Towards a Sociological Theory of Sport and the Emotions', in E. Dunning and C. Rojek (eds) *Sport and Leisure in the Civilizing Process: Critique and Counter-Critique*, London: Macmillan, and Toronto: University of Toronto Press.

Maguire, J. (1993a) 'Globalization, Sport Development and the Media/Sport Production Complex', *Sports Science Review* 2(1): 29–47.

Maguire, J. (1993b) 'Bodies, Sportscultures and Societies: A Critical Review of Some Theories in the Sociology of the Body', *International Review for the Sociology of Sport* 28(1): 33–52.

Maguire, J. (1993c) 'Globalization, Sport and National Identities: The Empire Strikes Back', *Society and Leisure* 16(2): 293–322.

Maguire, J. (1994a) 'Preliminary Observations on Globalisation and the Migration of Sport Labour', *Sociological Review* 42(3): 452–80.

Maguire, J. (1994b) 'Sport, Identity Politics and Globalization: Diminishing Contrasts and Increasing Varieties', *Sociology of Sport Journal* 11(4): 398–427.

Maguire, J. (1996) '"Blade Runners": Canadian Migrants and Global Ice-Hockey Trails', *Journal of Sport and Social Issues* 23: 335–60.

Malcolm, D. (1997a) 'Stacking in Cricket: A Figurational-Sociological Reappraisal of Centrality', *Sociology of Sport Journal* 14(3) 265–84.

Malcolm, D. (1997b) 'Cricket, "Racial" Stereotyping and Physical Education', *Bulletin of Physical Education*, 33(1): 8–14.

Malcolmson, R. (1982) 'Popular Recreations Under Attack', in B. Waites, T. Bennett and G. Martin (eds) *Popular Culture: Past and Present*, London: Croom-Helm/Open University Press.

Mannheim, K. (1953) 'Conservative Thought', in K. Mannheim *Essays on Sociology and Social Psychology*, London: Routledge and Kegan Paul.

Marcuse, H. (1955) *Eros and Civilization*, New York: Vintage.

Marples, M. (1954) *A History of Football*, London: Collins.

Marsh, P. (1978) *Aggro: The Illusion of Violence*, London: Dent.

Marsh, P., Rosser, E. and Harré, R. (1978) *The Rules of Disorder*, London: Routledge and Kegan Paul.

Martin, S. C. (1995) 'Don Quixote and Leatherstocking: Hunting, Class and Masculinity in the American South, 1800–40', *International Journal of the History of Sport*, 12(2): 61–79.

Marx, G. (1969) *Protest and Prejudice*, New York: Harper Torch Books.

Marx, K. and Engels, F. (1942) *Collected Works*, London: Lawrence and Wishart (2 vols).

Massey, D. (1994) *Space, Place and Gender*, Cambridge: Polity.

Mazrui, A. (1976) *A World Federation of Cultures: An African Perspective*, New York: Free Press.

264

McCrone, K. E. (1988) *Sport and the Physical Emancipation of English Women, 1870–1914*, London: Routledge.

McIntosh, P. (1993) 'The Sociology of Sport in the Ancient World', in E. Dunning, J. Maguire and R. Pearton (eds) *The Sports Process: A Comparative and Developmental Approach*, Champaign, IL: Human Kinetics.

McKay, J. (1995) ' "Just Do It": Corporate Sports Slogans and the Political Economy of "Enlightened Racism" ', *Discourse* 16(2): 191–201.

McKitrick, E. L. (ed.) (1963) *Slavery Defended: The Views of the Old South*, Englewood Cliffs, NJ: Prentice Hall.

Melnick, M. and Sabo, D. (1994) 'Sport and Social Mobility among Afro-American and Hispanic Athletes', in G. Eisen and D. Wiggins (eds) *Ethnic Experience in American Sport*, Westport, CT: Greenwood Press.

Mennell, S. J. (1989) *Norbert Elias: Civilization and the Human Self-Image*, Oxford: Blackwell.

Mennell, S. J. (1992) *Norbert Elias: An Introduction*, Oxford: Blackwell. (New edition published in 1998 by University College Dublin Press.)

Merton, R. K. (1957) *Social Theory and Social Structure*, New York: Free Press.

Messner, M. (1987) 'The Life of a Man's Seasons: Male Identity in the Life-Course of the Jock', in M. S. Kimmel (ed.) *Changing Men*, London: Sage.

Mills, C. W. (1956) *The Power Elite*, Fairlawn, NJ: Oxford University Press.

Moorhouse, H. (1989) 'Models of Work, Models of Leisure', in C. Rojek (ed.) *Leisure for Leisure: Critical Essays*, London: Macmillan, pp. 15–35.

Morgan, D. H. (1992) *Discovering Men*, London: Routledge.

Morgan, W. J. (1985) ' "Radical Social" Theory of Sport: A Critique and Conceptual Emendation', *Sociology of Sport Journal* 2: 56–7.

Mouzelis, N. (1991) *Back to Sociological Theory: The Construction of Social Orders*, London: Macmillan.

Mouzelis, N. (1993) 'On Figurational Sociology', *Theory, Culture and Society* 10: 239–53.

Murphy, P., Williams, J. and Dunning, E. (1990) *Football on Trial*, London: Routledge.

Nash, B. and Zullo, A. (1986) *The Baseball Hall of Shame (2)*, New York: Simon and Shuster.

Nelson, M. B. (1994) *The Stronger Women Get, The More Men Love Football: Sexism and the American Culture of Sports*, New York: Harcourt Brace.

Oakley, A. (1972, 1985) *Sex, Gender and Society*, London: Gower/Maurice Temple Smith.

Parker, S. (1976) *The Sociology of Leisure*, London: Allen and Unwin.

Parsons, T. (1964) 'Evolutionary Universals in Society', *American Sociological Review* 29: 339–57.

Payne, R. (1981) 'Comment on Margaret Talbot's "Women and Sport: Social Aspects" ', in B. Tulloh, M. A. Herbertson and A. S. Parkes (eds) *Biosocial Aspects of Sport*, Cambridge: Galton Foundation.

Peiss, K. (1986) *Cheap Amusements: Working Women in Turn of the Century New York*, Philadelphia: Temple University Press.

Peitersen, B. (1996) 'Comparative European Perspectives on Football Spectatorship', *Proceedings of the Symposium on Sport in the Civilizing Process and Violence in Football*, State University of Campinas, Campinas, Brazil, September.

265

Peitersen, B. and Holm-Kristensen, B. (1988) 'An Empirical Survey of the Danish Roligans during the European Championships "88"', Danish State Institute of Physical Education.

Perkin, H. (1989) 'Teaching the Nations How to Play: Sport and Society in the British Empire and Commonwealth', *International Journal of the History of Sport* 6(2).

Planck, K. (1898) *Fusslümmelei: über Stauchballspiel und englische Krankheit*, Stuttgart (reprinted by Litverlag, Münster).

Plummer, K. (1975) *Sexual Stigma: An Interactionist Account*, London: Routledge.

Popper, K. (1957) *The Poverty of Historicism*, London: Routledge and Kegan Paul.

Powell, R. E. (1993) 'Sport, Social Relations and Animal Husbandry: Early Cock-Fighting in North America', *International Journal of the History of Sport*, 10(3): 361–81.

Riesman, D. (1953) *The Lonely Crowd*, New Haven, CT: Yale University Press.

Riesman, D. and Denney, R. (1971) 'Football in America: A Study in Culture Diffusion', in E. Dunning (ed.) *The Sociology of Sport: A Selection of Readings*, London: Cass.

Rigauer, B. (1969) *Sport und Arbeit*, Frankfurt: Suhrkamp. (English edition, A. Guttmann (trans.) (1981) *Sport and Work*, New York: Columbia University Press.)

Risse, H. (1921) *Soziologie des Sports*, Frankfurt.

Robins, D. and Cohen, P. (1978) *Knuckle Sandwich*, Harmondsworth: Penguin.

Roderick, M. (1996) Review of Haynes, R. (1995) *The Football Imagination*, London, Arena; and Wagg, S. (1995) *Giving the Game Away*, Leicester, Leicester University Press, *British Journal of Sociology* 47(3): 726–7.

Rojek, C. (1985) *Capitalism and Leisure Theory*, London: Tavistock.

Rojek, C. (1989) *Leisure for Leisure: Critical Essays*, London: Macmillan.

Rojek, C. (1992) 'The Field of Play in Sport and Leisure Studies', in E. Dunning and C. Rojek (eds) *Sport and Leisure in the Civilizing Process: Critique and Counter-Critique*, London: Macmillan.

Rojek, C. (1995) *Decentring Leisure: Rethinking Leisure Theory*, London: Sage.

Roversi, A. (1994) 'The Birth of the "Ultras": The Rise of Football Hooliganism in Italy', in R. Giulianotti and J. Williams (eds) *Game without Frontiers: Football, Identity and Modernity*, Aldershot: Arena.

Rowe, David (1988) 'Play Up: Rethinking Power and Resistance in Sport', *Journal of Sport and Social Issues* 22(3): 241–51.

Sabo, D. (1985) 'Sport, Patriarchy and Male Identity: New Questions About Men and Sport', *Arena Review* 9: 1–30.

Sammons, J. (1990) *Beyond the Ring*, Urbana, IL, and Chicago: University of Illinois Press.

Sammons, J. (1994) ' "Race" and Sport: A Critical Historical Examination', *Journal of Sport History* 21(3).

Sayers, J. (1982) *Biological Politics*, London: Tavistock.

Seidler, V. J. (1992) *Rediscovering Masculinity*, London: Routledge.

Sheard, K. (1972) 'The Development of Rugby Football: A Sociological Study', unpublished MPhil thesis, University of Leicester.

Sheard, K. (1992) 'Boxing in the Civilizing Process', unpublished PhD thesis, CNAA.

Sheard, K. and Dunning, E. (1973) 'The Rugby Football Club as a Type of Male Preserve: Some Sociological Notes', *International Review of Sport Sociology* 5(3): 5–24.

Shearman, M. (1887) *Atletics and Football*, London.

Shilling, C. (1993) *The Body and Social Theory*, London: Sage.

Shorter, E. (1982) *A History of Women's Bodies*, New York: Basic Books.

Sipes, R. (1973) 'War, Sports and Aggression: An Empirical Test of Two Rival Theories', *American Anthropologist* 75: 64–86.

Small, S. (1994) *Racialized Barriers: The Black Experience in the United States and England in the 1980s*, London: Routledge.

Smith, M. (1983) *Violence and Sport*, Toronto: Butterworths.

Snyder, E. E. and Spreitzer, E. (1989) *Social Aspects of Sport*, Englewood Cliffs, NJ: Prentice Hall.

Spierenburg, P. (1991) *The Broken Spell: A Cultural and Anthropological History of Preindustrial Europe*, London: Macmillan.

Suttles, G. (1968) *The Social Order of the Slum*, Chicago: University of Chicago Press.

Suttles, G. (1972) *The Social Construction of Communities*, Chicago: University of Chicago Press.

Taylor, I. (1971) 'Football Mad: A Speculative Sociology of Football Hooliganism', in E. Dunning (ed.) *The Sociology of Sport: A Selection of Readings*, London: Cass.

Taylor, I. (1982) 'Putting the Boot into Working Class Sport: British Soccer After Bradford and Brussels', *Sociology of Sport Journal* 4: 171–91.

Taylor, P., Lord Justice, (1990) *Inquiry into the Hillsborough Stadium Disaster: Final Report*, London: HMSO.

Tester, K. (1989) 'The Pleasure of the Rich is the Labour of the Poor: Some Comments on Norbert Elias's "An Essay on Sport and Violence"', *Journal of Historical Sociology* 2(2): 161–72.

Thompson, H. S. (1979) *The Great Shark Hunt*, New York: Warner Books.

Thrasher, F. M. (1936) *The Gang*, Chicago: University of Chicago Press.

Tinbergen, N. (1953) *Social Behaviour in Animals*, London: Methuen.

Tomlinson, A. and Whannel, G. (eds) (1986) *Off the Ball*, London: Pluto.

Toulmin, S. (1972) *Human Understanding*, Vol. 1, Princeton, NJ: Princeton University Press.

Trivizas, E. (1980) 'Offences and Offenders in Football Crowd Disorder', *British Journal of Criminology* 20(3): 281–3.

Urry, J. (1990) *The Tourist Gaze: Leisure and Travel in Contemporary Societies*, London: Sage.

van Benthem van den Bergh, G. (1992) *The Nuclear Revolution and the End of the Cold War: Forced Restraint*, London: Macmillan.

van der Brug, H. (1986) *Voetbalvandalisme*, Harlem: De Vrieseborch.

van Limbergen, K., Colaers, C. and Walgrave, L. (1987) *Research on the Societal and Psycho-Sociological Background of Football Hooliganism*, Leuven: Catholic University.

van Stolk, A. and Wouters, C. (1987) 'Power-changes and Self-respect: A Comparison of Two Cases of Established-Outsider Relations', *Theory, Culture and Society* 4(2–3): 1477–88.

Vertinsky, P. (1990) *The Eternally Wounded Woman: Women, Doctors and Exercise in the Late Nineteenth Century*, Manchester: Manchester University Press.

Vertinsky, P. (1994) 'The Social Construction of the Gendered Body', *The International Journal of the History of Sport* 11(2): 147–71.

Walby, S. (1990) *Theorizing Patriarchy*, Oxford: Blackwell.

Warner, W. L. (1949) *Social Class in America*, Chicago: Science Research.

Weber, M. (1930) *The Protestant Ethic and the Spirit of Capitalism*, London: Allen and Unwin.

Weber, M. (1946) 'Class, Status, Party', in H. H. Gerth and C. W. Mills (eds) *From Max Weber*, New York: Oxford University Press.

Weber, M. (1972) *Wirtschaft und Gesellschaft*, 5th revised edn, Tübingen: J. C. Mohr.

Wenner, L. (1994) 'The Dream Team, Communicative Dirt and the Marketing of Synergy', *Journal of Sport and Social Issues* 18: 27–47.

Wheatley, E. E. (1994) 'Subcultural Subversions: Comparing Discourses on Sexuality in Men's and Women's Rugby Songs', in S. Birrell and C. L. Cole (eds) *Women, Sport and Culture*, Champaign, IL: Human Kinetics.

White, P. G. and Vagi, A. B. (1990) 'Rugby in the 19th Century British Boarding-School System: A Feminist Psychoanalytic Perspective', in M. A. Messner and D. F. Sabo (eds) *Sport, Men and the Gender Order: Critical Feminist Perspectives*, Champaign, IL: Human Kinetics.

Whitson, D. (1990) 'Sport in the Social Construction of Masculinity', in M. A. Messner and D. F. Sabo (eds) *Sport, Men and the Gender Order: Critical Feminist Perspectives*, Champaign, IL: Human Kinetics.

Willis, P. (1982) 'Women in Sport in Ideology', in J. Hargreaves (ed.) *Sport, Culture and Ideology*, London: Routledge.

Wiggins, D. K. (1977) 'Good Times on the Old Plantation', *Journal of Sport History* 4(3): 260–84.

Wiggins, D. K. (1979) 'Isaac Murphy: Black Hero in Nineteenth Century American Sport', *Canadian Journal of the History of Sport and Physical Education* 10(1): 15–33.

Wiggins, D. K. (1983) 'Wendell Smith, the *Pittsburgh Courier Journal* and the Campaign to Include Blacks in Organized Baseball', *Journal of Sport History* 10(2): 5–29.

Wiggins, D. K. (1986) 'From Plantation to Playing Field', *Research Quarterly for Exercise and Sport* 57(2): 101–16.

Wiggins, D. K. (1991) 'Prized Performers but Frequently Overlooked Students', *Research Quarterly for Exercise and Sport* 62(2): 164–77.

Wignall, T. C. (1923) *The Story of Boxing*, London: Hutchinson.

Williams, J. (1986) 'White Riots: The English Football Fan Abroad', in A. Tomlinson and G. Whannel (eds) *Off the Ball: The Football World Cup*, London: Pluto, pp. 5–19.

Williams, J., Dunning, E. and Murphy, P. (1989) *Hooligans Abroad*, London: Routledge.

Williams, R. (1976) *Keywords: A Vocabulary of Culture and Society*, London: Collins.

Willis, P. (1974) 'Performance and Meaning: A Sociological View of Women in Sport', unpublished paper, Centre for Contemporary Cultural Studies, University of Birmingham. Later published in revised form as 'Women in Sport in Ideology', in J. Hargreaves (ed.) (1982) *Sport, Culture and Ideology*, London: Routledge.

Wouters, C. (1993) 'Ja, ja, ik was nog niet zoo'n beroerde kerel, die zoo'n vrind had', in H. Israëls, M. Komen and A. de Swaan (eds) *Over Elias*, Amsterdam: Het Spinhuis. (Contains numerous quotations from Elias in English.)

Wrangham, R. and Peterson, D. (1997) *Demonic Males: Apes and the Origins of Human Violence*, London: Bloomsbury.

Wrong, D. H. (1961) 'The Oversocialized Conception of Man in Modern Sociology', *American Sociological Review* 26(2): 183–93.

Wurman, R. S. (1982) *American Football: TV Viewers Guide*, Newton Abbott: Access Press.

Yiannakis, A., McIntyre, T. D., Melnick, M. J. and Hart, D. P. (1979) *Sport Sociology: Contemporary Themes*, 2nd edn, Dubuque, IA: Kendall Hunt.

Young, K. (1988) 'Sports Crowd Disorder, Mass Media and Ideology', unpublished PhD dissertation, McMaster University.

Young, K. (1991) 'Sport and Collective Violence', *Exercise and Sport Sciences Reviews* 19: 539–87.

Young, P. (1968) *A History of British Football*, London: Stanley Paul.

Zurcher, L. A. and Meadow, A. (1971) 'On Bullfights and Baseball', in E. Dunning (ed.) *The Sociology of Sport: A Selection of Readings*, London: Cass.

INDEX

Abrams, P. 20
Adams, N. 194
Adorno, T. 242
affluence thesis 140
'agency–structure dilemma' 19–20, 114, 242
aggression: catharsis and 32–3, 34; drive/instinct 40–1, 247–8; *see also* violence
'aggro' (ritual aggression) 38; soccer hooliganism 141–2; theory of 159–61; in USA 161–5
Alcock, C. W. 98
Alcock, J. F. 98, 99
alcohol consumption 139
Allan, J. 147
Allport, G. W. 189
amateur ethos 118
American Civil War 200–2
American football 167–8, 215, 255; crowd violence 170–1, 177–8; masculinity and 229–30
ancient world 47–9
Andreski, S. 154
'anthropological' explanation for soccer hooliganism 141
aristocracy 45, 74, 91, 116–17
Arlott, J. 103
Armstrong, G. 141, 148
Arnold, T. 94
'athletic superiority' myth 216–17
Atyeo, D. 39
Auguet, R. 47
autonomy 4; commercialization and 109–10, 113–14; professionalism and 114–21; slaves 196; of sport 70–1
away-match travel 174, 176–8

'Baby Squad' 150, 152
Bairner, A. 151
balances of power 191–2, 227–8
balls 88
Banks, T. 128
Barcelona Olympics 1992 217
bare-knuckle prize-fighting 57, 59
Barkley, C. 217
baseball 81; black involvement 204–6, 214, 215, 217; campaign against segregation 212–14; crowd violence 166–7, 171
basic structure 71–2
basketball 215, 233
Bauman, Z. 19
Beamish, R. 202
Bedouin syndrome 150
behaviour: civilizing processes and 44; soccer hooliganism as learned pattern 143, 148–53
Belgium 157
Bendix, R. 187, 208
Berreman, G. I. 183
biological reductionism 232
Birrell, S. J. 179–80, 196–7, 219, 222–3, 225–6
black bourgeoisie 183–4, 193–4, 202, 217–18; sport and under colour-caste segregation 203–7
Black Muslims 210
Black Newspaper Publishers Association 213
Black Panthers 210
black–white relations 193–218; civil rights struggle 211–17; colour castes 203–7; emancipation and Civil War 200–2; 'ghettoization' 207–11; plantation slavery 194–200

270